HUMAN VALUES
AND
PROFESSIONAL ETHICS

This Page has been intentionally left blank

HUMAN VALUES AND PROFESSIONAL ETHICS

VALUES AND ETHICS OF PROFESSION

(Textbook for the Students of Engineering and Management)

Dr. Jayshree Suresh
Professor and Dean
School of Management
Faculty of Engineering and Technology
SRM University
(Under 3G Section)
Kattankulathur – 603 203
Tamil Nadu

B.S. Raghavan
Former Member of the Indian Administrative Service
Former Policy Adviser to UN (FAO)
Management Consultant
Chennai – 600 020
Tamil Nadu

S. CHAND PUBLISHING

S Chand And Company Limited
(ISO 9001 Certified Company)

S Chand And Company Limited
(ISO 9001 Certified Company)

Head Office: Block B-1, House No. D-1, Ground Floor, Mohan Co-operative Industrial Estate, New Delhi – 110 044 | Phone: 011-66672000

Registered Office: A-27, 2nd Floor, Mohan Co-operative Industrial Estate, New Delhi – 110 044 Phone: 011-49731800

www.**schandpublishing.com**; e-mail: **info@schandpublishing.com**

Branches

Chennai	:	Ph: 23632120; chennai@schandpublishing.com
Guwahati	:	Ph: 2738811, 2735640; guwahati@schandpublishing.com
Hyderabad	:	Ph: 40186018; hyderabad@schandpublishing.com
Jalandhar	:	Ph: 4645630; jalandhar@schandpublishing.com
Kolkata	:	Ph: 23357458, 23353914; kolkata@schandpublishing.com
Lucknow	:	Ph: 4003633; lucknow@schandpublishing.com
Mumbai	:	Ph: 25000297; mumbai@schandpublishing.com
Patna	:	Ph: 2260011; patna@schandpublishing.com

First Edition 2005
Revised Edition 2007, 2009, 2010 (Twice), 2012
Fourth Revised Edition 2015
Reprints 2016, 2018

Reprint 2021

ISBN: 978-81-219-2452-8 **Product Code:** H3HVE60ETHS10ENAD15O

PRINTED IN INDIA

By Vikas Publishing House Private Limited, Plot 20/4, Site-IV, Industrial Area Sahibabad, Ghaziabad – 201 010 and Published by S Chand And Company Limited, A-27, 2nd Floor, Mohan Co-operative Industrial Estate, New Delhi – 110 044.

Dedicated
to
Dear Students

This Page has been intentionally left blank

PREFACE TO THE FOURTH EDITION

We are greatly pleased that the book has been well-received and already run into three editions. The earlier editions took into account the syllabus and the course content of the subject of "**Human Values and Professional Ethics**."as envisaged by the Anna University in Chennai.

The Uttar Pradesh Technical University at Lucknow too has since included the subject in its curriculum with a detailed enumeration of the aspects to be covered. We have, therefore, suitably expanded the contents of the book to cover the course design of that University as well.

The book and the exercises and case-studies contained in it have been designed with bearing in mind the paramount consideration that regardless of the nature and category of the education offered – whether relating to humanities, sciences or professions such as engineering or medicine – its true purpose is creating an awareness of the vital importance of values sustaining human relationships and building character which Samuel Smiles has described as "the crown and glory of life"

It seeks to bring home the principle that the calibre and competence of, say, an engineer, an architect or a doctor, are derived not from the level and standard of his/her professional education alone, but also from his/her abiding commitment to, and practice of, the virtues and values of a good human being.

In short, a professional, requires knowledge and understanding about human as well as professional values. Before he becomes a good engineer through practice of good professional values or code of conduct or best practice, it is essential that he becomes a good human imbibing human values such as truth, transparency, integrity, sense of duty, discipline, helpfulness and accountability which are of universal relevance.

The first two chapters of the book are on human values and other chapters deal with professional values for engineers. Hope students will find the book useful

Dr. JAYSHREE SURESH
B.S. RAGHAVAN

PREFACE TO THE FIRST EDITION

Ethics is a general subject. Anna University and other Indian Universities introduced professional ethics for engineers in the Undergraduate course of engineering from this academic year. In India, ethics in general and for Engineers and Management Professionals, in particular, is a newly emerging academic field. Since it is not much developed in India we had to fall back upon US cases and situations. The availability of Indian cases are scant in engineering ethics. We are happy to contribute what is no more than a drop in the ocean of ethics. Through the medium of this book attempt is made to impact an Indian flavour to a subject that ought to command universal importance. While the book has been written keeping in mind the prescribed syllabus, it seeks, at the same time, to do justice to the current scenario as well so as to help the students understand the contents in the proper perspective. We hope that the community of students and faculty members will find the book interesting and useful. Suggestions for improvements are always welcome.

Dr. JAYSHREE SURESH
B.S. RAGHAVAN

ACKNOWLEDGMENTS

In writing this book, we have received help and guidance from a number of professionals in the field. Foremost among them is **Mr. T.R.Rajan**, Management Consultant, Chennai, who has toiled hard to edit the manuscript and put it in a proper shape. We are indebted to him for his total involvement with the project and his unstinted efforts to add significantly to the clarity of the various issues covered in the book.

Mrs. Charu Bharat Shah, who has helped in editing Revised Version of the book.

We benefited greatly from the many valuable suggestions received from Mr. M.R.G. Apparao, Mr. Shantikumar Jain and Ms. Maria Hohen – leitner Muller, CEO, MTG Montage Technik GmbH, Bayreuth, Germany, by way of broadening and deepening the treatment of the subject.

Among those who were a source of encouragement, we would like to thank Chancellor and Chairman Thiru T.R. Pachamuthu, Vice Chancellor Thiru Sathyanarayanan, Pro Vice Chancellor, Dr. T.P. Ganesan, Director R & VE Dr. Ponnavaikko, Registrar, Dr. A. M. Bala Subramaniam and Dean Professor R. Venkataramani of SRM Institute of Science and Technology. No less worthy of mention are the faculty and students of SRM School of Management.

But for the enthusiastic support received from our family members, it would not have been possible to complete this book on time.

Of course, the entire credit for conceiving and pursuing this worthwhile project to its conclusion belongs to our publishers who generously came forward to publish our work.

Dr. JAYSHREE SURESH
B.S. RAGHAVAN

FOREWORD

Professional Ethics First Edition

Following the introduction of "Professional Ethics" as a compulsory subject for study in the Under-graduate Course in Engineering by Anna University, Chennai from this academic year, the need has arisen for a well-written book, broadly based on the prescribed syllabus – a book that would be helpful guide to the engineering students in the colleges affiliated to the University. And this need is sought to be fulfilled by the two authors of this book on "Professional Ethics" – Ms. Jayshree Suresh, Professor and Head of the SRM School of Management and Mr. B. S. Raghavan former member of the Indian Administrative Service and presently a Management Consultant. By virtue of their deep knowledge and wide experience in the field of Management Studies, their refreshing thoughts on the art of winning and losing and dynamic personal insights into professionalism in engineering these two writers have made an impressive attempt to articulate in their work the essentials of professional ethics in general and its crucial implications with reference to engineering as a profession against the backdrop of the current global scenario.

The Introductory Chapter of this treatise presents a scholarly and in-depth analysis of the subject of "Profession, Professionalism and Professional Ethics". Students will find it to be an excellent starting point for their understanding of the issues of professional ethics in the proper perspective, besides getting to know the subtle differences between Ethics and Moral, Ethics and Religion and Ethics and Law, Ethics and Virtues etc. Various theories of ethics and factors impacting ethical behaviour and particularly moral issues confronting an engineer on a daily basis are interestingly discussed in Chapter II. The role of engineers, their responsibilities and commitments, their loyalty to their employees, the occupational confidentiality they have to ensure, the interest conflicts they have to resolve, their obligations to society at large, the organizational values they should uphold etc. have all been spelt out extensively in the subsequent chapters.

While highlighting the responsibilities of engineers, the authors have not failed to underscore the range of rights that engineers as employees are entitled to, The right of an employee to blow the whistle on the shenanigans resorted to by his employing company and its raison d'etre are spotlighted. If only because of the deleterious consequences that the public will be exposed to, if this right is underplayed. Even so the concept of Intellectual Property and the issues emerging from it including its moral status are examined critically in the context of the tentacles of globalisation presently encircling the world today (vide Chapter II).

Chapter III is significant to the extent that it sets out in vivid terms, the multi-dimensional role of engineers as managers, consultants, leaders and entrepreneurs.

With the onward tide of globalisation sweeping the world today and with our engineers working outside Indian or in multinational companies sprouting within the country, international ethical problems have cropped up demanding solutions in a multicultural setting. Canons of Ethics in the global market and Computer Ethics have become imperative to deal with Cyber Crimes, Cyber Scams and Software Piracy. This issue is penetratingly discussed in Chapter VII.

The final chapter is devoted to the amplification of the theme of Code of Conduct. As the authors have rightly observed, code of conduct is a part of code ethics and codes of conduct are guidelines for specific groups of professional to help them perform their roles responding conventionally to the compulsions of professional ethics. Towards, the end of the chapter, useful guidelines have unequivocally been suggested for developing codes of ethics, with a note of caution that any inclusion of values and preferred behaviour for every possible ethical dilemma should be discountenanced. Furthermore, this chapter is enriched with valuable Annexes comprising Codes of Conduct of different countries, sample Code of Conduct of some Indian companies and the Engineers Bill which reveal the lineaments of the theory and practice of professionalism in the domain of engineering and technology.

Ms. Jayshree Suresh and Mr. Raghavan deserve to be warmly congratulated for their having scripted this book, presenting as it does, a comprehensive overview of Professional Ethics. As a pioneering effort of theirs, their contributions is a noteworthy one which comes with a whiff of fresh air. Rich in contents, it carries a lot of valuable quantitative data sifted from different surveys and censuses. Extensive quotations from Western scholars and scientists embellishing the book at appropriate places are both lively and relevant. The real life situations and incidents narrated now and then add weight to the topic discussed and help a clearer understanding of the issue involved. Of much value are the case studies, tables and charts, besides the references, exercises and short and long questions at the end of each chapter, which provoke the thinking of earnest readers. Writing in an elegant, diction, their language being, rich, powerful and effective, the authors have made a valiant effort to reduce a mass of material to its essentials and have succeeded in bringing into prominence the thematic complexities. They deserve commendation for giving a balanced perspective of the whole gamut of views, ideas and points at issue that compel thoughtful consideration.

In sum , this work of quality has all the ingredients to make engineering students look into it as their most preferred text book on the dynamics of Professional Ethics even exceeding their expectations while evoking their passion and sustained interest. I expect it to prove to be a No. 1 Best Seller, for the reason that it instructs, inspires and illumines. It is the kind of book that does not think for the reader but the one that makes them think.

I wish the trend – setting venture of Ms. Jayshree Suresh and Mr. B. S. Raghavan every success. I should compliment M/s. S.Chand Publishers for publishing this work of notable worth.

S.V. Chittibabu.

2005

Dr. S.V. Chittibabu

Former Vice- Chairman , Tamilnadu State Council for Higher Education.

Former Vice – Chancellor

Madurai Kamaraj and Annamalai Universities.

PROFESSIONAL ETHICS AND HUMAN VALUES

SYLLABUS

1. **HUMAN VALUES** : Morals, Values and Ethics – Integrity – Work Ethic – Service - Learning – Civic Virtue – Respect for Others – Living Peacefully – Caring – Sharing – Honesty – Courage – Valuing Time – Co-operation – Commitment – Empathy – Self Confidence – Character – Spirituality.
2. **ENGINEERING ETHICS** : Senses of "Engineering Ethics" – Variety of moral issues - Types of inquiry – Moral dilemmas – Moral autonomy – Kohlberg's theory – Gilligan"s theory – Consensus and Controversy – Models of Professionals Roles – Theories about right action – Self interest – Custom and religion – Uses of ethical theories.
3. **ENGINEERING AS SOCIAL EXPERIMENTATION :** Engineering as experimentation – Engineers as responsible experimenters – Codes of ethics –A balanced outlook on law – The challenger case study
4. **SAFETY, RESPONSIBILITIES AND RIGHTS :** Safety and risk – Assessment of safety and risk – Risk benefit analysis and reducing risk – The Three Mile Island and Chernobyl case studies.

   Collegiality and loyalty – Respect for authority – Collective bargaining – Confidentiality – Conflicts of interest – Occupational crime – Professional rights – Employee rights – Intellectual Property Rights (IPR) – Discrimination.
5. **GLOBAL ISSUES:** Multinational corporations – Environmental ethics- Computer ethics – Weapons development – Engineers as managers – Consulting engineers and engineers as expert witness and advisors – Moral leadership – Sample code of Ethics like ASME, ASCE, IEEE- Institution of Engineers (India) – Indian Institute of Materials Management – Institution of electronics and telecommunication engineers (IETE) India etc.

CONTENTS

Chapter

1

Introduction

What is Value Education?

Let us first understand the term value education. As per the Oxford Dictionary the word ***Education*** means a process of teaching, training and learning, especially in schools or colleges to improve knowledge and develop skills. ***Value*** can be used both as a noun and verb. It means how much a particular thing is worth. It is the ***quality of being useful, worthwhile or important.***

Value education is a combination of two words value and education. The term can be looked at from two points of view. (1) Is Education of any value or worth? And (2) How can we add value to education ?

Government of India classifies a person as literate when he is able to put his signature. Now let us look at few examples, through which the meaning of term 'value education' can be understood.

1. ***Lakshmi*** is a 52-year lady working as a maidservant. She knows how to use a washing machine, wet grinder, mixer, vacuum cleaner, toaster, gas and other electrical appliances. She is honest and does her job meticulously. She is neat and clean. She does not know to put her signature and cannot read or write any language.. Does she qualify for value education?
2. ***Gopi*** a son of a rickshaw puller, went to Government school till 5th standard in Hindi medium and left the school as he found studies boring. He learnt to drive Autorickshaw and is making a living driving Autorickshaw. Does not cheat any customer. Does he qualify for value education?
3. ***Alex*** completed his Ph.D in Mathematics. Working as a lecturer in a college. Does not take classes regularly. On occasions, found taking classes after drinking. Does not teach well. Does he qualify for value education?
4. ***Abbas*** did his engineering and worked in a multinational company for 4 years. Went to USA for higher studies. He is the Chief Executive Officer (CEO) of a Textile division. Started a small-scale company to manufacture automobile spare parts. Runs his company ethically. Provided jobs to 400 people. Does he qualify for value education?
5. ***Bhargava*** is the son of a Purohit. Does not know how to read and write but can recite the scriptures and slokas and perform pooja. Does he qualify for value education?

If we use the official definition of literacy and the dictionary meaning of education, **Lakshmi** and **Bhargava** do not qualify to be called educated, but they have developed skills. This means that they have the necessary ability to understand the basic of value education. **Gopi** and **Abbas** already have value-consciousness ingrained in them. It will be easy to build upon it and make them role models for others. **Alex**, despite having a Ph.D, has no hold over himself and indulges in conduct which is the opposite of what human values and professional ethics should be. He will need to be put through an intensive and vigorous programme of coaching to bring about a beneficial change in his behaviour and conduct.

Before we go into the role of values in education, let us briefly take stock of the state of education as it has evolved over centuries and in its present form.

Education, obviously, does not consist in acquiring formal degrees or diplomas. In the sense of the ability to maintain good human relations, and cultivating a helpful and cooperative temperament and a sense of responsibility, one can possess all the essential attributes of education without formally going to school, college or university. The framework of the education system that we see in India today is one that had been superimposed by the British when they ruled the country. The ancient education models of the Indian sub-continent, exemplified by universities like Taxasila and Nalanda, covered in a holistic fashion the entire gamut of human development in all its dimensions. The glorious traditions of teaching and training were passed on from one generation to the next by extensively spread out gurukulas and ashrams with eminent and erudite preceptors (or ***acharyas*** who could be sages or rishis) heading them, setting an example of nobility and refinement.

The child went to a preceptor, called a ***guru***, and on being accepted as a disciple, became a member of the guru's household in the capacity of ***shishya***, serving him in a variety of ways while the guru imparted to him all that he needed to know in terms of knowledge, wisdom, religious scriptures, code of conduct, ways of solving life's problems and meeting challenges.

In the ***guru-shishya parampara,*** the day started with touching the feet of guru and taking his blessings. In the period we are talking of, many thousands of years before, the communication was oral. The student learnt what was taught to them through recitation,. He learnt the correct ucchara (pronunciation) and through the repetitive recitations acquired proficiency even in the Vedas. The process of imparting education was such as to provide a grounding in values also. The respect for gurus, parents and elders in general, discipline, and an innate sense of self-restraint and social commitment were also developed along with the knowledge of the scriptures. The guru explained the meaning of the slokas with examples from real life. It was education that brought about an integration of the student with the people and the society around him.

The Upanishadic education aimed at the all round development of personality, and preservation and dissemination of knowledge. All round development meant imbuing the students with all the dynamics of physical, mental and moral development. Students were instructed to speak the truth, practice virtue, be devoted to studies and work for the welfare of society.

The aim of the education system was to produce a rational individual, free from prejudices and pettiness, extending the hand of friendship, goodwill and affection to all, continuously adding to one's knowledge and intellectual attainments and striving to reach the highest goals in terms of self-improvement. It led to an individual's learning revealing itself through his thoughts, words and deeds. He was expected to fulfill his obligations to the family, society and country, and sacrifice his own wants and comforts for the good of all. True education was construed to be a life-long commitment which was in accord with dharma. Learning was not viewed as a way of making money or a gateway to riches.

One of the defects of the modern higher education is that the importance is on training in the acquisition of certain kinds of skills, and too little on the enlargement of mind and heart. There is an excessive stress on marks and grades, on one-upmanship, and on how to compete and succeed. Students are constantly in a state of stress and tension, driving them to take to drinking and drugs, which are harmful to health and morally degrading. In addition, they become the cause of waywardness, lack of concentration, loss of self-control, general apathy and indifference to one's duties and responsibilities. Thus, the limited span of life on the planet, instead of contributing to ennobling endeavours, is frittered away in trivialities.

Difference Between Education and Value Education

The true significance of education lies in two directions. First, in its formal and structured sense of acquiring it in institutions such as schools and colleges in terms of curricula and syllabi, it provides unlimited access to knowledge. The more knowledge one gains, the more it expands the mental and intellectual horizons and equips the individual to face life's challenges and make the maximum use of its opportunities.

Second, it facilitates the realisation and development of the potential within each individual for attaining the peak of human efflorescence which is nothing but another word for genius. The degree to which an individual benefits from both the attributes of education depends upon an environment fostering a thirst for knowledge and intellectual curiosity. These, again, are not ends in themselves, but are only a means to leading a life steeped in the highest values constituting the glorious human heritage. Without value-based education, human personality will be devoid of all that gives meaning and purpose to human existence. Value-based education not only guarantees success in the materialistic terms, but also contributes to a sense of spiritual fulfillment.

That is why the literary and cultural heritage in every language of the world has put the utmost emphasis on the adherence to ethics and values not just as an integral part of self-development facilitating achievement of one's goals in life, but also as a practical aid for leading a life free from stress and tension and fears and anxieties, and endowed with peace, harmony, goodwill and fellow-feeling, a positive and constructive attitude, passion for striving for the good of the society and a creative and innovative bent of mind.

Thus, cultivation, inculcation and fostering of human values can be said to be at the very heart of education in the best and broadest sense of the word. In the ultimate analysis, it is not the nuts-and-bolts of what one learns in class that is going to make a difference, but whether the learning has been put to wise use in the service of humanity.

This is the essence of the teachings and writings of the greatest minds and achievers who have lived in India. For instance, for Mahatma Gandhi, the purpose of education is to enrich the body (physical), mind (intellectual) and soul (spiritual) by means of rigorous training at five levels: (1) Moral; (2) Literary; (3) Physical; (4) Vocational: and (5) Spiritual. Cumulatively, he believed, they will raise the quality of life of the individual concerned and those he interacted with in whatever capacity.

Mahatma Gandhi explains how the five categories of training can be given. Character building through moral training is the fundamental first step . The purpose of moral training is to give a firm grounding in ethical principles and eternal verities. Literary training puts the student through various courses in different languages and subjects and helps him acquire proficiency in them. The ruling motto of physical training is "A healthy mind in a healthy body" (*Mens sana in corpore sano* as the Romans have long ago made it known.) The same idea has been incorporated in the more homely adage, "All work and no play makes Jack a dull boy"!

Gandhiji believed that every student should be trained in some useful manual vocation. These can be cooking, tailoring, farming, stitching, weaving, shoe making, carpentry etc. In his view, engaging oneself in useful and productive labour is also another form of meditation, keeping the mind focused on a concrete achievement and soothing to the nerves.

The content of the spiritual training is to develop a holistic understanding of the variegated facets of human existence, their purpose and their relevance to the duties and responsibilities devolving on an individual as a householder and as a citizen. It enables enable the person receiving it to work towards knowledge of God and self-realization. Gandhiji put this at the heart of the entire five-part scheme of training and was of the view that without the refinement and reinforcement of the personality brought on by spiritual awakening, education by itself was of no use and might be even harmful.

The time-honoured method of imparting spiritual training is to instill in the individual the quintessence of the teachings of the sages and saints and by recitation and memorization of the hymns and prayers, as also by treasuring the cultural heritage they have bequeathed to humanity. It goes without saying that the efficacy of the spiritual training depends on the life and character of the teacher. It is he, and he alone, who leaves a life-long imprint on the minds of his pupils through his way of living and the example he sets.

According to J. Krishnamurthy, "Education in the true sense is helping the individual to be mature and free, to flower greatly in love and goodness" [1] In his view, education is not merely about academic capacities but to bring about the good in human beings who will care, and will be the embodiment of love, consideration, sympathy, and generosity.

Rabindranath Tagore held the highest mission of education to be to help us realize the inner principles of unity of all knowledge and all the activities of our social and spiritual life. He believed that education should aim at multi-faced development of a human being – his intellectual, physical and spiritual and ethical development. He felt that education should be based on one's understanding of the philosophy of life. He emphasised the importance of close and harmonious relations with the natural surroundings and human society so as to promote efforts aimed at protecting ecology and environment.

Swami Vivekananda felt that true education is training both the head and the heart. Just as the intellect is the instrument of knowledge so is the heart the instrument of inspiration. According to him, education should build the fundamental traits of character such as honesty, compassion, courage, persistence and responsibility.

Dr. S. Radhakrishnan considered education as a creative process moving from being to becoming, from knowing to internalising, from self generated understanding to a network of interactional activities leading to knowledge (gnan) The purpose of education according to him is to provide a coherent picture of the universe and an integrated way of life. Education should go beyond information and technical skill.

Sri Sathya Sai Baba, in one of his discourses, has said, "In my view, the cultivation of human values alone is education. Whoever tries to understand the human values of Truth, Rightous Conduct, Peace, Love and Non-violence properly, and whoever practises these values and propagates them with zeal and sincerity can alone be described as a truly educated person."

If we judge modern education in the light of these yardsticks, we find that it is utilitarian and does not aim at the cultivation of character and the development of noble virtues. It is determined by the desire to pursue a career and lead a good and comfortable life. Education has come to be seen as just a matter of accumulating information databases and cramming of text-books for getting good scores in examinations. Education bereft of values is what is at the root of the drift and disarray that we see in the political, social, cultural and social spheres today. We have reached a stage of crisis of confidence and loss of self-pride driving us to ask with T.S. Eliot "Where is the wisdom which is lost in knowledge, where is the knowledge which is lost in information?"

Linkages of Value Education

Is it possible to remedy the situation and infuse the young minds with the needed idealism, respect of eternal verities, the can-do spirit, the determination and courage to be the game changers

1. Dr. V. Nithyanantha Bhat, Value –Based Education – The need of the Hour, Bhavan's Journal, Vol 56(3), September15, 2009,

and role models? The answer is undoubtedly yes, provided the linkages of value education with character, social commitment and social responsibility and nation-building is clearly understood. Since values embedded in education are of extreme importance for the development and building of character in an individual, let us start with the relationship (See Figure 1 below) between them:.

Figure 1. Relationship between Value – Education – Character

		Education	
		High	**Low**
Value	**High**	Very High Character	High Character
	Low	Low Character	Very Low Character

The above figure 1 shows the correlation between value-based education and the extent of its contribution to the formation of character. Character is the culmination of the process of implanting values in education. It can be expressed as a simple equation: **Education + Value = Character.** While a person with character will command universal respect and trust even if he is lacking in education, a person lacking in character, however high or numerous his educational attainments, will be looked down upon and face universal rejection and condemnation. Character is the sheet anchor of our lives, and without it life itself is not worth living.

Thus the main purpose of education is character formation. Character stands for integrity encompassing one's personal, intellectual and professional capacities, dedication to duty, trustworthiness, sense of responsibility, self-discipline, loyalty, selflessness, helpfulness, humility and patriotism.

Value Education as a Process

The process of education should bring out the talents and skills inherent in a child/individual and contribute to their being utilised in a meaningful way in the interest of the society, the nation and humanity as a whole. The focus here is on human development. Understood in its broadest possible connotation, it is the means of transforming all those having access to it into well-rounded personalities and socially aware citizens, with commitment to the following goals:

Social progress - greater access to knowledge, better nutrition and health services.

Economic advancement – resulting in inclusive growth, avoidance of regional or sectoral imbalances, the flow of benefits to all sections of the population.

Efficiency - in terms of resource use and availability. human development is pro-growth and productivity as long as such growth directly benefits the poor, women and other marginalized groups.

Equity - implying gender justice and safeguarding and conserving resources within and between generations.

Sustainability – preserving and augmenting the current assets for the betterment of future generations in ecological, economic and social terms. Thus, living in harmony with nature and environment is a vital dimension of the criterion of sustainability. It calls for a constant awareness of the dangers of depletion of resources, loss of biodiversity, and environmental degradation.

Ethics - denoting adherence to principles of respect for good citizenship, law, honesty, transparency, accountability, and the rights of others.

True education signifying the sum total of endeavours along the above lines leads to the building up high quality human capital in the sense of producing doers and thinkers of superior merits and accomplishments. But that alone is not sufficient guarantee of **human happiness and prosperity**, derived from freedom from hunger, poverty and disease, livelihood security, distributive justice, social virtues, mutual cooperation and the postulates laid down in the Preamble to India's Constitution. For all of the above to materialise, an essential pre-requisite is the adoption of a well-conceived and integrated system of value-based education.

Actually, there is a growing realisation that a country's state of development is not just a function of its economic growth, measured by means of gross domestic product (GDP). The President, Mr A. P. J. Abdul Kalam, has proposed adopting a National Prosperity Index (NPI) which he defines as the sum total of GDP, a minimum stipulated level of quality of life and ***value systems derived from the country's cultural heritage and ancient civilisation***.

Economists have been working on concepts such as Net Economic Welfare and Genuine Progress Indicator, while some years ago, the Bhutan King coined the novel term of ***Gross National Happiness*** (GNH) as the most appropriate index of a nation's standing based on the premise that true development of human society takes place when material and spiritual development occur side-by-side to complement and reinforce each other. The four pillars of GNH are the promotion of equitable and sustainable socio-economic development, preservation and promotion of cultural values, conservation of the natural environment, and establishment of good governance.

All this discussion is only meant to drive home the immense benefits accruing to society by having education rooted in a bed-rock of values. Thus fortified, education prepares the students for the battle of life, and instills in them the courage of conviction and determinations to work, and, if need be, fight, for establishing a society which will uphold moral and ethical tenets and the universal rights of human beings as proclaimed in international charters.

A number of education commissions and committees set up by the Government of India since Independence have gone in depth into the deficiencies of the education system implanted on the Indian soil by colonial rulers. Their main purpose was to create an English-educated class to be used to further the interests of British Imperialism. The Radhakrishnan commission (1948), Kothari Commission (1964-66), S.B. Chavan Committee, and most recently the Knowledge Commission have made a number of recommendations for carrying out extensive educational reforms. Their thrust is towards inculcating in all those coming within their scope the qualities of impeccable charcter, pride in oneself, a passion for social service, self-confidence, intellectual vigour, identification with the needs and aspirations of the people, charity, compassion, and a capacity to think for oneself along the right lines on the challenges of the knowledge, communications, technological and social revolutions – in sum, what Gautama, the Buuddha laid down as the eight-fold path of right thoughts, right views, right intentions, right speech, right action, right living and right effort.

Content of Value Education

On the basis of process of value education that we have discussed so far, let us now identify what should be the content of the value-based education.

1. Dharma – Right Conduct
2. Artha – Right Wealth
3. Kama – Right Desire
4. Moksha – Right Exit (Liberation)
5. Health -Yoga- Pranayam - Meditation
6. Prayer –Japa – Swadhyay – Satsang
7. Charity
8. Shaucha – Cleanliness

9. Santosha – Contentment
10. Tapasya
11. Communication

Related Terms

Body - Sukh – Suvidha - Sanyam - Swasthya - Nyaya - Tripti - Vishwas – Samman – Samadhan - Samridhi - Abhay - Akhand Samaj - Vyawastha - Sah-astitva.

To understand the relationship between these terms let us classify them into different categories.

Relationship/ Self	Body	Mind	Soul
Self	**Human body** **Swasthya**	**Sukh** **Suvidha** **Sanyam** **Tripti** **Vishwas** **Samridhi**	**Astitva**
Others	**Vyavashtha** **Nyaya** **Samman** **Samadhan**	**Akhand Samaj**	**Sah-astitva**

Body: It is a combination of chemicals. It consists of various systems, which are independent and dependent on each another. The body, mind and soul should be kept aligned.

Sukh: means **Happiness**. According to Bertrand Russell[2] happiness depends partly upon external circumstances and partly upon one self. Dr. Timothy Sharp[3] says. " Happiness is nothing more than a few simple disciplines practiced every day. While misery a few errors of judgment and bad habits repeated every day". Generally shanti follows sukh. Wherever there is such there is shanti.

We should not confuse pleasure with happiness. It is necessary to understand the difference between them. Pleasure is derived by using any or all of the five senses. The good feeling one gets, is pleasure; where as, without the use of these 5 (five) senses, the good feeling one gets is happiness. One is materialistic and the other is non-materialistic. Happiness is long lasting.

Suvidha: means comforts. In new era Sukh and Suvidha go together. Better the suvidhas higher the sukh. If I own refrigerator, air conditioner, car which are suvidhas, I am a happy person. These are the materialistic pleasures and should not be confused with the happiness. Later on it is dealt in detail.

Sanyam: means self-control. To be happy, control what you can control and accept what you cannot control. Not to worry or feel about things which are not under your control. Trying to change the unchangeable will lead to frustration and disappointment. In an organization, your manager shouts at you in front of your other colleagues. There is no reason to be mentally upset about it. What he speaks, when he speaks and how he speaks is not under your control. But what is under your control is whether to remain, calm, loose your temper, become upset. When you develop sanyam, then you remain calm. Lord Krishna in Bhagwad Gita says to Arjuna, you must treat sukh and dukh, respect (maan) and insult (upmaan) same. You cannot control, the external, but what is under your control is self-control. So control your mind, body and language.

2. Bertrand Russell, The Conquest of Happiness, Unwin Books, London, U.K., 1968

3. Timothy Sharp, The Happiness Handbook, Strategies for a Happy Life, Macmillan, 2007

Swasthya: means health. There is an age old saying that health is wealth. If you are sick you cannot earn wealth. Prayanam and meditation, physical exercise like walking, cycling, help the body to be in good health and condition.

Nyaya: is justice. When the economic development takes place, the injustice is done to the environment. The agriculture land and the forests get converted into buildings. Global warming is a phenomenon, which the universe is facing due to the injustice done to the environment. The natural law is " jo jaise beej dalega aisa hi payega". What you sow you reap. This is the natural justice. We need go to the courts for justice. Whatever one does, one has to look from the point of Nyaya. Are Nyaya fair and just? Opposite of Nyaya is Anyaya.

Tripti: Tripti means santosh and satisfaction. When you are thirsty and drink water you feel tripti. When the desires are fulfilled one is trupt.

Vishwas: means trust and confidence. It means, shraddha (faith). It is a value that we have for an activity before embarking on it.

Samman: means respect. Give respect to others and automatically you will receive it. What you sow, you reap. You should respect others, as you want to be respected by them.

Samadhan: through negotiation we can arrive at a Samadhan, which is solution. When the parties compromise then, the samadhan is easy to achieve. It is a WIN- WIN -WIN situation. I Win, You win and we all win. Samadhan can be looked at from two different ways:
(a) negotiation with other people and coming to a WIN-WIN situation, and (b) which is mental i.e. realising and accepting the facts of life, the mind is said to have made a samadhan, becomes serene. Gautama Buddha having realized the reality became very peaceful.

Samridhi: means well being. Sukh and Suvidha bring Samridhi.

Abhay: means fearlessness. One should not be afraid of death which is inevitable. A fearless person will be courageous.

Sah-astitva: Sah means together astitva existence. It is co-existence. In the given situation of terrorism, besides academic excellence, the focus of education should be on the spirit of cross cultural harmony without disturbing the delicate balance in its traditional art and craft, festivals, life-styles and social value system of the people. The value-based education must help the students to balance the traditions with modern and pick up the best of the modern and adapt rather than blindly adopt the modern values.

Akhand Samaj: Akhand means whole and samaj means society. It means that society is one and should not be divided. Vasudevkutumbam means the whole universe is one family. There is only one religion, the religion of ***Love***. There is only one language, the language of ***Heart***. There is only one caste, the caste of ***Humanity***. There is only one law of ***Karma***. There is only one ***God***. He is Omnipresent.

One should not give room for the differences based on language, religion, caste or nationality. Develop the feeling that all are the children of God. You may worship god in any form of your choice, but always bear in mind that God is one. Cultivate love and promote unity and harmony among all

Vyavashtha: means arrangements. If the arrangements are made well then there will be order and peace and happiness for all.

To integrate all the above terms, an attempt is made to conceptualize as a model given below : .

Figure 2. A Model to understand the relationship between the terms

ENVIRONMENT – Physical – Natural, Plants, Animals, Water, Air etc.

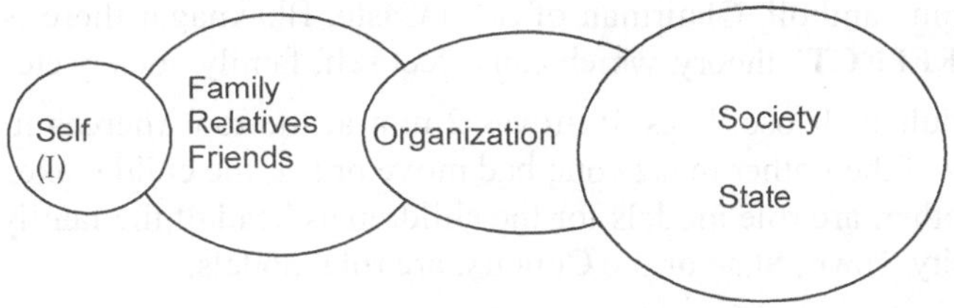

This model depicts the relationship between the various elements of the universe. The size of the circle is the indicator of the size of the component in the universe.

Self (I): The elements of self (I) are body, mind and soul (consciousness). Consciousness is above body and mind. It is the awareness and consciousness, which needs to be realized. Above our head we have starts, sun moon and below earth, do they have any life? Can you say how old is sun? When was it born? But as a body we take birth and celebrate birthday. Let us not forget that we are here for a short span of life.

Consciousness is like a conveyor belt in which thoughts and memories arise in a never ending and steady stream in our mind. Just as bags on a conveyor belt come in different shapes, sizes, colours, conditions, so also thoughts and memories appear in mind. The memories of unpleasant experiences, traumatic events, pleasant incidents disturb the mind. An air traveler picks up his bags, he claims ownership over them and proceeds to his destination. Just as the bags on a conveyor belt make their appearance and disappearance, similarly thoughts arise and fade. Unlike the air traveler, do not make the mistake of claiming ownership of the thoughts or memory, it is only when you pick up a thought or memory, hang on to it and claim it as your own that you suffer the consequences.

Like the air traveler who picks up only his bags and ignores all others, focus only on the thoughts that you require. Let all other thoughts pass by Practice to discard the thoughts you do not need.

Family: Of all the institutions that have come down to us from the past none is in the present day so disorganized and derailed as the family. The family has failed to provide the fundamental satisfaction and created discontent in minds of children. The education that a child imbibes in a well-ordered household is impossible to obtain in hostels. To day parents in fast moving world, leave children as young as 6 months of age in crèches. Let us not forget that children form 80 percent of their mental make up in the first Six years. Family plays a very important role in development of values.

A girl asks her father, how much is one hour of your time worth? Father was wondering why, his daughter is asking this question? He thought for a while and said Rs. 500 per hour. Then she asks father to give her Rs. 200. She collects Rs. 200 from her father, goes inside her room and comes with Rs. 300 which she already had. Father was perturbed. Girl then hands over Rs. 500 to her father and requests, father, can I have one hour of your time? This is to show how important it is to spend time with the children. Money or gift cannot be substituted by time.

Children observe behaviour of their parents and develop their values. Parents should from the beginning in the world of religious philosophy, teach the child the importance of moral values. It is important that the child learns to differentiate between the right and the wrong and the good and the bad.

Actually at the formative stage of a child, the parents better teach children the above difference. However, in to days world, TV and other media, influence mind of children. As soon as the child enters a school, the child picks up very soon the habits from other children.

Children pick up things very fast from what the parents do, rather than what the parents say. According to Bipin Tamboli, Chairman of Steel Caste, Bhavnagar there is what he calls it as a " **PENDULUM EFFECT**" theory, which can affect self, family, society etc.

Take a pendulum. It oscillates. It moves 2 mm at the top whereas it moves 10 cms at the bottom. Similarly, if the Father makes one bad move or act, the child makes 10 bad acts (moves). The Father or Mother, are role models for the children as head of the family. Similarly a Teacher, Head of community, Town, State or the Country, are role models.

Relatives: constitute extended family. They influence the values in the young age. Masaji – Mousi (maternal - second mother),Mama – Mami,(maternal) Kaka-Kaki, Fai - Fuvaji(paternal) cousins can influence. They spend their vacations and meet during the festivals and occasions and develop strong ties with each other. They learn values during their stay. The bondings between them become strong.

Friends: Once the child is takes birth, mother has the influence followed by father and then siblings. During the school and college days, friends influence the values. Birds of same feather flock together. Students with similar values, skills form into groups. School friendship is ever lasting case study at the end of the chapter brings out the role of friends and its impact on development of values.

Organization: After education, person starts going for work to earn livelihood. At this stage, organizational values start influencing them. There will be conflicting situations faced by you; the conflict is between self and the organizational values. Sometimes, you have to take a call. Some people compromise on personal values while some leave organization when there is a conflict between the personal and the organizational values.

Society: Human beings are social animal. They would like to get accepted by the society. Media plays a very important role in a society. The responsibility of mass media is very high. They should highlight values through mass media. They are powerful and influential. Movies also play a dominant role. Through movies also values can be show cased. It is again a powerful media for the youths. The film hero and the heroin influence the values.

State: plays a dominant role in the life of a person. They regulate, and control the society. Laws are passed and the society has to follow these to avoid the conflicts and in case of conflict, get the justice. State is for the benefit of people, for the people and by the people. A good corporate governance by the state will bring peace in the society. State manage people. The various laws are formulated, implemented and controlled through the regulation.

Environment: One has to develop respect for the environment. From the environment lot of lessons on harmony, order, and other values can be picked up. For example: Learn to give from nature, as it always gives. Fruits even though we pelt stones, mango or apples fall. Pet animals also have values. As human beings we need to respect nature and protect the environment. The natural resources are also limited so their usage and conservation has to be developed as a value.

The goal of all human beings is to be happy and remain happy throughout their life. Is it possible to achieve this? What is happiness? And how do you define happiness? Some of the issues are dealt later on.

HAPPINESS = UNIVERSAL PEACE

Happiness is, when one is at peace with oneself. When one is at Peace with oneself, peace with others becomes easy. This is the beginning of universal peace.

The absence of conflicts and friction between the various elements depicted in the model will bring about the universal peace. With the implementation of Input – Output model one can achieve goal of happiness.

INPUT – OUTPUT MODEL

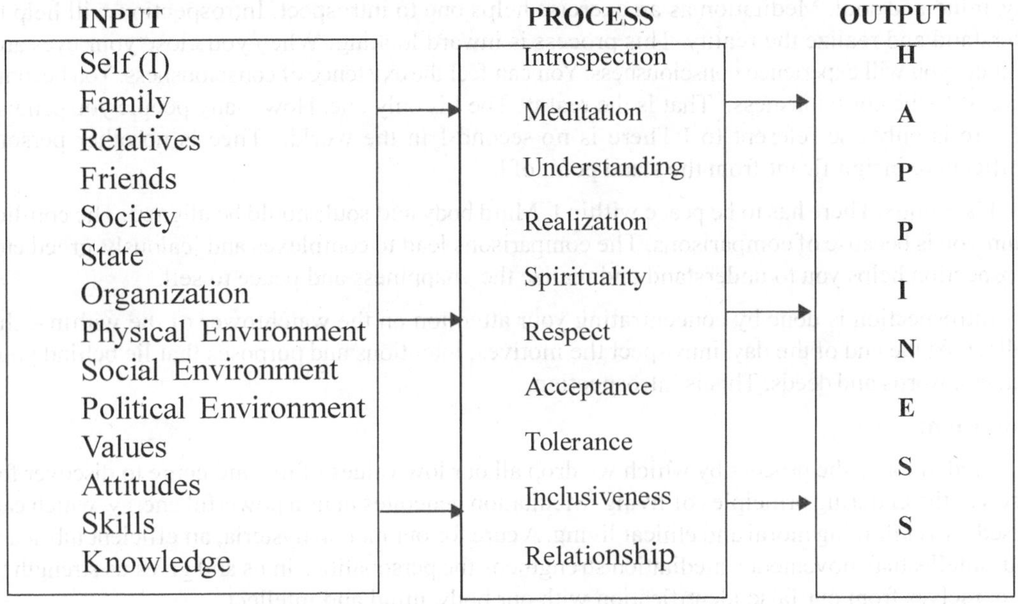

Issues:

How do you measure Input and Output? What is the Ratio between input and output? It is very difficult to measure in mathematical terms the relationship between the input and the output. At the end it is the experience, which is important.

Differentiate between **tolerance** and **acceptance**. What is the difference between these terms? Tolerance is marginal and compromising while acceptance is total. In spite of the differences we tolerate while in the case of acceptance there are no hard burns. When we accept person with all his or her limitations we develop tolerance in us. Accept what you cannot change.

Co- existence. For co-existence acceptance and tolerance are required. Adjustments will also help in the peaceful co-existence. Co-existence results in peace.

Conflicts are due to the ego. The ego comes in between and creates conflicts.

If the process involves Inclusiveness, the output will be unity, harmony and happiness for all. In contrast for exclusivity, output is conflict. Differences, which are divergent in nature, should be converged and result will be universal happiness.

There is a Hindi film song:

"Andhere me jo baithe ho
Nazar un per bhi kuch dalo
Aere o roshniwalo"

Means that people who are sitting and enjoying the light should also look at the people who are sitting in the dark. The concept of inclusiveness is manifested in this song.

The inputs like family, organization, state, society may create conflicting situations. At the end of the chapter, there are a few cases, which illustrates this point. How should one react to them and take decisions, which brings in happiness for self and others. Before taking any hasty decisions, the process should be used to analyse the situation and then take decision, which will be holistic, in harmony, and the output will be happiness. Let briefly understand each one.

Introspection: This is the first step to understand the self. Who am I? The I that we refer to is body, mind and soul. Meditation as an exercise helps one to introspect. Introspection will help to understand and realize the reality. This process is inward looking. When you close your eyes and meditate, you will experience consciousness. You can feel the existence of consciousness. You become aware of I , the consciousness. That is the reality. The I is only one. How many people you can use I? There is only one referent to I There is no second I in the world. Thee is no other person, significant or insignificant from the stand point of I.

I is unique. There has to be peace within I. Mind body and soul should be aligned. The conflict within you is because of comparisons. The comparisons lead to complexes and jealously, greed etc. Introspection helps you to understand and realize the happiness and peace to self.

Introspection is done by concentrating your attention on the watchtower of the within – the intellect. At the end of the day, introspect the motives, intentions and purposes that lie behind your thoughts, words and deeds. This is introspection.

Meditation:

Meditation is the process by which we drop all our low values of life and come to discover for ourselves the enduring principles of living. Meditation generates in us a powerful energy, which can be used for reinforcing moral and ethical living. A cure for our mental hysteria, an efficient lubricant in our intellectual movements, meditation strengthens the personalities in us and gives us strength to free ourselves from our false identification with our body, mind and intellect.

Meditation is a process of inner self-discipline by which through constant practice the doer learns the art of keeping his mind at one and the same chosen line of thinking to the strict and severe exclusion of all other dissimilar currents of thoughts. Ultimately he succeeds in bringing his mind to a complete stillness as in sleep, in which, unlike in sleep, he has his entire awareness brightly lit up.

Through the process of meditation we can cure our psychological complex, anger, passions, cowardice etc. It helps to grow, live, prosper and smile. You should be regular, sincere and pure.

Understanding:

The issue is understanding of what and how? The understanding will lead to the realization resulting in the happiness.

What is Body, Mind and Soul? How are they related? How do you align them to get the happiness? Body and Mind are physical and mental in nature while soul is spiritual. Soul is above mind and body.

There is light in the darkness.
There is silence in the speech
There is truth in the falsehood
There is happiness in unhappiness.

Nature has integrated the dichotomy of the two opposites and one can see that how they co-exist and lead to harmony. In between speech there is silence and both blend together. Similarly the relationship between light and darkness can be understood by the moon and sun. The integration is beautiful without conflict. One cannot see any conflict and both co exist. When nature can have that order why not human beings? These relationships are universal in nature. Neither religion nor human beings can separate them. Light and silence for example is same for a Christian, Muslim or a Hindu.

On the understanding of this fundamental truth, all the other process becomes easier to follow.

Alignment of Individual with the Group

Alignment	I	WE
I	Easy	Difficult
WE	Difficult	Very Difficult

Realization: The process of introspection and understanding will bring in the realization of what is the reality. Everything becomes simple and there are no conflicts. To Gautama Buddha the knowledge dawned and he realized the universe. The world became different on the realizations. The relationships also get connected. How I, we, and universe are connected. We are all part of the universe. I as consciousness is limitless in terms of space and time. On realization , the anger and hatred disappears and love will emerge.

Spirituality: Spirituality is well above, the body, mind and soul. It is not only understand I but also the universe. I as a part of universe. Spirituality should not be mixed with religion. It is above all religion. The aim of religion is to remove all the asymmetries, which are there in the world and move towards the universal peace. Self that has introspected, understood and realized the reality becomes spiritual. The spirit lives even after the death that is what is spirituality about. Soul of Christ, Mohammed, Krishna, Rama etc has all attained spirituality and is worshipped. Gandhi, Mother Theresa are the recent examples of spirituality. The higher purpose of life and the meaning of the world emerge. You become aware of your position in the world. The awareness shapes your beliefs and daily actions.

Spiritualism is a condition wherein the seeker through intelligent training of his inward impulses and judgement, controls and guides his outward actions and behaviour in such a way that a harmonious integration of his personality is achieved. It is a subjective self-growth and self-development, which ultimately ends in the self-discovery. It grows and flourishes in the sadhana of the individual.

Respect: Once the hatred, greed, jealousy go, the respect will automatically emerge. Respect for not only humans but also animals and other forms of life. You giver respect and you will receive respect. We worship sun and water. Worship is a form of respect. If we abuse, the environment, and the nature will abuse us.

Acceptance: Acceptance is total acceptance of the reality. Once the acceptance is made, the differences melt. The acceptance means what ever be the nature, we accept it. It is whole hearted. After looking at the pros and cons only, the acceptance is arrived at. It is born out of logical and rational thinking.

Tolerance: Tolerance will require compromises. The principle behind this as, as long as it does not harm, we will tolerate. Should the society and state tolerate terrorism?

Inclusiveness: All are equal and should be provided with equal opportunities. When the inclusiveness is practiced, the differences will get eliminated. The sharing will automatically become the nature of all. Everything becomes part of you. Environment is also included.

Relationship: The relationship include not just intimate relationships, but all forms of interpersonal interaction we experience daily in our lives. It includes, parents, grandparents, friends, extended family members (cousins, aunts, and uncles), social acquaintances, work colleagues, community, society, and teachers.

Relationship deals with not only between the humans, but also environment. In all the components of the model presented there is continuity. Each is inter connected and part of another component. When the relationships are good, the family, relatives, friends, society and state is happy.

How to Improve Your Relationship?

Timothy suggests that to improve the quality of your relationships, practice mutual **SUPPORT**, which is essential.

S = your strengths and of others

U = unconditional love

P = praise

P = positivity

O = openness

R = respect

T = trust

MEDITATION EXERCISE

Slogans to be told before Meditation

The atmosphere around me is being purified by the Divine Power.
The Divine Power descends upon me and I am being purified.
May the Almighty, protect me, day and night, in all places, in all my activities, to attain good health, long life, enough wealth, prosperity, wisdom and peace.
Salutations to Mother, Salutations to Father. Salutations to Guru.

Meditation

Give Autosuggestion and seek Blessings

By the Grace of Divine Bliss, I will enjoy good health, long life, and enough wealth, Prosperity, Wisdom and Peace. (3 times)
By the grace of Divine Bliss, I will be a man of values. (3 times)
By the grace of Divine Bliss, I will get a good rank in the professional course. (3 times)
By the grace of Divine Bliss, I will get a good job. (3 times)

Seek blessing and be blessed by the Divine Power

Mother
Father
Brother and Sisters
Class Teacher
Subject Teachers
Elders in the family
In my lifetime I will not hurt others, or myself physically or mentally.
I will help others to the extent Possible.
May the whole world enjoy prosperity, happiness, wisdom and peace?

Om Shanti Shanti Shanti

Five minutes of Meditation in the morning and evening will make the difference to the students in terms of concentration and performance.

Activity:

How to be Happy?

Wisdom, Knowledge, curiosity, interest in the world, love of learning, good in judgement, open-mindedness, critical thinking, ingenuity, originality, social intelligence, emotional intelligence, perspective. Courage, valor, bravery, perseverance, diligence, integrity, honesty. Humanity, love: kindness, generosity, loving. Justice, citizenship, loyalty, teamwork, fairness, equity, leadership.

Temperance: self control, discretion, cautious, modesty.

Transcendence: appreciative of beauty and excellence, gratitude, hope, optimistic, spiritual, faith, forgiveness, mercy, playful, humour, passion, enthusiasm,

1.From the above-mentioned list of qualities or you can add any other qualities, identify and choose any of your 5 strengths.

2. Write them down on a piece of paper or diary.

3. Write down at least 3 to 5 ways you can apply your strength, or utilize them in your daily life, in your relationships, for your own happiness.

Adapted from: Dr. Timothy Sharp, Happiness Handbook, and Macmillan, 2007

4 H Model

1. Holistic
2. Harmony
3. Humility
4. Happiness

All the human beings should practice to implement the 4 H model. It is difficult but when nature can do it why can't we? All it needs is to change the view and one can see everything falls in line and peace will emerge.

The goal of education is to promote unity, equality and peaceful co-existence with fellow human beings.

The India human values are: Sathya (Truth), Dharma (Righteousness), Shanthi (Peace), Prema (Love) and Ahimsa (Non-Violence).

Education should teach them simplicity and humility. Through social service, compassion, civic responsibility and community service, human values could be inculcated.

1. Holistic: The issue here is how do I take a holistic picture. The input – output model with process will help to become holistic. You will start your views by looking at a whole rather than parts. This will bring in universal peace. When you connect the components of the model and understand the relationship you develop holistic approach. This is inclusiveness of environment, society and State. You are not greedy or selfish when you take a holistic approach. The conflicts are eliminated. The process is a long one but result in happiness.

2. Harmony: There should be harmony in the universe. It is like a musical orchestra. When all the instruments are played in tune with other the resulting music is melodious and pleasant to hear. The relationships should be harmonious in nature. Each one of the components has to be in harmony with all the others. Like State should be in harmony with the society and individuals. Harmony will result in the happiness. Harmony of thought, deeds and actions is required.

To live in the harmony with the external world does not mean acceptance. A man is said to be living in harmony when his dancing steps on the path are turned to the constant hum of the eternal tune of goodness, charity, love, sacrifice, kindness and patience.

Practicing harmony is not done in the sanctuary of your home or in the moments of success. It is practiced in the din and roar of the market place while you are heaving and sweating with exertion upon the narrow footpaths of uncertain chances in life.

3. Humility: With the values, the humility will automatically come. Once the knowledge is realized and spirituality attained, no special efforts are required to be humble. The more you become humble, the acceptance is higher and so the respect.

4. Happiness:

What is happiness?

Is happiness an object, attribute, place, time and relationship. Let us take up one by one. A leaf is an object and green is an attribute of leaf. There is no object as happy, nor attribute like green colour. There is no place, which will make you happy. Any place can make you happy or unhappy. Similarly there is particular time when you can say that at 5 p.m. everyday, you become happy. It means rest of the time you are not happy. This is not true. You cannot call relationship as happiness. Every relationship has its own friction. In this world we have time, place, objects, attributes and relationships and none of them can be called happiness.

When are you happy?

Is it when your desires are fulfilled? Happiness is not due to something nor due to the efforts, it is in spite of you. You become happy even when all the desires are not fulfilled. This shows that you need not fulfill desires to be happy. . One does discover a moment of joy in spite of unfulfilled desires. Your heart is always in happiness. You want to be happy always, now and forever, in all places and in all situations. If this is true then, you have to assume that happiness is you experience despite all your desires. In a moment of joy you feel secure and happy. Security of money, power, influence, name, health and friends. You see yourself differently when you are happy. Whenever you are happy you are whole. It is the wholeness that you experience which is called happiness. That wholeness is your nature. This means that happiness is your nature.

All human beings desire happiness and make efforts to secure it. The degree and level of happiness, however widely varies from person to person. This indicates that happiness depends more on a state of mind of a person, than on the material like health, wealth or status. It is necessary to differentiate between pleasures and happiness. . Pleasure is derived from satisfaction of senses and is temporary in nature whereas happiness is more permanent. While pleasures are secured through fulfilling our desires of senses, happiness is achieved through training our mind by realizing our supreme self.

What causes unhappiness? (a) Jealousy (b) Attachment (c) Discontent (d) Fear (e) Ego and (f) Desire. For instance a glass of refrigerated water is a cause of happiness in a hot summer but the same is a cause of unhappiness in winter even for an extremely thirsty individual. Thus our happiness or unhappiness is mainly determined by our state of mind and our mental attitude.

Relationship between Religion, Spirituality. Science, Education and Human Values:

To understand the interrelationship between religion, education and human values we need to clarify all the three components. Education and Human values have already been elaborately dealt earlier. Let us now understand the term religion and the issues that we need to look at it. Does religion play any role? Can it integrate?

Figure 3

Anatomy of a religion[*]

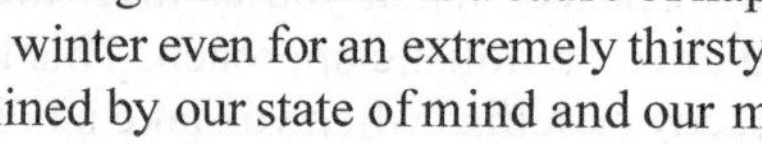

[*]Source: Bhavan's Journal, Volume (56), No. 4, September 30, 2009, pp. 34.

1. **Spirituality**
2. **Theology**
3. **Legends – Mythology – Personalities**
4. **Rituals – Sacraments**
5. **Social customs – Festivals – Institutions - Clergy**

The anatomy of a religion can be represented as rings surrounding a central core of spirituality as depicted in the figure. The outmost ring consists of the institutions, the temples, churches, mosques, the social customs, dress and dietary habits, religious festivals etc. This is the external face the religion presents to the world. In the next layer inside are the various rituals and sacraments that the followers are expected to observe. Usually, this facet of a religion is not open to everyone, but only to its adherents. The third layer is perhaps the most significant of all. It includes the legends and mythologies associated with the various prophets, saints and deities of the religion. The personalities, ideals ad beliefs introduced in this layer often are the factors determining the character of the religion.

In the next inner layer immediately surrounding the spirituality is theology dealing with its beliefs regarding God, origin of the world, soul, death, life after death etc. Typically, theology involves abstract concepts and theories, which the average followers may not totally relate to but is, expected to accept on faith.

Each religion has its own style of adding sugar and spices and serving spiritual truths in an appetizing way to satisfy the spiritual hunger that is in all humans. Just as many different culinary styles have evolved around the world, each capable of providing the nutrition necessary for the human body, so too many religions have developed to cater to the nutrition and needs of the spiritual body.

Religion like food is a matter of choice. Largely determined by the culture in which we grow up. Young people enjoy ethnic food from different parts of the world. Chinese dinner, Italian lunch, continental or Indian breakfast. How wonderful it will be if our understanding and tolerance of religions grows to the extent that we can attend service in a church one-day, pray in a mosque on the next and worship at a temple on the following day!

The distinction made today between religions are mostly superficial and not meaningful from a spiritual point of view. Like the Berlin wall, the barriers that exist between religions are artificial and unjustly divide people from people. Spirituality on the contrary, unites all.

Science, spirituality and religion have each a complementary role to play in our lives and are by no means intrinsically incompatible. The material science, with its focus on matter and energy, blesses us by making our material life more comfortable.

Spirituality, the science of life and knowledge, blesses us individually with inner happiness and collectively with communal harmony. Religions, at their best, serve the mankind by rendering spirituality more readily comprehensible and accessible to the average person.

One must realize the fact that all the religion are one. The main purpose of all the religions is to unite mankind and not divide the humans. Religion does not mean, going to the churches, mosques, or temples or any other place of worship, fulfilling certain formalities and feeling that your religion is the one and the only true one. The conflicts and misunderstanding among the followers of different faiths stemmed from a flawed conception of religion itself. Religion is the realization, not talk nor doctrine, nor theories, however beautiful they may be. It is being and becoming, and not hearing or acknowledging, it is the whole soul becoming changed into what it believes.

Ekam sat vipra bahuda vadanti means there is only one Truth. Different men of religious learning describe this one truth in different ways. Religion is should not be confused with the attempt to attain universal acceptance for one's own faith. The former will expand while later will contract and develop narrow view. A Christian without abandoning his own faith can become a better Christian so also others. No religion should be denied.

People should not think that their path alone is the true and rest is all false faiths.

One must spiritually grow up and become a universal human or divine being with love and sympathy for all. Such a person will have necessarily risen above all barriers of caste, creed, race, religion, colour, sex, nationality etc. A good example is Mother Theresa.

Each soul is potentially divine in nature. The goal of the religion should be to manifest this divinity within by controlling the internal and the external. Seeing God in everybody and serving them. This realization will lead to universal brotherhood and not religious brotherhood. In the end, the education that you receive from the religion will help to develop and respect human values.

How Add Value to Education?

To learn how to add value to education, let us look at the lessons that one can learn from the life of Mahatma Gandhi and Swami Vivekananda . This will help to answer the question of what human values we need to add and how it can be added.

Lessons on Human Values Derived from the Life of Mahatma Gandhi:

1. **Simplicity:** He used to wear loin cloth, steel rimmed glasses, and rough sandals.
2. **Spiritual**: He did not practice any religion apart from human activity.
3. **Ahimsa**: He believed that the way people behave is more important than what they achieve.
4. **Character building**. He regarded character building above all other learning. He regarded character building as the ideal foundation and if the foundation was firmly laid, they would be able to face life in a much better way.
5. **Power of prayer**: Worship and prayers are no superstition. Prayer is means to cleanse the heart of passions.
6. **Gita and Ramayana** are guide of conduct.
7. **Vegetarianism:** believed in nature's remedies for all illnesses, taking only fruits and nuts for food, practicing yoga, brahmacharya, self help including cooking and washing going for long walks He used to draw his energy from God. Surrender to God. It is better to try and fail for a cause that you believe in, than to succeed in some alien cause.
8. **Liberty** is better than learning. It is better to remain illiterate and break stones for the sake of liberty than to go in for a literary education in chains of slavery.
9. **No job is mean.** One should not bear injustice in the name of working or doing ones duty, but rather break free and do a job even of lesser value. Every one has to earn their livelihood from their work.
10. **Regular exercise and strict diet control** to keep fit. He used to regularly practice yoga. One should always find time for exercise as one does for meals.
11. **Self-reliance and dignity of labour**. He worked for the uplifment of untouchables (Harijans and did not believe in caste. His vision was a self-reliant India where Christians, Hindus, Muslims and Harijans could live in harmony and work towards a better world.
12. **Love** for mankind.

Gandhi had the inherent qualities of truth, purity, self-control, firmness, fearlessness, humility, unity, mutual respect, self-discipline, peace and renunciation. His life and preaching's can give us what we all strive for throughout our lives for a true sense of satisfaction and happiness synchronizing the individual goals to that of the Nation's.

West has gone through the cycle of dependence on force and material things of life and has become disillusioned. They want a return to the spirit. The East has not yet gone through materialism and hence has not become so disillusioned. Unfortunately, there is a rush for material at the cost of human values.

Lessons on Human Values Derived from the Life of Swami Vivekananda:*

The secret of the success of Swami Vivekananda was his values. It is the essence of morality what helped to control the mind and build a strong will power to alter fortune.

He has given prescription of Seven habits, when practiced will add value to the education and the success for the youth.

1. **Faith:** The issue will be faith in whom and in what? The faith in (a) ***aptitude*** of oneself. There is no point in having faith in others without your faith in yourself. You should be honest and straightforward with yourself. (b) Faith in your ***talent*** will result in development of self-respect. The faith will help to look up and will become a source of hope. This kind of reflection bonds your love for yourself and will enhance your goal in life. (c) Faith in your ***skills*** to do anything you aim in life.
2. **Character:** Along with the character, physique is also important. To develop good physical strength sports, games are to be played. To build character, spirituality is necessary. The body must be made strong.
3. **Love:** Love is required in youth. They must forget all quarrels, jealousy and hatred amongst themselves. Attitude of forget and forgive. Uplift others who are behind.
4. **Positive attitude:** If you hold yourself in low esteem in your capacity, you will build up pessimism in your thoughts, which positively give birth to an unenthusiastic attitude to wards everything. Strength is life whereas weakness is death. The strength of body mind and spirit should be acquired. Youth should not loose heart and become weak. One must remember that every negative thought saps the tremendous energy within and weakens them and every affirmative and constructive thought leads them to progress, development and success.
5. **Punctuality:** Punctuality is the secret of all success. The youth must be punctual in all walks of life. They must develop an art of finishing each specific task within the specified period of time. To follow the principle of punctuality is to follow the principle of steadfastness. Without steadfastness there is no progress.
6. **Responsibility:** Youth are the makers of their won destiny. So they must be prepared to take every responsibility. They should not waste time regretting the events of the past. There is unlimited future before them.
7. **Good habit:** Good thoughts and deeds will inspire hope. Take up one good thought, deed that may lead you to one good habit. Cultivate one good habit that may mould your whole conduct. From good conduct emerges good fortune.

To activate your inner spirituality in your family or college or society help your friend selflessly. Extend your help in every possible way to someone who needs it the most. Visit an orphanage or a handicapped children's school with your friends and spend some time with these children who need love and care. You do not have to donate money always because money is not everything. The joy that you will receive from such actions will transport you and your mind to a different and higher level. The smiles on the faces of the lesser fortunate children will teach you and inspire you to smile in the most difficult times. Your mind will automatically feel less stressed. This way you become nobler and diviner.

---

* Swami Sudarshananda, Towards a Life of Values, Bhavan's Journal, Vol. (56) No. 13, February 15, 2010, pp.

What is Life?

There is only one life that is present in stones, mineral, plant, vegetables, birds, animals and humans. There is but one life, all life must be regarded as sacred. All have right to live. You cannot take away that which you cannot give since you cannot give life to a dead creature, you have no right to take away the life of a living one. All killings must be stopped for universal peace. Together we must survive.

Cases:

The cases given below are hypothetical situations. These are developed for the purpose of class discussion. You are required to take a decision and justify the decision. The concepts that are presented in this chapter should be used to arrive at a decision. There are no right or wrong decisions.

Case 1: SELF (I)

Ms. Rosy got an admission in Lucknow University for engineering in computer science. She had to stay in the ladies hostel in the University. On Sunday's morning she went to church to offer her prayers.

The University had announced a compulsory meditation camp on Sunday.

What should Ms. Rosy do?

Case 2: Self – Family

1.Ms. Rosy's mother Mary was orthodox. Rosy was the only daughter When Rosy was small, every Sunday she had to go to church. Rosy's father was a south Indian Mr. Subramanian. He did not go to church but went to temple nearby.

Ms. Rosy called up her mother to inform and ask her what she should do. Mother said not to attend the meditation camp but go to church. When she asked her father, he said that Meditation would do her good so she should attend the meditation camp.

What should Ms. Rosy do?

2. There was a bania family settled in Delhi. Family consisted of two sons, two daughters, husband and wife. The eldest son Krishna fell in love with a Russian girl got married and settled down in USA. Second daughter Ms. Ketty got married to a Sardarji and settled in Punjab. Third son was doing his Engineering in south and stayed in the hostel. Last daughter Reema was studying in the XII standard in a CBSE School. Reema had a boy friend by name Rafiq. Rafiq used to help out Reema in her studies and used to visit her place.

During one of visits to India, Krishna met Rafiq. He took an objection that Rafiq should not visit their house. He told him on his face that you should not visit our house.

What should Mr. Rafiq do?

What should Reema do?

Do you think what Krishna did was acceptable?

Case 3: Self-Family-Relatives

Ms. Shashi after completion of 12th standard wanted to become a Doctor. In the family mother Suryakumari was traditional orthodox but with modern thinking, Father Dwarkadas had modern out look. Father had not studied so he was keen to make all children study well. Shasi had two brothers and a sister all younger to her. When she wanted to do medicine, relatives took the objection stating that she will touch the dead bodies daily and come home. She has to take daily head bath. Relatives said that they would not visit home.

What should parents do?

What should Shashi do?

How do you differentiate between a value and the custom in this case?

Case 4: Self – Family – Relatives – Friends

Mr. Sharad had completed his schooling from Bharatiya Vidya Bhavan. There were 12 friends who had studied together from LKG to 12th standard. They moved very close together. After they completed each one went into different fields. Commerce, engineering etc. One of them Mr. Honal who went to US after completing his engineering, met with a serious accident and had brain injury. Immediately his parents and sisters went to US and he survived. All the friends prayed for his health. They all went to Tirupati Balaji together and prayed for the life of Honal. She had a girl friend Sonali with whom he was moving. Sonali's relatives and family were advising her to break off from Honal.

This group of friends did not get into the habit of drinking and smoking. In between one of them started smoking, but all the others couselled and saw that he left his smoking habit.

After about 6 months he returned to India not fully fit. He required physiotherapy and was in depression and frequently said that he wanted poison and that he wanted to end his life. Friends go in batches to meet him and take him to beach and make him feel comfortable and that he is required in the group.

If you were a relative how will you help Honal?

If you are Sonali what will you do?

What can you apply from this chapter to help Honal?

Case 5: Self – Family - Relatives – Friends – Organization

1. Mr. Firoz , Mr. Vivek and Ms. Celina were appearing for their viva voce examinations. They were the students of final year of Engineering. All the three were from different sections. They had different guides under whom they completed their projects. When the valuation of written report was done by external, it was found that all the three had the same photocopy of the report.

An enquiry was conducted with all the guides and students. It was found that Ms. Celina had given her report to other two. The other two students were asked to resubmit the project. Ms. Celina stood by her friends and helped them to re do the project.

Do you think what Celina did was right?

What should college administration do to prevent this in future?

2. Mr. Abraham completed his Mechanical Engineering Degree from university in North India and through campus got selected in a large multinational company. He had to report for his work in Bangalore. He was not familiar with Bangalore city. All his family, relatives and friends were in North India. He was coming to the city for the first time.

The company had given all directions in detail. He had to find a place to stay, which was nearer to the place of work. He stayed in a hotel and searched for the house on rent .He approached a few residents.They said they would not give their house on rent to a bachelor. A few of them said that they would not allow cooking while others said that they would prefer only vegetarians.

What should Abraham do to get the house on rent?

As an organization how you can help Abraham?

As family, friends and relatives staying in the north, how will you help Abraham?

Case 6: Self – Family – Relatives – Friends – Organization – Society

1. Mr. Wilson daily went for a morning walk at 4 am along with his wife. One day he found a girl baby abandoned on the street. The baby was crying and appeared to be just born and left on the street. Mr. Wilson was a member of Rotary Club. He had three children. Two girls and youngest was a boy. They were 17, 12, and 5 years old. Kavita , Vetri and Arjun was the youngest.

He has been reading in the newspapers about the newborn being left near the hospital or in front of some house. He was aware of an orphanage nearby being run by Hindus. The husband and wife were wondering as what they should do? Wilson suggested to take the baby home, but wife said how will other children react? Should he take baby to the house how will friends and relatives react?

As Mr. Wilson what will you do ?

As Kavita eldest daughter of Wilson when father comes and informs you that during the morning walk he saw an abandoned baby girl, what will be your advice to your father?

2. Mr. Ebinezer was 40 years old. He was working as a peon in a shop. He earned a meager salary of Rs. 400 per month. He had two children both boys, 10 and 12 years old, studying in a corporation school. He had a problem in his heart, which required surgery, which will cost him minimum 4 lakhs. He and his family went to church not very regularly but on some festival days.

Ebinezer approached church authorities to help him with finance. Church authorities examined his attendance records and found that he was not coming to the church regularly. He did not know what to do. Meanwhile the shopkeeper happened to be follower of Sathya Saibaba. He informed Ebinezer about hospital that was being managed by Sai trust in Puttuparthi. It was state of the art hospital with all the latest medical equipments and senior surgeon as doctors. The hospital was known for cardiac facilities.

Ebinezer went to the Satya Sai Hospital and the doctors examined him and identified the problem and operated him free of cost. He got the best of the medical treatment at free of cost.

Identify the human values that Satya Sai Trust is advocating.

Case 7: Self – Family – Relatives – Friends – Organization – Society – State

1. Heavy rains lashed city of Mumbai. Life came to a standstill. The whole city was in floods. People could not reach their home and were on the roads. Transportation came to a grinding halt. Instead of waiting for the help from the state Government, the community started actions. They formed kitchens and fed the people. What ever they had in their houses were brought and community kitchens were started. The people came to the rescue. There were no differences in caste or religion. The Swaminarayan cult (a religion based organization) took initiative and fed people in masses. The spirit of co-operation instantaneously came on the surface and all the differences were forgotten. The support from the state also started coming.

2. On September 23rd, 2010 terrorist attacked the people on Chatrpati Shivaji station and two of the posh hotels of Mumbai, Taj and Oberoi as well as small restaurant where foreigners especially targeted towards Jews. The staff of the hotels rescued guests without bothering for their life. The Maharashtra State police, Fire service came together to act. Many of the lives were saved.

Through this situation what are the values that you can identify?

How do you train and educate the students to face these types of crises?

Can you think of similar situations where self, family, relatives, friends, organizations, society and state have come together and worked for universal happiness?

3. Mrs. Javasi amma was 25 years old when her husband expired. She had two sons and a daughter with 12, 7, and 5 years old. Eldest was a son and second was a daughter. Husband used to iron the clothes and had a mobile cart (bandi). The family did not know what to do. Somebody suggested that you enroll in the church and they will pay you some amount to take care of the family. She responded. All the children went to the corporation school. She started ironing clothes and both sons also started the same occupation. She was grateful to the Christian community and the society. The State Government allocated land on which she put up huts for her as well as her sons.

Do you think what Javasi Amma was right?
Identify the values that society, Government exhibited in this case.

OBJECTIVE TYPE QUESTIONS

Fill up the blanks:

1. _________ _________ Said that Education is building the character
2. Four H Model consists of _______ _______ _________ _________
3. Body is _________. Mind is _________ Soul is __________
4. All speech has _________ in between.

True or False:

1. The person is happy when the body and soul are not aligned.
2. Alignment of Self and I is difficult.
3. There is no light in the darkness.
4. Tolerance and acceptance are same.
5. There is no difference between sukh and happiness.

SHORT QUESTIONS

1. What is happiness?
2. What is pendulum effect?

Topics for Debates and Discussions:

1. Does only literacy mean education?
2. Character is more important than formal education
3. The role of formal education system in India
4. Education without moral values is of no use.
5. Education is means and not and end of character.
6. In the current environment of greed, corruption, violence and terrorism how to develop harmony with oneself and mother earth.
7. A discussion on the relationship between Religion – Spirituality – Science.
8. Discuss the views of Mahatma Gandhi, Rabindranath Tagore and Swami Vivekananda, Krishnamurti, on Education.
9. Compare the modern and the ancient upanishadic education.
10. Identify the human values of Satya, Dharma, Prema, Peace, and Ahimsa. From the life of Gandhiji.

EXERCISES

1. Recitation of passages from Bhagvad Gita, Bible and Quran.
2. Meditation and simple exercise of yoga. Pranayam.
3. Playing out door games.
4. Visit and Working in the agriculture fields.
5. Carpentry, stitching, tailoring.
6. Through videos, exposure can be given or
7. Invite a farmer, a carpenter, and a tailor to the class to demonstrate.

8. Invite a painter, a musician and a religious guru of different religions to motivate the students.
9. Students can attend a religious discourse of the various religions and submit a write up
10. Student can visit any one of the vocations they like and submit a report on the problems faced by them and offer solutions. Offer their help to assist them and solve the problems.
11. Design content for a course on value education.
12. Students should take up a social service project. Visit orphanages. Do community service.
13. Social projects to provide Sociocare, Medicare, Healthcare, Agricare, Educare, and Sanitarycare, Infrastructure care could be taken up by the students.
14. Apply existing technology or develop low cost technology and find low cost solution to social problems.
15. Compare and contrast the values of Mahatma Gandhi and Swami Vivekananda.

Chapter

2

Human Values

UNIT I : HUMAN VALUES : Morals, Values and Ethics – Integrity – Work Ethic – Service - Learning – Civic Virtue – Respect for Others – Living Peacefully – Caring – Sharing – Honesty – Courage – Valuing Time – Co-operation – Commitment – Empathy Self Confidence – Character – Spirituality.

This is an Introductory chapter. **Learning Objectives :**

- To understand the basic terms of Morals, Values and Ethics
- To examine relationship between these terms
- To understand how these terms are related to Human Values
- To identify the different Human Values and understand its importance and role

What are Morals?

Morals are the standards, norms or principles of right and wrong. They are basically principles which help to guide our behaviour and accept behaviour of others. The issues relate to: Are these standards based on science? In other words how scientific are these standards? Who develops these standards? How do they develop?

When we are children, we hear and read different stories and in the end there is a question what is the moral of the story? All the Jataka Tales and other stories: remember Tortoise and Hare story . This means that the lesson is learnt from the story. There is a subject of moral science in school. The objective of story telling is, through the story the moral lesson of what is right and what is wrong is learnt.

What are Values?

Value comes from the Latin word 'valere' which means to be of worth, to be strong. As per dictionary, value gives the following meaning: relative worth, utility or importance, degree of excellence, quality, intrinsically valuable. Value literally means something that has a price, something precious, dear and worthwhile, hence some thing, one is ready to suffer and sacrifice for, if necessary one is ready, even to die for it.

Values are a set of principles or standards of behaviour, that are regarded as desirable, important and held in high esteem by society .They are based on the moral norms or standards. Value is the importance or usefulness of something. Since we give importance , we try to protect values. We value money and jewellery, so keep it under lock. Values reflect personal attitudes and judgements,

Morals are the Standards of Right and Wrong.

decisions and choices, behaviour and relationships, dreams and vision. They give rise to beliefs, thoughts, feelings and actions. Higher the benefits, higher the value and higher the value, higher the respect. Value guide us to do the right things and be morally sound. The basis for values are morals. There are different types of values like economic value , time value , psychological and moral or philosophical values. Values can also be classified as personal values , social values, behavioural values, moral and spiritual values.

What is Ethics?

The term ethics is from the Greek word ***ethos*** (Character), refers to the philosophical science that deals with the rightness and wrongness of human actions. Ethics refer to the most important values and beliefs of an individual or a society. These beliefs help shape the character of the people in that society, teaching them what is good and bad. Ethics implies knowledge of these basic principles and the responsibility to make the appropriate choice when necessary. Many philosophers argue that ethics implies values that are universal and are not tied to one society or time period. Ethics is concerned with what is good and right for society. These principles of ethics are based on practice.

Ethics is a manifestation of morals and values in the form of decision. It is an applied moral science. Just as organization behaviour is application of psychology to the behaviour , ethics is an applied moral science. Morals are the standards and values are bundle of morals . By using the principles of morals, you construct a bridge of values and using the bridge of values cross the bridge and take the decision to move forward.

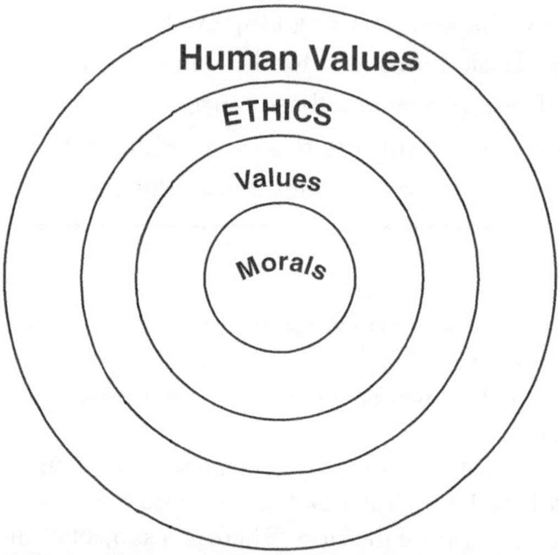

Let us understand the terms moral, value and ethics with the help of an illustration. After completion of Engineering, you may take up a job in a company. After joining the company, you observe your colleague in the office always busy making personal phone calls. What are the alternatives you have? Tell him as a good friend that what he is doing is not right or to keep quite or to tell the higher officials about his behaviour. The decision that you take is ethics. The question is : Is it ethical? The decision is based on your beliefs and value system. The moral value, time value and economic value is used to take the decision. The values are dependent on morals. Morals are the principles what you think is right or wrong. According to the principle of Moral , what your friend is doing is wrong. Because time is allocated for the company and you are paid for doing work in the company and for the company. Doing

Ethics is concerned with what is good and right for society.

personal work and getting paid by the company is not morally right. However, what is morally right is not necessarily ethically right. Further on investigation , you find that your colleague's mother is very sick and he is calling up to find out about the health condition of his mother and to give instructions. This means that ethically his behaviour is right even though morally it is wrong. Do you respect your mother, do you value her? As stated earlier ethics is manifestation of your values. The value of care and respect determines your behaviour. Here there is a moral dilemma about decision.

MORALS + VALUES + ETHICS = HUMAN VALUES

What are Human Values ?

Human values are the values of the human beings for the human beings and by the human beings. Morals and values are the foundation of human values. Just as a building has a foundation of concrete, the building of human values rests on morals and values. Human values can also be defined as values of life. Human is a form of life.

In a profession , the human values identified and used are called, **Key Ethical Principles (KEP)** examples are : Honesty, Integrity, fulfilling Commitments, abiding by Agreements in letter and spirit, being fair and open minded and willing to admit errors Caring and Compassionate, respect for human dignity, Responsible, pursuit of excellence and being accountable for decision and its consequences.

Let us take few of the human values and understand what it is and how important they are.

Integrity :

The dictionary meaning of Integrity is the quality of being honest and morally upright. It is the state of being whole or unified. Thus integrity is an act of honesty. There is a close relationship between integrity and honesty. The consistent honest behaviour develops integrity in an individual. The moral of honesty results in integrity. The person is said to be having human value of integrity when his behaviour and action matches, He does what he says. There is no contradiction between what he says and what he does.

Integrity helps the other person to predict your behaviour and action. If there is consistency in what you say and what you do, people will have belief in you. Lack of integrity, results in unpredictable behaviour and action. Mahatma Gandhi did what he preached. For example in the office, you observe your boss always coming late and insisting on others in the office to come before time or on time. He orders fine for coming late. What value you give to his orders ? Some people set examples by their actions. Don't talk about cost cutting and cost optimization to the rank and file, and then fly business class or stay in 5 star hotels.

This value will help the engineers to gain confidence from management and help him to move up the ladder. All the organizations are looking for this value in employees.

Work Ethic:

We say work is worship. This belief gives lot of value to work and regards it as a god. Many of the large organizations have code of ethics for the employees. The code specifies the work ethics. For example reporting time 8 am, Lunch 1 – 2 pm, specifies dress code. A person with work ethic will observe these rules. He does what is expected out of him. Work ethics are laid down by the organization to bring uniformity in the behaviour of workers, managers and all other employees.

A good work ethic creates a work culture in the organization and increases the productivity.

This value will help the engineer to work hard and discipline himself and build team in an organization.

Integrity is an act of Honesty. Work is Worship. Service is Responsibility.

Service:

Service is the work involving the use of the head, the heart and the hand, for the welfare of others, irrespective of their status, caste or creed. It is a social value and contribute to the development and offers ample opportunities for the development of one's character and personality. The value of service is dormant in all the human beings.

Service is going beyond the call of duty . To offer help and your time voluntarily without expectation of any return is doing service. It may be internal within the organization or outside the organization helping some Non Government Organisations (NGO's) or similar organizations. It is said that service to humanity is service to God. There are several service organization like Rotary Club, Lions Club etc. who do lot of social service. During famine, floods, fire or any other emergencies also, service may be provided. A person who values human, will offer the services. Many organization believe "Service is our motto", this means that they believe in serving their customers, employees, suppliers and society. Lot of satisfaction is derived from selfless service. Service is a responsibility of humans toward civil society.

Service will help engineer to build his personality and win the respect in the society. It will help to network with customers and people .

Learning :

When you perform some action then you learn in the process. Learning itself is a process. Learning is a value derived from the actions and decisions. The new concept of Learning organizations has emerged . These organizations adapt quickly to the external environmental changes and are considered to be dynamic in nature. One must also know how to unlearn. Sometimes to learn something we are required to unlearn something. It is very difficult to unlearn and comparatively easy to learn. There is a saying that habits die very hard. This is an attitude towards life. There is an opportunity to learn from everything even failure. Organizations want people who possess high level of willingness to learn. It is a fact that we do not know everything. You are fool if you think that you know everything. It is not possible at all. Learning takes place in the individual. Once you learn to do something, it is very difficult to forget. For example cycling or swimming.

The value of learning will help engineer to develop and grow in an organization. He will become more adjustable and develop open mind to accept the opinion of others.

Civic Virtue:

This is a social value. A human being is a social animal. He lives in a society and is a part of the society. While working in an organization he lives in a civic society. Civic society means civil society. As a member of the society he has to take care of the people and surroundings. For example not to create noise pollution, throw garbage , violate traffic rules and be a nuisance value to the other members of the society. As a member of a society he has certain responsibilities towards society. Every individual has to become a responsible Indian citizen. He must confirm to the natural law as well as rules laid down by the society for the peaceful existence of all human beings.

Indians score low on the civic sense. They have habit of throwing garbage outside, throw the used things anywhere and everywhere. The attitude of ' so what' is engraved in them. In slums people live in lot of dirt and unhygienic conditions.

Civic virtue makes humans, habitually neat or pure without any dirt, filth or corruption. It is freedom from dirt, filth, adulteration and corruption. It shows respect for the dignity of a human person. It helps us to keep our surroundings neat , clean and free from diseases. This virtue helps people to live a healthy life with clean environment. Cleanliness is next to Godliness.

You are fool if you think you know everything
Civic society means civil society.

This value will help to keep surrounding neat and clean and be considerate to others and co-operate with others.

Respect for Others:

This is a human value which is based on the principle of equality. All the human beings are same and deserve the same respect irrespective of economic, political or social positions. One must treat all human beings as fellow friend , listen to them, and not hurt anybody. This comes out from the golden principle of *'do unto others what you would like others to do for you'.* You have to put yourself in the position of other person. Give respect and take respect. When you give respect to other human beings, they in turn will reciprocate and return the same, Vice versa when you disrespect others, they will also return the same. Respect is like a mirror. Mirror reflects your own image. Similarly respect comes back to you in return.

Respect for others lead to tolerance. One has to respect the beliefs, views, attitudes temperaments or behaviour of others when these differ from our own. It enables us to adjust our relationship with each other and work together for a common purpose. It helps to cultivate the spirit of accommodation, dialogue and interaction. The respect for others helps to avoid all misunderstanding, animosity and conflict. It overcomes communal riots, racial prejudices and cultural biases. It helps to accept the differences in a spirit of understanding and friendliness. The result is peace and harmony among people and nations.

Respect for others will automatically come on the realization that there are no differences between the human beings. All are made of same chemicals and have common nature. The differences are man made in the minds of people.

An engineer, by practicing this value will win respect from other employees and management.

Living Peacefully:

You must live in peace and allow others also to live the same way. Living peacefully require immense amount of patience, adjustment, give and take, emotional control etc. Harmony is required for peaceful living. Where there is harmony there you will find peace. It is a social value. This is derived from the civic sense. In villages, one finds peace. There is absence of rush and people keep cool and calm. In temples also there is divinity and peace. Once you practice this value, terrorism and hatred will disappear.

A person with this value will not create problems for others. These days this value is very important.

Caring :

This is a human value which delivers satisfaction to others. Human psychology is such that every one wants attention and recognition. When, human being is ignored, he feels lonely , feels left out and develops an inferiority complex. He faces a low esteem He craves for attention. Love and care to other humans , make them wanted and results in attention. When you are baby, your mother is very loving and caring. As such, women are loving and caring. This value builds confidence in human beings. It brings around oneness amongst all. These values lead to communication and result in involvement of people in an organization. You have to show concern for fellow human beings.

This value helps to create, attitude of mother and not find fault with others and develop a feeling of caring. It will help to reduce conflicts in the organization. People also will be happy to get attention and the performance of subordinates will increase.

Sharing:

Sharing is the ability to give to others what we possess. This stems from the attitude of caring. When we start caring we also share. Caring and sharing are used together. There is togetherness when

Sharing is the ability to give to others what we possess.

things are being shared. When we start sharing, we get more and more . After sharing there are no expectations as it expects nothing in return. Sharing helps us to overcome selfishness and create spirit of magnanimity . Bill gates shares his wealth by donating huge sums of money for the welfare and cause of the human beings. One can develop habit of sharing by showing whatever they have and sharing with others. It is not only sharing of things but also joy or sorrow. A friend in need is a friend indeed. It is a social value.

This value will unite people of different caste and creed and create atmosphere of family in the organization. It will help in team building and performance.

Honesty:

Honesty means truthfulness. It is a personal core human value. It is a quality within an individual that urges a person to be true to oneself and to others. It does not permit any deception. A person will be honest when he has the ability to stand up for conviction and honour commitment. The result of the practice of honesty establishes character and reputation as a trustworthy individual and brings respectability. When a person is honest he leads a peaceful and a happy life. Honesty is the best policy.

A honest person speaks truth and accepts full responsibility for work done. He does not cheat other person. One needs to be honest with oneself. We feel that we have cheated others , but in fact you are cheating yourself rather than others.

It will bring pain but also happiness of being truthful. Recognition will automatically come for the sincerity.

Courage:

Courage is required to set realistic expectations with the employees and management. Some decisions that will benefit the organization in the long term may some time need sacrificing gains in the short term. Here it requires courage to face the losses in the short term.

Life has many challenges and they must be faced with courage. Courage is the ability to face the strains and setbacks. It is dynamic and motivates one to fight for principles and values. True courage is linked with deep faith. It drives people to achieve the impossible. Courage helps people to face the disaster with calmness, poise, tranquility, fearlessness and confidence. It makes person capable to own mistakes, The quality of courage helps to build confidence in an individual. The other term is valour. It is a personal value developed over time.

By practicing this value, entrepreneurial qualities and risk taking abilities will develop.

Valuing Time:

We must understand the value of time. Just as money has value , time also has value.

Time = Money. Just as you value money and spend carefully and plan finance, you must plan the time. It is a resource and needs to be utilized and not wasted. It cannot be stored and it just flies. In India we take time for granted. If somebody invites you at 8 am, we go at our leisure time and say 'so what.' , in spite of being late. This attitude reveals that you do not have value for other's time.

Imagine there is a program: Thousands of people are waiting and the chief guest arrives, one hour late and does not bother to inform the organization that he will be delayed and what time he can be expected. Chief guest, an hour late and thousand hours go waste. We must become more sensitive to time. When you start valuing time, you plan it well and avoid wastage. Time needs to be invested properly. Money when invested gives return, similarly time when invested delivers money and hence time is money. We need to use time for personal growth and find time for reading and meditation.

Time can be sold or purchased. When you employ a servant, you buy her time. In contrast when you work for somebody, you sell your time. We pay on the basis of time spent. This clearly

Time is money - save both.

shows that time has value and can be measured in terms of money.

This value will help to earn more, as time is money and value. You will develop discipline, timeliness and practice to be on time and not to waste time of others and yours.

Co-operation:

Co-operation means coming together. In human beings , the result is lot of energy and synergy. The value of togetherness is reflected in co-operation. Co-operation can achieve much more than an individual. Co-operation develops strength which is much greater than the strength of an individual. In the current stage, the individual performance and competition are in vogue. Generally, the psychology of human being is to come together when faced with crisis.

This value will help for the growth of the business. The achievement will be more by co-operation, rather than confrontation. It will result in peace.

Commitment:

Commitment is a very important value which is expected from employees of an organization. Commitment results in devotion of time and money . The value of commitment makes humans responsible. In an organization, communication, sharing and caring attitude, culture and climate create commitment. Commitment of time, job, duty, money etc .This value will get recognition and attention from the management. It will make you work hard and achieve more.

Empathy :

Empathy is the value of being considerate. You have to put yourself in the shoes of other person to know where the shoe pinches and to experience the same feelings and express the same. Empathy helps to change the attitude. The actions change when you try and empathize with other person. You understand the problems and experiences and become considerate. This will develop attitude of being in others shoe. Subordinates look forward for this value in their superiors.

Self Confidence :

Self confidence is the strength and value of an individual. It is inherent and internal in self. The encouragement and support from the family, organization, peers result in self becoming confident. Rewards also make person more confident.

Self confidence implies trust in oneself and in one's ability. It helps to enrich the character. The result is positive approach and develop self respect and optimism. It is supposed to be the first secret of success. This is personal value.

This will help engineers to deliver performance and achievements.

Character:

Character is the light which shines when the sun is down and all other lights are out. It is that power with which we can win victory even when losing battles. It is the awakened divine in man before whom all heads bend, it shines even in poverty. Robbers can break open and rob everything in the world, but not character. When we have lost everything but not character, we have not really lost anything. Everything made by man can be destroyed by man but not character. That is the strength of character.

One can build one's own character. The role of education is to develop character. Character transmission is the essential mission of education. One can build or lose character.

You will gain respect all round by inculcating this personal value .

We are the master of unspoken words but a slave of spoken words
One can build one's own character

Spirituality:

Spirituality is the realization and understanding of who you are? It brings alignment of mind with the body. Meditation and Yoga help to become spiritual. You realize the truth and understand the reality. These are also known as moral values. They are related to an individual's character, nobility and personality conforming to what is right and virtuous. It reveals a person's self control, self purification and inner quality. They depict a person's spiritual convictions and profoundness.

Some examples of moral and spiritual values are: detachment, faith, loyalty, non-violence, obedience, prayer, purity, renunciation and truthfulness. Examples of reforms at Tihar Jail initiated by Kiran Bedi is indicative of a move towards wholesome and spiritually sound leadership. Such leaders become channel of divine energy who comfort the disturbed. Spritually mature leader trust not only his own lonely power but take energy from cosmic unitary flow of energy.

It helps to achieve extraordinary from ordinary people. Also, make you calm the mind and concentrate. This is the highest order of all the values. Once this values are practiced all the other will follow suit. The emotional balance will be achieved and full control over the mind and body is gained. One achieves state of Sthitpragya, experiences joy and happiness. Once you become happy, you will make others happy.

Conclusion:

The different Human Values discussed in this chapter are not independent of each other. They are not water tight compartments but are inter dependent There is a relationship between them. Some of them like honesty and integrity are used interchangeably.

Inculcation of these Human values makes an engineer humane and be successful in the career as well as in life.

EXERCISES

1. Develop a news item, short story, magazine article, literary piece, skit, street play, folk-song, poem, film, biography, photo, painting, T.V. or radio serial depicting the various human values.
2. Recall in your mind instances when you had practiced these values in your life.
3. Prepare an assignment of the positive effects of the Human values.

QUESTIONS

1. Discuss the various human values and in what way it will help Engineers ?
2. Why time is a value ?
3. How important is the value of spirituality ?
4. How moral, ethical and human values are related ?

REFERENCE

Dr. S. Ignacimuthu, SJ, "Values for Life". Better Yourself Books, 8th print , 2004

Chapter

3

Engineering Ethics

UNIT II : ENGINEERING ETHICS : Senses of "Engineering Ethics" – Variety of moral issues - Types of inquiry – Moral dilemmas – Moral autonomy – Kohlberg's theory – Gilligan"s theory – Consensus and Controversy – Models of Professionals Roles – Theories about right action – Self interest – Custom and Religion – Uses of ethical theories.

Learning Objectives

- To understand the term "Engineering ethics"
- Types of Inquiry.
- Moral dilemmas.
- Theories of Moral Development – Kohlberg & Gilligan.
- Need for Consensus and Controversies.
- Theory of Right Action.
- To understand the concept of Self interest.
- Role of customs and religion.
- Uses of ethical theories.

This chapter serves as an introduction. It explores and discusses the concepts and issues relating to professional ethics. It examines the relationship of ethics with morals and religion. It describes the term 'professional ethics'. The role and importance of the professional ethics are discussed. There is an illustration of an ethical company. There are a few cases about situations faced by engineers.

PROFESSION

Definition of Profession

The term 'profession' is used in a variety of ways. When people ask of a person 'what his/her profession is, it is often a polite way of asking his/her job or occupation. In this usage the terms 'occupation', 'job' and 'profession' are used synonymously. The term is also used in sports and games to differentiate between amateurs and professionals. Here the term ' professional' means that the activity engaged in is one's principal career from which one expects to derive one's income and livelihood. In another sense, professional work is work that is done skillfully. People say of workers who perform well that "They do a thorough professional job".

The Latin term ***professionem*** originally meant the making of a public declaration. In medieval Latin, it referred to a person taking religious vows to join the clergy. The English word 'profession' comes directly from Latin and until the sixteenth century it meant only the public taking of religious vows. Later on it came to mean an occupation, in which learnt knowledge is applied to the affairs of others, especially in medicine, law, divinity and university teaching.

Is there any difference between professionals and non-professionals? Under communism the difference between professionals and non-professionals would not exist. Communistic ideology means that every worker, whether he be a physician or coal miner, always should be striving to promote the well being of the society at large. Consequently there would be no special group of professional occupations. The difference is sharp in a society that follows an individualistic ideology, such as free-enterprise system. In such a society, professionals, unlike non-professionals, have specific responsibilities towards their occupation, clients and public.

In the Western society, medicine has had professional character since ancient Greek times, when physicians took the Hippocratic oath, pledging to protect their art and to use their medical skill only for the promotion of health. Medicine was followed by law, architecture, engineering, accounting, journalism, business and many other occupations, which partook of the character of being a profession to varying degrees. When architects, accountants, managers, engineers are independent practitioners taking clients, their status tends to be ***strongly more professional*** than when they are employees.

Characteristic of a Profession

Professionals can be defined by three characteristics: they are experts in a chosen field, they are expected to use their expertise 'responsibly' and they identify themselves as professionals, "professing" membership of a distinguished group. (As mentioned earlier, the word originally alluded to membership in a religious order).

(1) ***Expertise***: Theoretical and practical knowledge gained through education and training in the chosen field makes him/her an expert. It requires acquisition of special knowledge and skills through extensive formal education, systematic studies and training. It also involves continuous education and updating of knowledge.

(2) ***Use of knowledge and expertise for public good:*** Like medicine for promoting health, 'law' is towards protecting the public's legal rights and 'engineering' towards promoting the public's health, safety and welfare. This is the main plank of 'responsibility'.

(3) ***Membership*** of an organization or society: These ***organizations*** are usually controlled by members of profession. They lay down the rules for standards, evolve and enforce a 'code of conduct' and represent the profession to the public and Government. Because of professional associations and rules governing their membership, public can assume that any certified professional be it a physician or an engineer or an accountant, he/she will have at least a minimal degree of knowledge and skill competency.

Who is an Engineer?

The dictionary defines an engineer as one who designs, makes or works with machinery. The definition had remained largely accurate till a couple of decades back when most engineers worked either on a factory shop floor or at the site of work. The dichotomy in definition happened after the IT came to dominate the work scene. The new technology created a new breed of engineers. Since the only machines that boys and girls got to see and use were the computers, and the only tool they knew to handle the mouse, this crew of engineers got designated as software engineers. As opposed to these are the ageing, shrinking set of hard core, hard up engineers of the nut and bolt economy. After understanding the term profession and engineer we can say that an Engineer is a Professional.

E – R –P = Expectation – Reactions – Pressures need to be managed. One who successfully manages ERP has mastered his mind

PROFESSION AND PROFESSIONALISM

The general dictionary meaning of the word profession is 'a vocation or calling, especially one that involves some advanced learning or science' it is a noun. The term professional is an adjective of profession. When used as a noun, professional also describes a person. Professionalism refers to the qualities, competencies and skills etc of professionals. It has behavioral connotations and refers to the manifestations of a professional.

The understanding of the term profession makes it easier to relate profession and professionalism. When the criteria of profession are applied to one's vocation or calling, it makes for professionalism. In Sociology many descriptive criteria of professionalism have been put forward. These include:

> The work is white-collar, above-average education, above-average pay, there is an explicit code of ethics to which those in the occupation subscribe, entry is limited by licensing procedures, those in the occupation have an association that is dedicated to maintaining standards, the service provided is indispensable for the public good, those in the occupation work as independent practitioners and income does not depend much on deployment of monetary capital.

A sociologist studying professionalism of a specific occupation prepares a particular list of such factors and then stipulates that occupation is to count as a profession only if it follows most of the factors on that list.

An occupation moves from just being an occupation to being a professional occupation through stages. Professionalism, it should be understood, is a relative condition. Professional status normally develops around an occupation. In a profession, unlike in an occupation, often it is hard to know that a person is incompetent until it is too late. If incompetence is immediately apparent, one can dismiss the employee before much damage is done. Engineering clearly calls for professionalism because serious defects in an engineer's work may not surface until years after the work is completed. The degree of professionalism can vary from professional to professional in the same profession; for example, from engineer to engineer. The degree and rigours of professionalism also varies from profession to profession, like medicine to engineering to journalism.

Whitelaw* sharply contrasts bureaucratic submission to one's employer with the independence he sees as inherent in professionalism. In fact, he defines professionalism and employee status as *logically incompatible*: "so long as the individual is looked upon as an employee rather than as a free artisan, to that extent there is no professional status."

In Whitelaw's view, only consulting engineers qualify as professionals. According to him, the mass of engineers working as employees within corporate or governmental bureaucracies cannot be considered professionals until they are protected by an engineering bill of rights ensuring them the freedom already enjoyed by self-employed engineers. Examples of these rights are "the right to refuse unethical activity without prejudice or loss of contract" and "the right to freedom from surveillance, psychological manipulation, and other job evaluation techniques." According to Whitelaw's definition, one is not a professional engineer if one acts merely on the basis of an employer's orders in matters where the public good is concerned. Being a professional involves the freedom to act according to one's own judgment about conduct.

Florman* on the other hand argues, "It is essential that professionals should serve rather than filtering their everyday work through a sieve of ethical sensitivity," Professionals have the task of meeting the expectations of their clients and employers. Professional restraints should be laws and government regulations rather than personal conscience. He believes that Engineers are obliged to bring integrity and competence to whatever work they undertake. But they should not be counted upon to consider paramount the welfare of the human race.

Professionals should do a professional job.

Professional engineers should be viewed as meeting two general criteria: (1) attaining standards of achievement in education, job performance, or creativity in engineering that distinguish engineers from engineering technicians and technologists. (2) accepting as part of their professional obligations at least the most basic moral responsibilities to the public as well as to their employers, clients, colleagues, and subordinates. This latter criterion lends to the term *professionalism* a moral dimension consistent with the fact that "unprofessional conduct" is often used as a synonym for "unethical conduct".

ETHICS

The term ethics, derived from the Greek word ***ethos*** (character), refers to the philosophical science that deals with the rightness and wrongness of human actions. Ethics refers to the most important values and beliefs of an individual and/or a society. These beliefs help shape the character of the people in that society, teaching them what is good and bad. Ethics implies knowledge of these basic principles and the responsibility to make the appropriate choice when necessary. Many philosophers argue that ethics implies values that are universal and are not tied to one society or time period.

Ethics is concerned with what is good and right for society. Some of the universally accepted ethical principles are ***: honesty, integrity, fulfilling commitments, abiding by agreements in both letter and spirit, being fair and open minded and willing to admit mistakes, being caring and compassionate, having respect for human dignity, responsible pursuit of excellence and being accountable for one's decisions and their consequences.*** Definitions and practice of these principles, however, tend to be contextual and change with time and societal norms.

PROFESSIONAL ETHICS

Professional ethics refer to the ethical obligations that people in professional occupations have to follow because of their professional status. It encompasses how professionals ought to behave in their professional work and not merely how they conduct themselves.

Every occupation involves its own ethical obligation. Thus, firemen have a special obligation to rescue people from burning buildings even when it can be dangerous to themselves to do so, and farmers have a special obligation to see that the food they produce are safe to consume for the intended consumers. These are related to occupational ethics. The professional ethics need to be seen as differing in their source and character from those of non-professional workers. This can come about only if professional ethics is based on a concept of the professions that succeeds in differentiating them ethically from other occupations.

The term professional ethics is interchangeable with engineering ethics. Engineering Ethics are deals with:

(1) the moral issues and decisions confronting individual and organizations engaged in engineering and

(2) related questions about the moral ideals, character, policies and relationships of people and corporations involved in technological activities.

Engineering Ethics is the activity and discipline aimed at understanding the moral values that ought to guide engineering practice, resolving moral issues in engineering and justifying moral judgements concerning engineering.

In ethics, the major issue is: who decides what is ethical? What is good for an individual may not be necessarily good for others or for the society. What is good at one point of time may not be good at all the times and in all situations. The understanding of the relationship between similar concepts will, to some extent, help answer these questions.

Professionals are persons with expertise and knowledge.

ETHICS AND ITS RELATIONSHIP WITH SIMILAR CONCEPTS

Ethics and Morals

People have a variety of notions of 'right' and 'wrong'. These notions manifest themselves in a number of ways. Some of these beliefs pertain to simple matters such as manners or taste; other to more general matters such as customs and laws and others guide the most fundamental aspects of human life. These are the beliefs that shape one's character and determine what others think about one as a human being. One's moral beliefs say more about one as an individual than any other aspect of existence. Whether one is rich or poor, old or young, one's moral beliefs do more to define one's life and personality than anything else.

The issue here is ***whether ethics and morals are same. Or are there differences? If yes, what are the differences?*** The terms 'morality' and 'ethics' are often used interchangeably, but the distinction between the two is important to any serious study of ethical matters.

The clearest distinction can be understood by noting that there is a large school of thought referring to 'situational ethics'. There is, however, far less scope for 'situational morality'. Morality usually is far less relative. What distinguishes morality from ethics is that morality tends to be more universal and prescriptive. For this reason, the notions cited above, about manners, taste, customs and even laws may be considered ethical beliefs, but they are not always part of a moral code. When ethical views and moral beliefs come into conflict, morality must prevail, because moral beliefs are generally far more universal and fundamental.

A person who cheats at cards may be considered unethical, but that does not necessarily mean that the person is immoral. Being immoral is a much greater character flaw than is being unethical. A person may behave unethically on occasions and in certain circumstances, but to be immoral is to possess fundamental if not permanent character flaws that render one untrustworthy in most situations.

Some people are considered 'amoral' as distinct from 'immoral'. This means that a broad system of beliefs does not guide their behaviour. This is not to suggest that they do not have a set of "do's" and "don'ts" in life. Only that their behaviour and beliefs are not guided by the generally accepted universal systems that provide justification for human actions.

A morally correct decision often depends on the circumstances of the person making it. Even with the same moral standards, two individuals may consider different decisions to be appropriate, if their individual circumstances are different. ***Ethical subjectivism*** argues that what is ethically right or wrong for an individual depends on the ethical principles he or she has chosen. In other words, for people who subscribe to ethical subjectivism what is ethically right or wrong is entirely a personal matter. While a person lives by the principles he chooses, it is not necessary that these principles are universally ethical. To be accepted as universally ethical, they must withstand public scrutiny and cease to be a personal matter.

An issue that arises in a moral debate is a genuine moral issue, i.e. a question having to do with the relevance or application of one or more moral principles. It should be noted that there is a broad and a narrow sense of the term "moral issue." Often times the application of moral principles to particular situations is relatively non-controversial. For example, let us say *Compound X* is a virulent carcinogen and is emitted in large quantities by *Company B* into the atmosphere, then most people would probably agree that this practice should be stopped. The general prohibition against knowingly harming other people would necessitate this conclusion. But on the other hand, suppose *Compound X* produces only mild respiratory problems in a very small percentage of the population and that discontinuing the practice is so prohibitively expensive that it would force the plant to discontinue a product line and lay off a large part of its work force. And further, there is already a serious unemployment

Ethics is concerned with what is good and right for society.

problem in the town and many employees may have to leave town to find alternative work. Then there would be serious disagreement as to what should be done.

A conceptual issue is resolved by coming to agreement over the proper definition or scope of a term. A moral issue is resolved by agreement over the proper application of one or more moral principles. It is also important to keep in mind that the resolution of factual and conceptual issues may be just as controversial and just as difficult as the resolution of moral issues—sometimes even more so. In many situations it is difficult or impossible to determine the relevant facts, especially when the factual issues have to do with the prediction of the likely consequences of events in the future. Scientists may simply disagree over the likelihood of a meltdown in an atomic power plant or the probable effects of storing toxic wastes in a particular location. Similarly, arguments over the definitions of "bribe" or "proprietary" may be very difficult to resolve. Nevertheless, people can disagree over moral issues, so let us examine these disagreements in more detail.

In considering issues in engineering ethics, a distinction is at times made between morals and ethics. When this distinction is made, the term morals is taken to refer to generally accepted standards of right and wrong in a society and the term ethics is taken to refer to more abstract principles which might appear in a code of professional ethics or in a textbook in ethical theory. However, the terms moral philosophy or moral theory would refer to a set of abstract moral principles as appropriately as the term ethics, so it may be more practical to use the words interchangeably. Both the terms refer to standards of right conduct and the judgments of particular actions as right or wrong by those standards.

Moral and ethical statements must be distinguished from two other types of statements, namely those in etiquette and those in law. Referring to a rule of etiquette, we might say, "You should compliment your host or hostess after a good meal." Here we have used the word should, and this suggests that we have made an ethical judgment. However, there are at least two important differences between statements of etiquette and statements of ethics. First, moral and ethical statements are generally thought to have greater importance than statements of etiquette. Most of us probably feel that a violation of a rule such as "An engineer should protect the safety of the public" is much more serious than a violation of a rule such as "You should not eat peas with your knife." A second difference between ethics and etiquette is that ethical norms cannot be changed by books of rules or by authoritative bodies, but rules of etiquette may be.

Some believe that moral beliefs can be acquired. According to some, there are six ways of acquiring moral beliefs: ***authority, ,logic, sense experience, emotion ,intuition and science.*** If one is taught to obey parental authority in ones' early years, one will generally find it easier to accept other authorities in later years.

For most people, parental authority is their first exposure to subordinating personal desires to some other's influence. If one learns to control one's desires, one can then substitute other influences for parental authority in later years. Ones' ability to respond to any kind of moral guidance is dependent upon one's ability to control one's own actions.

The factors that influence beliefs usually change as people mature emotionally and intellectually. Moral development need not be linear in nature. Moral philosophers have never agreed on the main source of morality but they agree only that moral theories and moral actions are a necessary part of being human.

Ethics and Values

Value is what makes actions, character traits and objects good or bad. Examining the moral qualities of people or actions and their non-moral properties inevitably raises the qualities of the nature or source of those values. What is 'value'? It takes two possible forms. The first and the simplest provide a list of values, such as courage, honesty, beauty and compassion. The second attempts to answer what exactly is meant by courage or beauty or friendship. It may seem relatively

Ethics and Morals shape the character.

simple to compile a list of values, but difficult to answer the second part of the question. The list of values may differ from time to time and culture to culture. One cannot know what particular values are unless one knows the nature of value in general.

Values are unquantifiable attributes that have to be assessed only by our behaviour and signals that we constantly send out. Any one therefore needing to know about the values that drive his/her life needs to introspect. Values and ethics are not different from our whole identity. We are what we practice and our practices are a manifestation of our values. Our ethics and value systems really define **who** and **what** we are.

Corporate Values

These are the values of an organisation. Generally, the founders and the top management leadership inculcate these values in an organisation through written statements, actions and practices. They drive the policies ,strategies and operations of the organisation.

Values are basic assumption about which ideals are desirable or worth striving for. (Vijay Sathe; 1985). Value represents preference for the ultimate end states. Values are key determinants of attitudes, which in turn affect work related (and all other) behavior (Becker and Conner 1986,Finegam 2000). Values together with ethics, beliefs and norms make up the culture of an organisation. And culture affects not only managerial behavior within an organisation but also the decisions they make about the organisation's relationship with its environment and strategy. Consciously chosen values are the guiding force for organisational effort. In the ever changing era of politico-economics and technological scenario any number of policies or rules cannot ensure the righteous human action It is the well defined values which can lead human action in desired direction. According to Jack Welch "Strategy and system don't get you results; their values and people do."

Example can be cited here is the success of the Hero group. This is largely due to customer service and excellent relation between distributor and the company. This level of relation with distributor can't be ensured by mere policy and rules. This is the result of deep rooted value of customer care.

Transformation Through and With Values

In the changing business enviroment, values are the guiding force for many companies. There are several Indian companies, which have transformed themselves as world class players during emerging business context. *Bajaj Auto* had benefitted from the system before economic reforms through long waiting lists for its products.After the opening up of the economy, the company faced problems at the market place.After losing subsantial market share initially,the company regained its leaderdhip position by innovative strategies. During this transformation two values were guiding the process - customer delight and avoiding debt at all costs. *Bajaj Auto* has grown with rate of 1852 percent in last 10 years!!!

Growth of HDFC is again a case worth mentioning. It was established with the objective of solving India's housing problem. Basic guiding value was solving the Indian housing problem. HDFC committed itself to the development of house construction activity. In order to live up to this value, HDFC helped even its potential competitor like ICICI to start their House Loan division. It has reduced the processing time to the level of 24 hours in order to serve the customers better. With the strong middle class values, HDFC carved out extraordinary results from ordinary people. HDFC is still the leading housing finance company and HDFC bank is considered one of the most efficient banks in the country thanks to its grounding on values.

There are other exemplary cases of Indian companies, which have shown the relevance of the corporate values by outperforming even MNCs in highly dynamic markets.Dr.Anji Reddy made a personal mission to put his company on the world map for its R and D capabilities in pharmaceuticals.This mission emanated the corporate value of being a research-based company. To-

Ethics and Morals both refer to right conduct.

day, Dr. Reddy's Laboratory (DRL) has 10 new chemical entities (the largest declared by any Indian Pharmacompany) in various stages of development.

Value of co-operation has spread in thousands of families in the Gujarat by Gujarat Co-operative Milk Marketing Federation. It was conceived as a co-operative and continues to be so. This is a case of using economics to drive social change.GGCMM has adhered to the values inculcated by its founder Dr.Kurien.Today it is undisputed market leader in milk and milk product markets,a complex business having huge inventory and handling a highly perishable commodity.

One more example of transformation in the Indian corporate sector can't be overlooked in this discussion. That is a 48-year-old developmental finance institution's transforming into a Universal bank with asset worth rupees one lakh crore. This transformation was guided by the value of creative reconstruction. With the objective of reaching close to the customer ICICI has made huge investment in technology to make ICICI bank a technology led operation.

Value of integrity, ethics, customer orientation and independent thinking are embodied in Wipro.Azim Premji (Chairman of Wipro) himself delight his customers many times with his customer centric attitude and non-negotiable integrity. Even as late as 1999, Premji would visit shopkeepers around India to gather customer feedback. Value of encouraging independent thinking in this organisation is expressed by encouraging entrepreneurship by cross-fertilization of the talent and fostering diversity. That's why it is no surprise that in Wipro's diaspora one can count more than a hundred who now head businesses as diverse as IT consulting and networking to strategic investment and BPO the world over.

Any discussion on management by values in Indian context would not be complete without reference of Infosys, the most respected and admired company in India. This company has convinced Indians that if you set your mind to it, business can be done ethically. Mr. Narayan Murthy and his founding partners of the company paved the values of integrity, wealth sharing and learneability in the organization. It is the first company in India to show human capital in its balance sheet and start an HR audit. This is a company which has produced hundreds of millionaire thanks to its core value of wealth sharing.This is implemented in the form of employee stock option. In order to ensure the highest quality of corporate governance, it is the first to introduce a 'protection of whistle blower' policy. That means the company encourages employees to bring to the notice of the management any wrong practice going on any where in the company. Few companies would dare to introduce such a step to ensure ethical behavior across the organisation.Indian corporate sector, often characterized by certain surveys as having lower ethico-moral standards and poor corporate governance, offers a number of examples of corporate houses who have earned respect the world over by managing themselves on a good value base.

Ethics and Virtues

Virtues are principles of goodness and righteousness in character and conduct that lead a person towards moral excellence and away from moral depravity. A virtue is a reflection of good character because it is a pattern of action. Confucius identified five virtues: charity, righteousness, propriety, wisdom and sincerity. He considered virtue as a means between the extremes of excess and deficiency. Aristotle distinguished between theoretical and practical virtues. According to him the three theoretical virtues are wisdom , science and truth; the practical virtues are art and prudence. Art is the ability to know how to produce or create things and prudence is the ability to know how to act well in life. It means exercising common sense and sound judgement in practical matters, carefully considering the consequences of one's actions. These five later got expanded into seven virtues: viz. prudence, temperance, justice, courage, faith, hope and love.

Values together with ethics, beliefs, and norms make up the culture of an organisation.

Corporate values are the values of an organisation.

Current ethics deal with rules, principles, obligation and consequences. Virtue ethics focus on what is important to both the individual and society and being a good person.

It is not sufficient to know what a person should do, but the concept of virtue focuses on what sort of a person he or she could become. This concept tries to explore the traits, which help a person to lead a life that is satisfying from an ethical point of view. Virtuous acts are done willfully and not by chance. Also, virtuous acts are not done out of self-interest or because they maximize pleasure. For instance courage, tolerance, generosity and honesty. Moral education is very important because it helps people to become virtuous by being taught to be virtuous and also by modeling one's behaviour after virtuous persons. Institutions like family, religion, school and other legal and social institutions are of central importance in teaching virtues and making it possible for the virtues to be taught. The problem with the concept of virtue is that complete ethical viewpoint cannot be based solely on virtue. Ethical principles have an equally important role to play. Thus both ethical principles and virtues need to be considered together. It may thus be correct to say that virtuous people who lack ethical principles are ethically blind but ethical principles without virtuous people are empty.

Ethical problems in companies result in dilemmas because they usually represent a conflict between an organization's economic performance and its social performance. For an organisation, social performance implies various obligations, such as protecting employment, safe working environment and pollution control. Since considerable expenses are often involved in discharging these obligations, organisations often find it convenient to ignore them. Instead, they become obsessed with the economic performance as measured by revenues, costs and profits. It is thus important to appreciate the existence of this conflict. Since people run businesses, it is important to ensure ethical behaviour at an individual level. Only then the collective actions of individuals can result in ethically correct responses from the organisation as a whole.

Ethics and Law

Law is that which is laid down, obtained or established. It is a body of rules of action prescribed by a controlling legal authority and having binding legal force. It is more often than not a written code of rules that must be obeyed by people under a given jurisdiction or those people will be subject to sanctions or legal consequences. Law is a solemn expression of the will of a supreme power, an authority.

Law is different from ethics. Ethics has been defined by judges as " knowing the difference between what you have a right to do and what is the right thing to do" Ethics involve following not only the letter of law but also its spirit. Ethics are not codified in books. They are that which is moral. Ethics deal not only with conduct but also with motives and character. Ethics constitute a higher standard than that of law. Law dictates the minimum standard of behaviour required of a person by a given society, whereas ethics go beyond what is required. Law comes from principles of morality; morality does not descend from law. Morality is that which pertains to character, it governs conduct not by legislative action or by force but by conscience and a desire to adhere to general principles of right conduct. Morality is a strict belief or conviction in the mind that is independent of legal proof or positive law. Law is essential to preserve society; ethics and morality are essential to sustain it at a higher plain.

Ethics are concerned with human values. Often, these values are reflected in jurisprudence and in laws. Legal theory has always concerned itself with morality. It has been recognized that law can be used for good or bad. It can be good if it is just and is derived from the laws of nature. One is morally bound to obey just laws but not unjust laws. Laws are developed by humans and do not automatically merit respect.

Virtues are principles of goodness and righteousness in character and conduct.

The role of law on enforcing morality is another ethical dilemma on the relationship between law and ethics. Law has an interaction with moral opinion. There is a conflict between the individual conscience and the law. Should morality be legislated and enforced by law? When law and conscience conflict, which should be obeyed? Laws originate from moral conviction;. which moral convictions should be incorporated into the legal code? Who decides which moral convictions are to be incorporated into laws: judges, the people or both?

There are many cases in ethics and in law where conceptual issues are crucially important. One of the crucial questions in the abortion debate is whether the fetus is a "human person." A normal adult human being is unquestionably a person, but what about a fetus? If we say a fetus is a "potential person," do we want to say that "potential persons" have the rights of actual persons?

Moral and ethical statements should also be distinguished from laws. The fact that an action is legally permissible does not establish that it is morally and ethically permissible.

Suppose an engineer discovers that his/her company is emitting a substance into the atmosphere that is not currently regulated by the Pollution Control Boards. Suppose further that the engineer reads some scientific literature that indicates the pollutant causes respiratory problems and may cause other serious health problems. Should she reveal this information to authorities? Whatever your views on this matter, it is clear that the mere fact that emitting the substance is legally permissible does not mean, it is morally right to do so knowing that it can cause harm. It does not, however, settle the issue fully.

Just as legality does not imply morality, illegality does not imply immorality. It would be illegal to introduce very small amounts of a chemical into the atmosphere if doing so violates pollution standards, but one might make a good argument that there are cases in which it is not immoral to do so and the standards at times are too strict and fail to balance costs and benefits in a rational way.

We can draw a Venn diagram of the relationship between law and morality as follows:

Figure 1

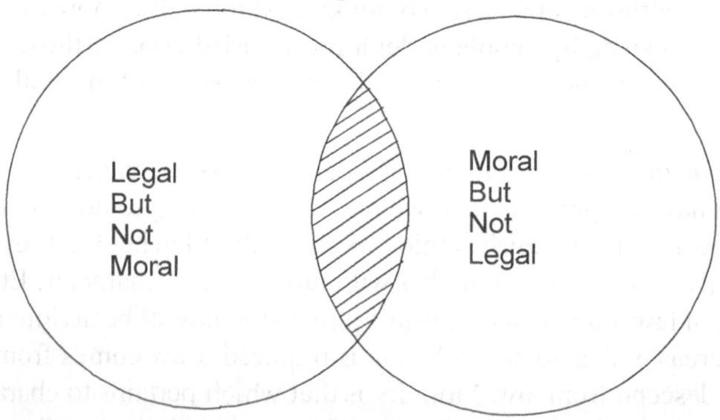

In the above diagram , the shaded area covers those actions that are both legal and moral. The area on the left cover those actions that are legal and not moral and the right area relate to actions that are moral and are not legal.

The legalities lay down the minimum ethical standards. Dr. Klaus Leisenger, President and Executive Director, Novartis Foundation for Sustainable Development, advises companies to go beyond the minimum standards of ethics, laid down by the law to change the image of big pharma companies. The big pharma companies have a big *'bad image'* problem since they are seen as greedy people making profits from people's illnesses and diseases. He believes that stakeholders including

An action legally permissible may not be morally and ethically permissible.

Non Governmental Organisations (NGOs) should be consulted for ensuring corporate social responsibility. The intellectual property and related issues that are legal in nature need to be communicated to them.

The moral, ethical and legal issues are thus closely related and often heavily overlapping. Later in the book, their interrelationships will be explored further through case studies.

Ethics and Religion

The relationship between religion and ethics is controversial. The range pf opinion is wide. For some, religion destroys ethics. For others, ethics depends upon religion. For still others religion and ethics are the same. All religion-based actions are not ethical. God means good. In the name of God, animals are killed and offered as an offering. Many consider this highly unethical. Some claim that religion is unnecessary or irrelevant to ethics. To them, ethics is much more stable in content than religion

The writings in the religious scriptures are accepted as ethical without any doubt by the strict followers of a religion. Ethics is born out of religion. Religion backs up ethics. In Jainism there is concept of Ahimsa. Which means that no living being should be killed or hurt. Thus even killing of mosquitoes, ants is prohibited. In India large part of our ethical standards are borne out of religion. The concept of Dharma and Karma dictate our ethics. More details are dealt in the theories of ethics while dealing with Indian theories.

Ethics and Facts

The issue here is whether whatever is factual is ethical. There is no question of hiding a fact. Should a fact be kept secret or keeping a fact secret is unethical? An organisation keep lots of factual information in their records. It says employees not to reveal the information to anybody outside the organization. Should the employee abide by this or if he gives the information outside is it unethical on his part?

The other point is of factual issue, i.e. an issue having to do with the truth or falsehood of factual claims. It is important to distinguish different kinds of issues, because they are resolved in different ways. A factual issue is resolved by investigation or empirical research. The truth cannot be determined empirically or mathematically.

A distinction between that which is either true or false and that which can be neither true nor false will help to resolve the issue.

Ethics and Rights

Ethics and human rights are closely related. Whenever there is violation of human rights, it is considered as unethical .The general consensus is that both the individual and the society at large have rights that each must recognize. The issues are: What are the rights of the individual in relation to society? What rights may the collective social body claim to be individual's? When people form a society, how are the respective rights of both the individual and society at large to be structured?

In order to provide a more precise and objective guideline for respecting the moral rights of individuals, some moral philosophers have refer to a **Doctrine of Rights**. A 'Right' may be defined as an entitlement to act or to have another individual act in a certain way. Rights serve as a protective barrier, shielding individuals from the unjustified infringement by others. The rights for implementing the ethics related to respect for persons are the rights to freedom and those physical and non-physical conditions necessary to realise one's well-being as he or she defines it.

In the 'Respect for Person' (RP) morality, these basic rights ***may not be sacrificed*** for greater overall utility. One individual's (or group's) rights may be overridden to protect another individual's

Law is essential to preserve society.
Ethics helps to build a character.

(or group's) rights that are considered to be more basic, but not merely to provide ***greater utility*** for the other individual or for the group. This is the most important difference between RP morality and utilitarianism.

If an individual's rights may be overridden only to protect a more fundamental or basic right of another individual, those rights that are most fundamental must be known. This requirement calls for a hierarchy of rights. These can be classified into a three-tier hierarchy of rights. The first tier includes the most basic rights, the essential preconditions of action: ***life, physical integrity, and mental health***. The second tier includes rights to maintaining the level of purpose-fulfillment an individual has already achieved. This tier includes ***the right not to be deceived or cheated, to have one's possessions stolen, to be defamed, or to suffer broken promises***. The third tier includes those rights necessary to increase one's level of purpose-fulfillment. It includes the right to such things ***as property, self-respect, and nondiscrimination.***

To apply RP morality, the following sequence is followed:

1. Determine the audience of the action or policy. The audience whose rights are affected would ordinarily be the same as the audience under the utilitarian analysis.
2. Evaluate the seriousness of the rights infringements each action will impose.
3. The course of action that produces the least serious rights infringements must be chosen.

Rights-infringements can be measured in three dimensions. First, some rights are more basic than others. The 'right to life', for example, is more basic than the right to property. Second, an action that abrogates a right altogether is more serious than one that merely limits it. Taking away all of an individual's property, for example, is a more serious rights-infringement than taking away some of it. Third, there is a difference between an actual and a merely potential rights-infringement. An action that actually produces a disease, for example, is a more serious rights-infringement than one that merely increases the risk of having it.

There are two principal difficulties with RP morality. First, it is sometimes difficult to apply in a way that leads to a clear conclusion. In some cases, any alternative open to an engineer may involve interference with an individual's or company's rights, and it may not always be clear which rights should have priority. This is especially true if the rights violations are merely potential rather than actual or if the action is only a slight infringement of a right. Let us look at an example discussed earlier. Suppose a pollutant, which has been shown to cause mild respiratory problems in some people, is emitted into the atmosphere. However, installing the pollution control devices necessary to stop the emission will be so expensive that the plant may be forced to close and many jobs will be lost in an economically depressed community. What does RP morality tell us to do here? It is clear that the hierarchy of rights is not sufficient to resolve the dilemma. The threat to health might be considered a threat to a basic right, but the threat to this basic right is not an extremely serious one. The threat to economic well-being might be considered a threat to a second-tier right, but the threat to this right is more serious and more certain and may affect a larger number of people. The methodology so far presented does not provide adequate guidelines for resolving such dilemmas.

A second problem with RP morality is that moral judgments implied by it sometimes appear implausible because they conflict so strongly with overall welfare or utility. Products can always be made more safe by expending great amounts of money. Automobiles could be made safer if they cost Rs 1,00,00,000 each, but few people could afford to buy them. The decision to construct cheaper automobiles means that a number of individuals will die who otherwise might not die, so that the basic right to life of these individuals will be violated. Yet most people are probably inclined to believe that the decision to produce cheaper but less safe automobiles is the right one, and this decision is most easily justified from a utilitarian perspective.

Responsibility is a pre condition for moral behaviour.

Ethics and Responsibility

Responsibility is a precondition for moral behaviour. Persons are judged morally praiseworthy or blameworthy only if they are responsible for their actions. It is commonly said that persons can reasonably be held responsible for what they do only if their actions are done freely. In moral evaluation and legal decision-making, persons are usually excused from responsibility for their actions if the evidence suggests that they acted without the ability or opportunity to choose to act differently. The concept of responsibility includes the responsibility of others along with self. The responsibility is delegated and others are also held responsible. With corporate decision-making structures as the focus, we find that many of the difficult ethical choices corporate managers must make involve conflicts regarding who is responsible for a given activity. Managers and engineers alike have different obligations depending on their role within the corporation. Thus, one of the obligations at issue is role morality, which is concerned with duties individuals have, based on the specific roles they have assumed within the corporation.

Corporate role morality takes as given precisely what classical moral theory wishes to evaluate, the worthiness of the duties assigned by one's role. Unfortunately, one of the pressing problems in legal scholarship on corporate social morality involves the fact that as laws change, so do the roles within the corporate hierarchy. Thus, there is a need for individuals within corporations to take a more active interest in their obligations as professionals, as well as to protect society at large.

An example of choosing social responsibility over law is the guns-for-hire classified advertising by 'Soldier of Fortune". In an article, Don Tomlinson asks: "What are we first: professionals or human beings?" While placing guns-for-hire advertisements was not illegal, it was immoral, and people died because of the advertisements. Soldier of Fortune acted irresponsibly toward the public, and "Law cannot shield anyone from the most basic duty all human beings owe all other human beings: respect for life. Law and ethics are not one and the same. Further, using law as a justification for conduct which is socially irresponsible is socially irresponsible itself."

Responsibility, rights and religion from the professional engineer's ethics point of view will be elaborated on later in the book.

Corporate Social Responsibility (CSR) has become a buzzword. Organisations have many social responsibilities. The regulations guiding the organization in this matter are either feeble or rudimentary. Businesses have realised that by being socially responsible corporate citizens they stand to gain economically. Gone are the days where we looked at the objective of businesses as only profit earning. Indian Companies like Infosys, Wipro, Polaris and Tatas are supporting the primary education in the country. Orchid is educating rural people. There are numerous such examples.

Ethics and Environment

This branch of ethics is known as environmental ethics. It involves concern for environment. Ethical principles are applied to resolve problems and challenges of the relationship of humans with environment. Is it possible to prevent broad damage to the biosphere while accommodating the economic needs of a growing population? The answer is ' no' unless the world adopts a new paradigm for environmental ethics – one based on common values. Once people agree at a values level, they can begin to communicate and develop solutions to perhaps the greatest challenge faced by humanity.

Companies should look at the whole manufacturing process to see what can be improved in line with social and ethical policies. It's good for the company to always look for better ways of doing things. One company has a concept called Design for Environment. For example, they try to make sure that 80 per cent of packaging is reusable. The concept of reverse logistics is also emerging. Companies are collecting the damaged and used products packages and recycle them to avoid environmental damages.

Do not allow mind to be carried away for a ride by the string.

Richard Sullivan, group resources director, *Xerox UK*, says: "The link between global awareness and employee morale has become much stronger recently. People say they put these things higher on the agenda." The company surveys staff annually on motivation and satisfaction, and acts on the results. "Five years ago 70 per cent of staff agreed that Xerox was environmentally responsible. Last year, 95 per cent agreed," says Sullivan. "We have a goal to produce waste-free products in waste-free factories to enable customers to work in waste-free offices. We have reduced landfill by 75 per cent since 1993 and have a target of zero landfill...Our design and development people try to ensure that all our products are recyclable. This helps our sales people to feel much better about our products and to differentiate between ourselves and competition...We believe there is a direct correlation between the policies, our results and staff retention. Many factors influence motivation and morale, so it is difficult to measure, but I am convinced they are having a positive impact. We all like to feel we work for a company that has a good reputation for its contribution to the protection of the environment."

A major leakage of a poisonous gas in an industrial plant caused death of Five workmen besides injuring Fifteen others. The "occupier" of the industrial plant pleaded that he had exercised all due diligence to prevent the escape of the gas and that the leak was attributable to an act of God. Will he succeed?

The Occupier will not succeed. The Supreme Court, in a landmark judgement in M.C.Mehta and others vs. Union of India, held that an enterprise which is engaged in hazardous or inherently dangerous activity and any industry which posses a potential threat to the health and safety of the persons working in the factory and those residing in the surroundings areas owned an absolute and non-delegatable duty to ensure that no harm results to anyone on account of any hazardous or inherently dangerous nature of the activity which it has undertaken. The court further ruled that the compensation must be correlated to the magnitude and capacity of the enterprise so as to have deterrent effect.

Recently, *Coca-Cola's* bottling plant in Palakkad in Kerala has been embroiled in major environmental issues. The coke plant was first accused of generating hazardous waste and disposing it off without treating. Then it was alleged that the plant was drawing excess groundwater, leading to water shortage and nearby wells drying up. The Kerala Government has asked the plant to stop functioning till the onset of monsoon. The company claims it has invested Rs.100 crores plus in the Kerala State. *Coca-Cola* has closed down the plant temporarily. *Coca-Cola* is sourcing from its Bangalore plant. The empty bottles from Kerala are being sent to its plant in Bangalore till the bottling plant in Kerala resumes operations. It costs Re. 1 per bottle more for freight. The attack on Iraq by the US was the first incident that triggered boycotting of *Pepsi* and *Coke* in the State, which has a strong base of leftist parties. This case shows the impact of environmental issues on the performance. What should *Coke* do?

WHY STUDY ETHICS?

In the recent past, a spate of controversies have erupted in the Corporate world, both abroad and in India. We have read stories about downfall of *Enron, Andersen, Xerox Corp* in America and *Home Trade, Madhavpura, CRBSecurities* in India. Are these reflection of the 'degeneration of society'? In the present circumstances, we need to give space to the issue of values that we are going to carry with us into our lives – personal and professional.

As per the Transparency International (TI), Corruption Perceptions Index (2003) (CPI) India ranks 83rd out of the 133 countries in which the level of corruption was measured. The degree of corruption was measured on a 10-point scale with highest score of 10, which meant (Highly Clean) and 0 (Highly Corrupt). Finland got the score of 9.7 whereas Indian score was 2.8. The score relate to perceptions of the degree of corruption as seen by business people, academicians and risk analysts.

You have to give up something of value to get something of value.

Ethics and business do mix. It may come as a big surprise to some, but successful, leading companies are convinced that this is so. A consultancy firm that advises on environmental, social and ethical policies, says that 81 per cent of companies in a survey of the food and electronics industries believed that such policies were bringing them market advantage. The study, 'Turning Obligation into Opportunity', says 77 per cent of the sample of 25 companies in each sector claimed they saved costs through more efficient business processes. The policies, said 73 per cent, had improved staff morale, 67 per cent believed would protect their market share. The finding is in line with an Ethical Investment Research Service survey which said that ethical funds were less risky than traditional ones. Brian McBride, vice-president and general manager of *Dell UK and Ireland*, says: "The average age at Dell is 32. Young people are very vocal on these issues and they see the company you work for as a statement about the sort of person you are."

Many of us are of the opinion that ethics are fundamental and do not require a formal education. It is believed that ethics are inherently present in all human beings. Ethics are universal values. Then why do these issues come up and for what benefit? For example, a thief knows that what he is doing is unethical that is why he does not want anybody to notice when he steals.

Recent times have witnessed exponential business growth in India. With many positive aspects like professionalism and competition it has had some negative impacts also. These negative features are in the form of mismanagement and poor corporate governance at organisational level and in the form of stress at the individual level. This is seemingly the result of wrong prioritisation of objectives at individual and organisational level. Importance of the values needs to be stressed for proper prioritization of the individual and organisational objectives and fundamental upliftment of the collective human consciousness.

If organizational values are well defined and clarified this will be of great help in decision-making and prioritising the expectations to be fulfilled. Well-defined and accepted values can guide organisations to the right path in the right manner with collective consciousness.

Organisational values are aggregate manifestation of individual values. Integration of both is essential for excellence in corporate performance. No organisational strategy for excellence can be implemented unless the implementators have the values for doing so along with the knowledge, skills and attitude. If this has been understood properly, corporate world can be a platform for fulfilling the highest potential for an individual. Connecting human values to organization strategy can bring extraordinary holistic results in long term. This understanding makes a strong case for the study of ethics.Management Gurus have realized this need and are advocating an ethical approach to business. They argue that a business entity, based on a strong value system and principles, is in the long run, more likely to survive and thrive.

Thus, a study of Ethics helps:

(a) Bringing clarity in thought and help in reasoning.

(b) Reinforcement of ethics.

(c) People who want to be ethical. (*They would like to keep their conduct good in order to rise in their own self-esteem. Thus, if it can be explained to them that some of their actions are not consistent with what is ethically expected of them, they would gladly change.*)

(d) People becoming virtuous.

(e) Adjusting to and adhering to organizational values

(f) Reduce and avoid stress.

(g) Build character

(h) Facing moral ethical dilemmas with confidence.

Organisational values are aggregate manifestation of individual values.

The study of professional ethics helps develop skills that are helpful at all stages. By combining readings on ethical theory with case studies, classroom discussion, and clarification through writing, it is possible to strengthen skills in moral reasoning and resolving conflicts.

WHY PEOPLE ARE UNETHICAL?

Individually most of us intuitively know what is good and what is bad. In spite of this, people act unethically. Unethical acts are the result of five factors.

(1) Unawareness

(2) Insensitivity to issues

(3) Selfishness

(4) Faulty reasoning and

(5) Pressure

Because of these reasons, people, in spite of knowing ethics, become unethical in their acts. The ethical values break down when you are not aware of what is unethical or you feel that it is not very important and ignore by being insensitive to the issues. Sometimes self-interest overrules ethics and one feels that one has done right thing. Many a time you give wrong justification for an unethical act especially when done under pressure. For example, a student may copy when there is threat from the school or parents that he would be punished severely for failing in the examination. Under pressure, he may copy. Similarly when there is strong requirement for money, one may go for pick pocketing or defrauding. The person, in these cases is aware that what he did was wrong.

CAN MORAL VALUES BE INCULCATED?

Looking closely at the many value driven organisation a general assumption can be made that value at the organisational level is initiated , nurtured and established by the leadership. Wholesome organisation can be created by an enlightened leader who has attained higher levels of consciousness.Such enlightened leader can transform the large manpower toward creative direction.Bhagwad Gita says that "Mahjanah yen gatah sah panthah" i.e. whatever the great men of society do others imitate, whatever the great one prove, other follow unconditionally.

Apart from individual leadership, efforts have been made to institutionalize the desired values in formal ways. Experiment of *Bohram and Bancwala* on *Malaysian Airlines* is an exemplary work. This study outlined the value awareness programme and value inculcation programme.Concept of character competance as basis for creative organization had also been introduced This was given in view of the gaps between the statement of values and state of values..

While corporates pay a lot of attention to core competence but hardly pay attention towards their character competance.. They have suggested that ethical sensitivity can be inculcated through development of ethics based management model with roots in character competence. By proper education and training, behaviour of individuals can be moulded and modified so that it is consistent with ethical principles.

STRUCTURED WAY TO APPROACH ETHICAL PROBLEMS

(Adapted from A&M University, Texas)

Dilemmas force hard moral choices. They cause us to deal with values. If we have to deal with dilemmas in an organised manner that allows us to explain and defend our decisions and not start from ground zero with each new problem, we need to:

- Think about what we mean by such terms as good, bad, right, wrong, and necessary.
- Consider, at the most general level, what kinds of actions are morally permissible. Is war ever justified? Can a price tag — any price tag — be put on human life? Is it ever permissible to eliminate a species?

Sensitivity to customer is the hallmark of ethics.

- Bring the general and theoretical to specifics which relate to the here and now of the real world. Is capital punishment a moral way to deal with those who are guilty of murder? Was the Persian Gulf War justified? Was it morally permissible to drop atomic bombs to end World War II?

This process allows us to get in our minds clear ideas about what is right and what is wrong and helps us decide what to do in other cases. Then we have to make important distinctions. We have to distinguish between:

- Conventional and Reflective Morality - Is what we have always done what we ought to do?
- Morality and Law - Just because it is legal, is it right?
- Morality and Prudence - Can we morally do it, just because it is in our best interest?
- Morality and Economics - Is the most economic decision the most moral decision?
- Morality and Obedience to Authority - Is following orders that are not proper a legal or a moral defense?
- Morality and Mere Opinion - Are you obligated to search further for a reason to justify actions than mere opinion?

This takes you back to the start of the list and the considerations of what morality really means.

Follow the above system when you analyze ethical dilemmas and you will be able to completely encircle the problem and approach its solution from many directions. But remember: You usually have to give up something of value to get something of value, and with ethics, there frequently is no absolute right answer, just a personal best answer, and it all comes down to you

SUM UP

Most of us understand ethics as related in some way to values such as honesty, harmony, integrity etc. The dictionary recognises ethics as a subject dealing with the rules of ideal human behaviour. But for ethics to really emerge as an exact science, a majority of us would have to accept accountability for defining and demonstrating a code of ethical behaviour that would engender a culture in which the individual, the family, the community and the society can endure — without the threat of disintegration.

'Culture' may be defined as an organised process of human behaviour that holds the individual, family, community or society together. The more ethical a culture, the greater its integrity and harmony, the greater its security, and the greater its resistance to change. The greater its resistance to change, the more enduring, necessarily, will that culture be. The inertia of large populations is nothing but a natural and ethical social-safeguard against the risk of change induced by dubious leadership.

The major economic systems of our times — capitalism and communism — have both addressed the goal of creating an ideal social culture through their respective philosophies. Significantly, the fundamental differences between these systems have never centered on whether or not a society needs the vehicle of business to drive its development. Their differences have only been related to the manner in which capital is to be owned or profit to be shared. And given that preoccupation, these systems, possibly, have overlooked an important principle that the successful growing business has thrown up: that we can not attain quality in mass production without defining and testing a prototype of quality! In effect, business seems to have laid down the first golden rule of ethics: That if we can not do without a prototype for the development of something relatively less complex like a product, we certainly stand no chance of developing the ideal society without defining and testing the qualities of the ideal individual in the first place. We thus have *per force* to deal with the concept of ethical leadership by acknowledging that behavioural change flows from the individual, through the family and community, to society and not the other way round.

Good governance enables ethics.

To quote Peter Drucker, the management guru: "The most important reason for focusing on business management is that it is the success story of this century. It has performed within its own sphere. It has provided economic goods and services to an extent that would have been unimaginable to the generation of 1900. And it has performed despite world wars, depressions, and dictatorships. The achievement of business management enables us today to promise — perhaps prematurely — the abolition of the grinding poverty that has been mankind's lot through the ages. It is largely the achievement of business management that advanced societies today can afford mass higher education."

There is also increasing evidence that business is not resting on its achievements but exploring, even if gradually, new ways of rising to the challenge of providing ethical leadership to society. In an article titled 'New Age for Business' that appeared in the October 1990 issue of *Fortune*, Frank Rose reports and comments on a new framework that is emerging for viewing and understanding business —a new paradigm that will carry humankind beyond the industrial age—to the mental and spiritual enrichment of those who take part in it. The article highlights the following: "Visionary thinkers are rejecting the by-the-numbers approach to enterprise and seeking a new paradigm for viewing the world. Is there Love and caring in the workplace? Is profit motive less than pre-eminent? Major corporations are buying in."

The disciplined managers of this new concept of business would present an image, which would be in sharp contrast to that of the conventional business executive. To these managers, being business-like would mean being considerate and caring; being financially secure would mean understanding the function of money and profit in business and life rather than relentlessly accumulating the same, being enterprising would mean taking on new and greater responsibility in society and being publicly accountable for it; and sooner or later, being good managers would necessarily mean being good husbands or wives, good parents, good citizens and good leaders. They would then serve as exciting role models for the development of our future generations and raise the vision of an enduring corporate culture extending itself to an enduring global culture. And incidentally, business would have also established ethics as an exact science.

After looking at various concepts of ethics, let us now explore and first understand some typical issues faced by individuals and organisations.

MORAL ISSUES

An engineer has to confront almost on a daily basis the types of moral issues, which Tilak and Sundeep Vani faced in the Case study given at the end of this Chapter. These are only illustrations. They become a major issue only when decisions need to be taken. These decisions are difficult to make and there would be a sense of guilt associated with such decisions when they go against the basic instincts of one's conscience.

The moral issues may be faced at the ***micro*** level within the organization or ***macro*** level at a societal level. The impact of the decisions taken will differ from level to level. Whereas a micro level issue affects only one's organization and people, a macro issue will have impact on the whole society. Some ethical issues may affect an engineer's professional and personal life. In the beginning of one's career, the impact will be felt more on one's professional and personal life. As one reaches higher positions, one would influence policies and the effect will be much larger. A person's ethical responsibility increases as one moves up the ladder.

Certain cases get wide publicity and are widely discussed. A few examples were given in the previous chapter. Let us take up some illustrative examples to understand where and how moral problems arise in the engineering profession.

1. More than a year back, a portion of the Metro rail, which was under construction near Taramani in Chennai, gave way and fell on a car passing underneath and seriously injured the occupants. Who is to be blamed? Who is responsible? Any lapse in procedures?

Ethics stem from values.

2. Chemical effluents are let out into the open near Aminjikarai in Chennai. Are the people who let it out or the Government, which does not get them to stop to be blamed?
3. A building plan made as per prescribed norms, gets rejected. Why?
4. An electrical item when tested does not confirm to the ISI standards. What do we do?
5. Russia has developed world's first floating nuclear power plant. What will be its impact on the environment? Could they be allowed to sell such plants to other countries?

In each of these instances, an engineer will get contradictory opinions from within the company, competitors, governmental agencies and his own conscience. He faces severe moral and ethical dilemmas about what action he should take. What should one do when there are such vast differences in the opinions and judgments of different people? Should one follow the laid down law? The moral problems arising in these situations are not straightforward. They are indeed very complex.

According to an Article published in the A & M Texas University site, as with any other higher-order intellectual activity, resolving moral problems requires that we be both analytical and imaginative. In the **analytical** mode, we sort out the component parts of ethical problems. This activity helps us in knowing what kinds of solutions are appropriate. However, resolving ethical problems often requires something more. In the **imaginative** mode, we can think as creatively as we can about ways of resolving moral problems. This creative activity takes many forms, including imagining creative new ways of reconciling conflicting moral claims.

Factual, Conceptual, and Moral Issues

Let us begin by considering some of the analytical devices that are useful in resolving moral issues. It is important to distinguish different kinds of issues, because they are resolved in different ways.

The first kind is a **factual issue**, i.e. an issue having to do with the truth or falsehood of a claim or an assumption. For example, in the case relating to the Compound X in the Case 2 given in this chapter, the *question whether Compound X is a health hazard or not is* a factual issue. If Sharad could come up with information that Compound X really is *not* any hazardous and that Pollution Control boards would not be concerned with it at all, then he would have no problem. He could simply forget the whole thing. If he cannot determine whether or not Compound X is hazardous, or if he finds out that indeed it is a serious health hazard, then he has a complex problem in his hand. It is necessary to know the distinction between that which is either true or false and that which is neither true nor false. *One gets into really deep waters in case something is neither true nor false!*

The second kind of issue is a **conceptual issue**, i.e. an issue having to do with the meaning or scope of a term or concept. The primary example of a conceptual issue in this case is the question whether the use of the information gained at Company A for the problem at Company B would constitute a use of proprietary information.

What, precisely, is the scope of the term "proprietary information"? Company A might have defined this term so precisely in the agreement, which you have signed that there is no room for doubt in this case. However, the document may be too generally worded to provide an easy answer to this question. Yet the problem that you face is vitally affected by the question whether the information that you would pass on to Company B would be "proprietary information."

Moral issues deal with what is 'right' and 'wrong' from an ethical point of view. A factual issue is usually resolved by investigation or empirical research. But often times, the truth cannot be determined empirically or mathematically! The issue then is whether whatever is factual or conceptually right is ethical. There is no question of hiding a fact. Should a fact be kept secret or is keeping a fact secret itself unethical? An organisation has lot of factual information in their records. Invariably,

> **Cost of ethics : Engineer has multi-faceted responsibility.**
> **Code of ethics needs to be mentioned, supervised and enforced.**

employees are required to give an undertaking not to reveal any information to anybody outside the organization, unless specifically authorised to do so. Should the employee abide by this if the information pertains to some 'unethical act' by the organisation or if, in his opinion, revealing it could be beneficial to the society at large? (*as was the case in the Sharad incident mentioned above.)*

Types of Statements

People often think of ethical reasoning as fuzzy and imprecise, and it is certainly true that the qualitative thinking that goes on in ethics is not susceptible to the same kind of precision that can be achieved in mathematical sciences. Often, however, ethical thinking is unnecessarily confused, and much of this confusion is due to the failure to distinguish between three kinds of statements that are made in ethics.

Factual statements are either true or false and can be confirmed or refuted by empirical observations. The claim that a product will produce accidents because of faulty design is a factual claim, although it can be crucial in a moral debate. For example, two engineers could agree on the moral principle that unsafe products should not be put in the market, but disagree as to whether Product X will produce accidents. We might describe this disagreement as to whether Product X should be marketed as a disagreement over professional ethics, but actually the disagreement hinges on different factual claims. Factual claims can be as controversial as moral claims, and it is crucial in a moral disagreement to first determine the disagreement over facts.

Conceptual statements are statements about the meaning or scope of certain terms. Discussions of conceptual issues are very important in ethics. One of the best-known examples of a conceptual issue is the question in the abortion debate as to whether a fetus should be considered a human person. This depends on how we define the term person, and many people believe the abortion debate hinges on this definition. The definition cannot be settled by appeal to facts about the fetus, although these facts may influence our definition of a person.

To take an example from engineering, let us take the case of an American engineer employed by a U.S company, doing business in a foreign country. A representative of a firm from that country tells the engineer that he would not purchase their product unless he is given a substantial sum of money. Since the representative is not a government official, the payment would not be considered *illegal* in the U.S. under their Foreign Corrupt Practices Act. Although the engineer believes that paying bribes to anybody is wrong, he considers this to be paying extortion money rather than a bribe. He defines bribery as paying money to get a person to give *special (and inappropriate) consideration* to his product. He defines extortion as *demanding money to do what one ought to do or not do any way.* Thus paying money to get the representative to consider your product, when he ought to consider it any way, is paying extortion, not bribery. He also believes that bribery is wrong but paying extortion is not since in the latter case his product deserves to be bought any way; therefore, he pays the representative.

In this example, one may disagree with the engineer's relative moral evaluation of bribery and extortion. One could also disagree with him regarding his definitions of bribery and extortion. Both of these disagreements might be called moral disagreements in a broad sense, but only the first is a moral disagreement in the strict sense. The second is a conceptual disagreement. Thus we have a wider and narrower sense of the term 'moral'.

Moral statements are statements that something is right or wrong. There can, of course, be disagreement over moral statements. We have just now mentioned an example of a genuine moral disagreement, namely the disagreement over whether it is wrong to pay extortion. There are other examples of genuine moral disagreements. For example, some people may not believe it is wrong to pay bribes in a country where this practice is generally accepted. Engineers may disagree over the morality of killing civilians, so that one engineer could work on a particular defense contract in good

Moral dilemmas are the conflict between duty, right, good or ideal.

conscience and another could not. You can probably think of many other areas where two people can have genuine moral disagreements.

In discussing factual disagreements, one looks at factual or empirical considerations to resolve the problem. In considering conceptual disagreements, arguments are presented about the appropriateness of one definition as opposed to another. In evaluating moral disagreements, we need to look at broader and more basic moral principles.

Types of Inquiry (Three Types of Inquiry*[1])

Engineering ethics, like ethics in general combines inquiries into values, meaning, and facts. To find answers to moral dilemmas, knowing the different types of inquiry and theories will be of immense help. In professional ethics, there are three types of inquiry, which can be used to solve the ethical problem.

Normative inquiries, which are most central, seek to identify the values that should guide individuals and groups. ***Conceptual*** inquiries seek to clarify important concepts or ideas, whether the ideas are expressed by single words or by statements and questions. ***Factual*** inquiries seek to provide facts needed for understanding and resolving value issues.

First, and most centrally, engineering ethics involves ***normative*** inquiries aimed at identifying and justifying the morally desirable norms or standards that ought to guide individuals or groups. Normative questions are about what *ought* to be and what is *good* (bearing in mind that here our concern is with moral values).

Here are some examples of normative questions: How far does the obligation of engineers to protect public safety extend in given situations? When, if ever, should engineers blow the whistle on dangerous practices of their employers? For example, whose values should be given primacy in making judgments about acceptable risks in a design for a public transport system: those of the management, senior engineers, employees, government, public, or a combination of all these? Which particular laws and organizational procedures affecting engineering practices are morally warranted? What moral rights of engineers should be recognized in order to help them fulfill their professional obligations?

Intertwined with these practical questions, normative inquiries also have the theoretical goal of justifying particular moral judgments. For example, what are the reasons for engineers to have obligations to their employers, their clients, and the general public? How can professional ideals be justified in terms of more fundamental moral ideals? When and why is government justified in interfering with free enterprise?

Second, conceptual inquiries are directed toward clarifying the meaning of concepts, principles, and issues in engineering ethics. For example, what does 'safety' mean, and how is it related to the idea of 'risk'? What does it mean when codes of ethics say engineers should "protect the safety, health, and welfare of the public"?

What is a 'bribe'? What is a 'profession', and what distinguishes professionals? (*Later in this chapter we will explore the last question more fully.*) There it will become clear that, not surprisingly, our value judgments influence how we define "professionalism." Wherever moral concepts are at issue, normative and conceptual issues are tightly interwoven.

Third, factual inquiries-often referred to as descriptive inquiries-seek to uncover information bearing upon value issues. Where possible, researchers attempt to conduct factual inquiries using proven scientific techniques. They provide important information about the business realities of contemporary engineering practices, the history of the engineering profession, the effectiveness of pro-

* Mike W. Martin and Roland Schinzinger, Ethics in Engineering, Tata McGraw Hill, 2003

Violation of Human Rights is unethical.

fessional societies in fostering moral conduct, the procedures used in making risk assessments, and psychological profiles of engineers. Determining the facts in these areas, provides an understanding of the background conditions that generate moral problems. It also enables us to deal realistically with alternative ways of resolving those problems.

These three types of study are complementary and interrelated, as the following example illustrates. Consider a young engineer who becomes convinced that the level of pollutants her company is pouring into a stream is dangerously high, given that children are using the river downstream for swimming. She expresses her view to her immediate supervisor, who says her fears are unfounded because the pollution has caused no complaints in the past. Is she required to do more?

Obviously this question calls for a normative inquiry into what she ought to do-and why. But we will also want to know additional facts about the case, such as the nature of the pollutants being discharged, the costs of controlling them, and whether the engineer's conviction that they are dangerous is well founded. Hence a factual inquiry is called for.

Perhaps enough has already been said, however, to suggest that the engineer definitely should take further action, since her professional judgment has been overruled without a compelling reason. But should she merely request of the supervisor a more detailed response? Should she go above the supervisor to higher management? Should she write to the local authority, or would going outside the normal organizational channels constitute disloyalty to the company? And what is the basis for holding that she even has the right to a cogently reasoned response from her supervisor?

These are further *normative* questions since they call for making judgments about her responsibilities and rights. Answering them will require an understanding of the general moral obligations of engineers. And if this understanding is to be more than an undefended opinion or intuition, then it will have to be grounded on reasons provided by various specific moral principles.

Providing these reasons is the task of a more theoretical normative inquiry. But this inquiry will also involve clarification of ideas about safety, loyalty to companies, and professional freedom and autonomy. Thus it will involve *conceptual* inquiries.

Factual inquiries, moreover, enter the case yet again when we attempt to discover the realistic options open to the engineer, as well as to provide some estimate of their likely consequences. Those factual, descriptive inquiries will help us understand the business, social, and political realities in which the company operates. Only with this knowledge can we make a sound recommendation about what the engineer should do.

MORAL DILEMMAS*

If solutions to moral problems in engineering were always simple and clear, there would be little justification for taking valuable time to study ethics in the first place. But three sorts of complexity and murkiness may be involved in moral situations.

First, there are problems of ***vagueness***. It may be unclear to individuals as to which, if any, moral considerations or principles apply to their situation. An engineer starting a new job, for example, may have doubts about whether it is morally permissible to accept an expensive desk set as a gift from a salesperson with whom her company does business. Would this be regarded as accepting a bribe? Would it create a conflict of interest? Perhaps a conversation with a colleague will answer these questions. Perhaps the colleague may remember the test applied in earlier times: "If you can eat, drink, or smoke it in a day it is not a bribe!" But there will always be troublesome cases where there is considerable vagueness about whether the "gift" is an innocent amenity or an unacceptable bribe.

* *Ibid* pp. 15

Solutions to moral problems in engineering are not always simple and clear.

Second, and more frequently, there are problems of ***conflicting reasons***. It may be perfectly clear as to which moral principles apply to one's situation. The difficulty instead might be that two or more clearly applicable moral principles come into conflict (or that one principle seems to point simultaneously in two different directions).

Third, there are problems of ***disagreement***. Reasonable and responsible individuals and groups may disagree about how to interpret, apply, and balance moral reasons in particular situations. This disagreement becomes even more complicated within engineering corporations in which individuals must work together within authority-structured relationships, an issue to which we will return at the end of this section.

These kinds of moral problems are called ***moral dilemmas***. Stated more fully, *moral dilemmas* are situations in which two or more moral obligations, duties, rights, goods, or ideals come into conflict with one another, and it appears that not all of them can be fully respected. It is also possible for one moral principle to have two or more incompatible applications in a given situation.

Moral dilemmas occur frequently, although usually there is only moderate difficulty in seeing what should be done. We make a promise to a friend, thereby creating an obligation to do what we have promised. Then our parents fall ill and staying at home to help them prevents us from keeping the promise. The dilemma, which consists of a conflict between the duty to keep a promise and an obligation to one's parents, is usually resolved by an apologetic phone call to the friend. Or again, we may make a promise to our employer and another to a colleague, and it turns out that we can only fulfill one of them. Here the general duty to keep promises has two incompatible applications. Once again, an apology to the offended party may often settle the matter.

Dilemmas are not always so easily addressed. Resolving some of them can require searching, even agonizing, reflection. Contemporary engineering practice makes it virtually inevitable that most engineers will be confronted with moral dilemmas during their careers. Indeed, this is true of all professionals whether they be physicians, lawyers or teachers.

Steps in Confronting Moral Dilemmas

The problems of vagueness, conflicting reasons, and disagreement suggest the need for several steps in approaching dilemmas. The steps are distinct, even though they are interrelated and can often be taken together.

(1) Identify the relevant moral factors and reasons. What are the conflicting responsibilities, competing rights, and clashing ideals involved?

(2) Gather all available facts that are pertinent to the moral factors involved.

(3) If possible, rank the moral considerations in order of importance as they apply to the situation. (Sometimes this is not possible, and the goal is to find a way to meet equally urgent responsibilities and to promote equally important ideals.)

(4) Consider alternative courses of action as ways of resolving the dilemma, tracing the full implications of each. (Typically this involves making factual inquiries.)

(5) Talk with colleagues (or friends or other students), seeking their suggestions and alternative perspectives on the dilemma.

(6) Arrive at a carefully reasoned judgment by weighing all the relevant moral factors and reasons in light of the facts. (This last step is the most difficult!)

Study of engineering ethics helps develop skills that are helpful at all these stages. By combining readings on ethical theory with case studies, classroom discussion, and clarification through writing, it is possible to strengthen skills in moral reasoning and resolve conflict.

Moral autonomy is the skill and habit of thinking rationally.

MORAL AUTONOMY*

Should the study of engineering ethics aim at inculcating a particular set of moral beliefs? Not necessarily so. Of course, one proceeds in the faith that the study of engineering ethics will strengthen what is already imbued in the way of commitments to such fundamental professional values as honesty, respect for colleagues, and concern for public good. Nevertheless, the direct aim is to empower individuals to reason more clearly and carefully concerning moral questions. ***To invoke a term widely used in ethics, the unifying goal is to increase moral autonomy.***

'Autonomy' literally means 'self-determining' or 'independent'. But not just any kind of independent reflection about ethics amounts to moral autonomy Moral autonomy can be viewed as the skill and habit of thinking rationally about ethical issues on the basis of moral concern. This foundation of moral concern, or general responsiveness to moral values, derives primarily from the training we receive as children in being sensitive to the needs and rights of others (as well as of ourselves). Where such training is absent, as it often is with abused or neglected children, the tragic result can be an adult sociopath capable of murdering without compunction. Sociopaths, who by definition lack a sense of moral concern and guilt, are never morally autonomous no matter how 'independent' their intellectual reasoning about ethics may be.

Adult moral concerns, of course, can be evoked (or numbed) on specific occasions by any number of influences: friends, ministers, social events, novels movies, and inspiring teachers of whatever subjects. It would be surprising if the topics discussed in ethics courses did not call forth moral concern. Nevertheless the main goal of courses on applied ethics is to improve the ability to reflect critically on moral issues.

This can be accomplished by improving various practical skills that will help produce effective independent thought about moral issues. As related to engineering ethics these skills include the following:

1. Proficiency in recognizing moral problems and issues in engineering. This involves being able to distinguish them from, as well as relate them to, problems in law, economics, religious doctrine, or descriptions of physical systems.
2. Skill in comprehending, clarifying, and critically assessing arguments of opposing sides of moral issues.
3. The ability to form consistent and comprehensive viewpoints based upon consideration of relevant facts.
4. Imaginative awareness of alternative responses to the issues and creative solutions for practical difficulties.
5. Sensitivity to genuine difficulties and subtleties. This includes a willingness to undergo and tolerate some uncertainty in making troublesome moral judgments or decisions.
6. Increased precision in the use of a common ethical language, which is necessary in order to be able to express and defend one's moral views adequately to others.
7. Enriched appreciation of both the possibilities of using rational dialogue in resolving moral conflicts and of the need for tolerance of differences in perspective among morally reasonable people.
8. An awakened sense of the importance of integrating one's professional life and personal convictions-that is, the importance of maintaining one's moral integrity.

Most of us value moral autonomy for its own sake. Its exercise is central to what we think of

---

* *ibid* pp. 17

Ethics of care can be contrasted with ethics of rules and rights.

as the possession of a mature moral outlook, that is, one that is something more than second hand and passively adopted. Yet we also value it because we believe that it tends to lead to morally responsible conduct or is an integral part of being a responsible person. Certainly some faith in the ability of people to reflect on moral issues as morally autonomous individuals is presupposed in any attempt to engage in serious dialogue about ethics. And an affirmation of the individual's right to develop and exercise reasoned moral perspectives presupposes that most people have a large capacity for acting responsibly out of human values. It is in this spirit that we need to enter into the discussion of engineering ethics.

THEORIES OF ETHICS

There are different theories of ethics. The bases of these are philosophy, sociology economics, psychology, religion and customs. Some of them:

(a) Utilitarianism - *most good for most people.*

(b) Respect for People - *personal autonomy*

(c) Rights Theories - individual *human rights*

(d) Virtue Theories - *virtues are traits of character making*

(e) Situational Theory – based on situation and love.

Moral Theories

The basis of these theories is philosophy. In making judgments about right conduct, most of us recognize the ***value of moral consistency***. The requirements of consistency take several different forms.

(1) If a consulting engineer breaks confidentiality with her client because it is in her interest to do so but condemns another engineer for doing the same thing, we are inclined to say that she is inconsistent. She is not applying the same standards to herself that she expects everyone else to follow.

(2) We also expect a person to be consistent with her own moral standards. If she keeps strict confidentiality one time and breaks it another time, even when there is no important difference between the two cases, we again say that she is inconsistent.

(3) Finally, our moral beliefs must be consistent with one another. Our moral beliefs about confidentiality must be consistent with our beliefs about bribery, whistle blowing, and the environment. Ultimately, we must know how our moral beliefs in professional ethics relate to our beliefs about other moral issues.

One way to think consistently in this way is to have a moral theory, i.e. a set of moral principles, which systematically link moral beliefs to one another by means of a set of coherent moral principles. A theory in any area offers the opportunity to define terms in uniform ways and to relate a set of ideas to one another in a consistent manner. Moral theory does the same thing with moral ideas.

A moral theory can be conveniently divided into three parts.

First, there is a ***moral standard, a criterion or test*** of what is right or wrong. It has the general form:" Those actions are right that possess characteristic X." Thus, those and only those actions are right that possess some characteristic X. We could fill in X by a phrase such as, "producing the greatest total amount of human well-being" or "equally respect the humanity of each person." Obviously these expressions need further definition. What do we mean by human well-being? What do we mean by respect for the humanity of each person? These questions would have to be answered in an adequate moral theory.

Second, ***moral principles*** serve to categorize different types of actions as right or wrong. Moral principles have the following form: "Those actions of type Y are right (or wrong)." Such actions

Moral autonomy requires dependent reasoning.

are right because they conform to the moral standard by possessing characteristic X or wrong because they fail to conform. Examples of moral principles would be, "Bribery is wrong" and "Killing innocent people is wrong." These practices might be wrong because they fail to promote human well-being or because they fail to respect the humanity of each person. In any case, they serve to show the implications of the moral standard for a broad class of actions.

Third, ***moral judgments*** are statements about the rightness or wrongness of particular actions. Moral judgments have the following form:" Action Z is right (or wrong)." Examples of moral judgments would be "Ram should not have bribed the foreign official to buy his product" or "Ram should not have agreed to work on the defense contract" or "Sudha was right to have refused to sign that design." Moral judgments apply moral standards or moral principles to specific situations. They are thus the ultimate goal of moral reasoning.

Earlier, the need to test our moral views for overall moral consistency was given as one of the driving forces behind the search for a moral theory. From this standpoint it would be desirable to have a single moral theory in which all of our views could be encapsulated. However, moral philosophers have generally concluded that it is not possible to incorporate all of the moral views that are generally accepted in our culture into a single coherent moral theory. Rather, there seem to be two systems of moral concepts that are the most influential, although there are considerable areas of overlap. These two theories are ***utilitarianism*** and the ethics of ***respect for persons***. Let us consider each of these.

Utilitarianism

The moral standard of utilitarianism is: ***those actions are right that produce the greatest total amount of human well-being***. Utilitarianism has great intuitive appeal to many people because human well-being seems to be such a natural goal of human endeavor. In order to be plausible, however, utilitarians must define well-being. Yet people define well-being, or what some might call "good life," in different ways. For some it is physical pleasure, for others financial and professional success, and so forth. How do we resolve these conflicts?

One of the solutions that is most widely accepted by utilitarians is called ***preference utilitarianism***. According to preference utilitarianism, those conditions are promoted that allow each individual within society to pursue happiness as he or she defines it. Each individual may use his or her own preferences as a guide to action. But of course each person must also promote those conditions that allow others to pursue their own preferences. So, from the utilitarian perspective, each person has a double obligation: to maximize his own well-being, however this is defined, but only insofar as this is compatible with promoting those conditions that enable others to maximize their own well-being, however they define it. Only in this way will the utilitarian ideal be realized.

At least two conditions must be met if an individual is to pursue her well-being. First, each individual must have the ***maximum degree of personal freedom***; only in this way can she pursue well-being as she defines it. Second, she must enjoy the ***basic conditions of existence*** necessary to realize well-being, however it is defined. The most obvious such conditions are the conditions of physical well-being. For example, nobody can pursue their well-being if they are sick and cannot obtain medical care, or if they are subjected to unsafe working conditions, or are subjected to risk due to toxic emissions. Many non-physical conditions are also required for most people to realize their well-being, such as education and companionship.

A utilitarian analysis of a moral problem consists of three steps.

(1) The utilitarian must determine the audience of the action or policy in question—those people who will be affected for good or bad.

(2) The positive and negative effects of the alternative actions or policies must be determined.

(3) The utilitarian must decide which course of action produces the greatest overall utility.

Utilitarianism – most good for most people.

The utilitarian ideal is a persuasive one and has been very influential in individual morality and public policy in the twentieth century. It is an essential perspective in engineering ethics, where technological decisions are often made in terms of cost/benefit or risk/benefit analysis. These types of analysis are simply applications of utilitarianism. However, there are ***two major drawbacks*** to the utilitarian perspective on morality.

First, implementation of the utilitarian perspective ***requires extensive knowledge of facts***, and sometimes this knowledge is not available. This is especially evident in the case of cost/benefit and risk/benefit analysis. In order to balance the cost or negative utility of an engineering project, such as the Narmada Dam, against the benefit or positive utility, we must be able to calculate the long-term effects of the project on all the members of the audience. This requires an enormous amount of knowledge, some of which we do not have. Insofar as we do not know the long-term positive and negative consequences of an action or policy, we do not know how to evaluate it from a utilitarian perspective. Sometimes utilitarians are reduced to a "best guess" approach, and this is obviously not very satisfactory.

The ***second*** problem with utilitarianism is that it can lead to ***injustice to certain individuals***. A mining operation that is unsafe and leads to black lung disease for some of the miners may produce more utility than harm, from an overall standpoint, but it may be unjust to the miners themselves. Maximizing utility at the expense of individuals produces serious ethical problems which utilitarian theory is not well equipped to handle.

Respect for Persons

The moral standard of the ethics of ***respect for persons (RP) morality*** can be stated as follows: ***those actions are right that equally respect each human person as a moral agent.*** A moral agent is an individual capable of both formulating and pursuing purposes of his or her own and of being responsible for the actions taken to fulfill those purposes. Thus moral agents must be distinguished from things, such as knives or shovels, which exist to fulfill purposes imposed on them by moral agents.

The emphasis on respect for each individual is expressed in the Golden Rule: "Do unto others as you would have them do unto you." This moral maxim is found in one form or another in most major religious traditions. It forces a person to consider others by imaginatively placing himself or herself in the position of other members who could be affected by his or her actions. The Golden Rule is an excellent rule of thumb in many practical moral deliberations.

However, it can lead to seemingly perverse results, at times because it seems too permissive and sometimes because it seems too restrictive. Suppose an engineer who has *a rather carefree attitude toward danger* participates in the design of an automobile which is relatively inexpensive and fun to drive, but whose advantages are purchased at the cost of safety. He might justify participating in the design by saying (quite honestly) he would be willing to drive the car himself. While the Golden Rule might justify design of the car, we might still find problems with it from an ethical standpoint. Or perhaps an engineer orders the dumping of small amounts of chemicals into the local river, even though there is some evidence that the material may pose health problems. She justifies her action by saying, "I fish in the same river and eat the fish myself. I would be perfectly willing for other plants to do what our plant does." The Golden Rule might justify her action, but we might wonder about its moral permissibility.

In the above examples, the Golden Rule seems too permissive, but at other times it may seem too restrictive. Suppose an engineer discovers gross incompetence on the part of one of his colleagues, but refuses to report him on the grounds that he would not want to be reported (and probably loose his job as a consequence) if he were caught in a similar situation. Here the Golden Rule seems to prohibit actions that we might consider to be morally permissible or even required.

Golden Rule : Do unto others as you would have them do unto you.

To Sum Up

A review of the two most important moral theories lead to the following conclusions.

(1) It is probably impossible to unite all of our moral beliefs into a single coherent theory. Utilitarianism requires us to maximize the total amount of preference satisfaction, even if it means doing an injustice to individuals; RP morality requires us to respect the rights of individuals, even if it means promoting something less than the total amount of preference satisfaction.

(2) Given this fundamental divergence between the two theories, it is often best to analyze a complex moral problem from the standpoint of both theories. If the two theories converge, we can have some assurance about the proper course of action. If the two theories do not converge, a decision must be made as to which conclusion has priority. In general, moral philosophers have adopted the view that RP considerations should take priority over utilitarian considerations, except in those instances where the violation of rights is relatively minor.

(3) In addition to conflicts between the two theories, many problems that arise within a given theory are not adequately treated by the theories as they have been presented. These fall into two broad categories: relevance problems and conflict problems.

Theory of Kohlberg* -A Psychological Approach

Lawrence Kohlberg has set forth theories of moral development based on psychology.

Kohlberg developed theory of moral development based on the premise that morality is a form of reasoning that develops in structural stages .He asserted that one's maturity in moral decisions develops as one thinks about moral issues and decisions. With cognitive growth, moral reasoning appears, and moral reasoning allows children to gain control over their moral decision making process. For Kohlberg, moral judgment is the key ingredient in morality.

Building on the pioneering work of Jean Piaget, Lawrence Kohlberg (1927-1987) suggested there are three main levels of moral development.' They are distinguished by the degree of moral cognitive development, that is, by the kind of reasoning and motivation an individual adopts in response to moral questions.

Most primitive is the ***Pre conventional Level,*** in which right conduct is regarded as whatever directly benefits oneself. Individuals are motivated primarily by the desire to avoid punishment, by unquestioning deference to power, or by a desire to satisfy their own needs. This is the level of development of all young children and a few adults who never manage to go beyond it.

Next is the ***Conventional Level,*** in which the norms of one's family, group, or society are accepted as the final standard of morality. These norms or conventions are adopted uncritically as being correct because they represent authority. Individuals at this level are motivated by the desire to please others and to meet the expectations of the social unit, regardless of immediate effects on their self-interest. Loyalty and close identification with others have overriding importance. Kohlberg's studies reveal that most adults never mature much beyond this stage.

Finally, the ***Post conventional Level*** is attained when an individual comes to regard the standard of right and wrong as a set of principles concerning rights and the general good that are not reducible to self-interest or social conventions. Kohlberg calls these individuals *autonomous* because they think for themselves and do not assume that customs are always right. They also seek to reason and live by general principles, such as the Golden Rule ("Do unto others as you would have them do unto you"), which apply universally to all people in all cultures. Their motivation is to do what is morally reasonable for its own sake (rather than solely from ulterior motives), together with a desire to maintain their moral integrity, self-respect, and the respect of other autonomous individuals.

* *ibid* pp. 18

Morality develops in Stages.

Kohlberg's schema of moral development clearly connects with what was said earlier about the goals of studying ethics in college. To be morally responsible, one must be able and willing to exercise moral reasoning, and this in turn requires overcoming passive acceptance of the dominant conventions in one's society. Yet moral responsibility emerges from a foundation of early moral training by one's parents and culture. This early training, which involves submitting to the power of one's parents, makes possible later growth beyond complete self-centeredness (at the Pre conventional Level) and uncritical acceptance of customs (at the Conventional Level) toward respect for the rights of other people (at the Post conventional Level).

But how does Kohlberg know that these are the correct stages specifying moral development or growth? How does he know that his "higher" levels represent more advanced stages of moral maturity? He contends that advanced stages constitute a "better cognitive organization" that embodies more distinctions and represents a more universalized perspective. But why does that amount to moral progress, and not merely to increased intellectual sophistication?

The answer to these questions is not found by a mere appeal to facts about the number of people who reach each level. As we noted, Kohlberg thinks that relatively few people reach the Post conventional Level, and hence this schema does not record the path of moral development that the majority of people follow. Instead, Kohlberg seems to base his schema on the fundamental assumption that movement toward autonomy is morally desirable. This is consistent with the view expressed earlier that moral autonomy is an inherently valuable character trait essential for exercising moral responsibility. But it deserves emphasis that this is a normative claim, not a purely descriptive or psychological claim.

Could it be that Kohlberg bases his work on other moral assumptions that are somewhat more controversial? In particular, what should be said about his emphasis on abstract universal rules and rights?

Gilligan* -A Different Voice

One of Kohlberg's former students and colleagues has challenged his work on precisely this point and done so in a manner relevant to contemporary debates over male and female approaches to morality. In her book, *In a Different Voice,* Carol Gilligan charges that Kohlberg's studies are distorted by a male bias. Not only did he conduct his studies primarily with male subjects, but also according to Gilligan he approached his studies with a typically male preoccupation with general rules and rights.

Gilligan's own studies suggest that there is some tendency for men to be more interested in trying to solve moral problems by applying abstract moral principles. Males tend to resolve moral dilemmas by determining the most important moral rule, which then overrides other moral rules relevant to the dilemma. Women, by contrast, try harder to preserve personal relationships with all people involved in a situation. In order to do so, they focus greater attention on the details of the context in which the dilemma arises, rather than invoking and trying to rank general rules. Gilligan refers to this context-oriented emphasis on maintaining personal relationships as the ***ethics of care,*** and **contrasts** it with an ***ethics of rules and rights***.

Both males and females use both kinds of ethics. Gilligan wishes to draw attention only to a *difference in emphasis*, not a strict difference based on gender. Moreover, she does not attempt to answer the question of whether this difference in emphasis is due to biology (genetic determination) or to social conditioning.

In order to make Gilligan's criticism of Kohlberg clearer, consider the most famous example that Kohlberg used in his questionnaires and interviews. This example, called "Heinz's Dilemma," in-

* *ibid* pp.19-21

Right Action is duty

volves a woman living in Europe who will die from cancer unless she obtains an expensive drug that the doctors think will help her. Her husband, Heinz, cannot afford to purchase the drug. The local pharmacist is charging ten times the cost of making the drug. He also invented the drug and remains the sole source for obtaining it. The husband goes to everyone he knows seeking to borrow money, but he manages to raise only half the money needed to purchase the drug. When he asks the pharmacist to sell the drug at a cheaper price or to let him pay for it later, the pharmacist refuses. In desperation, Heinz breaks into the pharmacy and steals the drug. *Was the theft morally right or wrong?*

Applying his schema of moral development, Kohlberg ranked experimental subjects according to the kinds of reasoning they used about the dilemma (not dependent on their specific answers or conclusions). For example, the subjects who said that Heinz did wrong because he broke the law are reasoning at *the Conventional Level*, in which right conduct is regarded as simply obeying the law. Also at this level are subjects who said the husband did right because according to their religious beliefs God commanded that human life is sacred and God should be obeyed. By contrast, subjects who said that the wife's right to life is inherently more important than the property right of the pharmacist are, according to Kohlberg, reasoning at the *Post conventional Level.*

Women, interestingly enough, tended to cluster more frequently than men at Kohlberg's *Conventional Level* (a result that has subsequently been challenged). This was because they showed greater hesitancy about stealing the drug and searched for alternative solutions in terms of the context. For example, they recommended further attempts to reason with the pharmacist and to find creative ways to raise the necessary money. Kohlberg inferred that the women were overly preoccupied with conventional rules against stealing and that they were also wishy-washy in applying general principles about the right to live.

Gilligan, however, drew a very different conclusion from this data. She contended that it reveals a greater sensitivity to people and personal relationships, including the relationship with the pharmacist and the wife (who would not be helped if the husband ended up in jail for stealing the drug). She also saw value in the context-oriented reasoning used by women who did not locate the solution of the dilemma in abstract general rules ranked in order of importance.

Drawing on such reinterpretations of Kohlberg's experimental data, and combining them with her own studies of women, Gilligan offered a strikingly different schema of moral development. She recast Kohlberg's three levels of moral development as stages of growth toward an ethic of caring. Gilligan's recasting looked something like this:

The Pre conventional Level This is roughly the same as Kohlberg's first level in that the person is preoccupied with self-centered reasoning. Right conduct is viewed in a selfish manner as solely what is good for oneself.

The Conventional Level Here there is the opposite preoccupation with not hurting others and with a willingness to sacrifice one's own interests (*altruistic?*) in order to help or nurture others. Women are especially prone to fall prey to the cultural stereotypes that put pressure on them, always to be willing to give up their personal interests in order to serve the needs of others.

The Post conventional Level The individual becomes able to strike a reasoned balance between caring about other people and pursuing one's own self-interest while exercising one's rights. The aim is to balance one's own needs with the needs of others, while maintaining relationships based on mutual caring. This is achieved through context-oriented reasoning, rather than by applying abstract rules ranked in a hierarchy of importance.

Duty and Right are fundamentals.

How does Gilligan's theory of moral development relate to our emphasis of moral autonomy as a goal of studying ethics at the college level? Like Kohlberg' theory, it is entirely compatible. Note that autonomy was not defined as separateness from other people. On the contrary, it was emphasised that autonomy requires in dependent reasoning on the basis of moral concern. That concern is often best understood in terms of caring for others and trying to maintain personal relationships with them. Moral autonomy may well have as much to do with caring for other people within a community based on personal relationships (as Gilligan says) as it does with being sensitive to general principles and human right (as Kohlberg says). And it surely includes sensitivity to the subtleties of special situations (consistent with Gilligan's emphasis on context-oriented reasoning) along with an appreciation of general moral principles and rights (consistent with Kohlberg).

Theory of Right Action

The *Bhagwad Gita* is the most important part of the *Mahabharatha*. The Mahabharatha is the description of a war between the Kauravas and the Pandavas. Pandavas representing ethical people were few in numbers, whereas Kauravas were large in numbers representing the unethical. Ultimately the war was won by truth. Bhagwad Gita is a dialogue between Arjuna and Krishna. Arjuna is faced with a moral dilemma. He was a good archer and warrior. He refuses to fight with his opponents Kauravas, as they are his cousins, relatives and kinsmen. He was in an agonizing dilemma. Lord Krishna makes him understand the meaning of ***'right action'*** Through the *Bhagwad Gita* Lord says that the correctness of the action should be the primary consideration when doing any thing. He advices Arjuna always to act in accordance with Dharma (ethical living).In this instance, the right course of action is to fight. The doctrine of ***Duty*** is also brought out. The emphasis is on duty and action.

Hindu philosophy divides life into four stages. The first stage is for learning, the second for the family, the third is for meditation and study of scriptures and the final stage is one of renunciation of all worldly pleasures. Each of these stages has specified corresponding duties. Members of the family should always follow their duty. Children should respect and obey their parents' wishes. Husbands and wives ought to be loving and respectful, advising their families and teaching moral values.

Theory of Self-interest

This theory claims that self-interest plays a crucial role in determining ethically appropriate action. According to this psychological theory, human beings cannot help but act in their own interest. That is how they are constituted. Ethical theory claims that one should pursue one's enlightened self-interest exclusively. It contends that the only occasion one should take into consideration the interests of others is, when it is in one's interest to do so. A number of reasons have been offered by self-interest theorists to explain why one should act in one's own self interest. For one thing, it just makes good sense. People know what is in their own interest better than they know what is in the interest of others. If everybody pursued one's own interests exclusively and did not meddle in other people's business everyone would be better off. (Utilitarianism, on the other hand, claim that acting solely in one's self interest is never ethically acceptable.)

Very often there is a conflict and clash between the interests of self, organization and society. What is good for self may not be good for the organization and acceptable to society. *Vice versa* what is good for the society may not be good to self. The problem is how one balances between the two interests. Which should come first? This is situation dependent and varies from situation to situation. By and large, social interest for social good dominates.

Situational theory

Fletcher* advocates that all ethical decisions must be made in the light of individual circumstances and not according to moral or legal rules. He emphasizes love rather than law. The theory

* Fletcher, Joseph, Situation Ethics: The New Morality, Philadelphia, Westminster Press, 1966

Safety is a moral obligation.
Situational Ethics is based on inductive rather than deductive approach.

begins with the unique elements of a specific ethical situation rather than with any set of laws or rules that are to be applied in every situation. Situational ethics takes an inductive rather than a deductive approach to ethical decision making. According to him only one thing is intrinsically good, namely love. No law, principle or value is good in and of itself - not even life, truth, chastity, property or marriage. Love and justice are the same. Justice is distribution of love. Justice is love working itself out in a particular situation. Love is attitudinal rather than emotional therefore it can be commanded. Love is decisions made situationally not prescriptively. The rightness or wrongness of an action does not reside in the act itself, but in the whole complex of all the factors in the situation. Situational ethics has been criticized as too individualistic and subjective.

Indian theories

India is the largest democracy in the world with a secular constitution. All religions co-exist and equal respect is given to all religions. Religion is a way of life in India. The major religions practiced are Hinduism, Jainism, Sikhism, Islam, Christianity and Buddhism. Most of the ethical bases, customs and life style in India have emerged from these religions.

The Indian religious scriptures-Vedas, Upanishads, Mahabharata, Ramayana, Bhagwatam, Bhagwad Gita and eminent personalities like Buddha, Mahatma Gandhi, Ramakrishna Paramhansa, and Vivekananda have generally influenced social and ethical behaviour and attitudes in India. Indigenous religions like Buddhism, Jainism and Sikhism, besides Christianity and Islam also have had great influence on the thinking on ethics in India.

Vedanta is a school of Indian philosophy. The Upanishads, Bhagavad Gita and Brahma Sutra together form the essence of the Vedanta philosophy. The goal of Vedanta is to achieve the ultimate reality or Brahman, by breaking the cycle of birth and rebirth in three different ways:

(1) ***Jnana***, or the way of knowledge.

(2) ***Bhakti*** or the way of devotion.

(3) ***Karma*** or the way of action

There is an interesting argument that Jnana marga leads to tolerance; bhakti marga to intolerance and Karma marga is in between the two. Bhakti is the belief that all knowledge was codified in the past and will remain valid forever in the future. Jnana is the realization that knowledge is endless, impossible to comprehend in full. Bhakti needs focus.

It is perceived that Indian ethics is largely influenced by Indian philosophy and religion. It is important to note that most religious customs are based on scientific principles. The Indian literature of Vedas covers all the aspects of human life. What is surprising is what was written thousands of years ago is still relevant today.

The so-called Hindu ethics is based on the Scriptures. It has derived from the Hindu religion and Vedic texts and mainly practiced in India. Hindu ethics supply a complete moral code to good behaviour. Hinduism believes that it has behind it , a philosophy that is not only a religious doctrine but also a complete web of moral principles. It offers practical guidance, rites, prayers, festivals and social structure all aimed at social harmony and God realization. Hindu ethical philosophy has been evolving for four thousand years. Vedas are the oldest known literature in the world. It is primarily concerned with ***right action*** as a means to fulfillment.

Indian Philosophy has emerged from the forests and the philosophies that came to India from outside were from the deserts. Forest support innumerable flora and fauna while desert offers large vistas. Because of this India has a diversified culture. The institutions that came from outside to India from the desert background offered standard quality and large size. Our indigenous forest based variety is like a bazaar; it is disorganized but has always room for anything new. What India absorbs with ease, others would not even taste.

Ethics is dynamic.

Consensus and controversies

Which ethical theory is the best? In fact, each one of them has many insights to offer. We need to apply them in a complementary fashion and arrive at a consensus rather than look at the differences and highlight the controversies. There is no assurance that they will all help you reach the same conclusion. This shows that ethics is not as precise as mathematics. There will be disagreements.

Look at the controversy whether duty or right is more fundamental. We should be more interested in corresponding duty with right and *vice versa*. Thus, if you have right to life, then you have a duty not to kill you. Similarly if I have the duty to respect your freedom, then you have a right not to be interfered with. Do we adopt right or duty as the starting point for moral reflection? Some of these theories are contradictory. One should know when to apply which theory.

One should allow sufficient room for disagreements among autonomous, reasonable and responsible persons through tolerance and mutual respect. There must be a way to arrive at consensus in the midst of disagreements. Agreeing to disagree and arriving at some generalizations is essential for civilized living.

INFLUENCING FACTORS

There are many factors that influence the development of moral and ethical ideologies. These can be classified into external and internal. Self is internal while family, environment, society and culture as external. As an engineer, an individual plays different roles. These roles are played as an individual, as a member of an organization and as a member of the society. Moral and ethical ideologies are developed on the basis of past experiences and observations. As circumstances change, moral and ethical stances will also change. It might take a positive or a negative path. Shiv Kera says that values and ethics break under pressure, but one should not allow values to deteriorate.

Let us now take a look at these factors. Each factor is viewed from individual and organization perspectives.

Self

Simon * believed that a person is not morally educated unless he or she has developed within the self an understanding of what is good and right. Ethics and morality by definition comes from within, it is never imposed by an outside source

The Indian philosophy *Advaita* professes that there is only one ' supreme being' which is 'you'. The concept of ***Aham Brahmasmi*** is 'I am Brahman'. The concept of self is very powerful. In *Yoga,* which has become very popular in promoting health and peace of mind, self is everything. In the self, the whole world resides Self is complete and absolute. The concept of self has the most powerful influence on ethics.

Family

The institution of family develops and nurtures caring, sharing, protection and security ethics. The sense of care, concern and commitment of the family members for one another keeps the family together. There is a sense of responsibility and commitment. Usually, at the heart of family values is mutual affection. A family usually consists of parents and children. Family values are about the family, not about business or religion or politics, even though the family values interact with other values. For example, one set of family values may include belief in God as an integral part. Economic, educational and other social values interact with family values. A family does not live in isolation. However, family values are usually given the preference.

Environment

The environment consists of friends, educational institutions, society, residential and work locations. The environmental factors can be classified into external and internal. The internal are related

---

* Simon, Sidney B and Sally W. Olds, Helping Your Child Learn Right From Wrong: A guide to Values Clarification, New York, McGraw Hill, 1977

to the place of work while external are related to societal-local, national and global-environment, professional associations and societies like IEEE etc., government and public agencies, competitors and other industries, clients and customers.

This is a sensitive issue, which the society jointly has to face. Environmental protection has been integrated with ethics and there is an emerging branch of ethics called environmental ethics. For engineers it is important to anticipate the environmental impact of designs or processes. This topic is taken up in detail later on.

Society

Human being is a social animal. The society he lives in has a major influence on his behavior. He wants to be accepted by it. He fashions his behavior such that it is accepted by the society. After self, family, friends and then comes the society. The social norms are powerful tools to inculcate ethics. Professional societies and associations and their code of ethics play a major role in determining the ethical decisions. Code of ethics is dealt with, in detail in the later part of the book.

Customs

Some people do not believe that morality boils down to religion but rather than a function of what a particular society happens to believe. The theory of ***ethical relativism*** view that what is right is determined by what a culture or society says is right. What is right in one place may be wrong in another. Culture respects virtues like tolerance, compassion, honesty, integrity, corruption, cheating and loyalty, as well as more abstract ideals like peace, justice, fairness and respect for persons. In addition to these moral ideals there are institutional or organizational ideals of efficiency, productivity, quality, stability. Does a particular act serve or violate these ideals?

The culture in which engineer has lived and also the culture of the organization influences his ethical behaviour. We must accept that values, beliefs and attitudes differ from culture to culture.

With respect to customs, India has a long heritage, handed down through generations thanks to its very ancient civilization. The roots of customs are much stronger than in many other countries. The custom of touching the feet of god, elders, guru, mother etc. is a sign of surrendering one's self and respect. Another custom is to welcome people with the two palms held together with the fingers pointing upwards called – ***Namaste in Sanskrit and Hindi (or Vannakam in Tamil).*** These are all social customs, which are followed through the ages. Vegetarianism has emerged out of customs. One of the very important traditions is that of Ayudha Pooja when the equipments are worshipped. For example, a potter worships his wheel or a mechanic his tools. Each one pays his respect to the tools of his trade- the source of his livelihood. Each of these customs is aimed at inculcating in the people the ethics of respect for other human beings and one's profession.

Religion

The relationship of religion to ethics is controversial in different cultures. For some religion destroys ethics. For others, ethics depends upon religion. For still others, religion and ethics are same. The connection between religion and ethics in any particular society is a matter of convention. Most religions endorse the basic virtues of humility and charity. It has been observed that ethical content is fairly the same among various religious cultures. Some say that religion will work, while others say that religion is unnecessary or irrelevant to ethics. Some feel that religion is the cause of ill will and violence between persons professing different faiths.

To sum up

We have looked at the factors that influence ethical behaviour. Ethics is a very complex subject. It is a combination of Philosophy, Sociology, Economic, and psychology. Ethics is manifestation of self in the form of behaviour. The self gets influenced by various factors. These factors are mutually dependent. The various factors gets churned and jell with the self.

Factors influencing Ethical Behaviour

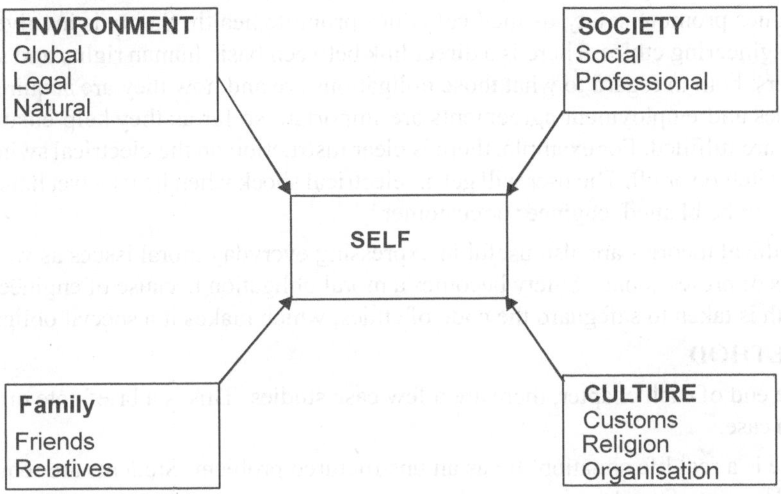

Ethics can be imagined in the form of a tree. Self is above the ground As stated in the psychological theory, ethics develops over the time. Roots are family, culture, society, environment etc. Observations, experiences are the soil and water. Just as a child learns to walk ethics is to be learnt. Ethics can change and develop for the better or for the worst. Hence it should not be looked as static but dynamic.

Ethics which is behavioural and decision related will differ when the person is alone than when in group. In a group, the ethics will get influenced by other members in a group.

USES OF ETHICAL THEORIES

Ethical theories are developed to illuminate, unify, and correct commonsense judgments and help to refine commonsense judgments. Cheating, for example is clearly forbidden. But is it always clear what cheating is? Is it easy to give a general definition: cheating is dishonesty in trying to gain something undeserved or is falsely representing one's work. But is it dishonest to work in groups on assignments? Is it dishonest to look at a previous examination paper that is widely circulated among students?

Ethical theories have three important uses: understanding moral dilemmas, justifying professional obligations and ideals and relating ordinary and professional morality.

Ethical theories aid in identifying the moral considerations or reasons that constitute a dilemma. Look at the issue of loyalty to employees and colleagues versus loyalty to the public. Duty ethics indicate a *competing* duty to protect the public on one side and to respect employer's legitimate authority to make management decisions on the other. Right ethics emphasizes the rights of the public to be protected and the rights of management to have their decisions respected. Ethical theories help to identify the kind of information which are relevant to solving moral dilemma. Theories also offer ways to rank the relevant moral considerations in order of importance and thereby provide at least a rough guidance in solving moral problems. It does not always mean that obligation to public always overrides all other obligations. However, generally engineering code of ethics states that the obligation to the public is paramount in understanding professionalism. The risk to life is more important than the economic benefits to corporates. The theories help to identify implications of alternative courses of action and provide a systematic framework for comparing alternatives. By providing frameworks for development of moral arguments, the theories strengthen ability to reach balanced and insightful judgments.

In addition to helping to understand and resolve moral dilemmas, ethical theories can be used to justify the general obligations for engineers and others involved in technological development. Engineering ethics promote safety, as medical ethics promote health. Safety is involved in most of the cases in engineering ethics. There is a direct link between basic human rights and safety obligations of engineers, both in regard to what those obligations are and how they are acquired. Laws, professional codes and employment agreements are important so far as they help ensure that the safety obligation are fulfilled. For example, there is clear instruction on the electrical switch, not to use wet hands to switch on or off. The user will get an electrical shock when he uses wet hands to switch on or off. Who is to be blamed, engineer or customer?

The ethical theories are also useful in expressing everyday moral issues as well as in justifying obligations of professionals. Safety becomes a moral obligation because of engineering code of ethics. An oath is taken to safeguard the code of ethics, which makes it a special obligation.

CASE METHOD

At the end of each chapter, there are a few case studies. This is a brief note on how to go about handling a case.

A case is a real life situation. It has an unstructured problem. Students are required to solve the problem. There are five steps in case solving.

1. ***Identification of problem.***: There may be one or many problems. The students may get confused between symptoms and problems. Symptoms are indicators of a problem(s) After identification of the problems, if there are more problems then prioritization of problems should be done.
2. ***Problem Analysis:*** The problem has to be discussed and the reasons for the problem to occur identified. Quantitative and qualitative analysis is done to identify the causes of the problem.
3. ***Identification of alternative courses of actions:*** The problem solver has to generate a few alternatives solutions.
4. ***Evaluation of alternative actions.*** This step involves evaluation of the various alternatives.
5. ***Justification of Choice of action and choice***
6. ***Action Plan***
7. ***Implication of the decision***

Tips for solving a case

While reading underline the salient features of the problem. Refer to the books, journals to find the alternative solutions to the problem. The analysis could be done using the statistics or qualitative support. Implication of the decision needs to be discussed and implementation plan developed. The implication is to be measured in terms of time, cost and effort. A case reader has to put him/herself in the shoes of the person who is facing the problem, become empathetic. You need to relate with the case and solve it. At every step of case analysis, information is required. Additional information helps to understand the scenario much better.

The case method helps to develop comprehension, analytical and decision making skills in students. It trains them to apply the theoretical concepts for solving the problem.

Case 1

Mr. Tilak Riswadkar after completion of Civil Engineering from Vasad joined the Post Graduate Diploma Programme offered by the National Institute of Construction Management and Research (NICMAR), Hyderabad. It was a Two-year course. After completion of the course, Tilak got a job from campus interviews in a Construction company of Chennai as engineer project manager. At the young age of 22 he took up job. He was the first one to get the placement. He had another offer from Dywidag from Bombay. He selected the job offered by the Chennai as the company was dealing in Building construction work. Tilak wanted to have more experience into building construction rather than going into infrastructure works like roads, bridges etc. and moreover as his uncle was in Chennai, he decided to take up the job. He was then transferred to Bangalore after undergoing training in Chennai. He did very well in his first job. He was a hard worker and within a short time, was known for commitment and decision-making. He was posted as a Planning Engineer.

When he was working in construction company , he got an offer from Moulik Associates, Ahmedabad to work on a Hospital project. His aim was to ultimately join his parents business and take it on further. So he immediately left his job at Bangalore and shifted to the project site at Udaipur. His parents Mr. Nitin Riswadkar and Mrs Shobhana Riswadkar owned Moulik Associates, a reputed Architectural firm in Ahmedabad and were the architects for the Hospital project. The project was very big and prestigious project for his parents' firm. Tilak's role on this project was that of quality checking, full time site supervision and project co-ordination. This was the right project to give him the right kind of experience Tilak wanted. The project started in full swing and enthusiasm. The construction execution contract was given to a very small time contractor of Udaipur by the clients. This was against the recommendations of the Consultants. And hence due to lack of experience of doing such large projects quality control on site had become a major issue. Tilak had to be very vigilant and strict about the quality aspects. This was not taken very positively by the contractor and client. The client always felt that what Tilak was doing on the quality aspect was not so important and they felt that it was affecting the progress of the project. This created differences of opinion between the Client and Tilak, which he reported to his firm. Tilak would not allow any type of loose work by the contractor and would ask the contractor to correct things on site. Now, being a small contractor with less resources for doing a large scale project the contractor could not cope up with the project progress with frequent correction. This was not taken well by the client who kept feeling that such small corrections were not necessary and could be allowed. As time passed by differences in such small matters increased between the client and Tilak.

Within a month many irregularities came to his notice. He found that materials were not as per specifications. He had to put his signature to pass the material. If he refused to sign, the material will get rejected. He informed the promoters of the project. There was no sign of any action. He had to sign against his morals to keep project on. He had option to withdraw from the project as site engineer. So one fine day thinking in betterment of the project Tilak decided to stop giving supervision services for the project and rather continue with only co-ordination works for the project.

QUESTIONS FOR DISCUSSIONS

1. What are the moral and ethical issues faced by Tilak?
2. Evaluate the actions of Tilak
3. What would you do in place of Tilak ?

Case 2

SHARAD is a chemical engineer who changed employment from Company A to Company B. Before leaving Company A, they asked him to sign a document by which he agreed to keep confidential any proprietary information which he acquired at Company A. Soon after he arrived at Company B, Sharad is assigned to solve a problem involving emission of a new chemical-Compound X, though noxious was not regulated by the Pollution Control Board. Sharad's new manager did not know whether to be concerned about Compound X or not. However Sharad realized that some of the proprietary information he had acquired at Company A might enable him to modify the manufacturing process at Company B. This information would be used in an entirely different way than it was used by Company A and would not harm the competitive position of Company A with respect to Company

B, but Sharad still wonders whether he should approach his new manager with a proposal that requires the use of this information.

QUESTIONS FOR DISCUSSIONS

What issues does Sharad face?

What should Sharad do?

Case 3

WHERE EFFLUENTS AND SEWAGE FLOW FREELY

Mr. Gopal was an electrical engineer working in the Tamil Nadu Electricity Board. His friend Mr. Venkat was civil engineer. Both of them had studied together in an engineering college. Both read a news item in 'The Hindu'

Fifty years old farmer Mani's face lights up when he recalls how in 1982 his farms on the banks of the Kosasthaliyar river yielded three crops of ragi, groundnut, paddy, moong dal, tomatoes and brinjal. Now, with intense pollution from industries and intrusion of seawater, it is a different story altogether. He and his family today survive by cutting firewood from the numerous thorny bushes that grow in the wasteland. "Even these sturdy palms that were so green and lush in those days are now withered and dry due to the mixing of salt and pollution in the water," the farmer says, pointing his finger at the effluent from the Ennore Thermal Power Station run by the Tamil Nadu Electricity Board going into the Kosasthaliyar river.

The river, which was always in the news during monsoon when floods would rise over the old causeway at Napalayam, cutting the traffic flow in and out of Chennai, stands today a spectacular symbol of industrial pollution and urban expansion. "With only effluents being let into the river by several industries in the Manali belt, the river has turned inhospitable for the fish which was once breeding in plenty,." said S. Manoj Babu, a social worker at Manali, who runs a night school, 'The Way", catering to 80 students.

A weir, which was built to prevent seawater intrusion into the river, has broken and now salt water enters the river unhindered. "This part of the river was a transit home for exotic birds and their numbers have dwindled." says a resident pointing out to the few egrets that still continue to haunt the river over the broken weir.

In the Manali New Town area, the problems that affect the river are two fold. They are pollution by discharge of residential sewage and sand mining. Walking near the bank of the river, slushy and caked with sewage. Mr. Manoj Babu shows the broken two-acre oxidation pond at Edayanchavadi. He said that there was a good system of sending the sewage sludge into the pond allowing for evaporation of water. "However, it was designed for a smaller population. With over 4,000 households in the area, there is imbalance in the inlet sewage water and the evaporation process," he said.

Another social worker Mohamed Vaseem said that the sand mining in the riverbed also ate into the bund that guarded the pond." Now the sewage water flows freely into the Koshasthalaiyar River. There were times when we, as youngsters, used to frolic in the river water. Today, we cannot even wash out feet in the water," says a resident. The sand mining has also aggravated the problem of pollution and flooding, say residents. For the numerous farmers like Mani, it remains a dream to see their land green on either side of the river's banks.

Mr. Gopal and Mr. Venkat ,now retired and working with a social organization, are wondering what action they should initiate ?

Exercise[1]

The exercise needs to be done in three stages. In the first stage, take 60 uninterrupted minutes out and try and draw three graphs:

1. your family life (infancy to date)
2. your study life and
3. the activities in which you have spent or currently spend your time.

These graphs can be descriptive. The number of ways and stages in which we can divide our lives is itself an interesting exercise. In the second stage , you have to return to your answers. This should be done preferably after a gap of at least one day. Re- read what you yourself have written. This can in itself be a rewarding experience. Make corrections/alterations in your graph. Retain the original – they are more instinctive whereas the latter ones will be more reflective. Share your answers with your chosen confidant. Read out the descriptions or explain the graphs. Answer all queries and clarify all points where the confidant may have doubts. Once that is done, the preparatory work for the next stage has been completed.

In the third stage sit down alone for around 40 minutes more and answer the questions. Try to be as honest as you can. After all this is an exercise in getting to know yourself. Careless and flippant answers will mean that you will end up fooling yourself. Remember that the others are seldom fooled once they have an opportunity to interact with you for a prolonged time.

The questions that you need to answer are as follows:

1. What are you ready to die for?
2. Who are the five most important people in your life ? Why ?
3. What are the decision that you have taken that lead to happiness for you?
4. If you are unconstrained by anything in life, what would you choose to do ?
5. What is your idea of an ideal vacation ?
6. Who will you be 10 years hence?
7. What idea have you liked the most ? Why ?
8. Of the values that you have inherited from your family which is the one that you have chosen and which is the one that you have rejected.

After writing out these answers, share them with your confidant. The confidant may only seek clarification on the issues that are unclear. Under no circumstances should the confidant try and make judgemental statements. At the same time the confidant have to be very attentive and empathetic.

At the end of the recitation of your answers and clarification, you can ask the confidant to try and enumerate what sort of person he feels you are. After going through this exercise , you may have learnt a few new things about yourself.

Case 4

Dr. Sundeep Vani did his B.Tech in Chemical Engineering from IIT Kharagpur. After graduation, he went to Rice University USA for a PhD programme. After obtaining his Doctorate he took up a job with ADA, a large Chemical company in the USA. After few years he got an offer from ADB, a much bigger company. ADB was a competitor to ADA in one of their product portfolios.

ADB was earlier involved in a case involving business ethics and two of their senior executives had been jailed for two offences-one relating to price fixation and the other for wrongful acquisition of competitive information. ADB had learnt from their mistakes and had an ethics policy in place. The company did not involve Sundeep in their product lines, which competed with his former employers. Some years back it was Sundeep who had developed the technology wherein the viscosity of the product was increased by 20%. The increased viscosity gave ADA an increase of 20% in market share. Most of it was from ADB. Now ADB wanted to increase its share. The Company had lots of information with themselves and systematic research could give them some idea. ADB was 10 times bigger in terms of size than ADA. There was not much co-ordination among various departments.

[1] Makarand Sahasrabuddha, Identifying values and ethics in oneself, Alumnus, IIM Ahmedabad, 36(1), February 2004, PP.26

Sundeep was assigned the role of technology management and product development. The products of new company were mostly used as raw materials in the production of food products. They were strong in the industrial market. The ADB was not known much in the consumer segment as ADA. Sundeep had taken legal advice before joining ADB. The lawyer had advised him that as long as he did not reveal competitive information of ADA, he was safe. Before leaving ADA, he had informed them that he was joining ADB. He expected that ADA might take up a legal action against him. As per US law, a person cannot reveal any confidential competitive information, which he obtained in the course of employment with an organisation to anybody outside it. If the Company is able to prove that an ex-employee has revealed such information, it would result in severe punishment for the person,

ADB appointed an outsider as a consultant to give them advice on technology management and product development. He had not revealed to them that he was an ex employee of ADA. ADA took up the case under Intellectual Property Rights violation. The ADB was put into lot of problems. They had to prove that they did not have knowledge about the consultant being from ADA.

Sundeep is wondering as to what role he can play in improving ADB's product lines, which he had handled for ADA earlier. He knew he was walking into a legal, moral and ethical minefield.

Questions for discussions:

Is it possible as Sundeep to help ADB?

What would you do if you were Sundeep?

Are the theories helpful?

Case 5 (A)

Johnson & Johnson: The Tylenol Crisis*

Crisis data:

- Sept 30, 1982 the CEO was given data that several deaths in the Chicago area might be linked to one of its products
- It was quickly determined that 7 people had died taking cyanide-laced capsules of Extra-strength Tylenol.
- The deaths were broadly reported in the press
- Additional deaths were also reported in other states that were falsely attributed to Tylenol.
- The Halloween season was approaching with the potential for copycat behavior.
- The consumer concern resulted in decline in sales of the drug.

Business data:

- From 1959 to 1982, the drug had been extensively promoted successfully as a superior treatment.
- It was distributed in tablet form of 350 milligrams and in capsule form of 500 milligrams. The "extra strength" capsule had no additional ingredients to make it effective. 70% of its product was "extra strength".
- The firm had captured 35% of a billion dollar market—three times the market share of its leading competitor.
- The drug represented 7% of its sales, and 17% of its profits.

Issues:

- What are the ethical dilemmas in the case?
- Did the firm act sensibly and reasonably in balancing economic, legal and ethical issues?
- Were the firms long standing ethical standards a useful guide to action?

Case 5. (B)

This case gives details about what happened later on and the actions taken by the company.

---

* Case from the web site

In 1982, seven people in the Chicago area died of cyanide poisoning between September 29th and October 1st, all after having taken Extra-Strength Tylenol capsules.

Oh No! Who committed the crime? 1982

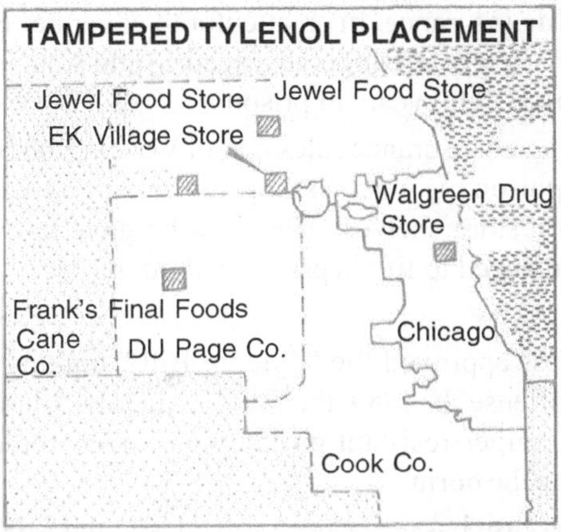

The possibility that cyanide had been inserted into the capsules during production was ruled out. Law enforcement believe that a person acquired bottles of the painkiller, tampered with the contents, then randomly selected stores where he would place one or two bottles back on the shelf. No one has ever been charged with the Tylenol murders.

James Lewis was convicted of attempting to extort $1 million from Johnson & Johnson after the McNeil offices in Fort Washington, Pennsylvania (a subsidiary of Johnson & Johnson) received an envelope with the word TYLENOL written across it; the extortion letter demanded a ransom of $1 million to be delivered to a Chicago post office box, and threatened more deaths if payment wasn't made. James Lewis received a 20-year sentence for extortion. Lewis remains a strong suspect in the deaths.

Oh No! What capsules did he use? Tylenol? 1982

Tylenol Extra Strength

The Johnson & Johnson credo was written in the mid-1940's by Robert Wood Johnson, the company's leader for 50 years. The J&J credo which puts customers first and stockholders last, helped Johnson and Johnson's handling of the Tylenol tampering crisis to be one of the best.

During the Tylenol Tampering Crisis Johnson & Johnson put customer safety first, before they worried about the companies profit.

The company immediately alerted consumers, via the media, not to consume any type of Tylenol product. They told consumers not to resume using the product until the extent of the tampering could be determined. Johnson & Johnson, along with stopping the production and advertising of Tylenol, recalled all Tylenol capsules from the market. The recall included approximately 31 million bottles of Tylenol, with a retail value of more than 100 million dollars.

In November of 1982, Johnson & Johnson reintroduced Tylenol capsules baring a new triple-seal tamper- resistant package. Johnson & Johnson provided $2.50-off coupons that were good to-wards the purchase of any Tylenol product. New pricing gave consumers discounts as high as 25 percent. Sales people from Johnson & Johnson were asked to make presentations to people in the medical community.

Tylenol is the number one over-the-counter analgesic in the United States

Oh No! Copycats! 1982 +

In 1986, Stella Nickell of Washington State killed her husband Bruce with cyanide-laced Excedrin in order to collect on his life insurance. In an attempt to cover her tracks, she also killed a complete stranger by placing three packages of tampered Excedrin and Anacin capsules on the shelves of three stores. Nickell was sentenced to 90 years in prison.

In 1993, Joseph Meling, an insurance salesman of Washington State, was convicted of murdering two people and trying to poison his wife. Meling tampered with capsules in six Sudafed packages, five of which he placed on store shelves. The sixth he gave his wife Jennifer, who survived the poisoning. Meling was sentenced to life in prison without parole.

Oh No! Aftermath 1982 +

In May 1983, Congress approved the "Tylenol Bill," making malicious tampering with consumer products a federal offense. In 1989, the Food and Drug Administration established a uniform national requirement for tamper-resistant packaging of over- the-counter products. Tamper-proof packaging has now become the norm.

The Tylenol poisoning case has never been solved, and the $100,000 reward offered by Johnson & Johnson remains unclaimed.

James Lewis was released from an Oklahoma prison on October 13, 1995. Lewis spent almost 13 years behind bars for extortion.

QUESTIONS FOR DISCUSSION

Evaluate the decisions taken by the Johnson & Johnson.

What are the ethical dilemmas in the case?

Did the firm act sensibly and reasonably in balancing economic, legal and ethical issues?

Were the firms long standing ethical standards a useful guide to action?

EXERCISES

1. Interview a practicing Engineer and ask him to describe a moral dilemma. Explain which theories can be involved to resolve the conflict.
2. An engineer from a company in Chennai is sent for submission of tender papers to Mumbai. He took drinks and submitted the drinks bill as laundry bill. Recommend action using theory.
3. Debate on "Ethics can or cannot be taught but should be learnt"
4. Debate on "Ethical behaviour of an individual is same when he is alone in a group."
5. Debate on "Should Ethics be promoted or imposed?

SHORT QUESTIONS

1. Define Ethics
2. Define Profession and professionalism
3. Differentiate between profession and occupation
4. Why engineering is a profession ?
5. What are the principles of ethics?
6. Ethics and Morals are same. - Discuss
7. What is Corporate Value?
8. What is moral autonomy?
9. What are the uses of ethical theories ?
10. Explain ethical dilemma with examples

11. How do you find a solution for a moral dilemma?

12. What is Golden Rule?

LONG QUESTIONS

1. Discuss the examples of Indian companies that believe in corporate values.
2. Discuss the need and importance of ethics or How does the study of ethics help you?
3. Compare and contrast the psychological theory of Kohlberg and Gilligan
4. Discuss the Right to Action theories
5. Identify the factors that influence ethics
6. Discuss the Indian theory of ethics.
7. What are the three types of enquiry?
8. "Self Interest is unethical "– Discuss the statement
9. Compare and contrast between Consensus and Controversy

REFERENCES

1. Aashish Pandey and Nisha Pandey : A paper published on Web entitled "Transformation Through Values : Study of Indian Organisation
2. A&M University, Texas USA
3. John Roth K (Ed), International Encyclopedia of Ethics, S.Chand & Company Ltd, New Delhi, 2000
4. Mike W. Martin, Schinzinger, Ethics in Engineering, Tata Mcgraw Hill, 2003
5. Fletcher, Joseph, Situation Ethics: The New Morality, Philadelphia, Westminster Press, 1966.
6. Simon, Sidney B and Sally W. Olds, Helping your child Learn Right From Wrong: A guide to Values Clarifications, New York, McGraw Hill, 1977.
7. Case from the Web
8. * Robert L. Whitelaw, Professional Status of the American Engineer: A Bill of Rights", Professional Engineer 45, August, 1975, pp. 37 – 38
9. * Samuel C. Florman, " Moral Blueprints", Harpers 257, October, 1978, pp.32

Chapter

4

Engineering as Social Experimentation

UNIT III : ENGINEERING AS SOCIAL EXPERIMENTATION : Engineering as experimentation – Engineers as responsible experimenters – Codes of ethics – A balanced outlook on law – The Challenger case study.

Learning Objectives

- To understand What is Social Experimentation ?
- To understand the responsibility of an Engineer as a social experimenter
- Role of Code of Ethics
- Importance of Law
- The Challenger Case Study

After a review of some of the major concepts of professional ethics, let us now focus on the roles and responsibilities of engineers and the engineering profession. In this chapter, we look at engineering as a 'social experimentation' and engineers as social experimenters. Their responsibility in different areas of engineering as social experimentation, product design and maintenance are discussed in brief.

ENGINEERING AS SOCIAL EXPERIMENTATION

Medicine is accepted readily as social experimentation because of its explicit preoccupation with human beings. In the case of engineering the argument goes thus: engineers experiment with things and processes and not with human beings; then how can it be regarded as social experimentation? The answer lies in the fact that there is always a strong human interface in the use of the process and results of these experiments and the beneficiaries are invariably humans.

Social experimentation is a research process. Engineering involves applied research and development. Experimentation ethics is the discipline that is concerned with the analysis of moral principles applicable in the conduct of research especially in relation to human subjects. It seeks to protect the rights and welfare of human subjects involved in the process. Research can do good; but also may cause harm. Research that causes harm is morally wrong. If avoiding harm is of primary importance, then many a research project with potential for doing good would be considered unethical since in the initial stages, some cause harm, but once proved successful will do good for the society. Therefore, the ratio of benefit to harm is the more reasonable criterion for justifying any experimentation. This principle of harm and benefit is called ***beneficence***.

Another relevant principle is ***autonomy***, which recognizes the rights of a person to information, self-determination and to liberty. A researcher has to provide all relevant information and then take the informed consent of a subject before asking him/her to participate in his/her project research.

Researcher should not subject a mentally ill or disabled person to experimentation without the due process.

For ethically sound. experimentation, an engineer should:

(1) Minimize the risk to subjects

(2) Make sure that risks are reasonable relative to anticipated benefits

(3) Obtain, prior consent from subject or their legal representatives

(4) Document the informed consent .

(5) Maintain, the privacy and confidentiality of the subjects and experiments

(6) Monitor the data throughout the experiment to ensure the safety.

(7) Provide safe exit to subjects.

Murphy's law states that if anything can go wrong, it will sooner or later. All technological products carry some potential danger, and therefore in engineering processes, there is always an element of risk, however small. In each and every stage of technology, process or product development, experiments are conducted. There are uncertainties at every stage. Engineers do not have the luxury of waiting until all the relevant facts are in before commencing work. At some point of time theoretical exploration and laboratory testing must be bypassed for the sake of moving the project ahead and gain time. The talent and ability to accomplish tasks with the available knowledge is crucial in an engineer. The final outcome of an experiment could be uncertain but monitoring throughout the experiment is essential. It is not sufficient for engineers to rely on handbooks alone. Engineering, like any other experimentation, demands constant monitoring, alertness and vigil on the part of the experimenters at every stage of a project.

Engineering as a social experimentation is not just a metaphorical notion. Any experiment in engineering has to consider its impact on the environment. Simulation studies are done but there are always risks associated with any experiment. Failures and mishaps are encountered in experimentation. Only after considerable research and experimentation, a product is ready to be put to use.

RESPONSIBILITIES OF ENGINEERS AS EXPERIMENTERS

Now let us look at the responsibilities of engineers as experimenters. Engineers are technical enablers or facilitators; they are far from being sole experimenters. Their responsibilities are shared with colleagues, management, public and others. They use their expertise to monitor an experimental project to identify risk, inform clients and public and to take appropriate corrective decisions. In the following paragraphs we discuss the general characteristics of a morally responsible engineer.

Conscientiousness

First and foremost is conscientiousness or being conscientious. It means commitment to live according to certain moral values. Conscientiousness implies consciousness. An Engineer has to be sensitive to a range of moral values and responsibilities that are relevant in a given situation; he should have the willingness to develop the skills and expend the effort needed to reach the best balance possible among various considerations. 'Open eyes, open ears and an open mind' are required to evaluate a given situation, its implications and determine who are involved or affected. He should not violate any rights, not breach any confidentiality, or tamper with data. He has to constantly play the role of a guardian of public interest.

Accountability

Accountability means being responsible, liable, answerable or obligated. It may be individual or collective. It assumes that there is a duty that one has to discharge. One can generally be held account-

Social experimentation is a research process.

able for the failure to do one's duty. Responsible people are expected to accept moral responsibility for their actions. In extreme cases, they may resign from their post.

Moral Autonomy

This concept is discussed in the previous chapter. The word autonomy comes from the Greek words 'autos' meaning self and 'nomos' meaning law. It denotes the absence of external constraint plus a positive power of self-determination. One should always act so as to treat persons as end in themselves, and never as means to ends. As an experimenter, an engineer is exercising his identity as a professional. Engineers may have to look for moral support from their professional societies.

Being Informed

Engineer has to show the commitment to obtain and properly assess all the information pertinent to meeting one's moral obligations. Conscientiousness is blind without relevant factual information. This has to be done on a continuing basis and confidentiality maintained. The cost-benefit analysis of information collection is to be estimated by the Engineer.

Awareness of Code of Ethics

As a social experimenter, an Engineer has to be aware of the codes of ethics of his profession. They help the engineer with a checklist and provide inspiration in the form of positive stimulus and guidance for decision-making. Since they are brief, they offer mostly general guidance. Engineering societies like, IEEE, ASCE, ABET, ASME have general codes of ethics for their members and many technologically advanced companies like Texas Instruments, TISCO, IBM etc .have developed company-specific codes. These tend to concentrate on the moral issues encountered in dealing with vendors, customers, governments etc. Texas Instruments publishes an ethics diary and provides on line consultation on ethical issues. Their ethics site has 'Quick Tests' answering queries on ethics such as (*Their site extols their employees "If you're not sure, ask. Keep asking until you get an answer*")

Is the action legal?

Does it comply with our values?

If you do it, will you feel bad?

How will it look in the newspaper?

From the perspective of engineering profession, the emphasis of codes should be on supporting responsible conduct, offering general guidance and promotion of mutual understanding rather than punishment. Preserving *status quo* and promoting business interests in violation of free competition should be avoided .It should be kept in mind that codes are but a small part of engineering ethics. Codes are not sacred writ and should always be open to critical examination. Codes should be applied with caution, keeping in view their limitations. (*Last chapter of the book deals with code of ethics in greater detail.*)

To create awareness and the implementation of the code of ethics, the engineering associations have to hold regular meetings, communicate the codes to all members , check for possible violations, enforce codes by rewards and punishment and review, update and report.

Importance of Law

In the first chapter we looked at the relationship between law and ethics. Here we will focus on law with respect to social experimentation.

Let us examine the role of law in the engineering ethics. Here we will focus only with respect to social experimentation. The law allows for the social experimentation, but it has to place emphasis on moral responsibility of engineers – an emphasis that goes beyond merely following laws and is especially vital for those working for the future technologies and its development. Laws lag behind the technological development . They look at the issue of compliance and regulation that can slow

Engineers are technical enablers or facilitators.

down the process of experimentation. It can form as limitations for the application. Lawyers do not have much knowledge about the engineering, they take long time first to understand , gather relevant information and deliver judgement. Experimentation is not a standard activity and standards cannot be applied. It calls for creativity and going beyond the existing standards. Laws insist on the compliance of minimum standards. In the Titanic case (given at the end of this chapter), while the minimum standards of having life boats was fulfilled by the shipping company, the numbers were not adequate to rescue all passengers. Thus, law can play only a limited role.

Let us now consider the major concepts, which an Engineer has to deal with in order to discharge his/her different roles and responsibilities After understanding the concepts of professional ethics, let us focus on the role and responsibility of engineering and engineers. In the Texas Instruments Ethics site, the professional ethics for engineers includes the issues of :

Entertainment, Gifts —Avoiding Bribes & Conflict of Interest

Signing Off on Engineering Documents

Mischarging Time — Financial Fraud

ETHICAL ISSUES IN DESIGN

Engineers at Bath University, England have developed a Compact Low Emission Vehicle for Urban Transport called CLEVER. The vehicle is three wheeled, tilting micro vehicle, which is only a meter wide, has a top speed of 50 mph and runs on compressed natural gas. The design is at research stage. The prototype needs to be developed and tested. The car is small and eco-friendly. The fuel consumption is predicted to be around 188 miles per gallon, a fifth of most cars. This car will outwit the smallest Smart car. CLEVER will combine the safety of a car with the maneuverability of a motorbike. This example shows how at the design and prototype stage, the environmental issues are kept in mind.

Mercedes Benz and Nokia have many of their engineering designs prepared in India. Our engineers have creativity and design costs are low. At design stage, lot of money is spent in R & D, so by designing in India, costs get reduced and conceptual skills are as good as in any advanced countries. But in the design processes ethically relevant decisions continually have to be made.

Social Responsibility Versus Legal Liability

Litigation associated with engineering design has escalated enormously over the last few decades. It has increased the intensity of debates over the question whether social responsibility or legal liability should have priority. Where do a design engineer and his/her company's responsibility end and the subcontractor's, manufacturer's and consumer's begin? The relationship between social responsibility and legal liability is complicated by the fact that laws are usually enacted only after a disaster. How can an engineering firm justify its actions based on current legal definitions? If a company's design has adverse affects on the public welfare, out of necessity, laws are enacted to ensure that appropriate safety standards are met. Or, at the very least, legal suits are filed so injured parties can be compensated and the culprits penalized. This phenomenon has become particularly critical regarding litigation involving engineering design and product liability.

The public has become increasingly aware that the benefits of industrial progress must be balanced against the growing need to protect the public from damages caused by some products and by-products of technology. Naturally, the spirited public debate puts engineers at the center of the controversy between product safety and social responsibility on the one hand and legal liability on the other.

How should we determine the engineer's and his/her company's social responsibility? Is it not their job to act as society's protector? Should social responsibility not precede any discussion of legal liability? And should a design engineer not take every precaution to ensure that his/her company's

Conscientiousness implies consciousness.

product is safe before it enters the market? Safety must be an essential design consideration, for as Christopher D. Stone notes in his '*Where the Law Ends: The Social Control of Corporate Behavior*', even if we put aside the defects in the impact of the sanctions, there still remains the problem that law is primarily a reactive institution. Law makers have to appreciate and respond to problems that corporate engineers, chemists, and financiers were anticipating (or should have anticipated) long before that the drugs their corporations are about to produce can alter consciousness or damage the gene pool of the human race, that they are on the verge of multinational expansion that will endow them with the power to trigger worldwide financial crises in generally unforeseen ways, and so on. Even if laws could be passed to deal effectively with these dangers, until they are passed a great deal of damage some perhaps irreversible can be done. Thus, it is socially dangerous in encouraging corporate managers to believe that, until the law tells them otherwise, they have no responsibilities beyond the law and their impulses (whether their impulses spring from the 'id' or from the balance sheet). We do not encourage human beings to suppose so. And the dangers to society seem all the more acute where corporations are concerned.

Social Responsibility for Public Safety

An engineer must often place his/her social responsibility over the objectives of his/her employer. "Just as we must know the rules of cricket to know what to do with the ball, so we must know engineering ethics to know, for example, whether, *as engineers*, we should merely weigh safety against the wishes of our employer or instead give safety preference over those wishes." Sometimes a cost/benefit analysis is not enough, especially when lives are at stake.

In his "*Explaining Wrongdoing*", Michael Davis emphasizes the need for professionals to distance themselves from a "microscopic" way of looking at their role within the corporation, to look up from their given tasks and role obligations to see the larger implications of the work they perform for society. Davis argues that problems associated with professional ethics center on these fundamental questions of social obligation. Using the catastrophic *Challenger* disaster as a case study, Davis shows that while no one broke the law, there was clearly wrongdoing on the part of a supplier's managers and engineers. "For an engineer, safety is the paramount consideration. The engineers could not say the launch would be safe. So, Lund, the man who knew should have delayed the launch. Seven people died, in part at least, because he did not do what, as an engineer, he was supposed to do. This is not simply limited to highly publicized disasters. In all fields of engineering, concern over safety, and the engineer's responsibility for ensuring it, is being emphasized.

In his "*Safety An Important Responsibility*", Carlton Robinson argues that safety is an especially critical factor for transport engineers and their managers. Given the volume of traffic on roads, safety must come before cost considerations in highway design and construction. Robinson argues that if, at present, increased safety is not the primary goal in engineering design and construction projects, it should be. Safety is a social, not primarily a legal obligation, and engineers and their managers must always keep their obligations to the public welfare at the forefront when making design and management decisions.

Quality engineering is an imperative. Thus, there is a need for responsible management of design projects, both in terms of ethical and creative engineering and corporate practice. The American Society of Civil Engineering Code of Ethics states "engineers must hold the public safety, welfare, and health paramount and use our knowledge and skill for the enhancement of human welfare." When engineers, managers, and their companies' corporate owners, as well as contractors, subcontractors and inspectors, take pride in and responsibility for their designs, the entire engineering profession benefits. According to Charlton Moorman, ethical engineering practice positively affects engineering creativity, and the "engineering profession benefits when ethics are followed and creativity is used by

Laws insists on the compliance of minimum standards.

the engineer. When not followed, bad public relations are a possibility for the engineer, the company employing the engineer and the profession in general."

As such, professional engineering societies play a significant role in ensuring that safety standards are maintained, and it is imperative that individual professional engineers adhere to what his/her society mandates. Michael Davis notes that in thinking like an engineer, one must remember the place of a code of ethics in the practice of his/her profession:

> 'Engineers should not only do as their profession's code requires, but should also support it less directly by encouraging others to do as it requires and by criticizing, ostracizing, or otherwise calling to account those who do not. They should support their profession's code in these ways for at least four reasons: First, engineers should support their profession's code because supporting it will help protect them and those they care about from being injured by what other engineers do. Second, supporting the code will also help assure each engineer a working environment in which it will be easier than it would otherwise be to resist pressures to do much that the engineer would rather not do. Third, engineers should support their profession's code because supporting it helps make their profession a practice of which they need not feel morally justified embarrassment, shame, or guilt. And fourth, one has an obligation of fairness to do his part in so far as he claims to be an engineer and other engineers are doing their part in generating these benefits for all engineers.'

Sometimes, despite engineers' meeting their design obligations, failures still occur. What is the engineer's responsibility once the design is handed off to a contractor, subcontractor or the consumer? Is the designer liable for aiding others in the use of a product? What criteria can the engineer invoke? In his " *Charity and the Duty to Rescue*", John Whelan says, "there is not a duty to aid; however, many failures to aid deserve moral criticism; and some of them deserve very serious moral criticism." He notes that one must distinguish between morally objectionable failures to aid and those that are merely failures of consideration. They are distinguishable by knowing what the obligations of the rescuer (or in this case, the engineer) are. "Knowledge (or any reasonable belief)...is relevant to any obligation. ...what matters [; however,] is whether you can do something about it." In determining whether you are obligated to do something to prevent harm to others, two of his six rules apply directly to engineering design:

(1) That there is sufficient professional reason to believe that you can prevent unreasonable danger at little cost to yourself; and

(2) That you do not have sufficient reason to believe someone else can prevent harm if you do not.

This raises serious questions about what constitutes safety and the concept of unreasonable danger as a design consideration. One of the problems is that engineers are often not trained to look at notions of "unreasonably dangerous products" conceptually. D. Muster uses the analogy of medical health practitioners to encourage a forensic approach to engineering. "Some engineers tend to ignore design considerations that cannot be quantified easily for analysis or, at least, they consider them to be of less importance than others which lend themselves readily to being modeled and analysed." For Muster, the real problem engineers face is that they are not properly educated in product liability law and the legal concept of an "unreasonably dangerous product," so they do not fully appreciate when they are ethically obligated to assist others in the product chain.

Strict liability for a defective product falls into three categories, and all three are significant in the chain: design, manufacturing, and marketing. In particular, Muster notes "A marketing defect is synonymous with the failure of a manufacturer to give adequate warnings and instructions for the

**The risks and benefits are based on the perception of probable gain and loss.
How safe is safe enough?**

proper use of his product." This is also true for the designer. When looking at whether there was an "unreasonable" danger, courts test the product as to whether it was: 1.) state-of-the-art, 2.) an unavoidably unsafe product, 3.) misconduct by the user, or 4.) misused with the foresee ability of the specific misuse at issue.

Like the other authors, Muster argues that safety is an essential design consideration. Given all the educational programs and literature available to engineers, "no designer can claim the information on which to base a safe design is unavailable." He further notes, as Stone does, that most design changes are directly attributable to product liability litigation, and that safe products lead to good business practice. Thus, safety is deemed as the absence of unreasonable danger. Anything short of that can be considered morally unacceptable. Yet, morally unacceptable conduct continues apace, as the amount of litigation escalates. What are the consequences for the engineering profession?

Legal and Social Consequences for the Engineering Profession

As stated above, claims against design professionals and their companies are on the increase. Even if the professional engineer feels he/she has done everything to avoid "unreasonable" danger, accidents happen, and designers are increasingly held liable for construction and product mishaps. Engineers must, therefore, familiarize themselves with the legal doctrines of informed consent, novel tort remedies and reforms, third-party liability issues, liability insurance, and legislative lobbying techniques.

The legal doctrine of informed consent is based on tort law. In "A History and Theory of Informed Consent," a "tort" is defined as "a civil injury to one's person or property that is intentionally or negligently inflicted by another and that is measured in terms of, and compensated by, money damages." Any failure to obtain informed consent in situations where it is legally required is considered a "tort."

In recent years, in the U.S, a novel theory of tort remedy, the "Hedonic tort," is gaining momentum, as litigation shows there is a widespread need both to do more than just cost-benefit analyses on products and to reevaluate corporate marketing strategies. The "Hedonic tort" remedy considers as its base, the theory of individual happiness, and its attributes include "quality of life factors such as environmental standards, quality of education, weather, and the amounts of time spent pursuing vocations." According to Jack Karns, individual happiness is based on three factors: "*a.* degree of moral virtue, *b.* degree of good fortune with which the individual is blessed, and *c.* [and most important for the design engineer's consideration] whether a tragic choice is made based on circumstances beyond someone's control." Hedonic damage suits could conceivably ruin a professional's reputation, and her financial well being. Thus, this theory of tort remedy could have significant impacts on product design, incorporating additional safety features in order to minimize such damage claims.

One of the problems associated with tort reform, however, is the issue of insurance. Because claims have increased substantially, battles over reform have escalated since the early 1980's. As Dennis Schapker notes, many firms have responded to these increased claims by dropping their insurance coverage. As of 1990, 21% of all design firms were uninsured. This percentage of uninsured firms does not bode well for the engineering profession as a whole. Thus, he argues that design professionals must get involved in the debate over tort reform. This call to action rises as designers are increasingly being held responsible for negligence in their work, including that of their subcontractor's, despite written contract disclaimers aimed at defending their interests. Civil Engineers should note that the privity of contract defense is no longer an absolute shield that design professionals may use to protect themselves from liability to third parties. Thus, engineers must understand tort law and liability insurance as never before.

While insurance is not a remedy for unprofessional behavior, engineers must know more about it. In his case study of an insurance carrier, Randall Horne notes that, "With the ever-increasing tendency toward litigation, clients have begun to view their design professional's liability insurance

Making ethical decision is element of profession.

as a potential source of full reimbursement for any damages they may incur." This can be a paralyzing concept for the engineer, to say the very least. Claims against designers result not only in financial loss, but also a loss of prestige, good will among clients and future business. "Although it may be difficult to assign a monetary value to these losses, it is not difficult to imagine that they could be career or at least business threatening." Thus, engineers must get involved, in their societies. The nature of engineering in the United States means that each state can create unique laws governing the practice of engineering. This has resulted in a liability crisis of the first order. While most recognize the need for engineers to place their social responsibility over issues of legal liability, many petty lawsuits make practicing as a professional a risky venture. If engineers get involved in the debate over legal liability, perhaps they can spend more time policing themselves, and less time in the court room. Mark Friedlander, a liability attorney in the U.S, argues that engineers and their societies must acquire the requisite knowledge about liability issues, and then lobby for legislation that will protect them from the ever-increasing litigation crisis. "Among the most costly and frivolous lawsuits are construction-site-accident claims. Engineers ordinarily have no responsibility for construction-site safety. Nevertheless, obtaining indemnity against these claims from the contractor, or defense under the contractor's general liability policy, is difficult. In my experience, such claims constitute the most frivolous malpractice claims filed against design professionals." If engineers are better educated about the litigation process, perhaps they can better serve society at large. The courts are siding with contractors, which means that the public feels engineers should continue answering for their designs on site. And maybe they should take a more active role. The only way to know for sure that their design instructions are being adhered to, is by getting involved, and by understanding both their social and legal responsibilities.

Implicit Social Contract Between Engineers and Society

Engineering is a form of social experimentation. As with every experiment, there is a risk of negative consequences as well as positive ones. We need only examine the way the quality and structure of life has changed over recent decades with the arrival of such phenomena as high-speed computers, new composite materials, new modes of high-speed transportation, and new advances in bioengineering to appreciate the potential impact on society of technological change. Unfortunately, such advances are not always accompanied by unalloyed blessings, and we must deal with the possible side effects. We must, for example, consider our needs for protection against invasion of privacy to easily accessible computerized records, or our needs for protection from the many drunken drivers who cause over 20,000 deaths per year.

As engineers test designs for ever-increasing speeds, loads, capacities and the like, they must always remember their larger societal obligation: protecting the public welfare. After all, the public has provided engineers, through the tax base, with an educational opportunity, and, through legislation, with the means for licensing and regulating themselves. In return, engineers have a responsibility for protecting the safety and well-being of the public in all of their design efforts. This is part of the implicit social contract all engineers agree to when they accept admission to an engineering college.

The Issue of Public Risk and Informed Consent

As technology advances, risks are unavoidable. Thus, the issues of risk and decision making confront all engineering professionals. Recognizing them will always be some measure of risk associated with engineering design, how do engineers know when those risks outweigh the possible benefits gained from their work? How do they make informed decisions?

Engineering, more than any other profession, involves social experimentation. Often one engineer's decision affects the safety of countless lives. It is, therefore, important that engineers constantly remember that their first obligation is to ensure the public's safety. This is a difficult assignment, for engineers are not typically autonomous professionals. Most of them work for salaries within a structured environment where budgets, schedules and multiple projects are important factors in the decision-making process.

Safety must be an essential design consideration.

The decision-making process is often complicated by the fact that most engineers have multiple responsibilities attached to their job descriptions. They are responsible for actual engineering practice (including research, development and design), for making proposals and writing reports, for managing projects and personnel, and often for sales and client liaison. In other words, engineers, by the very nature of their professional stature both outside and inside the corporate structure, cannot work in a vacuum. Graduation is not a license to merely tinker in an engineering laboratory. As an engineer advances, he will be given more authority for directing projects.

This is a natural phenomenon in the engineering community. Most engineers aspire to managerial positions, even if only on one specific project. There are many benefits associated with managerial authority, not the least of which are increased financial remuneration and job satisfaction. But authority comes with a heavy price tag: increased responsibility for decisions made. It is important to remember that responsibility always rests with the project leader.

Eventually, engineers and engineering managers have to make tough decisions about whether a product is safe for public use. Sometimes those decisions involve conflicts over technical problems versus budgets, and problems with schedules and personnel allocations. The engineering manager must first be an engineering professional. Before attending to profits, he must meet professional engineering code requirements and obligations to public safety. This requirement can create difficulties for the engineer.

The problems engineering professionals face involve how to define, assess and manage risk in the light of obligations to the public at large, the employer, and the engineering profession as a whole. Bear in mind that, above all, risk assessment is closely tied to the perspective that engineering is a social experiment, that engineers have an implicit social contract with the public they serve, and that professional societies and their codes of ethics play important roles in helping shape the engineering decision-making process.

Negligence and the Codes of Ethics of Professional Societies

What guidelines do the professional codes of ethics give engineers? The last chapter contains two such codes: the ASME, and the recently revised IEEE code adopted by the IEEE Board of Directors in October 1990. Note the emphasis in the first clause of the new IEEE code on the public's welfare, and the responsibility cited in the second clause for engineers to inform all affected parties of any inherent dangers or risks. This is very different from engineering codes of ethics written in past decades, where the primary concern was competitive bidding, advertising, obligations to employers and clients, and so on. While these are all important issues for professionals, they are less important than obligations to the public those obligations implicit in the engineers' adopted social contract.

In their recent book on engineering and ethics, Mike Martin and Roland Schinzinger cited earlier studies on the responsibilities of engineers. They summarize these responsibilities as involving the following considerations:

1. A primary obligation to protect the safety and respect the right of consent of human subjects.
2. A constant awareness of the experimental nature of any project, imaginative forecasting of its possible side affects, and a reasonable effort to monitor them.
3. Autonomous, personal involvement in all steps of a project.
4. Accepting accountability for the results of a project.

Martin and Schinzinger's implicit assumptions are:

(a) engineers are and should be held responsible for past actions;

(b) engineers are responsible for the roles they have played in projects;

(c) engineers are capable of making moral (and certainly technically correct) decisions autonomously; and

Safety is a social rather than legal obligation.

(d) as such, each individual engineer is accountable for the projects she/he works on. Thus, an engineer can be deemed negligent if she/he does not meet these criteria.

Conflicting norms and values in the design process

Conflicting norms and values often play a part in technological design processes. In that connection one may think of norms and values such as safety, sustainability, respect for nature, social justice and human welfare. These norms and values often, but not exclusively, emerge in the design process as demands, constraints, criteria and standards. In design processes it is often the case that such criteria clash. In other words, it often is impossible to select one design that scores as best with all criteria simultaneously. In such situations designers have to decide on the relative importance of the criteria and thus also of the underlying norms and values. Sometimes that is done in an ad hoc fashion and at other times with the aid of formal methods and models. The question is to what degree such choices - and the methods upon which they are based - are methodologically sound and ethically acceptable.

ETHICAL ISSUES IN MAINTENANCE

Maintenance of equipments both static and mobile, materials requires a schedule and a plan. The maintenance system is designed on the basis of perception of safety and past experience. The failure rate in the past serves as an indicator for the future maintenance plan. The engineer has to have preventive maintenance system ,routine maintenance and breakdown maintenance. The maintenance techniques differ from continuous process industry like chemical plants and the manufacturing which involves batch production. In former, the plant is shut down for complete checking. If there is urgent order, then the maintenance norms are violated to keep the production on to meet the urgent demand or delivery schedules. In case of Bhopal tragedy (Chapter V) the dilution on the maintenance resulted in the disaster. Quality control at every point should be complied with and the immediate actions to be taken to solve the problem.

Under safety aspects some of the maintenance issues are already dealt with. Just as cost is an important element of consideration in design, in maintenance, safety also play an equally important part. The cost of new acquisition and cost of maintenance are compared and decisions taken on maintenance. To save on the cost, maintenance quality is compromised resulting in accidents. Vehicles need to be maintained regularly for their smooth functioning. We witness a number of accidents due to brake failures. The reason for brake failure is poor maintenance. Maintenance involves replacement of worn out spare parts, change of lubrication. It involves inspection at regular intervals and taking relevant decisions. There is a saying that a stitch in time saves nine. Any noise in the machine calls for a check up. Genuine spare parts are to be used without compromise.

SUM UP

Safety is a very important responsibility of an engineer. Its relationship with risk is to be assessed for decision making. The risk and safety which are the two very important responsibilities of engineers needs to be managed properly and a balance to be maintained. The engineers have to act with responsibility, while performing the role of safety, quality or testing engineering. It is important to maintain safety quality through testing, inspections, audits, selection of technology, materials, process. The safety of all consumers, employees, visitors to be kept in mind while designing the product, process. The cases deals with these concepts in more depth.

CASE STUDIES :

The objective is to expose students to the intricacies and learn from the disasters and analyse what went wrong. One can examine, whether failure could have been avoided. The case studies except CERC are US based. These cases will help them to understand and appreciate the situations faced by engineers and the consequences thereof. The Titanic case introduces the concept of experimentation. The Challenger case is in detail giving the account of step by step. The alternative choices at each stage are given. The Three Miles Island case is about the chemical leakage. The impact is clearly brought out in this case. CERC is a simple case which depicts, the role of society as a watch

Safety is deemed as the absence of unreasonable danger.

dog for monitoring of safety standards in India. .The Three Mile Island, Chernobyl and CERC case studies are presented in the next chapter. Abstracts of few case studies from the web site of Texas A & M University are included in the end.

1. The Titanic Case:

As a social experimenter let us take an example of ***Titanic***.

Titanic, pride of the **White Star Line**, sank on

April 15th, 1912 after colliding with an iceberg on her maiden voyage between Southampton & New York, with the loss of over 1,500 lives. The memory of this great ocean liner, and the people who died that cold night, are kept alive in many ways, notably books, films, documentaries, websites etc.

HER STORY

Titanic was built at the *Harland & Wolff* shipyards of Belfast, Ireland under the auspices of Mr. J. Bruce Ismay, managing director of the White Star Line. Her keel was laid down on March 31, 1909. She was the second in a trio of the "Olympic Class" of ships. Olympic being the first and Gigantic, later renamed Britannic, the last.

She was launched on May 31, 1911, just past noon, to a formidable crowd of well-wishers. There was no formal ceremony as it was not customary for the White Star Line to christen their ships. After just sixty-two seconds the Titanic slid safely down into the River Lagan and on her way to the fitting out basin.

The scant shell of Titanic awaited the arrival of the hundreds of skilled workers who would fill out her interior. And fill it they did. Under the direction of Thomas Andrews (chief draughtsman of Harland & Wolff) and his assistant Edward Wilding, the ship was tailored with the most opulent furnishings money could buy. In fact, when Lord William James Pirrie (managing director of Harland & Wolff) met with J. Bruce Ismay in 1907 to discuss the building of three new colossal liners, it was verbally agreed that money would be no object.

Sea trials for Titanic began on April 2, 1912. This day marked the first time her massive boilers were fired and her immense engines began to move under their own power. Various maneuvers were performed to test how well the ship handled under certain conditions. With the trials successful, Titanic obtained her passenger certificate and was dutifully handed over to her owners. She steamed out of Belfast and was safely landed at her new berth 44 at White Star's dock in Southampton.

Titanic set out on her maiden voyage on April 10, 1912. Her Captain, Edward J. Smith was in command. He was known as "the millionaires Captain" and was one of the highest paid in the world. It was customary for Captain Smith to take the White Star Liners on their maiden voyage. This would be "EJ's" last voyage however, since he was planning to retire to spend more time with his wife and daughter. After taking on additional crew, passengers and mail in Southampton it was off to Cherbourg to take on more passengers. Titanic's last stop, at Queenstown, saw the loading of the last of the passengers and mail.

Among Titanic's First Class passengers were Mr. J. Bruce Ismay, Mr. Thomas Andrews, Mrs. J.J. ("the unsinkable" Molly) Brown, Grand Trunk Railroad president Mr. Charles M. Hays, President Taft's military aide Major Archibald Butt and the richest man in the world, Colonel John Jacob Astor along with his eighteen year old second wife Madeline. Other First Class passengers included the prestigious of New York and Philadelphia's Mainline society.

Second Class mainly consisted of professionals on holiday and families who may have booked First Class passage on other ships but were excitedly "forced" to downgrade to Second Class accommodations on Titanic (a coal strike had laid up most of the other ships). These passengers included Mr. & Mrs. Benjamin Hart and their young daughter Eva, Mrs. Allen Becker with her 3 children and Mr. Lawrence Beesley, a school teacher on holiday.

The passengers in Third Class or Steerage consisted mainly of Irish immigrants and those of

Insurance is not a remedy for unprofessional behaviour.

Mediterranean descent, planning to make a new life in a new country. Many of the families had 6 or more children. Among these passengers was Mr. Daniel Buckley, Mr. & Mrs. Frederick Goodwin and their 6 children, Mr. August Wennerstrom, Mr. & Mrs. Bertram Dean with their 2 children. Mr. & Mrs. Frank Goldsmith with son Franky came along with a family friend.

Life aboard the Titanic was anything but boring. First Class truly lavished in the great ship's lustrous surroundings. The beauty and elegance of her exquisite Grand Staircase, A La Carte Restaurant, Palm Court, Cafe Parisian, Smoking Room, Library, elegantly decorated Staterooms, elevators, state-of-the-art Gymnasium, Turkish Bath and heated Swimming Pool rivaled the most luxurious hotels of Europe. In Second Class the Library, Smoking Room and Dining Room were the enlightenment and enjoyment of many. There was even an elevator for the Second Class passengers. Such a thing was never heard of on another ship. Even Third Class, with its Smoking Room, General Rooms and Dining Saloons, rivaled Second Class on many another ship.

The evening of Sunday, April 14th, was reasonably uneventful. The sea was flat calm, the air was brisk but there was no wind. The night was a sea of stars for there was no moon to dim their view. Most passengers were now getting ready to retire for the evening. Some First Class passengers could be found in the lounge playing bridge and other card games. There was talk about a couple of ice warnings which had been received during the day from other steamers; no cause for alarm. It was also rumored that Titanic could quite possibly beat Olympic's Maiden Voyage speed in getting to New York. Many felt she would dock on Tuesday evening, April 16, instead of her scheduled Wednesday arrival. At 11:40 PM on April 14, 1912, she struck an iceberg about 400 miles off Newfoundland, Canada. Although her crew had been warned about icebergs several times that evening by other ships navigating through that region, she was traveling at near top speed of about 20.5 knots.

Less than three hours later, the *Titanic* plunged to the bottom of the sea, taking more than 1500 people with her. Only a fraction of her passengers were saved. The world was stunned to learn of the fate of the unsinkable *Titanic.*

At around 11:40 p.m., three pulls of the crow's nest bell along with lookout Frederick Fleet's immortal words, "Iceberg, right ahead", would forever change the course of history.

The events which followed cannot wane with time's passage. Never to be forgotten is the moral strength, valor and courage carried out by Titanic's passengers and crew during her last hours. Mr. Strauss, offered a place in boat #8 because of his age, refuses because *"I will not go before the others."* Mrs. Strauss refusing to leave her husband, desiring instead that they enter eternity together. The band on deck, playing cheerful ragtime tunes to calm the distressed crowds. The engineers never once abandoning their posts in an effort to keep the lights burning until the very end.

Even today it is staggering to imagine all the 1,523 gallant souls who stood by as the boats were being sent away, knowing that it would take a miracle were they to be saved. It is difficult to imagine the 705 brave survivors watching in terror and anguish as their husbands, wives, children and dreams all perished that night when the "Unsinkable" Titanic went down. Titanic had very few life boats. Life boats only helped 705 passengers to survive. What was wrong with the Titanic design ?

2. The Challenger Case Study

The Story of the *Challenger* Disaster*

Roger Boisjoly had over a quarter-century's experience in the aerospace industry in 1985 when he became involved in an improvement effort on the O-rings which connect segments of Morton Thiokol's Solid Rocket Booster, used to bring the Space Shuttle into orbit. Boisjoly has spent his entire career making well-informed decisions based on his understanding of and belief in a professional engineer's rights and responsibilities. For his honesty and integrity leading up to and directly following the shuttle disaster, Roger Boisjoly was awarded the Prize for Scientific Freedom and Responsibility by the American Association for the Advancement of Science.

* Source : onlineethics.org

Engineers are accountable for projects.

Boisjoly's discussion of the Challenger Disaster is separated into seven sections. Each section is then followed by some responses. Supporting material is also provided. You may want to consult some of it in deciding what you would have done in Roger Boisjoly's place at each stage of the story.

Boisjoly's discussion of the Challenger Disaster is separated into seven sections. Each section is then followed by some responses. Supporting material is also provided. You may want to consult some of it in deciding what you would have done in Roger Boisjoly's place at each stage of the story.

I. Discovering Leaks in the Primary Seal
II. Early Evidence of a Temperature Effect
III. Being Asked to Soften the Urgency of the O-ring Problem
IV. Frustration with Lack of Management Support
V. Temperature Forecast for Challenger Flight
VI. A Management Decision Overrides a Recommendation not to Launch
VII. The Explosion of the Challenger

I. Discovering Leaks in the Primary Seal

The significance of January 1985 as the starting point results from the observations made during the post-flight hardware inspection of Flight 51C. During this inspection I found evidence that hot combustion gases had compromised the primary seals on two field joints. My concern heightened as a result of the large amount of blackened grease I observed between the two seals. Subsequent to reporting the findings to my superiors, I was asked to proceed to the Marshall Space Flight Center (MSFC) in Huntsville, Alabama, to brief them with a preliminary viewgraph presentation which included my observations and an explanation of the scenarios that caused the seal erosion and hot gas blow-by.

Morton Thiokol was then asked to prepare a detailed presentation as part of the Flight Readiness Review for Flight 51E, which was scheduled for launch in April 1985. This presentation was given in February at three successively higher-level review boards with refinements in contents made at each level. I presented my belief that the lower-than-usual launch temperature was responsible for such a large witness of hot gas blow-by, but NASA management insisted that this position be softened for the final review board.

What is the problem confronting Boisjoly here? The shuttle is already behind schedule, and the leaks in the primary seal in Flight 51C in January 1985 occurred during the worst temperature change in Florida history — hardly everyday conditions. Which of the following actions would be appropriate to take at this point?

- Perform experiments.
- Consult personal advisors.
- Consult peers at work for advice.
- Take concerns to supervisor.
- Write memos far up the corporate ladder.

II. Early Evidence of a Temperature Effect

The final flight readiness assessment chart read as follows:

Conclusion: STS-51C consistent with erosion data base. Low temperature enhanced probability of blow-by.

STS-51C experienced worst case temperature change in Florida history. STS-51E could exhibit same behavior. Condition is acceptable.

STS-51E field joints are acceptable for flight.

These conclusions were accepted and the flight was certified ready for launch.

Later, I met with Arnie Thompson to discuss the blow-by scenario and the effect of cold temperature on O-ring resiliency, which is the ability of the seal to restore itself to a round shape when the squeeze on the seal is removed. Arnie proposed that subscale lab tests be conducted which would provide us with assessment data. The resiliency testing was performed in March and showed that low temperature was a problem. The results indicated that the seals would lift off their sealing surfaces for several seconds at 75 degree Fahrenheit and in excess of 10 minutes at 50 degree Fahrenheit. This data was discussed with Morton Thiokol engineering management but was thought to be too sensitive by them to release.

Another post flight inspection occurred in June 1985 at Morton Thiokol in Utah. This time a nozzle joint from Flight 51B, which flew on April 29, 1985, was found to have a primary seal eroded in three places over a 1.3 inch length up to a maximum depth of 0.171 inches, and the secondary seal in the same joint was eroded 0.032 inches. It was postulated that this primary seal had never sealed during the full two minutes of flight.

My former concerns now escalated because if this same scenario happened in a field joint, the secondary seal could also be compromised especially during a low temperature launch. A Flight Readiness Review presentation was prepared for Flight 51F, which was scheduled for launch on July 29, 1985. The presentation was given to NASA at MSFC on July 1, 1985, with an additional presentation on the overall status of the booster seals given the next day. The preliminary results of the O-ring resilience testing in March were presented for the first time during this meeting. All O-ring test samples were 0.280 inch diameter and compressed to 0.040 inches with a decompression distance of 0.030 inches at a 2-inch-per-minute rate as compared with a flight rate of approximately 3.2 inches per minute. The results showed that the seals did not lose contact at 100 degrees Fahrenheit; lost contact for 2.4 seconds at 75 degrees, and lost contact in excess of 10 minutes at 50 degrees. Test results also indicated that a 0.295-inch diameter seal lost contact for 2 to 3 seconds at 50 degrees, which meant that the 0.295-inch diameter seal performance at 50 degrees was similar to the performance of a 0.28-inch diameter seal at 75 degrees. Everyone on the program for the first time was now aware of the influence of low temperature on the joint seals.

My concern increased once again due to the lack of attention being given to this problem.

The bench tests showed that temperature can adversely affect the resiliency, and therefore the effectiveness, of the O-rings, yet management at Thiokol and NASA shows no interest in planning a design change. What general courses of action are reasonable for an engineer in this sort of situation ?

- Consult personal advisors.
- Gather knowledge of the problem.
- Perform more experiments.
- Consult peers at work.
- Take concerns to supervisor.
- Write memos far up the corporate ladder.
- Contact a professional society.

III. Being Asked to Soften the Urgency of the O-ring Problem

My notebook entry on August 15, 1985, reads as follows: "An attempt to form the team (referring to the Solid Rocket Motor seal erosion team) was made on 19 July 1985. This attempt virtually failed and resulted in my writing memo 2870:FY86:073. This memo finally got some response and a team was formed officially. The first meeting was held on August 15, 1985 at 2:30 pm." The memo referred to is the one I read to the Presidential Commission on February 25, 1986, which was written to the vice-president of engineering at Morton Thiokol on July 31, 1985.

The memo ended by saying, "It is my honest and very real fear that if we do not take immediate action to dedicate a team to solve the problem, with the field joint having the number one priority, then we stand in jeopardy of losing a flight along with all the launch pad facilities."

During this July period, NASA headquarters in Washington D.C. asked Morton Thiokol to prepare a presentation on the problems with all the booster seals. The presentation was prepared by MSFC on August 19, 1985, with Morton Thiokol personnel in attendance.

Morton Thiokol was then asked by MSFC in September to send a representative to the SAE conference in October to discuss the seals and solicit help from the experts. I prepared and presented a six-page overview of the joints and the seal configuration to approximately 130 technical experts on October 7, 1985. However, I was given strict instructions, which came from NASA, not to express the critical urgency of fixing the joint but only to emphasize the joint improvement aspect during my presentation.

NASA once again wanted the seal task force team to soften the urgency of the O-ring problem. If the word leaked that there existed a major malfunction in the solid rocket booster, Congress would likely lose even more faith in the Shuttle program. No cold weather launches were scheduled for the near future. Should Boisjoly continue to listen to NASA and play down the importance of the problem? Which of the following are good things to do in this situation?

- Consult personal advisors.
- Gather knowledge of the problem.
- Research company structure.
- Consult peers at work.
- Take concerns to superiors.
- Write memos far up the corporate
- Inform the media.

IV. Frustration with Lack of Management Support

After my presentation, I asked for help in the form of design improvement suggestions, but no one said a word. Bob Ebeling and I spent the remainder of the convention time meeting with seal vendors whom we had previously contacted for help. From the beginning, the Seal Task Team was frustrated from a lack of management support to provide the resources necessary for us to accomplish our task.

Morton Thiokol doesn't want to appear like a company with a flawed product, so they would prefer that Boisjoly play down the O-ring problem. While there have been a few cases of hot gas blow-by, almost twenty flights have flown successfully. Boisjoly has already written memos expressing his view of the seriousness of the joint problem. What can he do now?

- Consult personal advisors.
- Gather knowledge of the problem.
- Consult peers at work.
- Take concerns to supervisor.
- Write memos far up the corporate ladder.
- Inform astronauts of danger.
- Inform client (government) of danger.
- Inform the media.

V. Temperature Forecast for Challenger Flight

Accordingly, I wrote a series of very damning activity reports in which I left no room for error about how I felt concerning the lack of management support. Unfortunately, I never received any comments back and never knew if they had been incorporated into reports up through the management structure.

The evening meeting of January 27, 1986, was the concluding event preceding the launch disaster. The major activity that day focused upon the predicted 18 degrees Fahrenheit overnight temperature.

Contrary to everyone's expectations, it is now predicted that the next day's temperature in Florida will exceed the record cold experienced the previous year. The next day is the day scheduled for the Challenger flight. Boisjoly is firmly convinced that this extreme weather condition presents a major threat to the capacity of the O-ring seals to perform their function, and thus to the survival of the flight crew. Time is short. What actions are appropriate to take in such a situation?

- Consult personal advisors.
- Perform more lab tests.
- Gather knowledge of the problem.
- Consult peers at work.
- Take concerns to the top.
- Inform client (government) of danger.
- Inform astronauts of danger.
- Inform the media.

VI. A Management Decision Overrides a Recommendation Not to Launch

The major activity that day focused upon the predicted 18 degrees Fahrenheit overnight temperature and meeting with engineering management to persuade them not to launch. The day concluded with the hurried preparation of fourteen viewgraphs which detailed our concerns about launching at such a low temperature. The teleconference with Kennedy Space Center (KSC) and MSFC started with a history of O-ring damage in field joints. Data was presented showing a major concern with seal resiliency and the change to the sealing timing function and the criticality of this on the ability to seal. I was asked several times during my portion of the presentation to quantify my concerns, but I said I could not since the only data I had was what I had presented and that I had been trying to get more data since last October. At this comment, the general manager of Morton Thiokol gave me a scolding look as if to say, "Why are you telling that to them?" The presentation ended with the recommendation not to launch below 53 degrees. This was not well received by NASA. The Vice-President of Space Booster Programs, Joe Kilminster, was then asked by NASA for his launch decision. He said he did not recommend launching, based upon the engineering position just presented. Then Larry Mulloy of NASA (who was at KSC) asked George Hardy of NASA (who was at MSFC) for his launch decision. George responded that he was appalled at Thiokol's recommendation but said he would not launch over the contractor's objection. Then Larry Mulloy spent some time giving his interpretation of the data with his conclusion that the data presented was inconclusive.

Just as he finished his conclusion, Joe Kilminster asked for a five minute off-line caucus to re-evaluate the data, and as soon as the mute button was pushed our general manager, Jerry Mason, said in a soft voice, "We have to make a management decision." I became furious when I heard this because I knew that an attempt would be made by management to reverse our recommendation not to launch.

Some discussion had started between the managers when Arnie Thompson moved from his position down the table to a position in front of the managers and once again tried to explain our position by sketching the joint and discussing the problem with the seals at low temperature. Arnie stopped when he saw the unfriendly look in Mason's eyes and also realized that no one was listening to him. I then grabbed the photographic evidence showing the hot gas blow-by and placed it on the table and, somewhat angered, admonished them to look and not ignore what the photos were telling us, namely, that low temperature indeed caused more hot gas blow-by in the joints. I too received the same cold stares as Arnie with looks as if to say, "Go away and don't bother us with the facts." At that moment I felt totally helpless and felt that further argument was fruitless, so I, too, stopped pressing my case.

What followed made me both sad and angry. The managers who were struggling to make a pro-launch list of supporting data actually supported a decision not to launch. During the closed managers' discussion, Jerry Mason asked in a low voice if he was the only one who wanted to fly. The discussion continued, then Mason turned to Bob Lund, the vice-president of engineering, and told him to take off his engineering hat and put on his management hat. The decision to launch resulted from the yes vote of only the four senior executives since the rest of us were excluded from both the final decision and the vote poll. The telecon resumed, and Joe Kilminster read the launch support rationale from a handwritten list and recommended that the launch proceed. NASA promptly accepted the recommendation to launch without any probing discussion and asked Joe to send a signed copy of the chart.

The change in decision so upset me that I do not remember Stanley Reinhartz of NASA asking if anyone had anything else to say over the telecon. The telecon was then disconnected so I immediately left the room feeling badly defeated.

What is the situation that Boisjoly faces now? He has presented his case. NASA has acted in a way that was unprecedented in Boisjoly's experience. They have put the burden of proof on those who believed it was risky to fly rather than on those who felt it was safe to fly. Fearing that NASA will not continue to make Morton Thiokol the sole contractor for the Solid Rocket Booster program if they insist on holding back the Challenger flight, management has reversed the decision made by engineering. Boisjoly doesn't have the hard data that he has been requesting since last summer and which is now needed to prove that low temperature is a major contributor in hot gas blow-by, and his job appears to be at stake. He has had over a year to work on the joint problem and in that time ten shuttle missions have flown successfully. Is there anything else that can be done at this point?

- Consult personal advisors.
- Rally peer support.
- Consult peers at work.
- Take concerns to superiors.
- Write memos far up the corporate ladder.
- Inform the client (government) of danger.
- Inform astronauts of danger.
- Inform the media.

VII. The Explosion of the Challenger

I wrote the following entry in my notebook after returning to my office. "I sincerely hope that this launch does not result in a catastrophe. I personally do not agree with some of the statements made in Joe Kilminster's written summary stating that SRM-25 is okay to fly."

As it turned out, I didn't agree with any of his statements after I had a chance to review a copy of the chart. A review of the chart will produce the following conclusions from anyone having normal powers of reason. The chart lists nine separate statements, seven of which are actually reasons against launch, while one is actually a neutral statement of engineering fact. The remaining statement concerning a factor of safety of three on seal erosion is not even applicable to the discussion which had ensued for over an hour. Therefore, Morton Thiokol senior management reversed a sound technical decision without any re-evaluation of the data they had promised when they requested the caucus.

The next morning I paused outside Arnie Thompson's office and told him and the manager of applied mechanics, who was my boss, that I hoped the launch was safe, but I also hoped that when we inspected the booster joints we would find all the seals burned almost through the joint, then maybe we could get someone with authority to stand up and stop the flights until we fixed the joints.

It was approximately five minutes prior to the launch as I was walking past the room used to view launches when Bob Ebeling stepped out to encourage me to enter and watch the launch. At first I refused, but he finally persuaded me to watch the launch. The room was filled, so I seated myself on the floor closest to the screen and leaned against Bob's legs as he was seated in a chair. The boosters ignited, and as the vehicle cleared the tower Bob whispered to me that we had just dodged a bullet. At approximately T+60 seconds Bob told me that he had just completed a prayer of thanks to the Lord for a successful launch. Just 13 seconds later we both saw the horror of destruction as the vehicle exploded. We all sat in stunned silence for a short time, then I got up and left the room and went directly to my office, where I remained the rest of the day. Two of my seal task-team colleages inquired at my office to see if I was okay, but I was unable to speak to them and hold back my emotions so I just nodded yes to them and they left after a short silent stay.

Roger Boisjoly made a number of choices in the months leading up to the Challenger accident. He consistently took an ethical course of action, often risking his job. Nevertheless, he was unable to avert the January 28 launch. In 1988 Roger Boisjoly was given the American Association for the Advancement of Science Award for Scientific Freedom and Responsibility for his extensive and well conceived efforts to avert the shuttle disaster.

Supporting Material:

- Morton Thiokol and the Space Shuttle Challenger Disaster. Essay by R. Boisjoly.
- 7/31/85 Memo about O-Ring Erosion
- 8/22/85 Memo from A. R. Thompson on the Flight Seal
- What Went Wrong with the Solid Rocket Booster
- Morton Thiokol Wasatch Division Corporate Structure

Supporting Material:

- Morton Thiokol and the Space Shuttle Challenger Disaster. ***Essay by R. Boisjoly.***

ABSTRACT

A background summary of important events leading to the Challenger disaster will be presented starting with January, 1985, plus the specifics of the telecon meeting held the night prior to the launch at which the attempt was made to stop the launch by the Morton Thiokol engineers. A detailed account will show why the off-line telecon caucus by Morton Thiokol Management constituted the unethical decision-making forum which ultimately produced the management decision to launch Challenger without any restrictions.

The paper will continue with the post-disaster chronology of my working relationship with Morton Thiokol Management and conclude with a discussion on accountability, professional responsibility and ethical conduct which should be practiced in the work place, plus statements from the academic community about the plight of whistleblowers and my closing remarks.

NOMENCLATURE AIAA-American Institute of Aeronautics & Astronautics. FRR-Flight Readiness Review. IEEE-Institute of Electrical and Electronics Engineers. KSC-Kennedy Space Center MEOP-Maximum Expected Operating Pressure. MSFC-Marshall Space Flight Center. MTI-Morton Thiokol Incorporated. NASA-National Aeronautics and Space Administration. SAE-Society of Automotive Engineers. SRM-Solid Rocket Motor.

You may have already concluded that the Challenger disaster was the result of only the decisions made during the evening prior to and the day of launch. As a senior engineer involved with the SRM's since July, 1980, and specifically with the joints since 1981, I can make the following statements from personal observations.

The SRM Program at MTI was suffering from the lack of proper original development work and some may argue that sufficient funds or schedule were not available and that may be so, but MTI contracted for that condition. The Shuttle program was declared operational by NASA after the fourth flight, but the technical problems in producing and maintaining the reusable boosters were escalating rapidly as the program matured, instead of decreasing as one would normally expect. Many opportunities were available to structure the work force for corrective action, but the MTI management style would not let anything compete or interfere with the production and shipping of boosters. The result was a program which gave the appearance of being controlled while actually collapsing from within due to excessive technical and manufacturing problems as time increased.

This paper starts with January, 1985, which was the period of gross escalation of joint seal problems and continues with specific events that should have signaled either stopping the flights or as a minimum, changing the launch commit criteria to prevent launching below 53+ F (I2+ C).

Figure 1 shows the SRM joint configuration for purposes of this discussion.

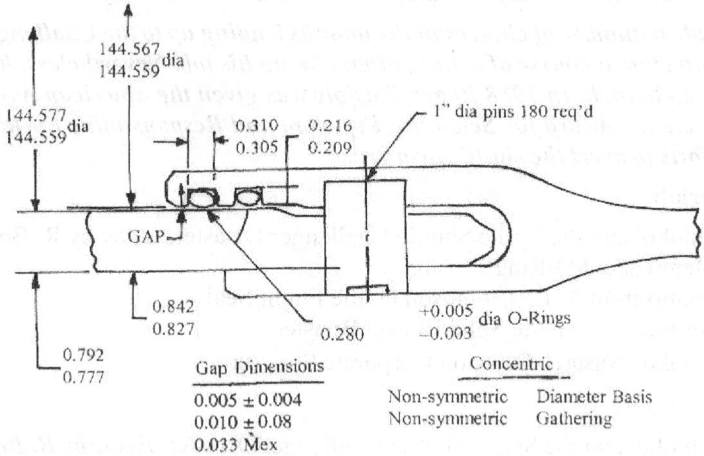

Inches	Millimeters	Inches	Millimeters
144.557		0.310	7.81
144.569	3672.15	0.305	
144.567			
144.559	3671.90	0.280	711
1.0	25.40	0.216	
0.842		0.209	5.40
0.827	21.20	0.033	0.84
0.792		0.010	0.25
0.777	19.93	0.005	0.13

All dimensions are in inches with SI units for nominals given in the supplementary table. The first O-ring to seal internal hot gases is called the primary seal while the other is termed the secondary seal. There are 177 load carrying pins plus three locating pins for assembly clocking. Pressurization of the motor to 1004 psi (6.92 x 106 pascals) causes the gap dimension to increase 0.042 inches (1.07 mm).

PRE-DISASTER BACKGROUND

The significance of starting with January, 1985, results from my observations made during the post flight inspection of hardware from Flight 51C which was launched on January 14, 1985. 1 found that hot combustion gases had blown by the primary seals on two field joints and had produced large arc lengths of blackened grease between the primary and secondary seals. Subsequent to reporting my findings, I was ordered to present MSFC a preliminary report prior to formal FRR meetings.

I participated in the formal FRR's for flight 51E which was scheduled for an April launch. The presentations were given at MSFC in February at three successively higher level review boards with exclusions and refinements in content made at each board level. I spoke about my belief that the low ambient temperature prior to launch was responsible for such a large witness of hot gas (approximately 5500- F [3040-C]) blow-by but NASA Program Management insisted on that position being softened for higher and final review board presentations. The ambient temperature was 18 to 22- F (-8 to -6-C) several days prior to launch and in the 60-- 65-F (16 to 18- C) range at launch time and resulted in a seal temperature of 53- F (12- C) -which was calculated after the damage was found.

Accordingly, the final FRR assessment chart read as follows:

- Evaluation Summary
- STS-51C primary O-ring erosion on two field joints
- STS-51C soot between primary and secondary O-rings on both field joints predicted after STS-11 observation, first time observed
- Evidence of heat affect on secondary O-ring of A68 (right hand) center field joint but no erosion —first time heat affect on secondary O-ring has been observed
- Conclusion
- STS-51C consistent with erosion data base
- Low temperature enhanced probability of blowby — STS-51C experienced worst case temperature change in Florida history
- STS-51E could exhibit some behavior
- Condition is acceptable
- STS-51E field joints are acceptable for flight

These conclusions were accepted and the boosters were certified for launch.

I returned to MTI in Utah and met with Arnie Thompson, who was the Supervisor of Structural Design and Analysis for the SRM case segments, to discuss the hot gas blow-by scenario and the affects of cold temperature on O-ring resiliency, which we defined as the ability of the seal to restore itself to a round cross sectional shape after the squeeze on the seal is removed. The preliminary resiliency testing, which was requested by Arnie Thompson, was performed in March and showed that a low temperature of 50- F (10- C) was a problem, as the seal material could not follow the rate of gap opening and lost contact with its mating surface. The significance of this data was that the seal erosion and blow-by problem was known to occur within 0.60 seconds during the motor ignition transient. The data was discussed with MTI Engineering Management, but was thought to be too sensitive by them to release to anyone.

Another post-flight inspection was performed in June, 1985, at MTI facilities in Utah on a nozzle joint from Flight 51B (SRM 16A) which was launched on April 29, 1985. The nozzle joint configuration is shown in Figure 2 with all dimensions in inches. The bore (radial) sea] is the primary seal and the face seal is the secondary seal in this joint.

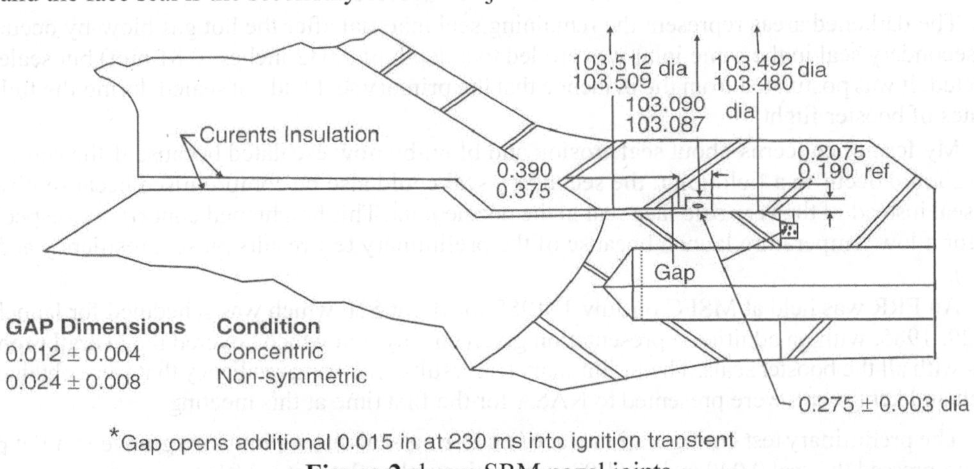

Figure 2 shows SRM nozel joints

Inches	*Millimeters*	*Inches*	*Millimeters*
103.512			
103.509	2629.15	0.275	6.99
103.492		0.275	
103.480	2628.54	0.190	5.05
103.090		0.024	0.61
103.087	2618.45	0.015	0.38
0.390			
0.375	9.59	0.012	0.30

This joint was found to have the primary seal eroded through in three places as shown in Figure 3 below.

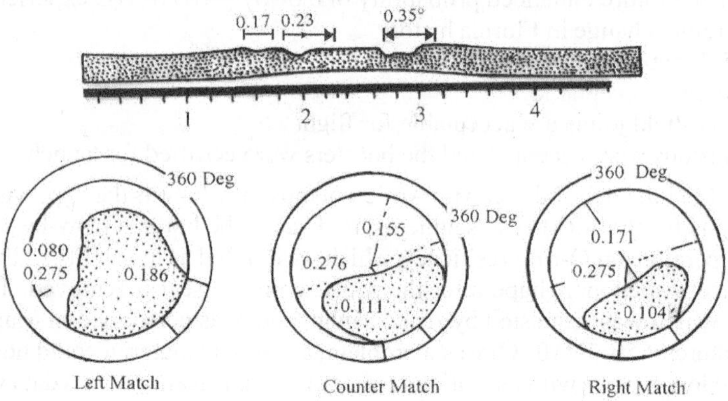

Inches	Millimeters	Inches	Millimeters
0.17	4.32	0.111	2.62
0.23	5.84	0.155	2.94
0.35	8.89	0.104	2.64
0.089	2.03	0.50	12.70
0.186	4.57	0.275	6.98

The darkened areas represent the remaining seal material after the hot gas blow-by occurred. The secondary seal in the same joint was eroded to a depth of 0.032 inches (0.81 mm) but sealed as expected. It was postulated from the evidence that the primary seal had not sealed during the full two minutes of booster flight.

My former concerns about seal erosion and blow-by now escalated because if the some scenario should occur in a field joint, the secondary seal could also be compromised because it was a bore seal instead of the very safe face seal in the nozzle joint. This heightened concern was especially true for a low temperature launch because of the preliminary test results on seal resiliency at 50-F (10-C).

An FRR was held at MSFC on July 1, 1985 for flight 51F which was scheduled for launch on July 29, 1985, with an additional presentation given on July 2nd which covered the overall problem status with all the booster seals. The preliminary test results on O-ring resiliency that were obtained in March and kept secret were presented to NASA for the first time at this meeting.

The preliminary test configuration placed an O-ring seal into a flight size groove in a flat plate and compressed the seal 0.040 inches (1.02 mm) with another flat plate. After temperature conditioning of the assembly, the plates were separated 0.030 inches (0.76 mm) at a 2.0 inch (5.08 cm) per minute rate to simulate a flight rate of approximately 3.2 inches (8.13 cm) per minute (slightly unconservative).

The test results showed no loss of seal contact at 100-F (38-C); loss of seal contact for 2.4 seconds at 75- F (24- C and loss of seal contact for in excess of 10 minutes at 50- F 10- C. The testing also showed that a larger diameter seal (0.295 in - 7.49 mm) lost contact for 2 to 3 seconds at 50- F 10- C. This showed that the larger diameter seal performed at 50- F (10- C) similar to the operational flight seal (0.280 in - 7.11 mm) at 75- F(24- C), which was why the larger seal was being considered for a short-term fix.

Everyone on the program, working with the joint seal problems, was now aware of the influence of low temperature on the field joint seals.

Again, my concern about the joints increased due to the lack of attention being given to this problem by MTI. My notebook entry on August 15,1985 reads as follows: "An attempt to form the team (I was referring to the SIRM Seal Erosion Task Team) was made on 19 July 1985. This attempt virtually failed and resulted in my writing memo 2870:FY86:073. This memo finally got some response and a team was formed officially. The first meeting was held on August 15, 1985 at 2:30 p.m." The memo I referred to is the one I wrote to the Vice-President of Engineering at MTI on July 31, 1985. The memo was stamped COMPANY PRIVATE by my boss and had a very limited distribution until I read it to the Presidential Commission on February 25, 1986. The memo reads as follows:

"Subject: SRM O-Ring Erosion/Potential Failure Criticality. This letter is written to ensure that management is fully aware of the seriousness of the current O-ring erosion problem in the SRM joints from an engineering standpoint. The mistakenly accepted position on the joint problem was to fly without fear of failure and to run a series of design evaluations which would ultimately lead to a solution or at least a significant reduction of the erosion problem. This position is now drastically changed as a result of the SRM 16A nozzle joint erosion which eroded a secondary O-ring with the primary O-ring never sealing."

"If the same scenario should occur in a field joint (and it could), then it is a jump ball as to the success or failure of the joint because the secondary O-ring cannot respond to the clevis opening rate and may not be capable of pressurization. The result would be a catastrophe of the highest order—loss of human life."

"An unofficial team (a memo defining the team and its purpose was never published) with leader was formed on 19 July 1985 and was tasked with solving the problem for both the short and long term. This unofficial team is essentially nonexistent at this time. In my opinion, the team must be officially given the responsibility and the authority to execute the work that needs to be done on a noninterference basis (full-time assignment until completed)."

"It is my honest and very real fear that if we do not take immediate action to dedicate a team to solve the problem, with the field joint having the number one priority, then we stand in jeopardy of losing a flight along with all the launch pad facilities."

The memo was signed by R. M. Boisjoly and concurred to by J. R. Kopp, Manager, Applied Mechanics, who was my boss.

During the July/August time period, NASA headquarters in Washington, D. C. asked MTI to prepare and present a summary of problems with all the booster seals on August 19, 1985. This was done and that is why I find it so incredible that top NASA management denies knowing anything about the problems with the joint seals, when questioned by the Presidential Commission.

MTI was then asked by NASA MSFC in September to send a representative to the SAE Conference in October to discuss the joint seal designs and solicit help from the technical experts in attendance. However, I was given strict instructions, which come from MSFC, not to express the critical urgency of fixing the joints but to only emphasize the joint improvement aspect during my presentation. I prepared and presented seven viewgraphs to approximately 130 technical experts at the conference. I then asked for help in the form of design improvement suggestions and stated that we were not asking for free advice but were willing to contract for work, but no one said a word. So Bob Ebeling and I spent the remainder of the convention time meeting with seal vendors whom we had previously contacted for help. In retrospect, I'm not surprised that no one responded to my pleas for help when I showed them the parameters of the joints. What they saw and heard were joint gap configurations (both static and dynamic) that were approximately an order of magnitude worse than anything they had previously encountered. I don't blame them for avoiding any comments and suggestions when asked.

The seal erosion task team was frustrated right from the start due to lack of management support to provide manpower and material resources necessary for us to accomplish the task of fixing the joints. Accordingly, I wrote a series of very damning activity reports in which I left no room for error about my feelings due to the lack of management support. The last such report written was on October 4, 1985 and reads as follows:

"SRM Seal Problem Task Team Status The team generally has been experiencing trouble from the business-as-usual attitude from supporting organizations. Part of this is due to lack of understanding of how important this task team activity is and the rest is due to pure operating procedure inertia which prevents timely results to a specific request.

The team met with Joe Kilminster on October 3, 1985 to discuss this problem. He wanted specific examples which he was given and he simply concluded that it was every team member's responsibility to flog problems that occurred to organizational supervision and work to remove the road block by getting the required support to solve the problem. The problem was further explained to require almost full-time nursing of each task to insure it is taken to completion by a support group. Joe simply agreed and said we should then nurse every task we have.

He did not understand that there are not enough people to do that kind of nursing of each task, but he doesn't seem to mind directing that the task nevertheless gets done. For example, the team just found out that when we submit a request to purchase an item, that it goes through approximately six to eight people *before* a purchase order is written and the item actually ordered.

The vendors we are working with on seals and spacer rings have responded to our requests in a timely manner, yet, we (MTI) cannot get a purchase order to them in a timely manner. Our lab has been waiting for a function generator since September 15, 1985. The paperwork authorizing the purchase was finished by Engineering on September 24, 1985 and placed into the system. We have yet to receive the requested item. This type of example is typical and results in lost resources that had been planned to do test work for us in a timely manner.

I for one resent working at full capacity all week long and then being required to support activity on the weekend that could have been accomplished during the week. I might add that even NASA perceives that the team is being blocked in its engineering efforts to accomplish its task. NASA is sending an engineering representative to stay with us starting October 14th. We feel that this is the direct result of their feelings that we (MTI) are not responding quickly enough on the seal problem. I should add that several of the team members requested that we be given a specific manufacturing engineer, quality engineer, safety engineer and four to six technicians to allow us to do our tests on a noninterference basis with the rest of the system. This request was deemed not necessary when Joe decided that the nursing of the task approach was directed.

Finally, the basic problem boils down to the fact that all MTI problems have number 1 priority and that upper management apparently feels that the SRM program is ours for sure and the customer be damned."

The Activity Report was signed by Roger M. Boisjoly on October 4, 1985 and given to my boss's secretary. Unfortunately, I never received any comments back and I never knew if the contents of my activity reports were incorporated into the reports up through the management organization to the top.

Telecon Meeting

The evening telecon meeting between MTI, MSFC and KSC on January 27,1986, was the final event preceding the Challenger disaster. The major activity that day focused upon the predicted 18-F (-8-C) overnight low and meetings with Engineering Management to persuade them not to launch below 53-F (12-C). I was driven to action for this cause because of my memory of my January, 1985, participation in the inspection of the hardware from the previous coldest launch which had massive hot gas blow-by. The discussion activity concluded with the hurried preparation of fourteen viewgraphs by various engineering groups which had less then an hour to respond for the scheduled evening telecon.

The following discussion is summarized to show the content of the engineering presentation. Figures labeled as viewgraphs show the major thrust of the telecon and contain the actual content of the originals as presented, with SI units added, while others are summarized to give general content for brevity.

The first viewgraph was a title page. The second viewgraph showed a table of post history of O-ring damage on SRM field joints. The third, fourth and fifth viewgraphs are shown as Figures 4., 5., and 6., respectively.

- field joint - highest concern
- erosion penetration of primary seal requires reliable secondary seal for pressure integrity
- ignition transient - (0-600 ms)
- (0-170 ms) high probability of reliable secondary seal
- (170-330 ms) reduced probability of reliable secondary seal
- (330-600 ms) high probability of no secondary seal capability
- steady state - (600 ms - 2 minutes)
- if erosion penetrates primary O-ring seal -high probability of no secondary seal capability
- bench testing showed O-ring not capable of maintaining contact with metal parts gap opening rate to meop
- bench testing showed capability to maintain O-ring contact during initial phase (0-170 ms) of transient

Figure 4. - Primary Concerns

Figure 4. was taken directly from the August 19, 1985 presentation to NASA headquarters. The last two statements show the reasons for both the high concern and for having a high probability of a secondary seal during the first portion of the transient time zone. The last statement was produced from testing at 50- F(10-C) which showed that a seal could maintain contact with its mating surfaces when compressed 0.040 inches (1.02 mm) and only 0.010 inch (0.25 mm) of compression was removed from the seal.

- a temperature lower than current data base results in changing primary O-ring sealing timing function
- SRM 15A - 800 ARC black grease between O-rings SRM 15B - I 100 ARC black grease between
- rings
- lower O-ring squeeze due to lower temperature
- higher O-ring shore hardness
- thicker grease viscosity
- higher O-ring pressure actuation time
- if threshold is reached, then secondary seal may not be capable of being pressurized if actuation time increases, threshold of secondary seal pressurization

Figure 5. - Field Joint Primary Concerns SRM 25

Figure 5. was the heart of the discussion at the telecon. The engineering issue was "Would the seals even actuate and seal due to changing their timing function?" This would place us in the category of having a high probability of no secondary seal capability while the primary seal would be experiencing massive blow-by erosion due to its inability to respond to the gap opening of the metal parts. The last two statements summarized the fear of loss of redundancy based upon my remembrance of the January, 1985 post-launch hardware inspection.

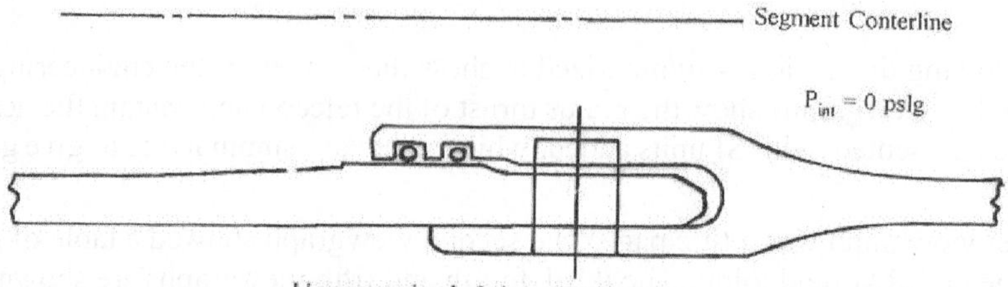

Unpressurized Joint - No Rotation

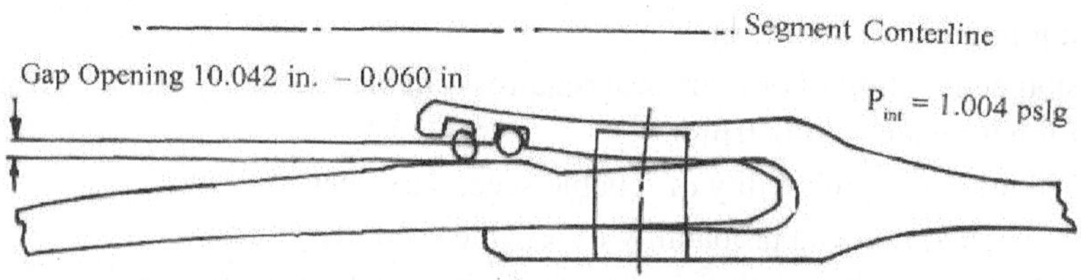

Pressurized Joint - Rotation Effect (exaggerated)

Figure 6 shows (given above) the field joint in the "as assembled" configuration, plus the pressurized configuration which shows the gap opening parameter due to outboard radial deflection of the case membrane. The differential deflection between the membrane and the stiffer joint causes the inboard clevis leg to deflect inboard opposite the rotation of the tong, which causes the gap at the seals to open. This results in the secondary seal lifting off its seat at full pressurization without considering seal resiliency parameters. The sixth viewgraph showed a comparison of hot gas blow-by by comparing ARC lengths of blackened grease and some descriptive phases for various flights at different launch temperatures. The seventh viewgraph was a table of O-ring shore hardness versus temperature. The eighth viewgraph contained the preliminary O-ring resiliency data in a tabular form. Up to this point in the telecon, I was asked several times by NASA to quantify my concerns, but I said that I could not since the only data I had was already presented and that I had been trying to get more data since last October (1985). At this comment, the General Manager of MTI gave me a scolding look as if to say, "Why did you tell them that?" The presentation continued with viewgraph nine which showed sub-scale test results of cold gas blow-by tests at 75- F (24- C) and 30-F (-1- C) which showed no leakage. This data was used as an argument by management to say that the joint sealed at 30-F (-1- C) but in fact, the tests were not seal tests at all, since the test ring was a solid block of metal which did not have the deflection characteristics of the full-scale joint and was never intended to test anything but incipient blow-by before any joint deflection occurred. Viewgraph ten contained a table of compression set data to aid in the visualization of seal permanent set characteristics. Viewgraph eleven, is shown as Figure 7, provided a comparison of O-ring squeeze for the Challenger joints (SRM 25) versus the previous coldest flight at 53- F (12- C) (SRM 15). Viewgraph twelve is shown as Figure 8. The DM designates development motors, QM is qualification motors and SRM is flight motors. This chart showed the current data base versus the predicted Challenger seal temperature of 27 to 29- F (-3 to -2). Viewgraph thirteen is shown as Figure 9. The third and fourth statements under the first bullet are actually disclaimers for the development and qualification test data because the joint putty had been altered after assembly and prior to horizontal test firings. Observed holes in the joint putty

Motor	*FWD*			*CTR*	*A*		*FT*		
%	*In.*	*mm*	*%*	*in.*	*mm*	*%*	*in.*	*mm*	
SRM 15A 61.1	.045*	1.14	15.8	.044	1.12	14.7	.041	1.04	
SRM 15B 11.1	.031	0.79	14.0	.039**	0.00	16.1	0.45	1.14	
SRM 12A 0.16	.028	0.71	13.22	.037	0.94	13.39	.037	0.94	
SRM 25B 13.91	.039	0.99	13.05	.037	0.94	14.25	.040	1.02	

* 0.010 in. (0.25 mm) erosion

** 0.038 in. (0.97 mm) erosion

Figure 7 - Field Joint O-Ring Squeeze (Primary Seal)

were repaired since it was thought that the horizontal assembly was very severe on the joints and is what caused the holes in the putty and that vertical assembly would not cause such holes to occur. The reasoning was generally okay but that reasoning was never tested until sometime in 1985 when it was found that vertical assembly could indeed cause holes in the putty. The major faulty thinking lies in the fact that no specific vertical assembly testing was performed to verify the original assumption and that made the original horizontal test firings a series of successful tests without any seal erosion.

Temperature of O-ring not only parameter controlling blow-by SRM 15 with blow-by had an O-ring temp at 53- F (11.7- C) four development motors with no blow-by were tested at O-ring temp of 47- to 52- F (8.3- to 11.1- C) development motors had putty packing which resulted in better performance.

Figure 9. Viewgraph thirteen is shown as Figure 9.

Motor	*MBT***		*Ambient*			*O-ring*	*Wide*
°E	*°C*	*°F*	*°C*	*°E*	*°C*		
DM-4	68	20.0	36	2.2	47	8.3	10 mph
DM-2	76	24.4	45	7.2	52	11.1	10 mph
DM-3	72.5	22.5	40	4.4	48	6.9	10 mph
DM-4	76	24.4	48	8.9	51	10.6	10 mph
SRM-15	52	11.1	64	17.8	53	11.7	10 mph
SRM-22	77	25.0	78	25.6	75	23.9	10 mph
SRM-25	55	12.8	26	-3.3	29	–1.7	10 mph
					27	–2.8	25 mph

* 1-D Thermal Analysis

** Propellant Mean Bulk Temperature

- at about 50-F (10- C) blow-by could be experienced in case joints
- temp for SRM 25 on 1-28-86 launch will be 29- F (-1.7- C) 9 a.m. 38- F (3.3- C) 2 p.m.
- have no data that would indicate SRM 25 is different than SRM 15 other than temperature

Figure 9. Conclusions

Viewgraph fourteen is shown as Figure 10.

- O-ring temperature must be & mac179; 53- F (11.7- C) at launch development motors at 47- to 52- F (8.3- to 11.1- C) with putty packing had no blow-by SRM 15 (the best simulation) worked at 53- F
- project ambient conditions (temp & wind) to determine launch time

Figure 10. Recommendations

This concluded the engineering presentation. Then Joe Kilminster of MTI was asked by Larry Mulloy of NASA for his launch decision. Joe responded the he did not recommend launching based upon the engineering position just presented. Then Larry Mulloy asked George Hardy of NASA for his launch decision. George responded that he was appalled at Thiokol's recommendation but said he would not launch over the contractor's objection. Then Larry Mulloy spent some time giving his views and interpretation of the data that was presented with his conclusion that the data presented was inconclusive.

Now I must make a very important point. NASA's very nature since early space flight was to force contractors and themselves to prove that it was safe to fly. The statement by Larry Mulloy about our date being inconclusive should have been enough all by itself to stop the launch according to NASA's own rules, but we all know that was not the case. Just as Larry Mulloy gave his conclusion, Joe Kilminster asked for a five-minute, off-line caucus to re-evaluate the data and as soon as the mute button was pushed, our General Manager, Jerry Mason, said in a soft voice, "We have to make a management decision." I became furious when I heard this, because I sensed that an attempt would be made by executive-level management to reverse the no-launch decision.

Some discussion had started between only the managers when Arnie Thompson moved from his position down the table to a position in front of the managers and once again, tried to explain our position by sketching the joint and discussing the problem with the seals at low temperature. Arnie stopped when he saw the unfriendly look in Mason's eyes and also realized that no one was listening to him. I then grabbed the photographic evidence showing the hot gas blow-by comparisons from previous flights and placed it on the table in view of the managers and somewhat angered, admonished them to look at the photos and not ignore what they were telling us; namely, that low temperature indeed caused significantly more hot gas blow-by to occur in the joints. I, too, received the some cold stores as Arnie, with looks as if to say, "Go away and don't bother us with the facts." No one in management wanted to discuss the facts; they just would not respond verbally to either Arnie or me. I felt totally helpless at that moment and that further argument was fruitless, so I, too, stopped pressing my case.

What followed made me both sad and angry. The managers were struggling to make a list of data that would support a launch decision, but unfortunately for them, the data actually supported a no-launch decision. During the closed manager's discussion, Jerry Mason asked the other managers in a low voice if he was the only one who wanted to fly and no one answered him. At the end of the discussion, Mason turned to Bob Lund, Vice President of Engineering at MTI, and told him to take off his engineering hat and to put on his management hat. The vote poll was taken by only the four senior executives present since the engineers were excluded from both the final discussion with management and the vote poll. The telecon resumed and Joe Kilminster read the launch support rationale from a handwritten list and recommended that the launch proceed as scheduled. NASA promptly accepted the launch recommendation without any discussion or any probing questions as they had done previously. NASA then asked for a signed copy of the launch rationale chart.

Once again, I must make a strong comment about the turn of events. I must emphasize that MTI Management fully supported the original decision to not launch below 53- F (12- C) prior to the caucus. The caucus constituted the unethical decision-making forum resulting from intense customer intimidation. NASA placed MTI in the position of proving that it was not safe to fly instead of proving that it was safe to fly. Also, note that NASA immediately accepted the new decision to launch because it was consistent with their desires and please note that no probing questions were asked.

The change in the launch decision upset me so much that I left the room immediately after the telecon was disconnected and felt badly defeated and angry when I wrote the following entry in my notebook. "I sincerely hope that this launch does not result in a catastrophe. I personally do not agree with some of the statements made in Joe Kilminster's summary stating that SRM- 25 (Challenger) is okay to fly."

After I had a chance to review a copy of Joe's chart, I realized that I didn't agree with any of his statements made to support a launch decision. I believe that anyone who has normal powers of reason will question the validity of Figure 11 as a document to support the Challenger launch.

Figure 11. MTI assessment of temperature concern on SRM-25 (51I) launch.

1. Calculations show that SRM-25 O-rings will be 20- F colder than SRM-15 rings
2. temperature data not conclusive on predicting primary o-ring blow-by
3. engineering assessment is that: colder O-rings will have increased effective durometer ("harder")
4. "harder" O-rings will take longer to "seal"
5. more gas may pass primary O-ring before the primary seal seats (relative to SRM 15)
6. Erosion experienced on SRM-15.
7. demonstrated sealing threshold is 3 times greater than 0.038.
8. if the primary seal does not seal, the secondary seal will seal
9. pressure will get to secondary seal before the metal parts rotate
10. O-ring pressure leak check places secondary seal in outboard position which minimizes sealing time
11. SRM-25 will not be significantly different from SRM-15.
12. MTI recommends STS-51I launch proceed on 28 January1986

Signed by Joe C. Kilminster, Vice-President Space Booster Programs.

The chart lists twelve separate statements. Statements 1, 2, 4, 5, 6, 8 and 9 actually support a no-launch decision. Statement 3 is actually a lie. There was no engineering assessment made during the caucus. Arnie and I continued to press for retaining the original decision of not launching below 53- F (12- C). Statement 7 addresses the erosion margin but erosion was not the primary topic of discussion that evening. We were all discussing whether the seals would even seal before hot gas blow-by would destroy them. This statement is the only one to support a launch but it was not part of the concern that night. Statement 10 neither supports nor is against a launch decision. It is simply a statement of engineering fact which states that when pressure is applied to an O-ring seal, it will move away from the pressure to the opposite side of the groove containing it. Statement 12 is a contradiction of statement 1 because everyone knew that 20- F (-7- C) colder seals were very significant as our preliminary test data had shown.

Therefore, MTI senior management reversed a sound technical recommendation without one shred of supporting data and without any re-evaluation of the data they had promised when they requested the caucus.

The next morning I paused outside Arnie Thompson's office and told him and my boss that I hoped the launch was safe, but I also hoped that when the booster joints were inspected that we would find all the seals burned almost all the way through the joint, and then maybe we could get someone with authority to take a stand and stop the flights until we fixed the joints.

Later, I was walking past the room normally used to watch the launches when Bob Ebeling stepped out to invite me to watch the launch. At first I refused because I didn't want to watch the launch, but he encouraged me to enter. The room was filled so I seated myself on the floor close to the screen and leaned against Bob's legs as he was seated in a chair. The boosters ignited and as the vehicle cleared the support tower, Bob whispered to me that we had just dodged a bullet. The reason Bob made this statement was that the propellant experts had told us that the boosters would explode at ignition if we developed a leak in the case. At approximately T+60 seconds, Bob again whispered to me that he had just completed a prayer of thanks to the Lord for a successful launch. Just 13 seconds later we both saw the horror of destruction as the vehicle exploded. We all sat in stunned silence for a short time; then I left the room and went directly to my office where I remained in shock for the remainder of the day. Two of my seal task team colleagues inquired about my condition at my office, but I was unable to speak to them and hold back my emotions, so I just nodded yes I was okay and they left after a short silent stay.

Within a day of the launch, one of my colleagues on the seal task force team told me that he was reviewing the video tape and thought he could see a plume of flame coming from a booster as it exited the explosion. My first thought was that one of the joints had failed, so I postulated several scenarios to fit the observations and one of them turned out to be what was found to cause the disaster. A failure investigation team was formed at MTI on January 31, 1986, which included Arnie Thompson and myself. The team was immediately sent to MSFC in Huntsville, Alabama.

POST-DISASTER TREATMENT

The first hint that there would be separation between the engineers and management occurred during the preparation for the first closed-door testimony to the Presidential Commission. I was given very little notice that a hearing would be held on February 14, 1986. I had approximately two hours total by myself prior to the hearing and was struggling to organize a set of notes to aid me during my testimony, while management had their Publications Department prepare a formal set of professional viewgraphs for their version of the events leading up to the launch decision. Meanwhile, at a pre-hearing meeting with management, the company attorneys advised us to answer all questions with only yes or no and not to volunteer anything freely. This advice was not followed by me nor Arnie Thompson and AJ McDonald and there were obvious tense feelings between management and us after the testimony session.

Approximately five days later at MSFC, two Presidential Commission members requested a closed interview session with Arnie Thompson, Joe Kilminster and me. During this meeting, I handed a packet of memos and activity reports to a commission member as a response to one of his questions and this action upset our company attorney. I sensed quite clearly from this time on that I had not endeared myself with MTI Management, since my memos would clarify the true circumstances leading to the disaster and would also counteract both NASA and MTI Management attempts to discredit our testimony up to that point. I thought it was unconscionable that MTI and NASA Management wouldn't tell the whole truth so that the program could go forward with proper corrective measures. Joe Kilminster then had a heated discussion with Arnie and me after the meeting. Joe strenuously objected to Arnie and me constantly correcting his technical version of what the data meant. Joe said that we were welcome to express our opinions but that he also was entitled to express his. We agreed but said we would continue to correct his version if his input was technically incorrect as it had been up to that time.

It was at this point that I realized that both NASA and MTI Management had been using me to supply them with the fine joint details. I had spent hours answering questions about how the joints worked, but I had thought it was pertinent to the failure investigation so I freely answered all questions and supplied all the information that made them appear to be very knowledgeable about the joints. I suspect that I fell into deeper disfavor with MTI Management after my public testimony to the Presidential Commission on February 25, 1986. Again, MTI Management had prepared beautiful color graph, viewgraphs and printed books, while I struggled with my original notes. However, this time they were not allowed to speak from their viewgraphs and were only allowed to submit the written material and answer questions. During my testimony, I directly rebutted MTI's General Manager's testimony concerning his statements about our supposedly non-unanimous engineering position at the telecon. My rebuttal was based on the fact that only Arnie Thompson and I were the principals involved during the continuing discussion at the telecon. Brian Russell and Bob Ebeling were the only other ones who spoke and they said only a few sentences. No one else said anything, either pro or con relative to launching, so I, therefore, consider all these people as non-entities and it matters not what they may say after the fact since they did not have either the conviction or the courage to speak out during the telecon. I know that Mason talked to some of those silent people after the disaster and interpreted what they said as support for the management decision to launch. I submit that his testimony as an example of management's deceit and half truth at its best by his attempt to discredit my previous testimony to the Commission.

We all gathered at MTI's resident office in Washington, D. C. after the testimony on February 25 and the intensity of bad feelings was so great that someone from management suggested that the company jet take us back to MSFC as soon as we gathered our personal belongings from the motel. Eventually cooler heads prevailed and we took a commercial flight the next morning. Later that some evening, management decided to send me back to Utah and keep Arnie Thompson at MSFC until the failure investigation was completed.

I was happy to return home because I wasn't pleased with the way MSFC Management was diligently attempting to find a condition other than low temperature which caused the disaster. For example, I witnessed NASA spend a two to three week side effort to prove that a Challenger joint close-out photo showed a twisted O-ring prior to mating. This was after I told them that the photo was only showing a track of smeared grease and not a twist because I had run a desk top test myself some time before to show that the O-ring could not twist as they were contending. I was proved right after their efforts failed to produce a twist in the O-ring and they finally admitted that the photo showed a smeared grease track.

In Utah I now began to sense the first signs of isolation from NASA, but I didn't fully recognize the situation and I continued to argue for full truthful disclosure while factions of MTI and MSFC Management were fully content to tell only half truths about the history of the development and production of the SRB's.

I realized for sure in mid-April that I was actually being isolated from NASA and the main redesign activity since mid-March while MTI Management was telling me of my great importance to the redesign effort. I was being asked to furnish technical design information for the new designs which was sometimes changed without my knowledge and was being presented to NASA by someone else with no copies of the final version of the presentation given to me for feedback. I was, in effect, actually isolated from the main redesign effort. Previous to my testimony, I always prepared and presented my own material and often my supervision gave me total freedom to do so because of their confidence in my abiIity. Unknown to me at the time, the President of Aerospace Operations at MTI had ordered that I should be kept isolated from NASA, and this was done with great subtlety to prevent detection by me and so I guess the company could say, if asked, "Yes, Roger Boisjoly still works here; in fact, he is the new seal redesign coordinator."

Working conditions kept deteriorating for some of us who had testified. Once again we were called to testify before the Presidential Commission in closed session on May 2, 1986. During the evening of May 1, we met with the President of Aerospace Operations at MTI, Mr. Ed Garrison, and he opened the meeting with a few general remarks about the upcoming session with the Commission. Then he addressed me and chastised me for airing the company's dirty laundry via my memos which I had given to the Presidential Commission. He also stated that MTI had suffered enough as a result of public disclosure but that we should continue to tell the truth, but we should consider the best way to state it before speaking. I quickly took exception to his remarks about me and said that I had simply tried to restore the truth in all testimony and I didn't consider my actions as airing dirty laundry. Bob Ebeling then spoke up with some support for me and he told Mr. Garrison that MTI should form a specific type of engineering development group. Garrison snapped at Bob and told him to stop and quit telling him how to run the company. We went into the Commission session the next day with conditions as tense as they had ever been and Chairman Rogers asked AJ McDonald and me about our current job assignments. We answered him and he was visibly upset because we were being punished for honesty in our testimony. The Commission then decided to release the closed session testimony to the public and MTI received tremendous criticism from the Congress, the Presidential Commission and the news media.

A few days later, AJ McDonald and I were invited back to Washington, D. C. by the Presidential Commission to review and comment on the final official accident analysis team report which was submitted to them by MSFC. The Commission had somehow found out that neither AJ nor

I had seen the final report. I submitted 12 pages of comments on the report and gave verbal testimony to four Commission members that the report findings were biased toward an attempt to downplay the effect of low temperature on the joint failure by trying first to focus blame on such things as assembly problems and other factors. The Commission members agreed with our comments and thanked AJ and me for our willingness to review and comment on the report at such short notice.

Major morale problems now started to develop within MTI as some of our colleagues perceived that our testimony was causing damage to the company, but we didn't agree with that assessment and decided to try to correct it by requesting a meeting with three top executives at MTI who could do something about the internal strife. A private meeting was held on May 16, 1986 with the CEO, the President of Aerospace Operations, and the Vice President of the SRM Program. The meeting produced a very candid discussion of problems from our side but it was essentially one-sided with management telling us very little. The CEO even made it sound like we were on probation and if we worked hard and proved ourselves during the redesign activity, then everything would be forgiven. His attitude was certainly consistent with his criticism of AJ and me in his previous statement to THE WALL STREET JOURNAL. I believe it was at this meeting that the CEO made the statement that the company was doing just fine until AJ and I testified about our job reassignments on May 2. He said that those statements caused the company more harm than all the previous releases.

AJ McDonald and I were supposedly restored to our former positions after MTI was scolded by some very angry U. S. Senators, but it was only a superficial restoration which the company skillfully reported in a press release as a promotion for AJ McDonald, who was to head the redesign activity, while my interface with NASA was restored. Actually, AJ got only his old job back without a promotion and was not heading the redesign activity, while some people who had remained silent received promotions and the same people who wouldn't face up to the original bad joint design were now directing the joint redesign effort. Simply put, the joints have been redesigned by top management with direction down to the working level engineer who must engineer the details to make it work.

I had been chastised and criticized before my colleagues and ignored generally both personally and professionally, but I still tried to make my voice heard for the best joint redesign. I was the only one who reviewed the joint seal proposal submitted to MTI by Gray Tool Company of Houston, Texas and finally secured them a chance to present their seal design to MTI Engineering and Management. Many engineers were supportive of the design but, unfortunately for Gray Tool, the primary redesign configuration decision had already been made by MTI Management and they only have a poor political back-up position at this time.

AJ McDonald, Arnie Thompson and I, along with MTI Management, were asked to testify at the House of Representatives Committee on Science and Technology hearings on June 17 and 18, 1986. The two days of preparations with attorneys and public relations people plus the testimony itself were almost more than I could withstand when combined with my treatment at MTI.

Approximately one month after my testimony to the House Committee, I could no longer endure the hostile environment at MTI, so I took some time off at the recommendation of a company executive. During this period of being absent from MTI, I realized that I could not subject myself again to the hostile environment, so I informed them that I would not return to work. I was then placed on extended sick leave from July 21, 1986 until January 18, 1987 at which time I qualified for long-term disability. I currently receive 60% of my former salary and for my disability case, my compensation will stop after two years, which is January 18, 1989.

Memo from Roger Boisjoly on O-Ring Erosion
Morton Thiokol, Inc
Wasatch Division
Interoffice Memo
31 July 1985
2870:FY86:073

TO:
R. K. Lund
Vice-President, Engineering

CC: B. C. Brinton, A. J. McDonald, L. H. Sayer, J. R. Kapp
FROM: R. M. Boisjoly
Applied Mechanics - Ext. 3525

SUBJECT: SRM O-Ring Erosion/Potential Failure Criticality

This letter is written to ensure that management is fully aware of the seriousness of the current O-ring erosion problem in the SRM joints from an engineering standpoint. The mistakenly accepted position on the joint problem was to fly without fear of failure and to run a series of design
evaluations which would ultimately lead to a solution or at least a significant reduction of the erosion problem. This position is now drastically changed as a result of the SRM 16A nozzle joint erosion which eroded a secondary O-ring with the primary O-ring never sealing.

If the same scenario should occur in a field joint (and it could), then it is a jump ball as to the success or failure of the joint because the secondary O-ring cannot respond to the clevis opening rate and may not be capable of pressurization. The result would be a catastrophe of the highest order-loss of human life. An unofficial team (a memo defining the team and its purpose was never published) with leader was formed on 19 July 1985 and was tasked with solving the problem for both the short and long term. This unofficial team is essentially nonexistent at this time. In my opinion, the team must be officially given the responsibility and the authority to execute the work that needs to be done on a non-interference basis (full time assignment until completed). It is my honest and very real fear that if we do not take immediate action to dedicate a team to solve the problem with the field joint having the number one priority, then we stand in jeopardy of losing a flight along with all the launch pad facilities.

R. M. Boisjoly
Concurred by:
J. R. Kapp, Manager
Applied Mechanics

Memo from A.R. Thompson on the Flight Seal
Morton Thiokol, Inc
Wasatch Division
Interoffice Memo

2871:FY86:141
22 August 1985
TO: S.R. Stein
Project Engineer
CC: J.R. Kapp, K.M. Sperry, B.G. Russell, R.V. Ebeling, H.H. McIntosh, R. M. Salita, D.M. Ketner
FROM: A.R. Thompson, Supervisor
Structures Design

SUBJECT: SRM Flight Seal Recommendation

The O-ring seal problem has lately become acute. Solutions, both long and short term are being sought, in the mean time flights are continuing. It is my recommendation that a near term solution be incorporated for flights following STS-27 which is currently scheduled for 24 August 1985. The near term solution uses maximum possible shim thickness and a .292 +.005/-.003 inch dia O-ring. A great deal of effort will be required to incorporate these changes. However, the O-ring squeeze is nearly doubled for the example (STS-27A). A best effort should be made to include a max shim kit and the

.292 diameter O-ring as soon as it is practical. Much of the initial blow-by during O-ring sealing is controlled by O-ring squeeze. Also more sacrificial O-ring material is available to protect the sealed portion of the O-ring. The added cross-sectional area of the .292 diameter O-ring will help the resilience response by added pressure from the groove side wall.

Several long term solutions look good; but, several years are required to incorporate some of them. The simple short term measures should be taken to reduce flight risks.

A. R. Thompson ART/jh

Why was Roger Boisjoly so concerned about O-Rings? These seemingly insignificant pieces of rubber played a critical role in the joints between segments of a **solid rocket boster** (SRB).

The challenger on the morning of its national launch (1) The External Tank (2) The Solid Rocket Booster

The two SRBs attached to a space shuttle orbiter provided eighty per cent of the thrust necessary to propel the shuttle into space. About two minutes after a normal launch, the SRBs would detach and parachute back to the ground to be reused in subsequent missions. Several cylindrical segments make up the 149.1-foot- (45.4-meter-) tall SRB. Each joint between these segments contains two O-rings, positioned concentric with the SRB. The O-rings must be in perfect condition to prevent hot gasses from leaking through the joints of the SRB.

The Challenger: What Went Wrong

Within a second of the launch of Challenger on January 28, 1986, the first signs of failure of a joint in the right SRB were visible. Puffs of black smoke, whose color suggested that 5800-degree gases were eroding the O-rings, spewed out of that joint three to four times each second. At the end of the first minute, a small but steady flame was evident.

Atmospheric and aerodynamic conditions directed the flame plume onto the surface of the **External Tank** , used to supply liquid hydrogen and liquid oxygen fuel to the shuttle's engines during the launch. The flame eventually breached the tank, and a massive amount of hydrogen and oxygen burst into flame. At 73 seconds, a nearly explosive burn of the hydrogen and oxygen quickly resulted and claimed the Challenger with its crew.

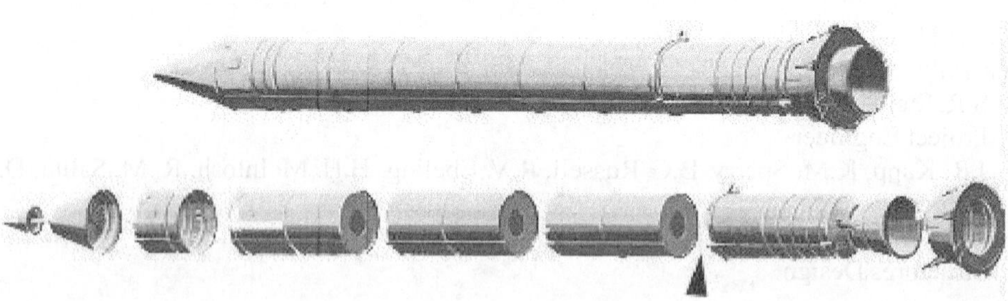

Above: A Solid Rocket Booster and its segments. The aft field joint (arrow) failed in the Challenger's right SRB

A Solid Rocket Motor Joint. Its parts are colorized in this diagram for clarity. In pink is the **tang,** which joins the **clevis,** colored orange. 177 huge steel pins (yellow) hold the joint in place. The O-rings shield the joint from 5800-degree gases inside the booster.

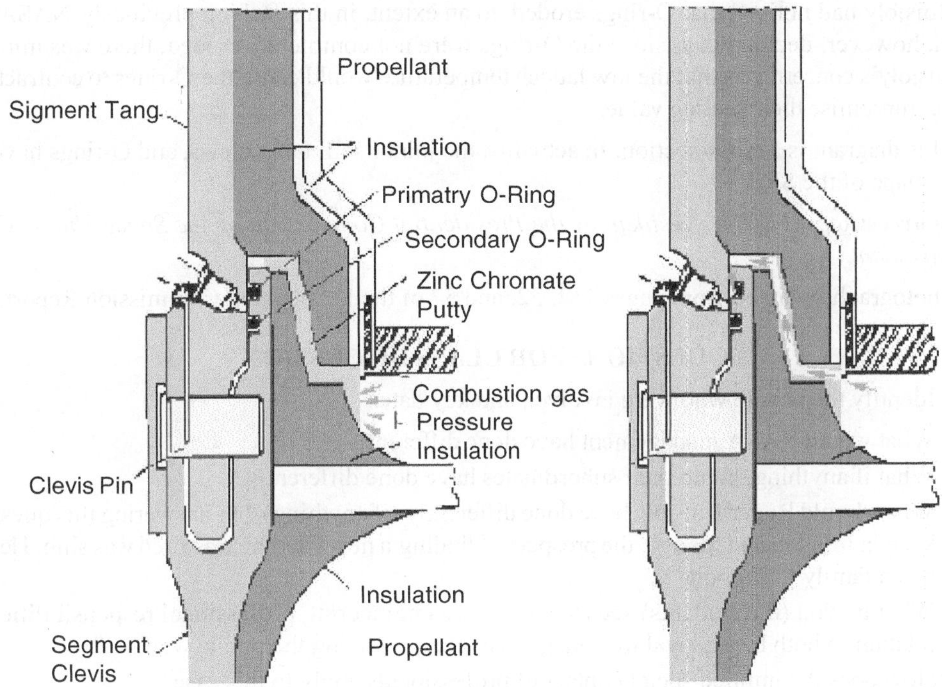

On the left scenario, hot gases (red arrows) are shielded from the joint by the zinc chromate putty. On the right, immense pressure creates a blowhole in the putty, allowing the O-rings to move into the positions needed to seal the joint as the gap between tang and clevis expands. Through the blowhole, gases penetrate and wear away the O-rings.

Morton Thiokol Organizational Chart

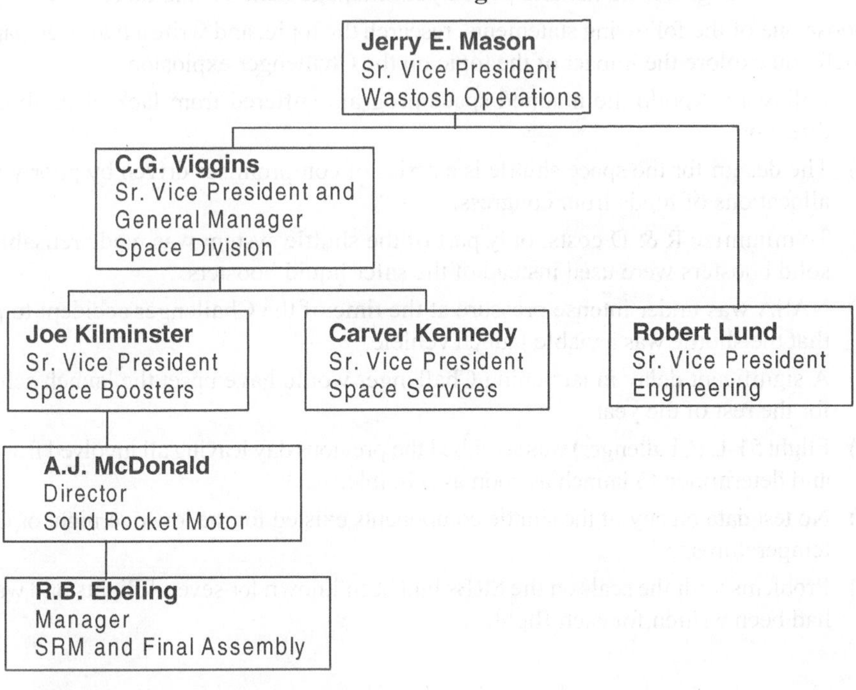

Boisjoly had noticed that O-rings eroded, to an extent, in this fashion previously. NASA and Thiokol, however, decided that, since the O-rings were not completely eroded, there was minimal risk. Boisjoly's concern was that the low launch temperature would cause the O-rings to contract and further compromise their sealing value.

This diagram is a cross-section. In actuality, the joint itself, tang, clevis, and O-rings have the circular shape of the SRB.

Sources: *Report to the President by the Presidential Commission on the Space Shuttle Challenger Accident.*

Photographs adapted from pages 112, 52, and 57 of the Presidential Commission Report.

QUESTIONS FOR CLASS DISCUSSION

1. Identify the people who were involved and key dates.
2. What would NASA management have done differently ?
3. What if anything, could their subordinates have done differently ?
4. What should Roger Boisjoly have done differently (if anything) ? In answering this question, keep in mind that at his age, the prospect of finding a new job if he was fired was slim. He also had a family to support.
5. What do you (the students) see as your future engineering professional responsibilities. In relation to both being loyal to management and protecting the public welfare ?
6. How does the implied social contact of professionals apply to this case ?
7. What professionals' responsibilities were neglected, if any ?
8. How could the chains of communication and responsibility for the shuttle program should be made to function better ?

EXERCISES

1. Take off your engineering hat and put on your management hat and do reverse.
2. Choose one of the following statements, research the topic, and write a two page paper in which you explore the impact of the topic on the Challenger explosion.
   (*a*) Following Apollo the manned space program suffered from lack of funding and direction.
   (*b*) The design for the space shuttle is a series of compromises driven by poorly timed allocations of funds from congress.
   (*c*) To minimize R & D costs, only part of the shuttle system was made reusable and solid boosters were used instead of the safer liquid boosters.
   (*d*) NASA was under intense pressure at the time of the Challenger accident to prove that the shuttle was a viable launch vehicle.
   (*e*) A significant delay in launching Challenger would have upset the launch schedule for the rest of the year.
   (*f*) Flight 51-L (Challenger) was scrubbed the previous day leaving all involved frustrated and determined to launch as soon as possible.
   (*g*) No test data on any of the shuttle components existed for the low overnight or launch temperatures.
   (*h*) Problems with the seals on the SRBs had been known for several flights and waivers had been written for each flight.

(*i*) Concerns about the O-rings were never revealed to the NASA administrators who has the final launch authority.

(*j*) Morton Thiokol initially recommended against launch, but when pressured by NASA reversed its decision.

(*k*) The anti-freeze plan left large sheets of ice and icicles all over the launch structure. An analysis done at Houston showed no danger at lift-off due to falling ice.

(*l*) Rockwell could not guarantee the shuttles safetly, but did not veto the launch. Their ice analysis showed some possibility of danger.

(*m*) The ice team recommended against launching, but was overruled by Mission Control.

3. Divide the class into small groups, no more than three to a group. Each group is to choose one of the four roles outlined below and develop a statements outlining the position represented by those in your role on January 28, 1996. Develop two statements : (1) what you think was the position of those in your role, and (2) the position that those in your role should have taken.

(*a*) NASA Management: You want to launch the Challenger as soon as possible. The delays are not only embarrassing, but threaten your funding and customer base. Challenger must launch on Tuesday to preserve the schedule. An analysis done by your engineers at Houston shows that the ice on the pad should not strike the Challenger when it lifts-off.

(*b*) Thiokol Engineers : You believe it is not safe to launch, but have no hard data to back this up. Limited data from a previous cold weather flight indicates that temperature is important. Basic physics tells you that the O-rings will lose elasticity with decreasing temperature. You feel that both NASA and your own management are trying to solve the problem with a bureaucratic solution, when an engineering solution is called for.

(*c*) Thiokol Management : You must listen to your engineers, but at the same time you must please your primary customer. There is talk in Congress of awarding a second source contact. The last thing you want to do is admit your product is defective. NASA is pressuring you to launch. It would be very damaging for your company if a delay is blamed on your SRBs.

(*d*) Rockwell Management: You are concerned about the amount of ice on the pad. Analysis by your engineers does not entirely agree with that done at Houston. Like Thiokol you must satisfy your customer. You would prefer not to launch, but are not sure that your reason to delay is good enough. Your objective is to try to convince NASA to delay without them pointing a finger at you as the cause.

4. Working in three person groups, develop a realistic procedure for making launch decisions which would have avoided the Challenger accident. Remember that the procedure must create a concensus among individuals and organizations with different objectives, backgrounds, and priorities. Part of your work will require that you develop a methodology to determine potential risks and benefits for launching the shuttle is less than ideal conditions. Remember that in the real world, personalities are often the dominant factor in a decision.

5. Working in three person groups, consider the problems of or Allan McDonald and Roger Boisjoly. Develop a strategy to convince Thiokol management and NASA management that your safety concerns were valid. Consider the points of view of all of those who are pressing to launch. Remember that management often tends to view engineers as extremely competents in a specific area, but lacking a good understanding of the big picture.

Synopses of Case Studies adapted from A&M University,Texas

1. **The Aberdeen Three:** In 1989, three engineers working on developing chemical weapons at a U.S. Army facility, the Aberdeen Proving Ground in Maryland, were indicted for a criminal felony. They were tried and convicted for illegally handling, storing and disposing of hazardous waste in violation of the Resource Conservation and Recovery Act form 1983-1986. This case shows the importance of the engineering profession's social and environmental responsibilities, in both legal and moral terms. In addition, it serves as an important case study in the escalating public concern over environmental and toxic waste, and the ways in which government is called upon to regulate engineering business. Aberdeen Three is particularly useful for students of environmental engineering; however, it also is a useful case for showing engineering students their responsibility to the public at large.
2. **Accepting Gifts and Amenities:** Most engineers probably believe that accepting small favors (such as inexpensive pens) from vendors is permissible. By contrast, most engineers probably believe that accepting large gifts or amenities is wrong. Drawing the line between permissible and impermissible instances of accepting gifts and amenities is not always easy, however. This case invites students to think about the issues involved in such decisions. It is particularly suitable for senior-level engineering courses.
3. **American Society of Mechanical Engineers (ASME) vs. Hydrolevel Corp.:** In 1971, McDonnell and Miller, an engineering firm, used an interpretation of an ASME code to undermine a boiler control device competitor, Hydrolevel Corp. As a result, Hydrolevel sued McDonnell and Miller, the Hartford steam Boiler Inspection and Insurance Company, and ASME on the basis of restraint of trade. In the ensuing trial, which went all the way up to the U.S. Supreme Court, Hydrolevel's lawyers argued that two key ASME subcommittee members acted not only on the conflicting self-interest of their companies, but also in violation of the Sherman Anti-Trust Act. The case of ASME vs. Hydrolevel Corp. shows how easily individuals, companies, and professional societies can find themselves embroiled in expensive legal battles that tarnish the reputation of the engineering profession as a whole. The case is appropriate for all engineering upper-level curricula, for it discusses not only conflicts of interest and various engineering codes of ethics, but also illustrates the roles of engineers within their professional societies.
4. **B.F. Goodrich Air Force A7-D Brake Problem Case:** In 1969, following brake failure at June, 1968 flight tests, and because of the ensuing accusations by a former B.F. Goodrich employee, Kermit Vandivier, regarding qualification test report falsification and ethical misconduct on the part of specific B.F. Goodrich personnel, Senator William Proxmire (D-Wisconsin) requested a governmental inquiry into the brake qualification testing performed by B.F. Goodrich. The case is one of the most famous in the literature on whistleblowing. Yet, other ethical issues raised by the case involve engineering responsibility for failed innovation, how easy it is for events to escalate (in this case, to a formal Congressional hearing) when people fail to communicate and get their facts straight, and how innovative design often makes testing procedures obsolete, or worse yet, shows that they were in fact erroneous from the onset. While valuable for all engineering students, the case is particularly well suited for design, materials and professionalism courses.
5. **Gilbane Gold:** This case focuses on a popular videotape that depicts a hypothetical—but nonetheless realistic—account of the experiences of a young engineer who is caught between his obligations to his company, Z-CORP, and to the public. The issue at the center of the controversy has to do with the fact that Z-CORP is discharging arsenic and lead into the city sewer system. The case is suitable for courses in environmental engineering, and in courses exploring professional issues, such as an engineer's obligations to his company and to the public.
6. **Kansas City, Missouri Hyatt Regency Hotel Walkways Collapse:** As the United States' most devastating structural failure, in terms of loss of life and injuries, the Kansas City Hyatt Regency walkways collapse left 114 dead and in excess of 200 injured. In addition, millions of dollars in

costs resulted from the collapse, and thousands of lives were adversely affected, all because of disputed conversations between and engineering design firm and a fabricator, and negligence on the part of the contracting engineering firm. The case provides a vivid example of the importance of accuracy and detail in engineering design and shop drawings (particularly regarding revisions), and the costly consequences of negligence in this realm. The case is particularly useful in structural design, statistics and materials classes.

7. **A Plow for Mexican Peasant Farmers:** Mechanical engineering students in a capstone design course are asked to design a plow that is suitable for use by peasant farmers in Mexico. The case shows how technological change, especially in third-world countries, can raise value issues. It illustrates the problems created by the intersection of design considerations and these value issues, and prompts students to come up with creative solutions to the problems. It is appropriate for design classes in mechanical engineering and is a model for projects in capstone design courses in other branches of engineering.

8. **Space Shuttle *Challenger* Disaster:** The fatal launching of space shuttle Challenger in 1985 resulted form a haphazard concatenation of economic considerations, political pressures and scheduling backlogs. The reality of a failed booster joint seal design took a back seat to these considerations, despite the protestations of design engineering Roger Boisjoly and others. Ethical issues raised by the case involve engineering responsibility versus management decision-making, as well as the ethics of post-hoc whistleblowing and negligence in design. This case is particularly useful to students in design, dynamics and structures courses. The case is dealt in detail in this chapter.

9. **T.V. Antenna Tower Collapse:** In this case, based on a real-world scenario, a television station was videotaping a crew raising the station's new television antenna tower. Unfortunately, on the day of videotaping, something went wrong with the lifting rig, and while the antenna was being hoisted the bolts failed. The result was a tragedy, with seven riggers falling 1200 feet to their death. The case raises serious questions about the design engineer's social responsibility to ensure safety on a construction site where riggers hoisting the antenna tower did not have sufficient technical expertise to know that they were endangered. Additionally, the case poses questions about product liability issues in engineering and ethics, particularly where knowledgeable bystanders, who could avert a tragedy by speaking up despite inferred liability, are concerned. What is the engineer's social responsibility as compared to legal liability? While valuable for all engineering students, the case is particularly well suited for statistics and structures courses.

10. **Trench Boxes and the Construction Site:** The use of safety equipment such as trench boxes can save many lives on construction sites. Unfortunately, trench boxes are not very cost effective, and because there is no legislation mandating their use, many contractors opt out of using trench boxes on construction sites. As a result, hundreds of worker's lives are lost each year, or at the very least, workers incur serious injuries because trench boxes are not operable on their construction site. The case raises the issue of legal liability for trench boxes versus the social responsibility of using them. What are the liability issues involved, and is it negligence to avoid their use? This case is of use to courses in geotechnical engineering, statistics, and construction engineering.

11. **XYZ Rubber Company and the Case of the Bursting Hose:** Since the 1940's, anhydrous ammonia has been used by farmers in the spring and early fall as a nitrogen fertilizer. Due to the toxicity of the ammonia vapors, however, serious accidents can result from its use. Such was the case in this study based on a real-world example. As a result of calamitous incidents involving hose ruptures, corporations were sued and forced to take their hoses off the market. Ethical questions raised by the case include what happens when professional codes and regulations lag

behind technological innovations; what precautions must engineers take when trying to balance the benefits new technologies bring against risks to public safety often associated with engineering innovation; and what are engineering and corporate responsibilities to the public for failed innovation. This is an excellent case for studying risk assessment and can be applied particularly well to cases in design, fluids, materials, and agricultural engineering.

EXERCISE

1. Debate on Is Engineering a Social Experimentation?
2. Visit onlinethics.org. it is on line Ethics Centre for engineering and science at Case Western Reserve University. USA.
3. Interview engineers in a company and understand the safety measures taken by the company.

SHORT QUESTIONS

1. What is social experimentation?
2. What are the issues involved in maintenance?
3. What is 'tort ?
4. How do you create awareness about the code of ethics?

LONG QUESTIONS

1. How does code of ethics help engineers?
2. Discuss the moral issues that engineer faces at the design stage of the product.
3. Discuss the responsibilities of engineers as experimenter
4. What are the lessons you learn from the Titanic story?
5. Identify the social and legal issues for engineers.

Chapter

5

Safety, Responsibilities and Rights

UNIT IV : SAFETY, RESPONSIBILITIES AND RIGHTS : Safety and Risk – Assessment of Safety and Risk – Risk Benefit Analysis and Reducing Risk – the Three Mile Island and Chernobyl Case Studies. Collegiality and Loyalty – Respect for Authority – Collective Bargaining – Confidentiality – Conflicts Of Interest – Occupational Crime – Professional Rights – Employee Rights – Intellectual Property Rights (IPR) – Discrimination

Learning Objectives:

- To understand the concept of safety and risk.
- How to assess safety and risk ?
- Three Mile Case Study
- To know the responsibilities of engineers as employees.
- To know the rights of employee engineer.

SAFETY

What does the term 'safety' mean? Some consider any thing to be safe if the risks associated with it and its use are judged to be acceptable. Next question is 'whose safety?'. Employees, customers, visitors? Is it possible to give a safety guarantee? Yes for some time perhaps. Safety is very important as can be seen from the preeminence it gets in most codes of ethics.

Safety is an objective as well as a subjective matter since most often value perspectives differ. Safety is frequently thought of in terms of 'something as fairly safe or relatively safe'. For example, when we say that airplane travel is safer than automobile travel, we mean that measured against passenger miles traveled, there are fewer mortalities and injuries in air travel. The safety norms or standards are mandatory / statutory which are as per various laws like pollution control, Indian Standard Institution etc. It can also be set up voluntarily by the firm. These standards can be higher than the minimum as per the law.

- Safety
  - Products (Consumers)
    - Product Design (Consumers)
    - Manufacturing Process (Employees & Society)
  - Services (Consumers)
  - Process at Work Place (Employees & Society)
  - Disaster (Employees & Society)

The line diagram shows that the concept of safety includes products, services, processes and disasters .It extends to finance, medicine and international affairs. For engineers the term safety would mean the safe operation of systems and the prevention of either human caused or process caused disasters.

Product safety: Engineers will have to design the product in such a way to reduce the accidents and ease of operations for the consumers. For example the product should have no sharp edges which will hurt the consumers and employees. The electrical appliances should be interlocked and covered fool proof to prevent electricity leakages and shocks. The label should carry clear, the usage instructions and in the event of failure, precautions to be taken. When the gas cylinder leaks, open the doors and windows immediately , not to strike match or switch on the light and avoid any friction. The product should be tested for safety. When the products are sold without proper testing for safety, accidents happen. No compromises on the safety quality standards. The Indian Standard Institutes regulate the safety quality standard which needs to be complied. The society also has a responsibility of Product safety. Consumer Education and Research Centre (CERC) case study deals with how the safety quality is tested by an independent body.

Services: Engineers have to educate and train the consumers of handling the products. The services include, pre sales and post sales. It includes installation and maintenance of machineries in the consumers work place. During repairs the original equipment spare parts to be used and avoid the spurious spare parts. The equipments have to be tested after installation and repairs. Adequate training should be given to the safety engineers, testing engineers and quality engineers. Safety audit to be carried out at regular intervals to prevent accidents.

Process at work place:

This includes the manufacturing process in the shop floor. The machine operations at the consumers place. The work place has the ***static equipments*** like machines and ***operating equipments*** which includes all the material handling equipments and the ***raw materials*** or components. The noise, and vibration checks for the equipments to be made. The work place should carry instructions about the safety precautions prominently displayed . Proper training should be given to escape in case of accidents. The shop floor should be kept clean and should not be oily or slippery to avoid accidents. The space allocation should be clearly marked. Yellow lines to be painted to show the place for movement of material handling equipments. All the equipments should be maintained properly. The trolly should have wheels, and proper brakes. Ladders should be stable ,insulated with shock absorbers, of proper heights to prevent worker from falling. The spill over from one area of operation to another should be avoided. The raw materials and components should be stored properly in bins. Gloves and shoes should be provided to persons who are handling the chemicals and other hazardous materials. Masks and caps to cover the head. In Pepsi when you enter the shop floor, you are required to wear a cap to cover the head. This is to be compiled with strictly even by the visitors.

The process should be designed in such a way to prevent mal functioning of equipment and process. The selection of technology is a crucial decisions. The manufacturing system, should take care of environment inside the factory that is domestic and also effluent which are discharged from the factory. The short term and long term safety should be considered. The gases and the water to be treated before releasing in the atmosphere. The execution of safety norms to be complied as per the environment , pollution and other regulatory bodies. Inspections to be done on continuous basis.

In handling of raw materials, (1) their properties should be clearly mentioned. If it is glass breakable etc. (2) If there are any harmful effects on human organs like eye, skin, throat and lungs, the user must be educated on these so that care can be taken. For Chemical companies there is a ***Material Safety Data Sheet*** (MSDS) which needs to be submitted. (3) Safety guidelines in handling toxic effects should be given. The room should be well ventilated and exhaust to be provided. Safety engineer should provide and promote the use of mask, shoes, gloves and take all the safety precautions. The inspection, storage and handling of the raw materials should be done with utmost care. The engineers should prepare procedures manuals to ensure safety. Appropriate selection of material should be done for the purpose of safety.

Disasters: Engineers should plan for disasters. Proper instructions, training and educating the users in the event of disaster is a must. In case of Titanic it was found that the life boats were not sufficient. In the event of failure of machine, how should you save your life. Fire fighting training should be given. The objective is the safety of humans in the event of failure or disaster. Simulation studies are used while training the people for disaster situation.

Almost all engineering companies assign safety one of the highest priorities. For example, in a construction company the safety policy is documented and all 'on site' employees are provided with safety helmets, safety shoes and safety belts. These are provided to unorganized labourers as well as all visitors. Apart from this, training is provided to safety officers in fire prevention and firefighting. Training programmes on safety are conducted especially for new technologies introduced. Training is provided to safety officers on a regular basis. Safety officers are required to visit the construction sites and conduct audit of safety measures and provide necessary training

Construction site personnel, be it an engineer or a labourer, are at constant danger of falling victims to an accident. Previously, safety was one of the most neglected aspects of the industry. Contractors used to avoid spending money on providing safety equipments. But now in the modern era, safety is considered as one of the main aspects of their quality policy. Companies feel that a safe worker (i.e. worker well trained in safety procedures) can benefit the company by saving precious man-hours lost to accidents. Many companies have detailed safety manuals, which are given and taught to every employee. This helps in creating awareness and minimizing accidents.

The Safety organisation in a construction company is usually structured as follows:

Chief Safety Officer

↓ Visits all sites in the country on a regular basis

Site Safety Officers

↓

Imparts training to people on site: - like preventing/ fighting fire, first aid, use of safety equipments like safety helmets, safety gloves, safety glasses, safety belts, etc.

Absolute safety, in the sense of a degree of safety that satisfies all individuals or groups under all conditions is neither attainable not affordable. The perception of safety also varies from person to person and country to country. Visitors from the West may not accept drinking water in India as safe while we would do so. In many countries, car seat belts are compulsory for passengers. In India, Fiats and Ambassadors did not have any seat belts. A sick person is more prone to suffer ill effects from air pollution than a healthy adult. The thresholds are significant because different people have different tolerances for specific conditions. An entire population living near an oil refinery may have a fairly high tolerance as far as automobile emissions alone are concerned. Safety standards vary from situation to situation.

The safety involves team. The team consists of Safety engineers, testing engineers and quality engineers. As a team they inspect and audit the equipments, work place, process, materials etc. Also their role includes promotion of safety and prevention of accidents.

Engineers must plan to disasters

CERC

A recent study of product testing was done on 14 brands of ceiling fans by Ahmedabad based consumer organization, Consumer Education and Research Centre (CERC)[1]. CERC has a full fledged large laboratories to conduct the tests and give the performance results. Every month they select a product. Earlier electric plugs, holders were taken up. They also take consumer items like atta, sauce etc.

CERC purchased 14 brands of ceiling fan from the market. 14 brands of 1200 mm ceiling fans were put through 22 tests. The test found that the fans tested consumed more power than specified under the standard. Also, none of the brands tested was efficient.

(1) Air delivery :They did not give as much air as they should for the power they consumed. The air delivery as per the standard is minimum of 200 cubic metres of air per minute. The entire test was computerized and the readings directly entered into the computer without any manual operation. The computer took the average of the readings and as per the standard calculated the air delivery at full speed.

(2) Power consumption: The power consumed by each fan at full speed should not be more than 50 watts with an allowed tolerance of +10 per cent provided the service value is a minimum of 4 as per the standard. At a time when all appliances are becoming more and more efficient in terms of power consumption all the fans tested consumed power well over the standard limit.

(3) Efficacy (Service Value): The best fans give the maximum air delivery while consuming the least amount of power. According to the standard service value should not be less than 4.

$$\text{Service Value} \; \frac{\text{Minimum air delivery (m}^3\text{/min)}}{\text{Maximum power input (watts)}}$$

None of the brands conformed to this parameter. The service value ranged from 2.64 of Ashok to 3.25 of both Bajaj and Orient. This means, none of the brands was efficient. A higher service value indicates higher efficacy.

(4) Safety (Suspension System) : The rod holding the fan and the clamp on top make up the suspension system of the fan. Although rare, the fan would be in danger of falling if the rod and the clamp are not strong enough. In the test, the suspension system of the fan should be able to withstand a tensile load of 1,000 kilogram force (kgf). That is, when the rod and the clamp are pulled with this force, they should not break. Almonard and Anchor did not conform to this test. In case of Almonard the screw broke. And for Anchor, the clamp broke. Crompton provided an additional safety cable to hold the fan in case the clamp breaks. This provides for extra safety, stopping the fan from falling down until the clamp is fixed again.

The construction test to check whether the fan is made well, proper insulation has been provided etc. There were large differences found in the finishes. Crompton was found to be the best in construction. Bajaj, Cinni, Orient, Khaitan and Polar also was good. In Anchor and Usha, the finish was poor and very poor in case of Almonard, Ashok, Remi and Shaan. The internal wiring except Shaan and Ashok provided adequate insulation with the wires properly fixed.

The brands were also tested for safety for protection against electric shock, the starting of motor operated appliances, temperature rise, leakage current, high voltage, insulation resistance, moisture resistance of the regulator, mechanical endurance, abnormal test, stability and mechanical hazards, mechanical strength, components, terminal for external conductors, screws and connections, creep-

CERC case, Insight, Consumer Magazine,Vol 24 No1, January – February, 2004, Consumer Education Research Society, Ahmedabad age distance and clearances, resistance to heat, fire and tracking and resistance to rusting. All brands conformed to these parameters.

(5) Markings: According to the standard , apart from the readings of air delivery, information like rated voltage, input in watts etc should be marked. None of the brands marked the air delivery value on the packing.

What can engineers learn about safety from this case?

What are the implication for the company? What should they do?

RISK

We say a thing is not safe if it exposes us to unacceptable danger or hazard. What is meant by risk? A risk is a potential that something unwanted and harmful may occur. We take a risk when we undertake something or use a product or substance that is not safe. Thus, a future possible occurrence of harm is postulated.

Risk like harm, is a broad concept covering many different types of unwanted occurrences. In regard to technology, it can equally include dangers of bodily harm, of economic loss, or of environmental degradation. Delayed job completion, faulty products or systems and economically or environmentally injurious solutions to technological problems in turn can cause these risks. New technologies have new risks. They look new but many of them have existed before. They are new in the sense they are now identifiable or public's perception has changed because of education, experience, media attention or reduction in risk. Technology has greatly reduced the harmful impact of natural hazards like floods, earth quakes etc. Risks and disasters are the result of a combination of many factors. They result from a combination of probabilities of certain occurrences and their consequences. The probabilities arise from uncertainties. While experimenting with new technology or new applications of familiar technology, risks may arise due to misapplied attempts and disasters may happen.

There are various factors, which influence risk.

(1) The risks taking ability of persons People can be classified into risk takers and being risk averse. Risk takers are daring and adventurous and take voluntary risks. Risk averse people tend to be conservative.

(2) Information available. Uncertainties are based on the information availability

(3) Cost –Benefit analysis.

Information is essential for taking calculated risky decisions, but obtaining information costs money. If it is very important information for taking the right decision, then the benefits must outweigh the costs. Without the information, will the decision be right? Risk takers are usually confident about their decisions, and often take decisions under uncertainty and without all the required information. The threshold limit of individuals for information varies from person to person. Some would be comfortable only when they have information of deeper depth and quality while others may be comfortable with minimal information. (*Later in this Chapter under the design stage we will discuss more on risk taking, legal liability and responsibility.*)

The risk and benefits are based on the perception of probable gain and probable loss. The typical risk – benefit value function drops steeply on the loss portion than it rises on the gain portion. The threshold is ascribable to the human habit of ignoring smaller hazards in order to avoid anxiety overload: it means that no value is attached to a first, small amount of loss, or that no effort is expended to overcome the loss. A smaller and similar threshold is added on the gain side to account for normal human inertia and certain amount of inherent generosity that often restrain people in how they set about seeking their own gain. The figure below explains the risk-benefit – value function.

Figure 1

Risk – Benefit – Value - Function

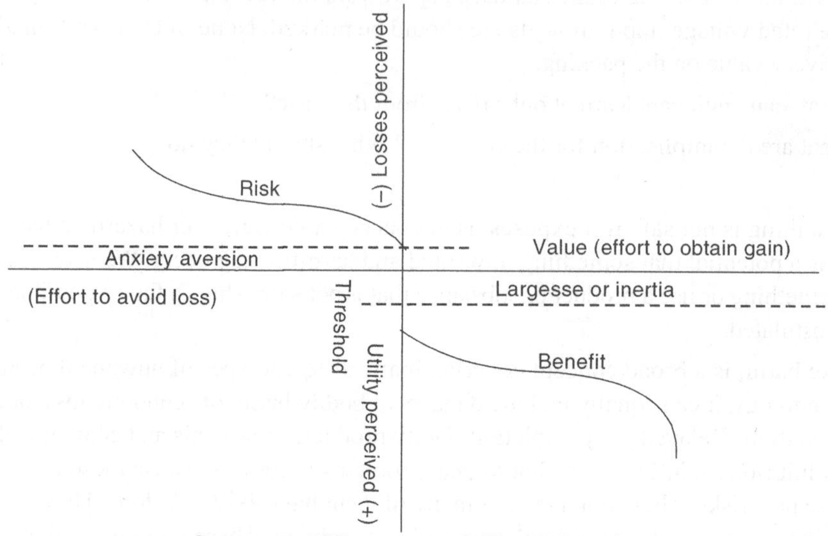

Source: p. 135 Mike W. Martin

In 1990 Theodore S. Glickman and Michael Gough assembled a number of papers, ***Readings in Risk***, as an introduction to risk definition, assessment, evaluation and management. Three papers in the series offer definitions of what we mean by risk, as relating to the engineering profession. These papers pose the classic question about technology-induced risk: "How safe is safe enough?" The answer to this question often depends on who is asked, whether the risk taken is voluntary or involuntary, what the near-term and long-term consequences are, and what the spatial distribution as well as expected probability of the risk is. As an adjunct, how we perceive and evaluate each given risk depends on factors such as the magnitude of exposure to the risk, whether the effects are reversible, and whether threshold levels of those risks exist.

Even if we can establish these parameters, we must remember that computations are based on our best available evidence, not necessarily *the* appropriate evidence. Our analyses often neglect the realities of uncertain inputs and exogenous disturbances to the system under study; therefore, probabilities entered in a numerical risk assessment are, at best, judicious engineering estimates. Nevertheless, we must perform risk assessments to establish what public risks can be undertaken, given the possible benefits from the technological advances being pursued. Where do we find our starting point in assessing risk?

Assessing Risk

We start with things we know. Risk assessment deals with setting magnitudes on the risks we know exist. This involves using tools such as fault- or event-tree analyses, and requires probability-based estimates (or sometimes knowledge) of the likelihood of a given fault or event. Once we have estimates, we can look at how best to minimize the risk.

Risk abatement addresses problems associated with how risks can be regulated or minimized. This means we have to address political questions associated with managing risk. Who should manage the risks? How should the risk be managed, and at what level in the hierarchy should risk be managed? This political analysis can only begin after the most accurate risk assessment possible is undertaken. Of course, this puts the greatest burden of proof on the engineers, and often stretches their capabilities.

Get down to business. Do it now.

In his "*Social Benefits Versus Technological Risk*", Chauncey Starr concludes that we are generally willing to take voluntary risks that are 1000 times (three orders of magnitude) as uncertain as involuntary risks. In Starr's studies, risk is generally proportional to the cube of the incremental wages involved in recognition for taking that risk. For example, doubling wages would tend to convince a worker to take eight times the risk. Further, there is a perceived separation of three orders of magnitude between involuntary risks (such as a corporations placing a toxic waste dump in your area) and voluntary risks such as smoking. Thus, studies show that people tend to overestimate the likelihood of low probability risks associated with causes of death. The converse is also true. Such tendencies lead to overconfident biasing (or "anchoring") in personal risk assessments, which in turn suppresses adjusting the assessment for the realities of the situation. In his study of 57 risk abatement programs at five different government agencies in Washington (including the Environmental Protection Agency and Occupational Safety and Health Administration), Starr shows that risk abatement programs cost from $170,000 to $3 million in cost/life in different agencies. But this presents a new problem how do you affix a price tag to a human life? This is not an easy task.

To assist in solving this problem, Norman C. Rasmussen, in "*The Application of Probabilistic Risk Assessment Techniques to Energy Technologies*", suggests a more basic definition for "risk," namely, "consequences/unit time." Rasmussen argues that risk is the product of frequency (events/unit time) and magnitude (consequences/event). For example, to compute whether you would have been one of the approximately 50,000 auto fatalities in a given year, multiply the number of auto accidents/year (about 15 x 106) times the death rate per accident (one in 300). Yet, to make Rasmussen's formula work, we must be able to differentiate between the unknown versus the "dreaded" risks. And within each category we must be able to differentiate whether those risks are observable, controllable, voluntary, short-term, fatal, increasing and so on, and attach an appropriate weighting factor to each of these considerations as they enter into our numerical risk assessment. According to Rasmussen's study, these weighting factors can vary between zero and 100, thereby making accurate risk predictions problematical indeed.

One of the most serious drawbacks to any risk assessment is perhaps the omission of totally random and exogenous inputs. Such random and exogenous inputs cannot be predicted at all, and yet, when performing the final analysis of a catastrophe, they are often the key items in the sequence of events that lead to the disaster. Most airplane crash and explosion disaster investigations have pointed to one or two exogenous causal factors, the absence of which would have prevented the disaster. These same causal factors, however, could not have been foreseen, and therefore the likelihood of their occurring could not have been predicted. One example of this is the real-world scenario involving the pilot who accidentally spills his coffee over the control console, thereby unwittingly setting off an "engine on fire" alarm, which in turn led to catastrophe. (This was popularized in the book and movie of the 1950's, "Fate Is the Hunter.") With all these drawbacks, you might ask, "Well, why bother?" The answer is that, we must still perform risk assessments to the best of our abilities in order to protect ourselves from those problems we do know about, or can foresee.

So, how can we answer the question, "How Safe Is Safe Enough?" We must first recognize that there is no single, simple answer. We are often choosing between unpleasant alternatives. There will always be some level of risk associated with engineering and innovation; therefore, any risk analysis should involve the following five steps:

1. Define all the possible alternatives.
2. Specify the objectives and measure the effects.
3. Identify the consequences of the actions taken.
4. Quantify the alternatives based on the best available information.
5. Analyze the alternatives to arrive at the best choice for cost/risk.

Never blame luck.

Once engineers and managers have established, to the best of their abilities, the costs versus benefits of the risks involved, they must manage that risk.

Managing Risk

In a recent article, Michael Davis notes there are five major problems associated with managing risk:

1. We must deal with uncertainties.
2. We are often forced into too narrow a focus on specific classes of risk.
3. A commitment is required to provide immediate solutions, instead of "going slow."
4. Our adversarial world promotes inflexibility in our risk analyses.
5. The nature of a risk management program does not promote consensus, collaboration or cooperation between all involved.

The last point, in particular, is important for the engineering professional. In recent discussions with engineering professionals at a large research and development firm, engineers (both managerial engineers and non-managerial engineers) note that engineering team players need to know all the particulars associated with the problem at hand. This includes budgetary and time constraints, promises made to clients, and realistic assessments of technological flaws.

Risk management is perhaps the most important aspect of the engineer's professional tool kit. It is important for the public, our corporations, and for the engineering profession at large. As Michael Davis notes, managers and engineers approach risk in different ways. Managers have to factor in such things as schedules, budgets and contract requirements. Engineers tend to place safety considerations above all others. Engineers need more training in balancing risk versus benefit, so they can better communicate their legitimate concerns about public safety. For both managers and engineers alike, the likely tendency is to look at their work through a microscope, and, accordingly, not to see the many complications that fall just outside the field of resolution we are viewing.

Microscopic vision is enhanced vision, a giving up of information not likely to be useful under the circumstances for information more likely to be useful. If a point of light at the other end, microscopic vision is like looking into a microscope at things otherwise too small to see. [Microscopia is neither near sighted nor myopic it's not a kind of blindness; rather, it's a kind of insight. A person with microscopic vision need only look up from the microscope.] ... Microscopic vision is a power, not a handicap, but even power has its price. You cannot both look into the microscope and see what you would see if you did not.

Thus, as Davis argues, risk management programs force us to look up from the microscope, so we are better equipped for avoiding tragedies due to failed innovation.

The decision-making process is never an easy one. The important thing all engineers must remember is that, their first obligation is to public safety. Some risk is unavoidable. Engineering professionals must learn how to convince their managers that minimizing that risk is worth the effort involved.

SAFETY AND RISK

An issue of great concern to engineers is how to balance quality and safety against cost. Engineers want to design a high-quality product, but business managers want to keep the cost down. This raises business, legal and ethical issues. The business issues center around what firms must do to compete in the market place. The legal and ethical issues concern what they should do.

It is necessary to understand the relationship between Risk – Safety – Costs – Price. The figure given below explains the relationship with examples. All these variables are in a continuum, which means that there are degrees in each of these variables.

Instead of fighting the darkness, bring in the light.

Figure 2
Safety

	High	Low
High	High Risk/High Safety High Cost – Price Air craft, Nuclear Power	High Risk/Low Safety Low cost High Price Automobiles
Risk **Low**	Low Risk / High Safety High cost — Medium Price Safety Valves, electrical Products	Low Risk / Low Safety Low Price Low Cost Computers

For example, the Indian Supreme Court has held that the risk associated with sensitive chemical and public utility nuclear plants could not be a ground for ordering their closure or relocation. Sabotage, attack by terrorists, earthquake etc., are all unforeseeable events. We have to strike a balance between the existing utilities, which exists in public interest on the one hand, and human safety conditions on the other.In modern times, we have nuclear plants, which generate electricity. Their structural integrity and operations are vulnerable to certain risks. However, generation of electricity is equally important and, within the prescribed limits, society will have to tolerate existence of such plants.

The Kerala High Court gave a judgment to close 10,000 tonne ammonia plant of the Fertilizers and Chemicals Travancore Ltd (FACT) in Wellington Islands near Kochi.

The High Court had observed that a major leak would result in the event of an air crash near the tank – as there is an airport nearby – an act of sabotage or an earthquake. This could lead to loss of human life on a tragic scale. The FACT employees filed a special leave petition in the Supreme Court. The Court appointed Engineers India Ltd (EIL) to re-examine all issues concerning the plant's safety and submit the report. The EIL felt that the plant could continue to operate subject to the Company taking up increased safety measures. The Bench took note of the report and the Company has taken the necessary safeguards and precautions to minimize risk factors.

The Bench observed that "if the arguments of the original petitioner. Law Society of India is acc epted, then no such utility can exist, no reservoir can exist, no nuclear reactor can exist. We do not discount such risks, but we have to live with such risks which is counterbalanced by services and amenities provided by these utilities.

The days when an engineer's only ethical commitment was loyalty to his or her employer have long passed. The expansiveness of technology is such that now, more than ever, society is holding engineering professions accountable for decisions that affect a full range of daily life activities. Engineers now are responsible for saying: "Can we do it, should we do it, if we do it, can we control it, and are we willing to be accountable for it?" There have been too many "headline type" instances of technology gone astray for it to be otherwise — automobiles that burn when hit from the rear, planes that crash when cargo doors don't hold, bridges that collapse, walkways that fail, space shuttles that explode, gas leaks that kill thousands, nuclear plant accidents, computer viruses, oil tanker oil spills, and on and on.

Everything we do involves risk...There are dangers in every type of travel, but there are dangers in staying home—25 percent of all fatal accidents occur there. There are dangers in eating—food is one of the most important cause of cancer and of several other diseases—but most people eat more than is necessary. There are dangers in breathing—air pollution probably kills 100,000 Americans each year, inhaling radon and its decay products is estimated to kill 14,000 a year, and many diseases like influenza, measles, and whooping cough are contracted by inhaling germs...There are dangers in working—12,000 Americans are killed each year in job-related accidents, and probably ten times that number die from job-related illnesses—but most alternatives to working are even more dangerous. There are dangers in exercising and dangers in not getting enough exercise. Risk is an unavoidable part of our everyday lives.

Since engineers have been accorded professional status and the privileges that go with it, since they have literally created our way of life, and since their designs require experimentation with subjects—sometimes many subjects and without their knowledge or permission—it is no wonder that engineers are being held accountable for their actions. And for engineers, the implications are inescapable. Handling ethical dilemmas and making ethical decisions are very important elements of being a professional.

Three Mile Island

Detailed Description of Accident

Immediate Reaction to the Accident

The Cleanup Operation

The Accident's Impact

Detailed Description of Accident

At 36 seconds past 4:00 a.m. on the 28th of March, 1979 the first of a series of pumps feeding water to the steam generators at the Three Mile Island nuclear plant stopped functioning.

It was later determined that this was caused by maintenance work being done on the Number 7 Polisher at the time. The steam produced by the reactor not only runs the generators to produce electricity but also serves to cool down the reactor core, reducing the risk of a meltdown. When the flow of the water stopped the temperature inside the reactor core increased. This caused the water inside the reactor to expand, increasing the pressure inside the pressurizer to 2200 psi, 100 psi more then the normal. As designed the increase in pressure caused the Pilot Operated Relief Valve to open (PORV) draining the steam and water from the reactor core in to a tank on the floor.

At this point the three emergency feed water pumps started. An operator noticed that they were running, but he did not notice that the valves on the emergency feed water lines were closed. The panel in the control room had lights to indicate that the valves were closed, one of the lights was covered by a yellow maintenance tag, while the operator did not notice the other light.

Despite the opening of the PORV the pressure continued to rise, 9 seconds into the accident the control rods automatically lowered as designed to halt the fission reaction. This halted the fission reaction but the latent heat of the radioactive material continued to heat the water. Even though this heat was a fraction of what is normally produced during the fission reaction, it was enough to potentially overheat the core. 13 seconds into the accident the PORV should have closed since the pressure in the reactor had dropped. The light indicating that the PORV was energized (i.e. open) shut off, leading the operators to assume that the PORV had was now closed. In reality the PORV was stuck open and steam and water was escaping from the reactor. This is known as a Loss of Coolant Accident (LOCA).

In the first 100 minutes of the accident almost 32,000 gallons of water, or one third of the reactors capacity escaped through the PORV. The accident at TMI could have been contained had either the PORV shut at this point, or the operators noticed that the valve was stuck open. During the initial stages of the accident Edward Fredrick and Craig Faust, the Control Room Operators were present in the control room. One of the factors which added to the severity of the accident at TMI was the inadequate training of the employees at the facility. The training was the responsibility of Met Ed and Babcock & Wilcox.

We should owe loyalties to values.
Engineer has responsibility towards colleagues, public and customers.

Over 100 alarms went off in the control room during the first few minutes of the accident. This added to the confusion without providing any useful information to the operators. Both Faust and Fredrick dealt with the alarms to the best of their ability based on the training they had received.

2 Minutes into the accident the pressure of the water in the reactor dropped sharply which caused the Emergency Injection Water (EIW) to be automatically activated. This sent about 1000 gallons of water per minute into the reactor coolant system.
The falling pressure coupled with constant reactor coolant temperature should have alerted the operators to the LOCA. Instead, fearing that the core would have too much water, Operator Fredrick turned off one of the EIW pumps, reducing the flow of water into the core to less then 100 gallons per minute.

8 Minutes into the accident it was discovered that the emergency feed water was not reaching the core because of the closed valves. Operator Faust proceeded to open these valves, allowing water to rush into the steam generators. It was later discovered that these valves were closed two days earlier during a routine test of the pumps. At 4:11 a.m. an alarm signalled high water in the containment building. This is the building where all the water draining from the core through the PORV is stored. In itself this alarm should have been a clear indication of a leak in the coolant system. When Fredrick was informed of this he recommended that the sump pumps draining water to the containment building be shut off.

By about 6:15 a.m., roughly 2 hours and 15 minutes into the accident, the level of water in the reactor had dropped below the level of the core. Unknown to the operators the core is now uncovered. It is essential that the core remain covered at all times to prevent it from over heating. Once the core over heats the zirconium alloy of the fuel rod cladding reacts with the steam to produce hydrogen gas. This is what happened in the TMI reactor, not only is the hydrogen produced flammable, but the diminishment of the fuel rod cladding increases the risk of radioactive contamination.

The water continued to leak out of the PORV until 6:22 a.m. when Leland Rogers, the Babcock & Wilcox site representative at TMI asked the operators if they had shut the block valve which is the backup valve to the PORV. At this point the PORV was shut after having remained open for 2 hours and 22 minutes. It is still unclear whether Rogers was responsible for the valve being shut. Edward Fredrick testified that the valve was closed at the suggestion of a shift supervisor coming onto the next shift. Based on increasing radiation levels, at around 7:00 a.m. a site emergency was declared, indicating the threat of release of radioactivity into the surrounding environment. As the radiation levels continued to increase, the staff of TMI-C was contacting local law enforcement and local energy providers. At 7:24 a general emergency was declared at the TMI site and the site began to be evacuated. By 11:00 a.m. all nonessential personnel were ordered off of the island, and the remaining technicians were forced to wear face masks to block any air bourne radioactive particles. At 1:50 p.m. the operators in the control room heard what they described as a loud "thud." While they dismissed the sound as well as the pressure spike indicated by their instruments as a malfunction, the thud was actually a hydrogen explosion inside the containment building. It is another several hours before the partially melted core is brought to a controllable temperature using water from the primary loops.

Immediate Reaction to the Accident

Shortly after the accident occurred, an incorrect reading reported traces of radioactive iodine-131 in the Goldsboror area. While the reading caused an immediate need for concern, the readings were later found to be erroneous. A build up in radioactive iodine in human's thyroids from inhaling radioactive particles or drinking contaminated milk remained the primary concern of the top officials including Governor William Scranton III. The Governor was incorrectly informed that the release of steam represented the primary concern to the surrounding environment, despite the fact that there was no indication that radioactive steam had escaped from the reactor core or the pumps feeding the core.

The evening of the accident, mayor of Goldsboro, Ken Meyers, met with his council members to discuss the possibility of an evacuation. The council members proceeded to go door to door through the town providing families with whatever information they could, mostly consisting of information they themselves had heard from news reports, as well as explaining the evacuation procedure should Governor Scranton declare a state of emergency.

Following the accident, numerous tests were conducted in attempts to conclude what if any effect increased radiation would have on the health of human, animal and plant life in the surrounding area. Through these studies, it was revealed that the majority of radioactive material had been contained by the core. Despite the immediate concern, however, a later government report indicated that there would likely be one additional death as a result of cancer due to increased radiation level in the surrounding area in a 30 year period.

The Cleanup Operation

During the cleanup operation at the Three Mile Island nuclear reactor there were issues of ethical misconduct on the part of both organizations and individuals that occurred. Professor Stephen Unger of Columbia University has discussed one such example in his book "Controlling Technology."

Background information

In order to further discuss these issues it is important to understand the relationship between the organizations and individuals involved.

The key individuals involved were:

Laurence P. King

Director of Site Operations, General Public Utilities

Richard D. Parks

Senior Startup Engineer, Bechtel Northern Corporation

Edwin H. Gischel

Plant Engineering Director, General Public Utilities

The task for cleaning up was given to an organization involving both General Public Utilities (GPU) and the Bechtel Northern Corporation. At the same time the Nuclear Regulatory Commission (NRC) was present on site to monitor the cleanup operations.

Laurence P. King was responsible for the site cleanup operations on the GPU side.

Richard D. Parks was employed by Bechtel as a senior startup engineer and seconded as an operations engineer to the Site Operations Department under Laurence P. King. His duties involved liaison with the NRC and ensuring compliance with licensing requirements. In addition he served as an alternate startup and test manager for the plant.

Edwin H. Gischel was the Plant Engineering Director and worked under Laurence P. King.

One of the issues later brought up was that the NRC worked too closely with the organizations directly involved with the clean up of the reactor. This tended to take away from the NRC's ability to regulate the safety and effectiveness of the operations. There were times when proposals would be unofficially approved by the NRC before the other organizations were able to fully develop or approve them. This, combined with the perception that the NRC was more concerned with expediting the cleanup process rather than ensuring it was done correctly encouraged people to cut corners.

The issue

In any industrial operation overhead cranes used for lifting heavy equipment play an important role. The polar crane used during the cleanup of TMI-2 had been damaged during the original accident. During the repairing of the crane various parts that were damaged had been substituted with replacements that were not exactly the same as the originals. In addition the crane had been modified to perform duties that exceeded the original manufacturer specifications. Due to the nature of the cleanup operation the changes made posed a hazard to not only the workers on site but also to people in the surrounding areas.

King received reports from both Parks and Gischel which stated concerns over the use of the Polar Crane. Prior to that King had already experienced difficulties with the cleanup operations. He felt that established engineering procedures were not being followed by other high level managers, particularly Bechtel people.

Based on what he had seen and the reports he received King decided that the crane should be carefully tested before being put into service. Top management at GPUN and Bechtel did not agree with King's assessment of the situation and felt that he was being overly cautious.

In reaction to the Gischel's report, King's superior ordered King to immediately fire Gischel. King refused and defended Gischel's position. At this point GPU's tactics turned nasty.

After suffering a stroke a year before, Gischel had seen a psychologist working under GPU. At the time, the psychologist suggested Gischel take a neuropsychological evaluation, but Gischel refused to take the test. Almost immediately following the release of the report, he again received a letter suggesting he take the exam. Robert Arnold, the president of GPU Nuclear, continued pressuring Gischel and in a clear violation of the doctor-patient relationship disclosed that he had knowledge of the topics of Gischel's meetings with the GPU employed psychologist. After a letter insisting Gischel take the exam from the board chairman of GPU, Gischel sent a sworn affidavit to Arnold explaining his take on the TMI cleanup operations and the events that followed. Gischel requested that Arnold forward the affidavit to the NRC which he did, but on July 1 after Gischel still refused to take the neuropsychological exam he was transferred to a different subsidiary of GPU.

Richard Parks also filed a sworn affidavit and submitted it to the NRC, and a harassment complaint filed against GPU Nuclear. Parks's complaint was filed on the grounds that a manager told him Parks's superiors were considering transferring him off site, he was demoted from his position as alternate startup and test manager, and was informed of a false rumor that his ex-wife (who was actually deceased) was trying to dig up dirt on Parks to get custody of their two children. The day after he filed his complaint Parks was suspended with pay on the grounds that his continued working would subject him to continued harassment from his coworkers.

In February of 1983 GPU Nuclear accused King of hiring employees away from GPUN for his own firm, Quiltec. Accused of a conflict of interest, King was suspended and locked out of his office while he claims that documents he wrote concerning the cleanup process were destroyed. King's secretary, Joyce Wagner, was also forced into suspension and within a month both king and Wagner had been fired.

The Accident's Impact

The numerous ethical questions surrounding the TMI cleanup procedure might suggest that nothing positive could have resulted from the incident. Beyond the questionable behavior on the part of the companies responsible for the cleanup, radiation presented a major problem for the cleanup crews as did algae that not only grew, but thrived in the contaminated water. There were important scientific as well as sociological issues that resulted from the accident. The following is based on Matthew L. Wald's article "After the Meltdown, Lessons from a Cleanup" that appeared in the April 24, 1990 edition of the *New York Times*

What the cleanup effort did prove was that, despite requiring 400 workers, over 4 1/2 years, and 970 million dollars, the cleanup of a nuclear disaster area is possible. Unlike the Soviet approach to

Confidentiality and conflict of interest involve external agents.
Confidentiality does not cease when employees change job.

the cleanup at the Chernobyl disaster site, where the reactor was encased in an enormous concrete structure, the cleanup of the reactor site and especially the reactor vessel at TMI provided many answers to questions surrounding the accident and even provided some hints as to the nature of exactly how stable reactor vessels are.

During the cleanup process the team learned that despite the 51% meltdown of the reactor core, that the reactor vessel was relatively undamaged. This indicated two separate points. First that it was far easier to have a meltdown to the core than expected, but secondly that at least in this case, the reactor vessel was able to withstand temperature much higher than anticipated.

Beyond scientific impact, however, remains the impact that the accident had on the public. Many analysts in the nuclear industry believe that the incident at TMI has meant the nuclear industry has only one more chance. Analysts feel that another nuclear accident on the scale of TMI will result in public outcry for the closing of the other nuclear plants around the nation.

Both the legal and medical ethics literature look at negligence in terms of what society and the law consider "reasonable" types of professional behavior, as well as the consequences of professional failures to act. In his recent article, Kenneth McK Norrie notes that negligence, through the standard of reasonableness, imports into the law an ethical *command* as an attempt to encourage certain types of safe ("reasonable") behavior and discourage other types of unsafe ("unreasonable") behavior. ... The more knowledge, skill and experience a person has, the higher standard the law subjects that person to.

In his article John C. Hall argues that we must take responsibility not only for our negligent acts, but for our failures to act as well. What is it the negligent man has to answer for?

CHERNOBYL

A far more serious accident occurred seven years later at Chernobyl, in what was then still the Soviet Union. At the time of the accident—April 26, 1986—the Chernobyl nuclear power station consisted of four operating 1,000-megawatt power reactors sited along the banks of the Pripyat River, about sixty miles north of Kiev in the Ukraine, the fertile grain-producing region of the southwestern USSR. A fifth reactor was under construction.

All the Chernobyl reactors were of a design that the Russians call the RBMK—natural uranium-fueled, water-cooled, graphite-moderated—a design that American physicist and Nobel laureate Hans Bethe has called "fundamentally faulty, having a built-in instability." Because of the instability, an RBMK reactor that loses its coolant can under certain circumstances increase in reactivity and run progressively faster and hotter rather than shut itself down. Nor were the Chernobyl reactors protected by containment structures like those required for U.S. reactors, though they were shielded with heavy concrete covers.

Without question, the accident at Chernobyl was the result of a fatal combination of ignorance and complacency. "As members of a select scientific panel convened immediately after the...accident," writes Bethe, "my colleagues and I established that the Chernobyl disaster tells us about the deficiencies of the Soviet political and administrative system rather than about problems with nuclear power."

The immediate cause of the Chernobyl accident was a mismanaged electrical-engineering experiment. Engineers with no knowledge of reactor physics were interested to see if they could draw electricity from the turbine generator of the Number 4 reactor unit to run water pumps during an emergency when the turbine was no longer being driven by the reactor but was still spinning initially. The engineers needed the reactor to wind up the turbine; then they planned to idle it to 2.5 percent power. Unexpected electrical demand on the afternoon of April 29 delayed the experiment until eleven o'clock that night. When the experiment finally started, they felt pressed to make up for lost time, so they reduced the reactor's power level too rapidly. That mistake caused a rapid buildup of neutron-absorbing fission by products in the reactor core, which poisoned the reaction. To compen-

Occupational crimes are secretive violation of laws regarding work activities.

sate, the operators withdrew a majority of the reactor's control rods, but even with the rods withdrawn, they were unable to increase the power level to more than 30 megawatts, a low level of operation at which the reactor's instability potential is at its worst and that the Chernobyl plant's own safety rules forbade.

At that point, writes Russian nuclear engineer Grigori Medvedev, "there were two options: increasing the power immediately, or waiting twenty-four hours for the poisons to dissipate. [Deputy chief engineer Dyatlov] should have waited...But he [had an experiment to conduct and he] was unwilling to stop...He ordered an immediate increase in the power of the reactor." Reluctantly the operators complied. By 1 a.m. on April 26, they stabilized the reactor at 200 megawatts. It was still poisoned and increasingly difficult to control. More control rods came out. A minimum reserve for an RBMK reactor is supposed to be 30 control rods. At the end, the Number 4 unit was down to only six control rods, with 205 rods withdrawn.

The experimenters allowed this dangerous condition to develop even though they had deliberately bypassed and disconnected every important safety system, including the emergency core-cooling system. They had also disconnected every backup electrical system, down to and including diesel generators, that would have allowed them to operate the reactor controls in the event of an emergency.

At 1:23 in the morning, the engineers proceeded with their experiment by shutting down the turbine generator. That reduced the electrical supply to the reactor's water pumps, which in turn reduced the flow of cooling water through the reactor. In the coolant channels within the graphite-uranium fuel core, the water began to boil.

Graphite facilitates the fission chain reaction in a graphite reactor by slowing neutrons. Coolant water in such a reactor absorbs neutrons, thus acting as a poison. When the coolant water in the Number 4 Chernobyl unit began turning to steam, that change of phase reduced its density and made it a less effective neutron absorber. With more neutrons becoming available and few control rods inserted to absorb them, the chain reaction accelerated. The power level in the reactor began to rise.

The operators noticed the power surge and realized they needed to reduce reactivity quickly by inserting more control rods. They hit the red button of the emergency power-reduction system. Motors began driving all 205 control rods as well as the emergency protection rods into the reactor core.

But the control rods had a design flaw that now proved deadly: their tips were made of graphite. The graphite tips attached to a hollow segment one meter (3.28 feet long), which attached in turn to a five-meter absorbent segment. When the 205 control rods began driving into the surging Number 4 reactor, the graphite tip went in first. Rather than reduce the reaction, the graphite tips increased it. The control rods displaced water from the rod channels as well, increasing reactivity further. All hell broke loose—The reactor exploded.

The explosion was chemical, driven by gases and steam generated by the core runaway, not by nuclear reactions; no commercial nuclear reactor contains a high enough concentration of U-235 or plutonium to cause a nuclear explosion. Medvedev, who had once worked at Chernobyl and who was on the scene within days, describes the explosion from the testimony of eyewitnesses.

Flames, sparks, and chunks of burning material went flying into the air above the Number 4 unit. These were red-hot pieces of nuclear fuel and graphite, some of which fell onto the roof of the turbine hall where they started fires...About 50 tons of nuclear fuel evaporated and were released by the explosion into the atmosphere...In addition, about 70 tons were ejected sideways from the periphery of the core, mingling with a pile of structural debris, onto the roof...and also onto the grounds of the plant...

Some 50 tons of nuclear fuel and 800 tons of reactor graphite...remained in the reactor vault, where it formed a pit reminiscent of a volcanic crater. (The graphite still in the reactor burned up completely in the next few days.)

Coolant water in such a reactor absorbs neutrons, thus acting as a poison. When the coolant water in the Number 4 Chernobyl unit began turning to steam, that change of phase reduced its density and made it a less effective neutron absorber. With more neutrons becoming available and few control rods inserted to absorb them, the chain reaction accelerated. The power level in the reactor began to rise.

The resulting radioactive release, Medvedev estimates, was equivalent to ten Hiroshimas. In fact, since the Hiroshima bomb was an airburst—no part of the fireball touching the ground—the Chernobyl release polluted the countryside much more than ten Hiroshimas would have done.

No commercial reactor in the United States is designed anything like the RBMK reactor. Cohen summarizes several of the differences:

1. A reactor which is unstable against a loss of water could not be licensed in the United States.
2. A reactor which is unstable against a temperature increase could not be licensed here.
3. A large power reactor without a containment [structure] could not be licensed here.

The absence of a containment structure is especially important. As Cohen point out about Chernobyl, "Post-accident analyses indicate that if there had been a U.S.-style containment, none of the radioactivity would have escaped, and there would have been no injuries or deaths."

But if the design of Russian and U.S. reactors is critically different, broad similarities between the two countries' management of nuclear-power development led both national programs into difficulty. In the U.S.S.R., writes Medvedev, "the ordinary citizen was made to believe that the peaceful atom was virtually a panacea and the ultimate in genuine safety, ecological cleanliness, and reliability." He quotes Soviet scientists and managers who waxed as enthusiastic in the heyday of nuclear power development as the U.S. AEC's Lewis Strauss. "Nuclear power stations are like stars that shine all day long!" academician M.A. Styrikovich claimed in 1980. "We shall sow them all over the land. They are perfectly safe!" The deputy head of the State Committee on the Utilization of Nuclear Energy, notes Medvedev, told the Soviet people that "nuclear reactors are regular furnaces, and the operators who run them are stokers"—an image corresponding to the glib coinage in the United States that nuclear power is "just another way to boil water."

Given such uninformed enthusiasm for technology, it isn't surprising that both the Soviet and U.S. nuclear power programs ran into difficulties, or that the difficulties in both cases were predominantly managerial. Nuclear power came to terrible disaster in the former Soviet Union because authority dominated there to the exclusion of informed technical discussion and judgment. "Accidents," writes Medvedev, "were hidden not only from the general public and the government but also from the people who worked at Soviet nuclear power stations. This latter fact posed a special danger, as failure to publicize mishaps always has unexpected consequences: it makes people careless and complacent."

Authority dominated in the early days of nuclear power in the United States as well. "The AEC and the JCAE," James Jasper notes, "placed themselves outside normal political accountability." Fortunately, both public and private sectors of the U.S. nuclear power industry learned the lessons of Three Mile Island and launched a major effort of improvement and regulation.

Three Mile Island and Chernobyl represent extreme instances of the problem that seems to trouble the American public more than any other about commercial nuclear power: its apparent danger. But risk is always relative. Friend and foe have estimated the relative risk of operating commercial nuclear power plants in the United States; their conclusions are instructive.

The most serious example of public exposure to radiation from a nuclear power plant is, of course, Chernobyl. The explosion at Chernobyl blew radioactive gas and dust high into the atmosphere, where winds dispersed it across Finland, Sweden, and central and southern Europe. "The sum if [Chernobyl] and exposures to people all over the world," writes Bernard Cohen, "will eventually, after about fifty years, reach 60 billion millirems, enough to cause about 16,000 deaths." (Millirem-mrem-is a measure of radioactivity; 1 mrem is estimated to increase one's risk of dying from cancer by about 1 in 4 million, corresponding to a reduction in life expectancy of about 2 minutes.) Cohen, a professor of physics and radiation health at the University of Pittsburgh, was responsible in the late 1980s for supervising the measurement of radon levels in some 350,000 U.S. homes. He puts Chernobyl's danger in context by pointing out that 16,000 deaths caused every year by air pollution from coal-burning power plants in the United States alone.

The rest of the world didn't choose to be irradiated by a badly designed and criminally misoperated Soviet nuclear power plant. Cohen's comparison is instructive but inappropriate. On the other hand, nuclear power serves useful purposes in the United States, and millions of Americans willingly buy the electricity that nuclear utilities generate. It ought to be appropriate to put nuclear-generated electricity in the context of other acceptable risks Americans take in the name of productivity, comfort, and convenience. Cohen does so, to startling effect:

RESPONSIBILITIES OF ENGINEERS

In the previous chapter the concepts of social experimentation, were discussed. In the beginning of this chapter we looked at the safety and risk and now move forward to responsibilities of the engineers. It is said that people with character accept responsibilities. Accepting responsibilities involves taking calculated and *not* foolish risks and being accountable. It means evaluating all the pros and cons of a situation. The focus in this chapter is on both internal and external responsibilities, which means responsibilities to employers and to the outside world respectively. It also examines issues of conflict, their causes and conflict resolution.

INTERNAL RESPONSIBILITIES

Imagine how many engineers would have worked as a team for how many years to build the *Titanic* and the *Challenger*! How many engineers are working in L & T, Infosys, and Wipro today! Team play is very important in experimentation and successfully building organizations. Team play involves, affection and respect for one another and a helping attitude. All the members of a team do not have the same capabilities. Just as our hand has five fingers of different sizes, a team consists of different types of people. Their individual goals need to be subordinated to the group's goals. Responsibilities herein are just as much professional responsibilities as those owed to public. Team play involves virtues of collegiality, loyalty, respect for authority and collective bargaining.

Collegiality

The central elements of collegiality are respect, commitment, connectedness and cooperation.

In Chapter II, we discussed the theory of respect. Respect is valuing one's peers for their professional expertise and their devotion to the social good promoted by the profession. This means affirming the worth of other engineers engaged in producing socially useful and safe products. Collegial respect is reciprocal. Commitment means sharing a devotion to the moral ideals inherent in the practice of engineering. Even when there is fierce competition, there should be a feeling that other engineers share a concern for the overall good. The underlying values are beyond just winning. Shiv Khera points out that *Greed, Fear* and *Pressure* affect our ethical values. Pressure to perform cannot justify unethical acts

Connectedness is the awareness of being part of a larger business system created by shared commitments and expertise. It is more than showing respect for peers. This sense of unity with other engineers evokes co-operation and support. It leads to net working. Collegiality is a virtue that strengthens one's motivation to live upto professional standards. It encourages shared values and is an essential character trait.

Loyalty

Loyalty is more than 'obligation' or 'duty', which are more specific. Obligation and duty are more 'formal responsibility' oriented. Their base is legal and positional. By contrast, loyalty is more a function of attitudes, emotions and a sense of identity. People may hate the job that they do and not like their employer, but they would still perform their duty as long as they are employees. Can they be automatically considered loyal? Which is a more desirable character attribute?

The relationship between engineers and employers is coming under increasing scrutiny in recent years. There are moral issues involved in the sense that loyalty to one's employer is considered by many as being more important than loyalty to the public. Engineers oftentimes have to choose between the two. In such situations what should he choose? Loyalty is important to an employer and it would be expected of all employees when they work for the him. A U.S. Court gives the definition of loyalty thus: "we have read into every contract of employment and it is an implied duty that an employee is to act solely for the benefit of his or her employer in all matters within the scope of employment."

This definition is useful because it tries to define the scope of activities a loyal employee should fulfill, as well as emphasize that the employee should work for the benefit of the company. Asking an individual to perform illegal activities for a firm would not be to the firm's long-term advantage since any illegal action would ultimately harm the firm.

Loyalty to the Company and Responsibility to the Public

The responsibility of an engineer to the public is paramount, many opine. However, it is too much to expect that obligation to the public should always override obligation to one's employer. Both obligations are important. When they come into conflict, it is necessary to examine the specific situation before deciding which ought to take precedence.

A professional's concern for public welfare may often place him in opposition to his employer. Many cases illustrating this conflict come from the engineering profession, since approximately 90 percent of engineers are employees. However, the employee rights issue is sure to become more widespread in all professional ranks. More physicians are being employed and many lawyers work for corporations and large legal firms. Chartered accountants work for accounting firms and corporations, and so do management accountants. Professionals are increasingly subject to organizational conflicts. The problems posed by the professional's rights at the work place are complex, because employers do have the legitimate right to expect loyalty, confidentiality and obedience from their employees, including professional employees. What rights should professionals have against employers?

We will begin this discussion accepting that all employees, including professional employees, owe unqualified loyalty to their employers. In a well-known article, Samuel Florman, an engineer, is concerned about what he calls "the deceptive platitude that a professional's primary obligation is to the public." According to him, the three problems that would develop from this 'platitude' are:

> First, ties of loyalty and discipline would dissolve, and blowing the whistle on one's superiors would become the norm instead of the last resort.
>
> Second, any engineer who declines a commission in deference to his scruples, furthermore, will only pass it along to a colleague of less refined sensibility.
>
> Third, as a class,engineers will have neither the ability nor the right to plan social change.

Florman's first criticism is directed especially at safety and risk issues. An engineer may want to introduce more safety features in a product, and management may not. It is obvious that any product can be made safer by adding more features. But there is a point where the costs of adding additional safety features would make manufacturing the product not worth the while. It is necessary to reach a confidence level where overt risks are dealt with, yet not all risks.

Florman is correct in remarking that if every engineer constantly demanded more protection for the public, no product would ever get out of a factory. There has to be some point where management can go ahead with a product. Florman's argument suggests that bickering and conflict would occur most of the time, or at least enough to be problematic, *Yet the claim that conflict would become the 'norm', as Florman suggests, is not necessarily true.* Secondly, there is a value to a corporation in having its employees bringing to its attention an obviously faulty product. It is hard to see how this type of behavior would harm the firm.

Now let us consider Florman's second argument. The fact that a second engineer might perform an immoral act refused by the first does not legitimize it. Immoral behavior will occur at times, nothing can prevent that. If enough engineers stood by their professional codes and refused to act immorally, Florman's second fear would be unfounded.

Now let us consider Florman's third criticism. What is an engineer's role in public policy issues? Broadly there are two shades of public policy issues. The first type involves deciding on alternative strategies, which will affect the public. An example would be the decision whether to build a nuclear power plant or not. A nuclear power engineer has neither the responsibility for deciding whether his company should build nuclear power plants, nor the responsibility for deciding whether the government should ban them. Florman is correct – engineers do not have responsibility for this type of decision. They can advise, but persons to whom the public has given the responsibility must make the decision.

There is a second type, a kind of obligation. Herein assurances are given to the public that whatever is done will be done within professional standards. Here an engineer does have an obligation to the public. It is necessary to distinguish between "solving problems and establishing goals." Goals are public policy decisions, and should be set by those given the power to do so. But engineers must uphold professional standards even when their employers object.

Let us now look at a couple of instances to understand the conflict between commitments:

(a) A policeman's wife is on her deathbed. He is by her side when he gets a call to handle a crime emergency where ten lives are at stake. What should he do?

(b) A surgeon is on his way to attend his only daughter's graduation, once in a lifetime event, which he had promised to attend. Minutes before the start of the ceremony, he gets an urgent call to operate on an accident victim to save his life. What choice does he have?

Choosing one option does not mean a lack of commitment to the other. The process of choosing between the two commitments involves priorities, responsibility and duty. Value based priorities help us to choose one commitment over the other. The issue is to whom do we owe our loyalties? Is it to an individual or the organizations? The answer is neither. We owe loyalties to values. Where value systems are conflicting, people find it difficult to co-exist in the work place.

Respect for authority

Authority relationships between employers and employees are normally necessary for avoiding the negative effects of unlimited individual discretion. An employment contract constitutes a promise on the part of employees to recognize legitimate institutional authority. The obligation to obey authoritative directives should not be considered as an obligation to suspend one's critical faculties and blindly follow those directives regardless of their moral content. Institutional authority is the right of employers and managers to exercise power so employees will meet their institutional duties, and is morally justified only where the goals of the institution are morally permissible and when the way in which it is exercised does not violate other moral duties.

A subordinate accepts his superior's authority. He holds in abeyance, his own critical faculties for choosing between alternatives and uses the formal criterion of the receipt of a command or signal as the basis for choices. This means that professionals should accept their superior's suggestions and orders without any critical review or consideration. At most, their reasoning should be aimed at anticipating commands by asking themselves how the superior would wish them to behave in given circumstances. All employees have limits to what they will accept from their employers, but within these limits the employee finds as relaxing his own critical faculties and permitting his behavior to be guided by the decision of his superior, without independently examining the merits of that decision. These claims for a virtually complete sacrifice of employee autonomy need a strong justification. A doctor who is told by his/her superior to watch costs (a legitimate request) is not in the same situation as a doctor requested to cut costs by not performing certain required procedures. The problem is whether limits can be set for professionals. The institutional authority is acquired, exercised and defined within the institution. It is an institutional right given to a person to exercise power based on the resources of the institution. Many codes of ethics state that the engineer's paramount obligation is to protect the public health, safety and welfare rather than the obligation of loyalty and faithful service to employers.

Apart from institutional authority, there is an authority because of the knowledge and expertise. The institutional authority should not be equated with expert authority. Expert authority is the possession of specialist knowledge, skill or competence to perform some task or to give sound advice. It is better to understand the difference between power and authority. Power is effective and goes beyond the authority. A highly respected engineer of proven integrity may have power within an organization exceeding institutional authority. Power is more related to influence. A leader, formal or informal, has more power.

Perceptually, there is a close relationship between the respect for authority and loyalty. It is assumed that higher the respect for authority, higher is the loyalty. Both are in a continuum and hence involve different degrees. But let us not confuse between these two concepts. Loyalty to the company should not be equated with obeying all orders of one's immediate supervisor. Acting for public commitment is more responsible than loyalty to the organization or employers. An engineer should remember that he has also responsibility to his colleagues, subordinates, public, and customers.

Collective bargaining

Collective bargaining is a process, which is used by companies to solve interpersonal problems between them and their employees. There are legal provisions for this system. It adopts a negotiation process. It has been dealt with under techniques of conflict resolution. An employer and his employees come together and sign an agreement which is to be honored by both the parties. Some guidelines for the negotiation process:

- Attack problems and not people
- Build Trust
- Start with a discussion and analysis of the interests, concerns, needs and whys of each party. Begin with interests, not positions or solutions.
- Listen
- Brainstorm; suggesting an idea does not mean one agrees with it. Develop multiple options.
- Use objective criteria whenever possible. Agree on how something will be measured.

Collective bargaining assumes 'unionism'. Every organization employing more than 20 persons could have a union. In some organizations, they have a single union. . More than one is also permitted. There may be formal and informal. Often employees may feel that employers are exploiting and cheating them. Unions are formed to take care of the interests of employees. There are engineering unions in organisations that have many engineers working. Some high level professional managers view Unions as a threat. Unions should be viewed as conduits for the expression of collective will. They have lot of bargaining power due to size. Unions can often prevent unethical acts of the employers. They give job security and protection against ill treatment.

Some professionals oppose unionism and feel that it goes against the principle of loyalties and respect for authority. There are arguments for and against unionism. Unions may go on strike. Many codes of ethics are against strikes. The issue is whether unions and collective bargaining practices are ethical or unethical. For example, a small-scale engineering firm employing 120 persons was on high growth stage with a 120% growth rate. When the eyes were on growth, certain signals from the employees were not taken notice of by the employers. In the hunger for growth, they missed feeling the pulse of dissatisfaction. The employers thought that growth was in the interest of all. Diploma engineers formed a union. An external union leadership entered the scene. They demanded a lot of amenities that the company could ill afford. Lot of time was expended on bargaining. The employees went on a 'go slow' strike. Production suffered, and the company's performance went down. The company had to be sold and the buyer closed down the company. All of them lost their jobs and livelihood. The union did not realize what they were doing was against their own interest. By the time they realized it was too late. For getting short-term gains, they lost long term benefits. The external union took care of them with some subsistence payments initially, but later that also stopped. In this case who is to be blamed?

EXTERNAL RESPONSIBILITIES

The issues with outside world involve confidentiality, conflict of interest and occupational crimes.

Confidentiality

Keeping confidence is one of the most central and widely acknowledged duties of any professional. Confidentiality implies that a communication is kept secret and will remains private. A person reveals sensitive information to another only because of the trust that the disclosed information will remain private and confidential. In codes of ethics of societies/associations, there are explicit rules requiring their members to maintain total confidentiality of any privileged information they are in possession of. A piece of information/communication that is conveyed to someone else with the expectancy that it will remain private is privileged. Anything disclosed which other people can have access to through other means is not. Ethical rules do not attempt to prevent general gossip. They cover only secrets revealed to professionals during professional work. Some laws protect professional confidence while there are other laws forcing the betrayal of confidentiality. Such situations create ethical dilemmas for the professions and professionals.

In case of engineers, design and drawings, process charts etc. are to be kept confidential. More so for consultants. We have a case in Chapter VI on this issue. What is confidential and what is not is the ethical question. One solution is to have a professional explain to the client in advance before commencing the work

When employees shift or change jobs, it is important not to leak out confidential information. This means that confidentiality does not cease when employees change jobs. Thus the relationship of trust between employer and employee in regard to confidentiality continues beyond the formal period of employment.

We have numerous cases like that of Sundeep Vani (See earlier Chapter) who face such situations. Many engineers value professional advancement more than long-term ties with any one company and so change jobs frequently. Engineers in research and development are especially likely to have trade secrets. Maintaining confidentiality is easier said than done.

Employers insist on specific undertakings before relieving employee from their jobs to prevent leakage of confidential information. Mr. Mordechal Vanunu, one of the world's best known whistle blowers, had to spend18 years in the Israeli prisons for leaking out secrets about Israel's nuclear weapon programmes till his release recently.

Texas Instruments provides guidance to its engineers to deal with the moral and ethical dilemmas through its website. Following situations have been taken from the. Website: http://onlineethics.org

Maintaining confidentiality is easier said than done.

The Responsibility for Safety and the Obligation to Preserve Client Confidentiality : Tenants sue their building's owner, and the owner employs an engineer who finds structural defects not mentioned in the tenant's lawsuit. Conflicting issues involve public safety versus client confidentiality.

Code Violations with Safety Implication : An engineer discovers deficiencies in a building's electrical and mechanical systems. It would breach client confidentiality (and the contract) to report them to a third party, but the engineer also has a responsibility to public safety.

Whistle blowing City Engineer : An engineer privately informs other city officials of an environmental threat, a problem her supervisor has ordered her not to disclose. The engineer is taken from the case, but is still advising another technician on the situation. The engineer has an obligation to both the supervisor of the company and to the public for the environmental health of the residents.

A Defense engineer blew the whistle , by taking objections to a subcontractor's poor performance. These objections were ignored and silenced by management. Under the circumstances what is the responsibility of Defense Engineer ?

Reporting : A engineer has signed an agreement with his employer to keep the hazardous information . He is confronted with a choice between keeping the secret or inform the public. The former is regarding keeping the information secret and later is in the public interest. As in the previous case, the responsibility of engineer is towards public and employer.

Recommendation letter: There is a conflict faced by a engineer when he has to write a recommendation letter for his friend who is another engineer. The letter is called by Board of Ethical Review (BER) . Should he write any negative comments about other engineer

A group of engineers leave their employer to start their own firm. The new firm contacts clients from their former employer. They start criticizing the capability of the other firm in providing competent services. The clients doubt the promotion done by the former company. Should engineers go to the clients of the former employers?

A engineer working in the public welfare department of Government defies immediate supervisor because he believes supervisor's instruction would pose an environmental health hazard.

Similarly a engineer working in a private firm is faced with a situation of Public welfare. To protect the interest of client, his supervisor orders to dispose hazardous waste.

Using Company Resources.: XYZ Corporation permits its employees to borrow company tools. Engineer took full advantage of this privilege. He went one step further and ordered tools for his unit that would be useful for his home building projects even though they were of no significant use to his unit at XYZ.

Conflict of interests

Conflict of interests is a situation in which two or more interests are not simultaneously realizable. In pursuing their lives, individuals establish goals and put into practice plans to achieve them. A goal to which an individual is committed is commonly called and 'interest' of that individual. Not all goals can be achieved. Individuals can set impossible goals that conflict with the nature of reality. For example, a student of below average intelligence setting the goals of getting A's in all his courses while working a full time job and playing a sport. Individuals can set goals that conflict with the goals of other individuals. For example, a burglar's goal of stealing gold jewellery is in conflict with the owner's goal of keeping it.

Professional conflicts of interest are situations where professionals have an interest, which if pursued might keep them from meeting their obligations to their employers or clients. Sometimes

Conflict of interest cannot be avoided.
Kickbacks imply conflicts of interest.

such an interest involves serving in some other professional role, say, as a consultant for a competitor's company. Other times it is a more personal interest, such as making substantial private investments in a competitor's company. This threat to meeting professional obligations makes it clear why conflict of interest has been given prominence in the codes of ethics in engineering, law and management. Conflict of interests may cause impairment in judgment and moral decisions. It is said that conflict of interests can arise under two conditions (1) the professional is in a relationship that requires exercising good judgment on behalf of the employer or client and (2) the professional has some additional or side interest that could threaten good judgment in serving the interests of the employer or client.

Conflict of interest can also arise in professional agent/client relationships – a consultant engineer hired by two clients with conflicting interests or a corporate director who is offered a job in a government agency that regulates his corporation. Professional-agent conflicts of interests raise moral concern because such conflicts make it more difficult for the agent to be objective in evaluating the interests of both sides, thus clients are less certain that the agent will act in their best interests.

Conflict of interest cannot be avoided; this is the law of nature. Conflict of interests is fundamental and it can be settled only by someone's interests having being sacrificed. Since conflict of interests is more fundamental to human relationships than ethics is about resolving conflict. Ethics is about deciding whose interests must be sacrificed. It should also identify and fulfill legitimate interests.

Employees have various obligations to their employees. Conflicts of interest arise when employees have a personal interest in a transaction substantial enough that it does, or might reasonably be expected to lead them to act against the interests of the organization. Conflict of interests arises due to a) Financial investments, b) Insider Trading, c) Bribe, d) Gifts, and e) Kickbacks. Let us look at each one of them briefly:

1. ***Financial investments***: Conflict of interests will arise because of financial investments in a competitors' or subsidiaries business. Unethical decisions are taken because of personal or organizational interest. For example, if you are an engineer and chief executive of a firm and another firm which has bid for a large project of your company. You have a financial stake in that firm which has bid for it. You have to decide to whom to award the contract? The tendency will be to award the bid to the company where you have stakes. Is it ethical? Under what situation it will be regarded as an ethical decision?
2. ***Insider trading***: This involves using privileged information unfairly. It may be done deliberately or innocently by slip of the tongue. When you are working for a company, you could have access to confidential information which others would not be privy to. If such information relates to the financial performance of the company and you use it to trade in the shares of the company, this would be considered insider trading. This happens often in the corporate world. As a senior executive of the company, is it right for you to do this? Is it ethical or unethical?
3. ***Bribes***: A bribe is a substantial amount of money or goods offered beyond a stated business contract with the aim of gaining an advantage. Bribes are generally given in secret. Bribes are illegal or immoral because they threaten fairness in competitive situations. Bribes are substantial unlike gratuities which are of smaller amounts. Traditionally, certain types of gratuities have been recognised as legitimate in the normal conduct of business, while others can bias judgment like a bribe does. There is no universally accepted definition of what constitutes a bribe. Many people regard a 'kickback' as a 'commission' for services rendered and not as a bribe. A gift of a new BMW after the conclusion of a deal may be viewed in many societies as an expression of gratitude rather than as bribe, even if some degree of *quid pro quo* is implied. A bribe signifies that the executive is serious and will behave himself to avoid upsetting a relationship in which he has invested. Bribes, therefore,

Conflict problem involves two or more moral principles.

may not be seen as corrupting although it should be noted that there is loss of face when exposed. Bribery is certainly corrupting when it occurs in rule-based societies or does not contribute to relationships that are essential to making the systems work.

4. ***Gifts***: Gifts are not bribes as long as they are small gratuities offered in the normal conduct of business. Often companies give gifts to selected employees of various government agencies they deal with or partners in trade. Many such gifts are unobjectionable. However, expensive gifts are intended as bribes, and still others create conflicts of interest that do not, strictly speaking, involve bribe. What is the difference? In theory these distinctions may seem clear but in practice they become blurry.

5. ***Kickbacks***: Prearranged payments made by contractors to companies or their representation in exchange for contracts actually granted are called kickbacks A classic situation is that of a purchasing agent for a company or government. being offered a payment in exchange for a contract. In the West this is considered unethical, and perhaps illegal. In many countries it is business as usual. Kickbacks are seen as corrupting in the West because they imply a conflict of interest. The purchasing agent is supposed to represent the interests of his company. If the agent is taking payments, his or her own interests interfere. The proper procedure is to look at the bids, investigate the companies, and choose the best deal. If they do not, the supplier is guilty of fraud and can be taken to court. The business relationship is based primarily on a framework of rules that most people believe in and take seriously.

   In a different kind of society, business relationships are personal. Rather than doing business with a company, one does business with a person and the relationship is based on mutual trust, which might have been built over a long period. When things go wrong, it is no use to call a lawyer. The agent must rely upon his personal relationship with another human being. Because a major part of the agent's task is to establish this relationship, there is no conflict of interest in doing so. One way a supplier can demonstrate his commitment to the relationship is to put money on the line. If the supplier has paid for the relationship, he is less likely to vanish when there is a problem. The agent who receives a kickback is therefore doing his job. Written contracts are traditionally not part of this process, because the concept of a contract presupposes an overarching framework of rules and laws that enforce the contract. Many people around the world do not believe in the legitimacy of any such framework, because they are not universalists as Westerners are. They regard it a piece of paper just. Any kind of enforceability must be based on flesh and blood, on a relationship of mutual trust and commitment between human beings. Since most modern businesses have accepted the Western practice of written contracts, some interesting anomalies result. For example, in some countries (e.g., Egypt), it is customary to write 'kickbacks' into the contract.

Conflict resolutions

As stated earlier, conflict is a struggle between at least two independent parties. Trust and a high level of ethical behaviour are essential for successful conflict resolutions. Arguments, yielding, yelling, stalling, threats, coercion are all images of conflict. There are three basic styles of conflict management: ***avoidance, competitive negotiation*** and ***principled negotiation***. Most people use more than one style, depending on the situation. Some people try to avoid dealing with conflict. In ***competitive negotiation,*** each party pressurizes the other to change. Control, coercion, threats, walkouts and lying are all approaches employed. It is a win-lose style. Both the parties come with their solution that is in their own interest. . This approach can be useful when the goal is more important than the relationship. Relationship is rarely improved by competitive negotiation. The goal has to be that important that one is willing to sacrifice the relationship. ***Principled negotiation*** calls for collaborative negotiation, but in a win-win style. It requires keen perception, good communication skills, creativity and most importantly trust.

Relevance and Conflict Problems

A moral issue involves doubts about the proper application of one or more moral principles to a situation. There are two common problems that we face in applying moral principles: **relevance** and **conflicting principles**. In a **relevance problem**, we are not sure as to which principle applies in a particular situation. For example, whether, applying a process you developed when you were working for Company A to a situation in Company B for whom you are working now, is use of proprietary information or not is a relevance problem. Its resolution depends on the resolution of the conceptual issue as to how we define "proprietary." In a **conflict problem**, we are faced with two or more principles, which apply to a particular situation, but the two principles would call for different and incompatible actions. For example, suppose an engineer feels that she has an obligation to stay with an employer who has been very supportive of her over a number of years, and at the same time she has a social urge to move to another company where she could participate in the development of environmentally safe products. Here she faces a conflict problem, because apparently either her obligation to her old employer or her urge to contribute her expertise to the development of environmentally safe products can be met.

A Method for Resolving Relevance Problems

Often, the answer to a conceptual issue provides the answer to a relevance problem as well. For example, the question whether the information the engineer used from his previous job to help Company B was "proprietary" or not is a relevance problem, but it depends on the definition of the term "proprietary." Once we know the definition of "proprietary" we can probably determine whether his action was wrong or not.

Since relevance problems arise when we encounter a situation in which the application of a concept is unclear, it makes sense to go back to situations in which the application of the concept was clear. Then, by comparing the similarities and differences between the situations, we can come to some conclusion about the propriety of applying the concept in the issue at hand. This method involves three steps.

First, set up a series of cases, ranging from a case where the concept clearly applies, through a series of ambiguous cases, to a case in which the concept clearly does not apply. Consider the situation described earlier. Since it is felt that using the information gained at Company A to help Company B with a new process is "theft of an idea" (and therefore wrong), it amounts to whether the information passed on is really "proprietary," The engineer should imagine a case where there is a clear transfer of proprietary information. We can call this the positive paradigm case, because it is a case in which the use of the term "proprietary" to describe the information that is transferred is clearly appropriate. Then he should imagine a case in which the term "proprietary" clearly is not appropriate as a description of the information that is transferred.

Second, the morally relevant similarities and differences among the various cases must be enumerated. There is no magic formula for determining what is and is not morally relevant. Rather, you must rely on your own sense of what is morally relevant. In case, for example, one of the characteristics of the positive paradigm case would probably be that it would give Company B a competitive edge over Company A. This is morally relevant because it relates directly to the fundamental reason that a company would want to keep certain information secret. Another characteristic of the positive paradigm case would be that exactly the same process is being transferred from Company A to Company B. By contrast, a negative paradigm case might be one in which there is no possibility of the transferred information putting Company A in an advantageous position with respect to Company B, and in which in fact the only transfer of "information" is in the limited sense that the original process started a chain of ideas in thinking that finally led to a new and creative process for Company B.

Professional ethics involves right, fairness, truth, perception, values and principles

Third, after enumerating the morally relevant similarities and differences in the various cases, you must determine the line of demarcation between transfers of information that should and should not be proprietary. In some instances this may be relatively easy to do, but in others no precise point of demarcation may present itself. This should not be surprising. Although we all recognize a difference between day and night, it may be difficult to say just when the point of transition from "day" to "night" occurs. Is it at 6:00 p.m.? Is it when we have to turn on the lights on our car? Is it when the evening news begins on T.V.? Is it when a trained observer can see the first star? Is it when a person with 20/20 vision can no longer see more than 20 feet ahead?

There may, of course, be different criteria for different purposes, but it is important to see that a certain amount of arbitrariness may be involved in setting the precise boundaries. This is not necessarily troublesome. It is no different from the situation in which we are attempting to find the point of demarcation between day and night. There is a clear difference between day and night, and there are many times which are either clearly day or clearly night. Nevertheless the precise point of demarcation may have to be established by convention. In the case of proprietary information, the courts ultimately establish these conventions. The conventions established by the courts may or may not be the most desirable from a moral standpoint, but in other areas there are no such conventions. In many cases, these conventions should be established by the professional community—for example, in determining how safe is safe enough.

Resolving Conflict Problems

Lata has a problem. A compound emitted from the stack of the plant where she is employed has been linked by several studies to respiratory problems that can be severe in a small percentage of the population. The Pollution Control Board(PCB) has not banned the compound, perhaps because it is relatively rare in industrial processes. Its elimination will be expensive, and it may force the elimination of the product line. This would lead to loss of a number of jobs in a small community that is heavily dependent on the plant for employment. An added dimension is that the product line could become very successful in the future, thus adding jobs in the community, which is in need of more jobs.

Lata's supervisor instructs her not to bring up the issue in hearings with the PCB officials. He believes he has a good chance of delaying any final action on the issue for several years at least, and by that time a modification in the process may eliminate the emission itself. He argues that the evidence for the health problems supposedly produced by the compound is questionable, and that the health problems are not fatal in any case. "I'm going to fight them as long as I can on this one," he says. How should Lata respond?

Lata finds herself in a conflict problem, pulled by two opposing obligations, both of which find justification in her professional code. On the one hand, the first Fundamental Canon" of the code of ethics of the National Society of Professional Engineers (NSPE) says: "Engineers shall hold paramount the safety, health and welfare of the public in the performance of their professional duties." On the other hand, the fourth Fundamental Canon of the NSPE code says, "Engineers shall act in professional matters for each employer or client as faithful agents or trustees." (Refer chapter VIII for the code of ethics).

Furthermore, the obligation to the public itself pulls her in two different directions. Lata rightly believes she has an obligation to protect the physical health of the community. But doesn't she have an obligation to be concerned with the economic health of the community as well? In fact, if the people of the community were asked to give advice to Lata they would probably side with the manager in advocating that the new product line be continued, with its promise of more jobs and wealth for the community. They would do this, even though they would also be the ones most likely to suffer

Engineers have to protect health and safety of the public

from the respiratory problems. This being the case, does Lata have a right to act in a paternalistic way toward her fellow employees, deciding that their economic well being is not as important as their health?

Conflicts between competing obligations, both of which appear to be valid, are common features of life. The conflicts that give us trouble are not those between good and bad, but between good and good, both of which cannot be fully realized. How should we approach such conflicts? Let us consider several ways in which conflict problems can be resolved.

1. *Finding the Creative Middle Way.*

When faced with two conflicting obligations, both of which appear to be justified, one approach is to try to find a way to satisfy both of them. While it is often not possible to satisfy both moral requirements in their original form, sometimes it is possible to satisfy them in a modified form. Now this may not seem possible, but we must not forget that most general moral rules have an "all other things being equal" qualification implicitly attached to them. Thus the first Fundamental Canon of the NSPE code should probably read, "All other things being equal, engineers shall hold paramount the safety, health and welfare of the public in the performance of their professional duties." But all things are often not equal. For example, the threat to the safety, health and welfare of the public may be both uncertain and minimal. That is, (1) whether or not the emissions are in fact harmful may itself be a matter of controversy, and (2) there is of yet, no evidence that the emissions produce fatal diseases, only significant respiratory problems in a certain small percentage of the population. Furthermore, as we have seen, the obligation to the community may include an obligation to its economic well-being. So the question is what in this case is Lata's obligation to the public.

This is not to say that Lata should unreservedly follow the instructions of her supervisor, for the same problem of specifying how the canon applies may apply to the Fourth Canon as well. What does it mean to act as "faithful agents and trustees" of one's employer? It cannot mean that the engineer is obliged to obey the employer no matter what the employer directs him to do. Virtually everyone would agree that an employee is not obligated to commit murder for an employer. Most people would probably agree that an employee does not have an obligation to vote in elections in accordance with what company management considers to be its best interests. Many would agree that employees do not have to observe a lifestyle that the employer considers "appropriate" for its employees. However, most would probably agree that the employee does have an obligation to be faithful and punctual in work attendance, to devote his energy and attention to the work assigned, and not to steal company property or use company property without permission.

The most obvious criterion for separating legitimate obligations of employees from illegitimate obligations is that the employee has an obligation to perform his assigned function in the workplace and not to do in his or her private life what interferes in a clear and direct way with on-the-job performance, unless a violation of an obligation to the public is involved. But one of the obligations to the public is surely protecting the health and safety of the public. This further explanation of the two norms means that they can be reconciled. According to these further specifications of the two guiding norms, if a product is a serious threat to the safety and health of the public and the employer orders the engineer to conceal this information, the engineer is obligated to disobey the employer, even if the employer is not breaking any law by concealing it.

However, the requirement for acting as "faithful agents and trustees" of the employer does seem to imply at least two limits on the actions of the employee. The first limitation is that the engineer should make his protests in as responsible a manner a possible. This requires respecting the corporate hierarchy where possible and making the protests in a private and non-confrontational way, if possible. The engineer should do everything possible to avoid embarrassing the employer and give the employer the opportunity to correct the problem, insofar as consideration of the well-being of the public permits. The second limitation is that the employee is not to protest about minor risks to the health and safety of the public, if these are in what we might call the normal range of risk.

There is an obvious way to minimize the conflict of these two norms. If there were a complaint mechanism whereby employees could register ethical concerns in a way that would be confidential and not embarrassing to the company, these two norms could be reconciled. If there is no such mechanism, Lata should try to find some way of raising her concerns to higher management in a confidential manner.

It is important to keep in mind that the encouragement to finding a creative middle way between the two norms is not necessarily a moral compromise. Remember that the two norms have great importance from a moral standpoint. If it is possible to still raise the concerns while not directly confronting her manager, Lata should probably take this option. The purpose of moral thinking is not to produce martyrs, but to satisfy as many moral concerns as possible.

2. *Employing Lower-Level Considerations.*

Let us suppose that Lata is unsuccessful in bringing her concerns to the attention of higher management. She feels, furthermore, that her obligation to be a "faithful agent and trustee" of her employer and her obligation to refrain from unnecessarily jeopardizing the jobs of other employees is about evenly balanced against the obligation to protect the public from a somewhat harmful emission. How can she decide?

Sometimes it is permissible in such situations to take into account considerations that might seem to be less relevant otherwise. Suppose you are considering hiring two engineers, one who is more skilled in one area and one in another. When the qualifications are evenly balanced in this way, you might be justified in bringing in other considerations that would not otherwise be relevant, such as the fact that one of the engineers is an avid tennis player. Since you also play tennis several times a week, you decide to choose the person who would make a good tennis partner. Such a consideration would not ordinarily be relevant, but in this case it might be.

Now carry this same logic over to Lata's case. If Lata really believes that her obligations are evenly balanced in this case, it may be justifiable to take into consideration which option is most likely to promote her career advancement. This is not to say that she has failed to consider her own well-being all along. After all, she is one of the employees who might loose her job if the plant closed. But if she observes her professional obligations as outlined in the NSPE code, she would not have made her personal well-being the decisive factor. Now, however, she may be justified in doing just that.

3. *Making the Hard Choice.*

It may not always be possible to reconcile opposing obligations or to drop down to a lower-level consideration. Sometimes no creative middle way is possible. For example, Lata may find that all the managers she approaches are unsympathetic to her concerns. She may also become convinced that the danger posed by the new emission is substantially more severe than she had at first supposed. In this case she may have to bring the issue before the PCB. She may be forced to make a hard choice.

Labeling a decision as an "ethical decision" may disguise the fact that almost every decision holds some ethical issue or impact. Perhaps a better approach would be to develop an ability to judge the ethical implications. What role do my ethics play in this decision? How do I recognize an ethical situation or problem? What are the warning signs that this may be a tougher decision with deeper issues and wider impact? Here are some guidelines from Texas Instruments (TI):

- Do I put a monetary value on this decision? Would I make this decision differently if cost were not a factor? Am I putting a monetary value on my ethics?

Responsibilities emerge from duties.

- Do words such as right, fairness, truth, perception, values, or principles appear in my reasoning when I am making my decision?
- Do I feel as if I need to search through TI's standard policies and procedures or contact a TI legal department representative for help with my decision?
- Do questions of fair treatment arise?
- Do my personal goals or values conflict with my professional ones?
- Could this decision generate strong feelings or other controversy?
- Would this pass the newspaper test? How would I feel if this were to appear in my local newspaper tomorrow?
- What does my heart tell me? Do I ponder this decision on the way home?
- Do I offer myself excuses such as everybody does it, or no one will find out, or I did it for TI?
- Does this decision really need to be made by someone else? Did I inherit it because someone else doesn't want to make it?
- How am I going to feel tomorrow if I do this?

If you face a tough decision and you feel as if you need help, there are many places to turn. Your supervisor or manager is generally the best for that is the one who understands your situation the best. But there are other sources of good information…the open door to higher levels of management. Know what's right. Do what's right.

Occupational crimes

Occupational crimes are illegal acts made possible through one's lawful employment. It is the secretive violation of laws regarding work activities. Many occupational crimes are specific instances of conflicts of interest, especially when the crime involves personal gain that constitutes or leads to the failure to meet professional obligations. Price fixing and industrial espionage are examples of occupational crimes. They impinge on various aspects of professionalism, loyalty, conflict of interests and confidentiality. Espionage is taken up in detail later on. Competitors come together and decide on the prices to be charged. These are called as pricing cartels. The price fixation leads to restraint of free competition and trade. It leads to unfair practices. Suppose the Government invites quotations for building a power plant. The companies, who quote for the work, come together and decide on the prices to be quoted. There are other instances of price fixation.

Endangering the lives of employees knowingly is yet another example of an occupational crime. An appropriate example is that of asbestos manufacture. Manville Corporation, a company manufacturing asbestos, knew that asbestos dust was harmful for the health of its employees. It could cause incurable lung cancer. For three decades, the company kept this information secret from the workers and the public who had the right to be informed. The company felt that as long as a man feels well, is happy at work, nothing was wrong. It was found that the asbestos related diseases developed after two to three months of exposure. It often led to nonmalignant asbestos disease or lung cancer. Many successfully filed cases to claim damages. Now companies manufacturing and selling asbestos have to take steps to protect their employees and mention the harmful effects of the product and prominently display the same in all advertisements and in shops selling asbestos. It is the same story in the case of cigarettes. It is mandatory to display prominently in all packages that cigarette smoking is injurious to health.

Espionage

This was covered briefly under occupational crimes. Now let us go a little more in depth into this. Espionage is secret gathering of information in order to influence relationships between two entities. It is clandestine in nature and is considered immoral. It may appear a bit contradictory that on the one hand we have the right to expression and information and on the other it is considered immoral to ferret out information. Since it involves 'stealing' of intellectual property rights, it is considered harmful and immoral.

Secrecy exists and is maintained for the advantage of one over another. Keeping information secret has always been an effective means of ensuring success. Keeping something secret is a right but acquisition of other's secret to your advantage is espionage which is not right and ethical. The element of secrecy is the distinction between standard intelligence gathering and espionage Most of the information is gathered overtly. Espionage, however, is carried out entirely in a covert manner. Espionage is the effort to discover by clandestine methods the secrets of others. It must be made clear that espionage is a secret act of information gathering and should not be confused with other covert activities such as sabotage and misinformation campaigns. In all forms of espionage, espionage agents called spies, who are trained and motivated individuals dedicated to their mission, carry out the act of secretly gathering vital information.

Engineers from one country or from one organization are sent out as spies. People who inform or sell information are traitors. A spy is required to conceal his own true identity and mission. They have to use some immoral tactics If caught, he has to deny his organizational affiliation. The ultimate goal of any spy is to steal secrets. For example, criminal acts like blackmail, bribery, coercion, burglary, murder are employed. This function is carried out in government and business organizations throughout the world. The practice is justified and accepted. Because of the clandestine nature of espionage and the fact that its ultimate goal is to steal secrets, it is perceived as most unethical and lawless activity. Using clandestine means to obtain secret information is ethically justifiable, however, if the end user of the gathered intelligence meets the goals and objectives of the society or organization in the larger interest. Espionage gathers the important information and places in the hands of authorities who use it to build a database of intelligence from which they can plan future decisions and actions. Almost all the countries and many companies have intelligence wings or set-ups for systematic gathering of the secret information.

Corporate Espionage—How Safe Are Corporate Secrets? (Source: the managementor)

Espionage is fast becoming a serious problem for corporates and causing immeasurable losses. Corporate or industrial espionage is the theft of trade secrets for economic gains. It involves theft of intellectual property such as designs, marketing plans, manufacturing processes, prototypes, formulas and software codes. The threat to businesses due to corporate espionage has been on the rise.

Some statistics American Society for Industrial Security has released statistics showing 589 occurrences of corporate espionage in 1,300 companies in the year 1996. The potential commercial value of this loss could be as much as USD 300 billion. In 1999, a survey by the American Society for Industrial Security and ***Price Waterhouse Coopers*** showed that Fortune 1,000 companies had lost more than $45 billion from the theft of trade secrets. A survey published by ***CSI/Federal Bureau of investigation (FBI)*** put the losses of US companies due to theft of proprietary property at more than USD 170 million for 2001! And this is a conservative figure, as 56 % of the companies surveyed did not report a figure. The ***White House Office of Science and Technology*** reports that corporate espionage costs US companies USD 100 billion per year in lost sales.

Assessing losses

It is difficult to find accurate statistics on corporate espionage for obvious reasons. No company wants to admit that it was a victim of corporate espionage. They are afraid that such a statement acknowledging a breach in their security would cause their stock price to plunge.

A bank in a similar position would be afraid of a detailed scrutiny of its policies and systems from the federal government. Small businesses are afraid of their trade partners halting any further business on learning about a lapse in security.

Who is a spy?

Any person with access to confidential information having present or future value is a suspect for corporate spying. According to estimates 85 % of corporate espionage crimes are committed by—

Rights, duties and responsibilities go together.
The motivation for the action must be mandated by professional ethics.

employees. A newly hired person could be a competitor's man. A disgruntled employee may go to your competitor with vital information he already knows, or has specifically gathered. The janitor or a member of cleaning staff may be bribed to hide a microphone in the conference room.

Other 'spies' could be independent contractors and consultants. Joint ventures are another danger-zone. The 1997 National Science and Technology Strategy has warned that technology transfers in the course of joint ventures with foreign companies raise concerns of economic and national security.

Travelling employees inadvertently become targets of corporate espionage. They continually complain about suspicious activities aimed at collecting information from them. There may be numerous cases of copying information from laptop computers, or even stealing of laptops.

What is the danger?

Corporate espionage poses a severe risk to any company's business. The various records that can be gathered to use against a company can include

- *Client lists:* These could be sold to a competitor or a sales person can use the information to start his own company. This would affect the profitability of the company.
- *Personnel records*: This information helps a rival to target or lure away key persons in the organizational structure. This would affect the processes in the company and hamper smooth functioning of work. It also results in important information being robbed through those employees who are lured away.
- *Research documents*: A company spends numerous hours and plenty of money in research. When the fruits of this hard labour get stolen, the company is robbed not only of the information, but unlimited resources and returns due on such investments. ***Four Pillars Consulting*** managed to steal ***Avery Dennison's*** technique of manufacturing adhesive diaper tags and saved years of experimentation and took away almost USD10 million in R&D from Avery.

Prototype plans: A prototype plan created for a new service or product contains valuable information about how the company plans to launch it, the marketing plans, the financial plans and other important information. This would be very valuable to a rival planning a similar launch as he could easily devise ways to counter it.

Pilferage of any such information can prove disastrous to the company besides providing vast monetary benefits to unscrupulous competitors. Also, this information can be used to commit scams and frauds like credit card defaults, extortion, blackmail or malice towards the company and/or its employees.

Contemporary Trends

With the advent of the Internet and computerisation of all data, espionage is also going hi-tech. In today's digital age anyone can copy information onto a floppy and e-mail it to an anonymous e-mail account to be retrieved later. Along with newer technologies of safeguarding information, are coming newer ways of breaching this security. Corporates and hackers are using newer technologies every day. It is important that corporates be aware of the technologies and practices being used against them.

The market has many high-speed storage devices with capacities measurable in gigabytes, but small enough to fit on a key-chain! These are increasingly becoming the preferred storage devices for corporate-information collectors. Chip designer ***ARM Ltd.*** is going to add high-security features to its processors to increase security of its smart-phones and wireless data services. Several models of ***IBM Think Pads*** come with integrated security chips and security software capable of locking data stored on a laptop. IBM is also launching a video security system to work in combination with the company's security infrastructure. This will help to identify patterns of security breaches quickly. These can also be used to review images of people accessing particular areas.

Companies can take various steps to counter espionage with technology. But, technology can always be breached. Hackers and spies find innovative ways to achieve their ends. For example, one surveillance application that is favoured by spies captures keystrokes, screen images and instant-messages. A wide scope of data can be collected through these and information including passwords, diagrams and documents may be compromised.

As long as a business is prepared to counter it, espionage can be controlled to a great extent. But withholding information, locking computer systems and frequently changing passwords can help the company, only to a certain extent.

The question remains, can a foolproof method be developed to safeguard a company's information from unwanted elements? The search continues.

The Bhopal Gas Tragedy Case

Many Decembers ago, there was a leak of poison gas from the Union Carbide Plant in Bhopal. Deadly methyl isocynate was inadvertently leaked into the atmosphere killing more than 20,000 people in the city of Bhopal. The parent company was held accountable for its actions. The company had to pay for the medical care of the survivors and their children, as well as a massive environmental cleanup. It was a case of corporate crime. Next chapter deals with this case in detail.

ALIGNMENT OF INDIVIDUAL – GROUP – ORGANISATIONAL VALUES

Alignment is the name of the game in business today. Every top-level executive is involved in alignment. Alignment brings order in the organization. There are bound to be differences of opinion among individuals and within groups, which have to be accepted as natural behavior. A leader is a person, who understands this and inspires people, and drives the organization towards a common goal

Alignment is a continuous process. The values of individual, group and organization differ and hence alignment becomes necessary. The issue is how one can successfully carry on the process of alignment. The process involves:

1. Constant two-way communication from top to bottom and bottom to top. What do you communicate? The organizational values need to be communicated clearly. In the first stage, create widespread awareness about the organizational values. Establish firm guidelines on 'Do's and Don'ts' within the organization. This helps in conveying to all the organizational expectations and areas of alignment. Induction training, which is usually given at the time of a person joining the organization, should cover organizational ethics. Formation of ethical committees like it, is being done in Wipro, Tata Group, Hindustan Lever etc.. helps in taking care of ethics in the organization. The ethics is promoted, nurtured and encouraged.
2. The whistle blowers are to be protected. These are the people who bring to the notice of employer, any unethical actions.
3. Like Texas Instruments , have consultation to resolve moral and ethical issues faced by the employees. When caught in a dilemma, an employee can contact the center and get moral support and help to resolve the conflict.
4. In some organizations Ethics Manuals are made available to employees. Some of them go into specific details such as "a long distance call to family from abroad is permitted only if the stay is above 3 days." Such manuals also clearly lay down the punishments for ethics violations.

Professional employees must be granted rights in the work place.

5. In the organization structure itself, there could be positions for ethics, just as you have Finance, Production etc.
   (Refer to the Annexure at the end of the chapter for Texas Instruments)

Case 1:

Ganga is a software engineer working for Alseac Technologies. She was thrilled to receive a job offer from their competitor, Novatex Systems, whom she greatly admired both as an industry leader and as an ideal employer. The position that was offered was just what she had always wanted. She discussed the offer with her husband Vish. He raised couple of questions, which began to trouble her.

He asked her about the big project that she had been working on. He reminded her that she was the driving force behind the project. He said, if you leave Alseac now, they could be in big trouble. Vish wondered whether her leaving would not be a let down to the company and the whole project team.

Vish reminded her about her criticizing their friend who had joined a competitor firm and taken away the accounts from his previous employer. Ganga had done well in Alseac and the company had treated her well. The issue is what is right for you to do, and not what the company would or would not do. Both are competing firms. It's like switching sides. It's not just loyalty to the company, but to the people you work with.

Novatex needed somebody right away. But they gave her some more time to think about the offer It was a big opportunity as far as she was concerned.

Her conversations with Vish had troubled her and she started wondering whether she would be right in accepting an offer which she had wanted so much.

Questions for discussion

1. What should Ganga Do? What ideals, obligations and effects should she take into account when making her decisions?
2 Would it be unprofessional of Ganga to drop everything and move to Novatex? Would it show lack of integrity? Could moving abruptly have negative career consequences for her?
3. Is it morally wrong, morally permissible or morally required to take up the new job? Examine Ganga's choice from a utilitarian point of view.
4. What does loyalty to the company mean and how important is it morally? Under what circumstances if any, do employees owe loyalty to their employees? When, if ever, do they owe loyalty to their colleagues?

Case 2:

Narendra grew up in a slum outside the city of Chennai. Through his hard work, talent and luck he completed his engineering from a reputed institution and joined Serve Ltd (SL). The company reimbursed him up to Rs. 2,000 towards house rent, utilities and services. This was done to avoid their employees staying in unsafe and poor quality housing. SL intention was to see that the employees live in a style that was appropriate to the company's image.

To claim the housing allowance, the employee was required to produce the rent receipt every month. Narendra worked hard and traveled frequently on business. He never entertained his colleagues at his home. From a casual conversation with a customer, Narendra's colleague Gautam came to know that Narendra was staying in Sowcarpet. Gautam knew that the area had only low rental houses. He kept quite and did not inform anyone till he confirmed his suspicions. On enquiries, Gautam found out that the rent in that area was in the region of Rs. 300 to 500 per month. Gautam reported the matter to their General Manager. He called Narendra and asked him how much rent he was paying. He said he was paying less than what the company gave him. He defended his action by asking what was wrong in staying economically. The G.M felt that Narendra's housing arrangement was not in keeping with his professional standing. It was insulting to say that an SL employee was staying in such type of a house. Besides, Narendra falsified the rent receipt every month, which he readily admitted.

Questions for discussions

1. Did Narendra act wrongly? Explain why or why not.
2. Was Gautam right in confirming and reporting the matter to the G.M? What would you do, if you were in place of Gautam and G.M?
3. Should Narendra be asked to leave? Should he be given some other punishment? What should be the punishment?
4. Is SL housing policy fair and reasonable? Is it culturally biased?

Case 3:

Preethi was working in Standard Limited for nearly a decade. It was a very large corporation. She liked the friendly work environment. Once she prepared a list and pinned it up on the board outside her office. Preethi did not want to be unfriendly. The list was:

Ethically Dubious Employee Conduct

1. Taking office supplies home for personal use
2. Using office telephone for personal, long distance phone calls
3. Making copies of personal documents on the office machine
4. Charging postage for your personal mail to the company.
5. Making non- official trips in a company car
6. Taking a full day off to attend a seminar for a day but attend it only for half a day.
7. Taking a taxi when the destination is a short walk away.

Questions for discussion

1. Review each item on the list and assess the conduct. Do you feel it morally acceptable, unacceptable or in between. Explain.
2. What obligation does employee have to their employers?
3. As Preethi, what will you do if you find fellow employee engaging in ethically dubious conduct?

RIGHTS OF ENGINEERS

Rights, duties and responsibilities go together. Rights and duties are two sides of the same coin. Along with rights go duties and responsibilities. It is difficult to isolate them. From duties emerge responsibilities. After gaining an understanding of the responsibilities of engineers vis-à-vis safety, loyalty, confidentiality, conflict of interest, let us now focus on rights. The concept needs to be looked from the points of view of both the employee and the employer.

Rights relating to 'Intellectual Property' are gaining increasing importance these days. Aspects relating to it are also discussed in this Chapter.

Before going into what professional rights are, let us understand the fundamental rights which are the basis for all rights. The Indian Constitution gives paramount importance to fundamental rights. Part III of the Indian Constitution deals with the Fundamental Rights of Indian citizens. The fundamental rights are recognized under Articles 12 – 35 of the constitution.

(1) Right to Equality Articles 14 – 18
(2) Right to Freedom Articles 19 – 22
(3) Right against Exploitation Articles 22-24
(4) Rights to Freedom of Religion Articles 25 – 28
(5) Cultural and Educational Rights. Articles 20 –31
(6) Right to Constitutional Remedies Articles 32 -35

Let us look at those rights which are relevant for our discussion. Article 14 mentions about the equality before law and Article 15 prohibition of discrimination on grounds of religion, sex, caste, sex and place of birth. Article 16 deals with equality of opportunity in matters of employment. Right to freedom in Article 19 deals with freedom of speech and expression. It gives freedom to assemble peacefully and form associations and unions. It gives us the freedom to practice any profession, or to carry on any occupation, trade or business. As citizens of India, we have been given these rights. It can be seen that the rights are the seed and freedom the fruit. Freedom is backed by rights.

Part IV A of the Constitution lays down the fundamental duties of Indian citizens.

(a) to abide by the Constitution and respect its ideals and institutions, the National Flag and the National Anthem;

(b) to cherish and follow the noble ideals which inspired our national struggle for freedom;

(c) to uphold and protect the sovereignty, unity and integrity of India;

(d) to defend the country and render national service when called upon to do so;

(e) to promote harmony and the spirit of common brotherhood amongst all the people of India transcending religious, linguistic and regional or sectional diversities; to renounce practices derogatory to the dignity of women;

(f) to value and preserve the rich heritage of our composite culture;

(g) to protect and improve the natural environment including forests, lakes, rivers and wild life, and to have compassion for living creatures;

(h) to develop the scientific temper, humanism and the spirit of inquiry and reform;

(i) to safeguard public property and to abjure violence;

(j) to strive towards excellence in all spheres of individual and collective activity so that the nation constantly rises to higher levels of endeavor and achievement.

These fundamental rights and duties become the basis for ethical behavior. They are applied to engineers also. The codes of ethics specify the details. The issue is whether engineers have a moral right to refuse carry out what they consider to be an unethical activity. How far are employers obligated to respect their rights to forsake coercion and condone the employee? Let us not forget the following:

1. An engineer has *human rights* by virtue of being a human or moral agent. He has a fundamental right to pursue legitimate personal interest and right to living.
2. He has *professional rights* by virtue of being a professional having special moral responsibilities. These include the right to exercise his professional judgment on the basis of his conscience, the right to refuse to engage in an unethical activity, the right to warn the public of dangers, the right to fair recognition and remuneration for his services.
3. He has *employee rights,* which includes the right to receive a salary of a certain amount, the right to perform contractual and non-contractual activities like choosing outside activity, privacy, and the right to demand protection from sexual harassment.

PROFESSIONAL RIGHTS

All employees have the right to expect fairness from their employer and to be treated with respect and dignity. Fairness is especially important in the area of hiring practices, compensation, promotion, privacy, discrimination, job security and sexual harassment.

The trend in the law is toward increased recognition of employee rights. Until as recent as three decades ago, even American law, considered the most protective of individual rights was governed by the common-law doctrine of "employment at will," where, in the absence of a contract, an employer can discharge an employee at any time and for whatever reason the employer considers relevant. This doctrine is highlighted in the Pennsylvania Supreme Court's position in the 1967 case of ***Geary*** *v.* ***United States Steel Corp.*** Mr. Geary was not educated as an engineer, but he had 14 years of engineering experience with U.S. Steel. Mr. Geary became convinced that a new type of pipe that U.S. Steel was using was unsafe under high pressure. He attempted to make his concerns known to management, but was rebuffed time and again. Finally a vice president listened to him and a detailed investigation vindicated Mr. Geary's position. However, for his efforts by which a costly blunder was rectified, the Company fired Mr. Geary on July 13, 1967, on grounds of insubordination. In a 4-3 decision, the Pennsylvania Supreme Court denied Mr. Geary a cause of action, reasoning as follows:

> "There is nothing here from which we could infer that the company fired Geary for the specific purpose of causing him harm, or coercing him to break any law or otherwise to compromise himself. According to his own statements, Geary had already won his own battle within the company. The most natural inference from the chain of events...is that Geary had made a nuisance of himself, and the company discharged him to preserve administrative order in its own house."

This case shows that even in the relatively recent past employees had little protection from their employers even when they wanted to protect their company's or the public's welfare.

A more important landmark case was the ***Pierce v. Ortho Pharmaceutical*** in 1980. Dr. Pierce, a physician, was involved in the development of a drug for treating diarrhea in children and the elderly. Dr. Pierce believed the drug contained an excessive amount of saccharin, and she objected to using the drug in tests on humans. Management overrode her objections, and she refused to continue working on the project. As a result, she was reprimanded and demoted. After resigning, she brought suit against Ortho, alleging that the company had pressured her to violate her ethical principles.
A trial court judge dismissed her claim, essentially invoking the doctrine of employment at will. However an appellate court found there were legal grounds for suit if her loss of employment was a violation of public policy. She appealed this ruling to the New Jersey Supreme Court. Dr. Pierce lost her appeal, but the decision was an important one nevertheless. In its majority opinion, the New Jersey Supreme Court said:

> "In certain instances, a professional code of ethics may contain an expression of public policy. However, not all such sources express a clear mandate of public policy. For example, a code of ethics designed to serve only the interests of the profession...probably would not be sufficient."
>
> The Court went on to say that, "employees who are professionals owe a special duty to abide not only by federal and state law, but also by the recognized codes of ethics of their professions. That duty may oblige them to decline to perform acts required by their employers."

The Court said that Dr. Pierce lost her case for two reasons. First, her resignation was premature. She had not actually been ordered to conduct the tests to which she objected. The tests were still in the future and would have required prior government approval. Second, her appeal to the Hippocratic oath was not an adequate support for her case. She should have appealed to the Code of the American Medical Association.

The wording of the court decision provides important grounds for asserting professional employee rights against an employer. At the same time, the assertion sets important parameters: the employee's action must be for public interest rather than for private benefit.

In 1981, the Illinois Supreme Court's ruling in the ***Palmateer v. International Harvester*** case affirmed the line of argument in the Pierce case. Mr. Palmateer discovered that International Harvester employees were using company property to store stolen goods. Instead of informing his superiors, he contacted the police, who instructed him not to go to his employers, but instead to continue informing them until an arrest could be made. He did as the police requested; as a result, company executives did not know of the illegal activity on their property until the arrests were made. When the matter was made public, Mr. Palmateer was fired for insubordination. In the ensuing suit against

Employees' rights can be protected by open door policy.

International Harvester, the company argued that Mr.Palmateer's action violated the Constitution's illegal search and seizure provisions. The Illinois Supreme court finally ruled against International Harvester, but did not prescribe a remedy. In granting Mr. Palmateer a cause of action, the court argued that if a corporation's actions violate public policy, the employee should be protected. But in a dissenting opinion Justice Ryan made the following comments:

> "By departing from the general rule that an at-will employment is terminable at the discretion of the employer, the courts are attempting to give recognition to the desire and expectation of an employee in continued employment.... In nurturing the shaping of this remedy, the courts must balance the interests of the employers with the hope of fashioning a remedy that will accommodate the legitimate expectations of both. In the process of emerging from the harshness of the former rule, we must guard against swinging the pendulum to the opposite extreme."

Justice Ryan's plea for balancing employee rights against the employer's rights to guide "the policies and destiny of his operation" should be given careful consideration, and we shall return to it shortly.

Although there is a growing trend to judicially restrict an employer's ability to discharge an employee at will, the trend still represents a minority position. Most of the judicial protection of employees from arbitrary discharge by employers has been afforded by creating a remedy in tort (injury) for unjust, abusive, malicious, or wrongful discharge.

The jurisdictions that support employee rights usually agree that a cause of action may be granted when the discharge violates a clear mandate of "public policy," but this term is difficult to define precisely, and there is considerable disagreement over its application. The courts which recognize the appeal to public policy tend to agree that discharging an employee because he exercises a right guaranteed by law, or because he refuses to undertake an illegal action, violates public policy. Thus discharged workers fired because they filed worker's compensation claims, refused to commit perjury, served on a jury, or refused to participate in an illegal price fixing scheme, have been able to obtain a cause of action against their employers. Whether or not discharging an employee for whistle blowing or upholding professional standards violates public policy is much more controversial.

The Pennsylvania case of ***Novosel v. Nationwide Insurance*** considers what this public policy exemption might mean. Novosel was an employee who was asked to assist his corporation in a lobbying effort that was to the advantage of the firm. Novosel refused and even spoke out for the opposite side. He was summarily fired. Drawing on the Palmateer v. International Harvester case, the court equated violation of "clearly mandated public policy" with "striking at the heart of citizens social rights, duties and responsibilities." Not assisting the corporation in a lobbying effort, and in fact speaking out against it, was protected activity.

Yet the actions by the Pennsylvania court have come under criticism. In a dissenting opinion one of the Novosel judges said, "my concern is that the panel has announced an extremely broad public policy exception." He gave three reasons for his reticence. First, This ignores the difference between the public and the private employee. While a public employee may well have to consider the public within the scope of their jobs, the private employee seems to, not have the public as a consideration. Second, the ruling fails to consider, "other public policy interests such as the economic interest of the public in efficient corporate performance." Third, the ruling does not take into account rights of the corporation and the corporation's legitimate expectation of loyalty.

A further important case is ***Kalman v. Grand Union Co*** case, wherein the Supreme Court of New Jersey held that a professional code of ethics might provide the foundation for a cause of action. A code of ethics might fit under the public policy exemption; however the whistleblower's motiva-

Whistle blowing means alerting.

tion is important. The motivation for the actions must be mandated by professional ethics, not the individual's personal ethics.

The Court said "...employees who are professionals owe a special duty to abide not only by federal and state law, but also by the recognized codes of ethics of their professions. That duty may oblige them to decline to perform acts required by their employers. However, an employee should not have the right to prevent his or her employer from pursuing its business because the employee perceives that a particular business decision violates the employee's personal morals, as distinguished from the recognized code of ethics of the employee's profession."

Mt. Heathy Board of Education v. Doyle dealt with an important issue in the controversy over employee and professional rights. How can one decide if an action is retaliatory in a mixed motive case where the person may have been retaliated against for a whistle blowing act, but the employee was also punished for a non-protected act, such as insubordination, or failure to achieve goals?

The U.S. Supreme Court did not want to make it impossible for an employer to release a disgruntled or non-performing employee. If the firm was unable to release employees who do not do their jobs, the costs of hiring anyone would become prohibitive. On the other hand, if an employee has blown the whistle on the employer, the employer should not be able to punish the employee. In Mt. Healthy case, the Supreme Court ruled that the employee must first show that she performed some type of protected activity. If she is able to do this, the burden of proof shifts to the employer. The firm must then prove that the disciplinary action was based solely on the non-protected activity; that is, once the employee has shown she was engaged in a protected activity, the firm must then prove that its act was non-retaliatory.

The attempt here was to both protect the employer from spurious retaliation charges, and also protect the mediocre employee who justifiably blows the whistle on her firm. In addition to protection through judicial modification of the common law doctrine of employment at will, some statutory protection of dissenting employees has emerged, primarily through whistleblowers' laws. In April 1981, Michigan became the first state in the U.S.A to pass a **"Whistle Blowers Protection Act."** The provisions are as follows:

> Any employee in private industry fired or disciplined for reporting alleged violations of federal, state or local law to public authorities can now bring an action in state court for unjust reprisal.
>
> If the employer cannot show that treatment of the employee was based on proper personnel standards or valid business reasons, the court can award back pay, reinstatement to the job, costs of litigation and attorney's fees. The employer can also be fined.

From the standpoint of strong advocacy of professional employee rights, the law is currently weak. It protects an employee only from discharge for reporting illegal actions, not actions that are contrary to professional ethics or conscience. Furthermore the penalties to employers are minimal. What is a fine of a few 1000 rupees to a big corporation? Nevertheless the law is significant as an indication of another departure from the "employment at will" doctrine.

Along with other countries, India also has whistleblower protection laws on the books. While the law only protects reporting to the employer or to government agencies, the protected report includes not only legal violations, but also "a code of conduct or ethics designed to protect the interest of the public or the employer." The assault on management autonomy will no doubt continue. Many people believe this assault is justified and that employees, particularly professional employees, must be granted more rights in the workplace. But we have seen that there are arguments in favor of protecting management autonomy as well. We must now examine the moral issues raised by these considerations. A good place to begin is by considering the philosophical arguments made on behalf of one side or the other in this debate.

A patent is registered in the name of the inventor.

EMPLOYEE RIGHTS

Firms and governmental agencies use various policies to protect employee rights. One of the simplest and most effective policies, especially suited to small firms and government agencies, is the*" open door" policy*. Managers make themselves available for hearing complaints on a regular basis and without prejudice to the complainants. This method is particularly appropriate where a single manager can correct the problem.

The Nuclear Regulatory Commission (NRC) of the U.S.A has introduced another method. This agency has instituted a procedure for handling what it calls ***Differing Professional Opinions*** (DPOs). If a professional employee has a complaint, there is a formal mechanism whereby the complaint can be registered. The employee is not limited to his/her area of responsibility and may raise matters dealt with by other parts of the NRC. A permanent record of all actions taken and formal comments made on a DPO are kept as the DPO travels up through the administrative ladder. Copies of all comments and responses to the DPO are made available for comment by the originator. Statements on each DPO and the NRC management responses to it consistent with security classification policy are placed in the NRC's public document room.

NRC also has an open-door policy to complement the DPO policy. Anonymity is allowed throughout the procedure, though this may decrease effectiveness. A panel is chosen each year to oversee and monitor the program and make recommendations on it. Although the DPO policy has many strong features, the provision regarding national security raises questions. A stern critic warns that Government agencies, including the NRC and its predecessors, have had a tendency to use "national security" to "cloak blunders or manipulate public opinion."

The same critic points out two ways security considerations could be used to subvert the DPO procedure. First, the security blanket might be used to cover up information that a complainant would need to justify her DPO. Second, the DPO might itself be a complaint that national security is being invoked to conceal information that should be made public. One possible solution would be to permit the originator of a DPO to request a special panel to rule on the legitimacy of invoking national security considerations; the panel should be composed of people outside government as well as inside.

A third approach for protecting employee rights is a ***corporate ombudsman***. An ombudsman can often register employee complaints in a confidential and anonymous way. The ombudsman or advocate must operate totally independently of the corporate hierarchy and should have direct access to top management and the board of directors. An ombudsman might not have sufficient expertise or power within a governmental or corporate bureaucracy to directly mediate a dispute between a professional and a manager, but he or she could facilitate mediation. While there is no assurance that every complaint will be accepted and acted upon, the employee should have confidence that he or she will be treated fairly and honestly. Obviously non-professional as well as professional employees could approach the ombudsman, although his or her services seem especially appropriate for professionals since they have considerable responsibilities, while often not being in positions of managerial authority.

Finally, some corporations have established ***a senior position for corporate responsibility.*** The person in this position and his department has the responsibility for the proper disposition of employee complaints. All employees would have access to this office, and it is expected to operate confidentially and in complete freedom from middle and lower-level management.

A small business, such as a small engineering firm, may not be able to make use of the more elaborate mechanisms proposed here. But perhaps a modified version of the NRC's DPO procedure would not be beyond their means. In any event, professional employee rights are an essential element in the proper performance of a professional's task in the workplace. As the number of professionals

Intellectual property is a patented invention, a trade secret or copy righted material.

becoming employees is growing, the issue of professional employee rights will become more and more important.

Whistle blowing

If an engineer decides that a current practice is unethical, there are at least three basic responses:

(a)"blow the whistle," either internally or publicly,

(b) resign, or

(c) keep quiet and do what the company wants.

There is a considerable literature on whistle blowing because it touches on a fundamental issue of employment: what, if anything, is the employee's duty to the firm? What exactly is employment, and how do an employee's obligations differ from those of someone working on contract? Two good case studies in this area are the Goodrich Aircraft Brake scandal and the Challenger Disaster mentioned earlier. Although prudential issues must be distinguished from ethical ones, this literature makes it clear that a would-be whistleblower must think carefully before acting. Whistleblowers often pay a substantial price, and their effectiveness is uneven.

The employee who would resign to avoid unethical conduct must also consider the duties of employees. Arguably, employment is indistinguishable from any other sort of work-for-hire unless it implies some degree of commitment, *albeit* both employers and employees often renege on their commitments. One can ask whether a company should immediately fire an employee who behaves unethically, or whether it should try to correct the behavior and give the employee a second chance. One can also ask the same question of the employee.

Whistle blowing is alerting relevant persons to some moral or legal corruption where relevant persons are those in a position to act in response if only by registering protest. An individual need not be a member of an organisation in order to blow the whistle. It presents a moral conflict between loyalty to one's employer or colleagues and the prevention of harm to third parties.

Let us look at it as a responsibility of professional people. Blowing the whistle on a person or activity is intended to bring to a halt some activity that will cause harm to the public. It is generally recognized that one should be loyal to one's employers and professional colleagues. Since whistle blowing by an employee appears to breach this loyalty by reporting the harmful activity to those outside, the employee who discovers misconduct is faced with a moral dilemma. Is the harm to the public greater than the harm to the corporation? Is it believable or sustainable? Has the internal channel been exhausted?

In the USA there is a law for the protection of whistleblowers called Whistleblowers Protection Act. Coleen Rowley exposed the Federal Bureau of Investigation's (FBI) handling of an alleged 9/11 hijacker; Enron's Sherron Watkins and WorldCom's Cynthia Cooper exposed the accounting shenanigans of their companies. They had a law protecting them. In the U K Public Disclosure Act provides similar protection. In India we do not have such a law, but steps are under way to enact one. By providing protection to whistleblowers, such an Act can ensure that organizations act on the message rather than against the messenger.

The Securities and Exchange Board of India (SEBI) has its own whistleblowers policy. According to it, all listed companies must formulate a policy, allowing employees to report illegal activities by those in positions of authority in their companies without any threat of a backlash. This is mandatory for all companies whose shares are traded on any of the recognized stock exchanges in India.

Well known corporates like Hindustan Lever, Tata Group of companies, Infosys and Wipro have internal set-ups which investigate and review matters where there are instances of suspected fraud or irregularities.

Who is a whistleblower?

They are people blowing the whistle on malpractices by companies and government. It could be:

A patent is registered in the name of the inventor.

- A criminal offence
- Breach of a legal obligation
- Miscarriage of justice
- Danger to the health or safety of any individual
- Damage to the environment, or
- A deliberate cover-up of information tending to show any of these.

Why whistleblowers?

They fill a gap in the existing system of curbing malpractices. The law of enforcement machinery may not have known the wrongdoings in a company, even if it did, it may not have enough information to bring about a conviction. It is an insider who can bring the fraud to the attention of the right authorities along with the information needed for a conviction.

Whistleblowers are people with a tough moral fibre and a strong desire to see that wrongs are corrected against all odds. . Their opponents are strong, capable of putting and ready to put these lone individuals through humiliation, ridicule, contempt, unemployment, and loss of social standing and to the extent of threat to life. There are some companies like Tatas and others who encourage the whistle blowers.

The Wipro Example

Wipro is an NYSE listed company. Which means it is listed in the New York Stock Exchange. Since they are listed with NYSE, they are required to follow Sarbanes Oxley Act, which deals with the whistle blowing policy and it is a new regulatory requirement under Securities and Exchanges Commission of the U.S(SEC). The Company has introduced a policy of Ombudsprocess. Earlier Wipro had a grievance redressal system which was functioning effectively. The new policy was framed as complementary to the existing system as per SEC requirement.

The company has selected six senior executives as ombudspersons. They have a demanding task ahead them. Their mission: Quality, Brand and Innovation and being Corporate Ombudsperson.

Wipro employees, numbering more than 25,000 are encouraged to voice their concerns on any issue, no matter how small it is. Some the issue do not amount to any whistle blowing, but the company wants employees to use the channel to voice their concerns. Company in turn attends to the concerns rather than brushing them aside. Nearly 85% of the concerns are of a personal nature.

The Ombudsprocess at Wipro works as follows: Employees and non-employees (mainly vendors) can raise a concern regarding any malpractice, impropriety, abuse or wrongdoing at an early stage and without fear of victimization, subsequent discrimination or disadvantage as per the spirit of the policy.

The whistle blower can mail, fax, telephone, write a letter or personally inform one of the five ombudspersons that the company has nominated or directly communicate to the Corporate Ombudsperson. The matter will be enquired by the concerned Ombudsperson. There is a Business Unit Compliance Committee that takes the decision on the matter based on the investigations. In some cases, the Ombudsperson can take action directly.

The Ombudspersons are senior enough to take action and there will be no vindictive action against the employees, which should make them comfortable in voicing their concerns. Their policies and procedures ensure confidentiality unless there is a criminal angle.

INTELLECTUAL PROPERTY

Because engineers are essentially designers, they create what is called intellectual property. It is important that they understand the concept and the issues surrounding it. In addition, the rapid development of biological and information technology has forced a rethinking of intellectual property law and ethics.

!Whistle blowers are the people with a tough moral fibre.

What is intellectual property?

In the narrow legal sense, intellectual property is a patented invention, a trade secret, or copyrighted material.

A ***patent*** grants an inventor exclusive rights to an invention for 17 years in exchange for disclosing it to the public. One cannot patent (or copyright) a pure idea, such as a mathematical theorem. The invention must be some product or process that embodies an idea. United States law defines it to be a method, product, apparatus, composition of matter, design for articles of commerce, or in certain cases a plant. The disclosure must be specific enough to allow a person skilled in the art to recreate and use the invention. To be patented, the invention must be useful, novel, and unobvious. It is "novel" if (a) it was not known or used in the United States prior to the patent application; (b) it was not patented or described in a publication anywhere in the world more than a year prior to the patent application. The invention is "unobvious" if the idea was not obvious to a person skilled in the art at the time of the invention. One cannot patent a "way of doing business" or anything that occurs in nature.

A ***trade secret*** is a secret formula, pattern, or device that is used in a business and provides a commercial advantage. A trade secret can be bought, sold and licensed. It differs from a patented invention primarily in two ways: (a) A trade secret remains intellectual property forever (not just 17 years), or until the secret gets out. An example is the formula for Coca-Cola. (b) While the law prohibits others from *using* a patented idea, it only prohibits others from *stealing* a trade secret. It is perfectly legal for another company to conceive the idea independently and use it. Reverse engineering is not theft of a trade secret, because an idea deducible by reverse engineering is not really secret. It is illegal, however, to obtain and use a secret idea from its owner without permission.

A ***copyright*** limits the number of copies others can make of a document or work of art without permission. It lasts much longer than a patent. A copyright held by an individual, for example, lasts 50 years beyond his or her lifetime. Ideas as such cannot be copyrighted and can therefore be discussed freely. Only a particular expression of ideas can be copyrighted. Software (source code or machine code) can be copyrighted, and recent law recognizes patents as well.

Who owns intellectual property?

A patent is always registered in the name of the inventor. The patent's *owner*, however, may be another person or a corporation. An employer normally owns any invention or trade secret conceived by an inventor who is working "for hire." This means basically that the employer is buying rights to whatever that person may produce in job-related work. Even an idea conceived in the garage at home belongs to the employer if it is related to the job. The 3-M employee who invented post-it notes for his church choir had to turn the rights over to the company. It is not always obvious who is working for hire. A full-time employee of a business or government agency almost always is, whereas a consultant may not be, depending on the specific arrangement. A Ph.D. student who is paid by a professor to develop a certain algorithm normally is not working for hire and therefore retains property rights to the algorithm, unless there is some specific agreement to the contrary. A professor who conducts research under a government grant is subject to the agreement under which the funds are granted. Traditionally a university faculty member retains rights to a scholarly article, but universities are free to modify this tradition in the employment contract and sometimes do. Inventors working for hire have limited rights, but a few things can be done to improve the situation. The inventor could make sure the patent is granted in his or her name and is mentioned in articles and grant proposals. Employment contracts that provide financial incentives for inventions can be negotiated.

Is Software Intellectual Property?

The legal status of software is confusing because it has gone through several stages of development and involves both copyright and patent law. Currently it is generally accepted that software can

One cannot patent 'The Way of Doing Business'.

be copyrighted, and that both algorithms and software can be patented under the category of methods or apparatus. A patent may be refused, however, for software that merely automates a procedure that was once done by hand, if that procedure can be viewed as a "way of doing business." A court battle between Apple and Microsoft established that Microsoft could copy the "look and feel" of the Apple desktop without violation of copyright. The argument was basically that Microsoft copied *methods* of entering commands, which are not protected by copyright. Lotus and Borland fought a similar battle over spreadsheet commands, with similar results. These rulings allowed the software industry to evolve toward standardized user interfaces. Software protection has broadened since then, but the rulings still seem to govern.

Can Life Be Patented?

The biotechnology revolution has brought much confusion to the intellectual property arena, but one principle seems to be observed consistently. One cannot have property rights to anything that occurs in nature. Apparent exceptions to this principle turn out not to be exceptions on closer examination. One can, however, patent a genetically altered organism. This was clearly established in a 1980 U.S. Supreme Court ruling in the case, *Diamond v Chakrabarty*, which remains the ruling authority. Given the triviality of human tinkering relative to the natural wonder that is DNA, one might liken this to changing the hubcaps on a Mercedes and claiming credit for the entire automobile Yet it is unclear that many conventional inventions do not have this character. The disclosure requirement for patents helps limit some of the excesses of biological patenting. In his much-discussed book *The Biotech Century*, Jeremy Rifkin reports that Philip Leder received a patent on a genetically engineered mouse that contains cancer-causing genes and on any mouse that might ever be engineered to contain such genes. This is an overstatement. The patent covers only a mouse that is engineered with a procedure similar to that described in the patent disclosure. A person skilled in the art must be able to derive the procedure used from the one described.

The *Neemix* Case Study

This interesting case study introduces some of the ethical issues surrounding the patenting of life. The story began when W. R. Grace received a U.S. patent on an insecticide, Neemix, derived from the seeds of the neem tree, which occurs naturally in India. Some Indians challenged the patent on the grounds that (a) neem seeds are natural and belong to everyone, and (b) neem extracts and their effects are traditional knowledge in Indian culture.

Some of the issues that arise are discussed in the ensuing paragraphs:

Can one patent a substance that occurs naturally in neem seeds? No. In fact, Grace did not seek a patent on the seeds themselves or any component of them. They patented a more stable form of the traditional extract. One might argue that their modification was too trivial, and the result too similar to the traditional extract, to be novel. But this is an issue of fact and law, not ethics. The related ethical issues are stated in the next two paragraphs.

Should U.S. patent law award Grace a patent for a neem-based product even if it is not novel? Current U.S law would in fact award Grace the patent in this case, provided neem extract was unknown in the United States, because the idea had not been patented or published in India. One might defend this policy on the ground that it grants the two countries symmetrical rights. Companies in each country can (and do) profit from intellectual property that originates in the other. (Grace did not seek and in any event would not be granted a patent in India.) Indian companies, for example, regularly sell unlicensed copies of video tapes from the United States. Current patent law therefore recognizes international boundaries. An alternative would be to regard the entire world as a single jurisdiction with uniform patent protection everywhere. A difficulty with this arrangement, however, is that Indians would be unable to patent their traditional knowledge anywhere (because it is not novel), but

One cannot have property rights to anything that occurs in nature.

Americans would be able to copyright the content of their video tapes everywhere (because it is new). The developed countries gain an unfair advantage because of the nature of their products. This issue must be addressed in any multilateral agreement on intellectual property.

*What if the product **is** novel?* New products based on natural substances have traditionally been granted patents without controversy. But one may still raise the next question.

Should indigenous people receive royalties from companies that profit, directly or indirectly, from their traditional knowledge? Note first that this issue is different from the issue of whether Indian folk knowledge could be patented in the United States. If Indians deserve payment for their knowledge, this is the case whether a single company or many companies exploit it in another country. As for the issue of royalties, one can observe that a subculture *within* the United States has no rights to royalties from domestic companies that use its traditional knowledge, either directly without modification or indirectly in the form of a patented product. This is precisely because the knowledge is traditional rather than new. If one accepts this situation, then it is hard to argue that people abroad should have rights to royalties from U.S. companies that use their traditional knowledge. As a practical matter, it is hard to say exactly to whom royalties would be paid, particularly in view of the fact that past generations should get most of the credit. There is a deeper argument, however, that goes to the heart of the intellectual property dispute. It asks what sorts of goods should be regarded as property in the first place.

The Moral Status of Intellectual Property

We tend to think of property rights as a recent advance in human history. In fact traditional conceptions of property tend to be more sophisticated than the modern one. Traditional societies usually recognize several kinds of property that are only partially interchangeable and whose disposition is closely regulated. One may be permitted to purchase a bride ("bride price"), but perhaps the payment can be made only in the form of cattle. There may be a form of money, but it buys only certain commodities, perhaps those traded with neighboring villages. Tools and certain other goods may fall under a system of "reciprocity," meaning that one can take them when in need and provide them to others in their time of need, with no strict accounting. Michael Walzer (1983) and others argue that more complex property systems are morally superior. In a society in which all property is interchangeable, one can use any form of economic power to acquire the assets of anyone who is less well off. One who has intelligence, artistic talent, or good looks ends up selling these assets to stay alive. This exacerbates the concentration of wealth and power. Modern societies sometimes recognize this problem, for example by trying to prohibit prostitution, partly in order to prevent exploitation of poor women. The efficiency of a single medium of exchange, however, drives Western-style economies toward assigning everything a price. One of the few reversals of this trend was the abolition of chattel slavery by European powers that established it three centuries earlier.

As technology-based manufacturing and distribution systems grew, businesses pressed for rights over intellectual property in order to provide an incentive to innovate. This is a recent development, as U.S. observance of intellectual property 150 years ago was much as it is in China today. Even here there is a recognition that pure ideas must be allowed to circulate without commercial restraint. But the rights of intellectual property owners have steadily increased.

A key issue is whether biotechnology signals a need to reverse this trend, much as in the case of slavery. Indians argue that traditional knowledge of healing and agriculture, like knowledge of mathematics, are part of our common human heritage and should not be subject to commercialization. In particular it should not be encumbered by patents, even in its refined or derivative forms. On the other hand, the patenting of variants could spur the development of affordable new remedies. Full resolution of this dilemma requires a more general analysis of property systems and their moral status. In the meantime, one might tentatively suggest the following test: if genetic or other engineering creates

Intellectual property rights provide an incentive to innovate.

a product whose *effects* go substantially beyond those of the traditional substance from which it is derived, grant the patent and commercialize the product. If the effects are substantially the same, grant no patent, but allow commercialization, at least until we figure out a better way to organize property. On this view, Grace's development of a more stable extract from neem seeds would not warrant a patent. The traditional effects of the seeds provide ample motivation to bring them to market. Developing a stable form is part of the cost of distribution. However, if Grace had converted neem extract into a new cure, the world would have benefited from providing Grace the incentive of patent protection.

In the past, pharmaceutical industry in India never valued a secret. Now the scenario is fast changing. A combination of impending changes in Indian patent laws and the growing importance of intellectual property have pushed some companies to get employees to sign confidentiality agreements,

Confidentiality agreements have not been limited to employees. Companies no longer use recruitment as a way to buy another firm's confidential information. For instance Orchid Chemicals, which researches new drugs, does not expect a potential recruit to disclose specific details of research carried out in the course of the existing job. They do not encourage knowledge transplantation. Companies are more interested in skills and competence.

In the three to five years the respect for intellectual property rights has grown rapidly. Companies have realized that intellectual property has greater value than the final product. Indian companies must realize that cost effectiveness is not just by low cost manpower, but technological innovations that need to be guarded.

Earlier companies had the practice of getting confidential information from scientists who changed jobs, now they discourage such practices. Companies that carry out considerable research and collaborated with overseas companies tend to respect data secrecy. The confidentiality agreements are made to ensure legal protection; for instance, if another company comes out with a product that suggested trade secrets had been stolen, the aggrieved party could approach the courts. The issue is can legal system provide enough protection? By that time the damage could have taken place. Legal recourses take time. The move towards data and information protection will increase in India as awareness increases and IPR Act implementation becomes more stringent.

Discrimination

Discrimination is the unequal treatment whether intentional or unintentional of individuals or groups on the basis of group membership that is unrelated to merit, ability or past performance. It is disgraceful to be discriminated because of one's sex, race, skin colour, age or religion. These are biological in nature hence does not make any sense. It does not create appropriate right organizational climate for the employees since personal conviction, self-esteem and self-image are basic human rights. Discrimination is not limited to individuals but also to law and institutions. Discrimination is found everywhere around us.

Imagine a situation where you are one of the members of a selection panel for an American multinational company. You are an Indian but working in the US for an American firm. There are two applicants, an Indian and a US citizen. The Indian in your view is slightly better suited than the American. Whom would you recommend? Will you accept whatever the selection is made or argue?

Case Study 1

Arun is a 47-year-old bio-engineer, a father of three children. He posted an envelope addressed to Mr.Narayanan, who was chairman of Pollution Control Board (PCB). Next day his company fired him. He was working for an engineering consulting firm, Suman Engineering that had been hired by Simco to help them with environmental protection measures. He pointed out that the documents and

Keeping secret is right but acquisitions of other's secret is espionage.

data submitted by Simco to the PCB were misleading. For two years, he tried to get his employees to listen to him, but they would not. His employers accused him of stealing the documents and sued him for defamation. A month after he was fired, he sent several documents supporting his point of view. A year later, his company dropped all legal actions against him and paid him a huge cash settlement. Arun withdrew his case.

Questions for discussion

1. Evaluate the actions of Mr. Arun. If you were Arun what will you do?
2. Do you think what the company did was ethical and correct?

Case Study 2

Indian engineer Satyendra Kumar Dubey was honoured with the Whistleblower of the Year 2004 Award by one of world's leading freedom-of-expression groups, the UK-based 'Index on Corruption'. Dubey, a former IITian (Indian Institute of Technology) who was working as an engineer in the Bihar section of the infrastructure project, was given the award for exposing corruption in the country's prestigious Golden Quadrilateral (GQ) highway project, an act for which he was allegedly murdered.

While announcing the award, Ursula Owen, editor Index on Censorship said: "Satyendra Kumar Dubey knew the risk he was taking but took it nonetheless. "Whistle blowing lies at the heart of free expression because corruption and secrets can be so harmful to the democratic process."

The award to Dubey was accepted by Prawal Gupta, an old friend who represents the UK chapter of the S K Dubey Foundation set up to campaign for justice for Dubey. Gupta, a London-based software engineer said that he received the award with mixed feelings — happiness because Dubey's sacrifice had received international acclaim and sadness because Dubey was not around to accept the award himself.

A fellow student at IIT Kanpur during the early '90s, Gupta said of the slain engineer: "Dubey was a very honest man. He liked to do things but would not take credit for them. He was a man who really believed he could do something. If anything was wrong he would not tolerate it. He believed things could be improved. Most of us talk about corruption for hours in our drawing rooms but don't do anything about it."

How did he blow the whistle?

Dubey was a graduate engineer from IIT Kanpur of 1994 batch. In a letter to the National Highway Authority of India, NHAI chairman Dubey had requested him to keep secret his identity, which was not done, resulting in his brutal assassination. The slain engineer had in another letter to NHAI chairman, copy of which was also released to the press, expressed his displeasure over leaking of his identity saying, this disclosure had exposed him to undesirable pressures and threats.

Dubey, in his letter to the Prime Minister, had questioned the process of procurement of civil contractors for the Golden Quadrilateral Project saying it was "manipulated and hijacked" by big contractors, who submitted forged documents to justify their technical and financial capabilities to execute the project.

"The big contractors have been able to get all sorts of help and secret information and documents from NHAI officials, and even note sheets carrying approval of the chairman have been leaked outside," The letter said that the NHAI officials showed great hurry in giving mobilisation advance to selected contractors for financial consideration. In some cases the contractors have been given mobilisation advance just a day after signing the contract agreement," it added.

"The entire mobilisation advance of 10 per cent of contract value, which goes up to Rs 40 crore in certain cases, are paid to contractors within a few weeks of awards of work but there is little follow up to ensure that they are actually mobilised at the site with the same pace, and the result is that the

Corporate espionage is risk to any business.

advance remains lying with contractors or gets diverted to their other activities," the letter said.

Dubey in his letter also highlighted the problems of sub-contracting by the primary contractors." Though the NHAI is going for international competitive bidding to procure the most competent civil contractors for execution of its projects, when it comes to actual execution, it is found that most of the works, sometimes even up to 100 per cent are sub-contracted to petty contractors in capable of executing such big projects," he said.

Dubey in his letter said that the phenomenon of sub-contracting was known to all in the NHAI but everyone remained silent.

"I have written all these in my individual capacity. However, I will keep on addressing these issues in my official capacity in the limited domain within the powers delegated to me," the letter said.

Dubey, in another letter to the project director, NHAI, Koderma, Jharkhand, on July 26, two days before he was to take over as project manager in Gaya, Bihar, expressed displeasure over the transfer saying it was baffling and would not serve interest of the project in Jharkhand.

In his letter, Dubey had drawn the attention of the project director to some alleged "irregularities" committed by contractors and consultant for the project. He had highlighted several instances of 'loot of public money' and 'poor implementation' of the project in Barachatti in Bihar.

Dubey had taken care not to sign his letters to the Prime Minister and the NHAI Chairman; he had appended his bio-data, which got leaked to vested interests who eliminated him.

In India the Whistle Blower Act has not been passed. The Act would ensure that the protection to the citizen/person complaining of corruption and to keep the complainant's name secret. It is obligatory to protect the identity of Whistle Blower. In the absence of the Whistle Blower Act, the State has a fundamental duty to keep the name of such person secret for the protection of his fundamental right to life.

Spurred by Dubey's tragic death, Supreme Court of India in response to a public interest litigation filed by a Non-Governmental Organisation directed the Central Government to come with specific measures to protect the whistleblowers who highlight corruption among public servants.

Questions for discussion

What should the Centre do?

Evaluate the actions of Dubey.

What are the alternatives Dubey could have thought of ?

EXERCISE

1. Debate on Employee Loyalty and Rights.
2. Debate on unions are boon or bane ?
3. Identify a whistle blower. Interview the person to learn from his experiences.
4. Identify the whistle blower act on the net and evaluate the act.
5. Debate on Discrimination advantages and disadvantages
6. Advantages and disadvantages of rights .
7. Discuss the moral issues that engineer faces at the design stage of the product.
8. How does one manage risk?
9. What are the lessons you learn from the Titanic story?

SHORT QUESTIONS

1. Define Safety
2. Define Risk
3. What is Collegiality?
4. What is Loyalty?
5. Differentiate between collegiality and loyalty
6. What is collective bargaining?
7. What is negotiation?

8. What are occupational crimes?
9. Differentiate between bribe and gift.
10. Discuss the various discriminations with examples which an engineer may face.
11. What is Intellectual Property Right?
12. What is the relationship between rights and duties?
13. What are human rights?
14. Briefly identify the rights relevant for engineers in the Indian constitution.
15. Who is ombudsperson?
16. Who is a spy?
17. What is Discrimination?

LONG QUESTIONS

1. Explain the relationship between safety – risk – cost – price
2. How will you resolve your moral conflict?
3. Explain the concept of Conflict of interest with examples from consulting engineers.
4. What is confidentiality and how will you maintain?
5. "Respect for authority creates lot of conflicts in employees" – Discuss the statement with examples.
6. What is espionage? Evaluate the pros and cons
7. Discuss the various rights of the engineers with examples
8. Discuss the implication of Whistle blowing
9. How does one manage risk?

REFERENCES

A & M University
1. Texas Instruments
2. Online ethics
4. John Hooker, Carnegie Mellon University, May 2000.

ANNEXURE

Advice from the Texas Instruments Ethics Office

Ethics Help-Line

The Help-Line is intended to provide advice for engineers, scientists, and trainees encountering ethical problems in their work. A principal goal of this Help-Line is to assist scientists and engineers in maintaining high ethical standards and in acting wisely when confronted with multiple and potentially conflicting responsibilities, even where this may lead to conflicts with organizational superiors.

The list contain a selection of advice from The Ethics Office at Texas Instruments Corporation.

Responsibilities, Rights and Obligations vis a vis the Company

- Company Resources Used for Personal Benefit
- Ethical Issues in Company Travel

Responsibilities, Rights and Obligations vis a vis Co-workers

- Favoritism in the Workplace

Don't expect anyone to be perfect.

- Gossiping at Work
- Individual Privacy
- Responsibilities as a Team Leader
- Responsibilities as a Team Member
- Sexual Harassment

Professional Ethics for Engineers

- Entertainment, Gifts – Avoiding Bribes & Conflict of Interest
- Signing Off on Engineering Documents
- Mischarging Time – Financial Fraud

Intellectual Property

- Intellectual property – Copyrights and Patents
- Proprietary and Other Sensitive Information
- Software Piracy vs. Legal Copying
- Software, Bringing Your Own to Work
- Benchmarking and Reverse Engineering

Confidentiality

Privacy, Confidentiality & Telephone Use

Advice for how to protect Proprietary Information and Sensitive Information by Monitoring the use of electronic data processing.

Policies and practices regarding telephone monitoring clarified.

How to deal with sensitive competitive information if gained accidentally Sensitive information belonging to another company must never be solicited or accepted by a Texas engineer unless there is an appropriate signed document, such as a non-disclosure agreement. But what if we receive that information accidentally through no intent or effort on our own?

"After Hours" Security Searches Help TI Safeguard Sensitive Information TI and the government are both very concerned over information security—particularly in high security areas. Violations have occurred in the past and TI must do whatever is necessary to maintain compliance.

Professional Secrecy is given in the Code of Ethics of Quebec Engineers of the Order of Quebec Engineers (OIQ).

Ethics Organization at TEXAS INSTRUMENTS (TI)

The TI Ethics Director is commissioned to ensure that all of the company guidelines remain aligned with ethical standards. His reporting chain is through an oversight group, the TI Ethics Committee, which reports to the Audit Committee of the Board of Directors. The TI Ethics Director is also responsible for updating the TI Ethics Committee, the Audit Committee of the Board of Directors, and the president and CEO on a regular basis.

The TI Ethics Committee was established in 1987 concurrently with the TI Ethics Office and consists of five high-level TI managers. This committee is chartered to oversee the activities of the TI Ethics Office, review and approve ethics-related policies, procedures, and primary publications, monitor compliance to laws and regulations as well as ethical practices, review any major ethical issues that may arise from time to time and approve appropriate corrective actions.

Chapter

6

Global Issues

UNIT V : GLOBAL ISSUES: Multinational Corporations – Environmental Ethics- Computer Ethics – Weapons Development – Engineers as Managers – Consulting engineers and engineers as expert witness and advisors – Moral leadership – sample code of Ethics like ASME, ASCE, IEEE- Institution of Engineers (India) – Indian Institute of Materials Management – Institution of electronics and telecommunication engineers (IETE) India etc.

Learning Objectives :

What are Multinational Corporations?

To understand the ethical issues and issues related to environment - computer and weapon development.

To be aware of tools for solving international ethical issues.

To get insight into the ethical issues faced by engineers in a role of consultant , Adviser , Manager, and Leader .

To be aware of code of ethics of different national and international associations.

To be aware of Engineers Bill, 2003

WHAT ARE MULTINATIONAL CORPORATIONS ? (MNCs)

Multinational corporations are known as MNC's. When a company operates in several countries, it is known as a multinational or transnational corporation. For example, Smith Kline Beecham, Unilever, Ford, Toyota etc. are MNCs. With Liberalisation, Privatisation and Globalisation (***LPG***), the number of MNC's have increased and in future will increase. This has resulted in certain global issues.

GLOBAL ISSUES

This chapter will discuss issues faced by global trade and increasing globalisation. This assumes importance since many Indian engineers are working outside India and *vice versa.* The awareness about global issues is necessary to help deal with various aspects of professional interactions. Cross-cultural issues and complex environmental issues are thrown up thanks to globalisation of business. The impact of weapons development is also covered. This Chapter presents some tools for solving international ethical problems. The Global Compact, which is an initiative taken by the United Nations is presented briefly.

Impediments to international trade in goods and services and investment continue to fall one by one every day. The free trade movement, the power of information age, technology, the shift of formerly communist and dictatorial states toward democracy and capitalism are all significant fac-

Multinational Corporations (MNCs) are also known as Transnational Corporations.

tors. Free markets, the means to supply them and the investments to support them have all gone global. As a result, the global trade has been increasing in double-digit percentages every year.

For most part of the world, this has resulted in more freedom, choice, income, economic growth, food production and longer life expectancy. But globalisation has also produced other major concerns. One is the shift in power from elected national governments to transnational corporations unaccountable to none and to such unelected global bodies as the World Trade Organisation, the International Monetary Fund and the World Bank. Another concern is the growing gap between the globalised 'haves' and non-globalised 'have-nots'. A third concern is the questionable performance of some transnational corporations and their suppliers, who have taken advantage of lower legal, environmental, corruption, labour and human rights standards in the less developed parts of the world. There are other factors at work as well. Technology has made business practices around the world effectively transparent and fast. There is no place to hide any more because of Internet, CNN.BBC etc. Values such as do not kill, lie or cheat are shared by most cultures around the world, specific practices vary between cultures (e.g. gender discrimination) and can cause difficulties for international operations. There is a need for ethical leadership from all sectors of society to maintain a level playing field and development of more international guidelines and law that can be effectively enforced.

Ethical Issues

In a global economy, many projects are often international. They bring together people from different traditions with different values and do business in different ways. Westerners sometimes have difficulty making the adjustment, because they are Universalists. They deeply hold the belief that all peoples should be basically the same (i.e., similar to them), although some may be further along the path of development than others. Whatever they may believe, peoples are in fact very diverse.

Cultures have developed fundamentally different and evolved equally legitimate solutions to life's problems. The key to working in a multicultural setting is to acknowledge the possibility of radically different approaches to life.

This is obviously a large topic, and attention here is restricted to a few behavior patterns that are considered unethical or unprofessional by Western standards. Engineers working abroad (or at home!) may encounter cronyism, nepotism, kickbacks, and bribes. Westerners view them as corrupting, and they are in fact corrupting in a Western context. They may or may not be corrupting in other systems, which can likewise be corrupted, but in different ways. Another cultural pattern that Westerners may find disturbing is the discrimination against women in business. The discussion here refers vaguely to non-Western cultures, but every culture has its own way of doing business and getting the job done. Before beginning an international assignment, the engineer should study the host culture and if possible the language. Some resources indexed by country may be found at http://ba.gsia.cmu.edu/jnh/culture.

Kickbacks

A classic situation is that of a purchasing agent for a company or a government. A representative of a potential supplier offers the agent a side payment in exchange for a contract. In the West this is unethical, and perhaps illegal in the case of government agents. In many countries it is business as usual. Kickbacks are corrupting in the West because they imply a conflict of interest. The purchasing agent is supposed to represent the interests of his company. If the agent is taking payments, his or her own interests interfere. The procedure is to look at bids, investigate the companies, and choose the best deal. This works because the system is based on rules and transparency. Bids, annual reports,

Values like do not kill, lie or cheat are shared by most cultures around the world.
Kickbacks are corrupting in the West because they imply a conflict of interest.

accounting statements and the like are expected to reveal the facts about the supplier. If they do not, the supplier is guilty of fraud and could be taken to court. Business relationship is based primarily on a framework of rules that most people believe in and take seriously. (The government enforces the rules, but enforcement is impossible unless most people are already inclined to obey them.)

In a different kind of system, business relationships are personal. Rather than doing business with a company, one does business with a person, who happens to work for a certain company. The relationship is based on mutual trust, which may be built over a long period. When things go wrong, it is no use to call a lawyer. The agent must rely upon his personal relationship with another human being. Because a major part of the agent's task is to establish this relationship, there is no conflict of interest in doing so. One way for a supplier to demonstrate his commitment to the relationship is to put money on the line. If the supplier has paid for the relationship, he is less likely to vanish when there is a problem. The agent who receives a kickback is therefore doing his job.

Written contracts are traditionally not part of this process, because the concept of a contract presupposes a framework of rules and law that enforce the contract. Many people around the world do not believe in the legitimacy of any such framework, because they are not universalists as Westerners are. They regard a piece of paper as just that. Any kind of enforceability must be based on flesh and blood, on a relationship of mutual trust and commitment between human beings. Because most business people have accepted the Western practice of writing contracts, some interesting anomalies result. For example, in some countries (e.g., Egypt), it is customary to write kickbacks into the contract.

Cronyism

In much of the world, one routinely lets contracts to one's friends. The reason, again, is that business is based on trust relationships with individuals. They take different forms in different countries. In China one speaks of *guanxi* (the Putonghua word for "relationship"), which is a long-term association based on mutual obligation. In Mexico business relationships reflect bonds of friendship and affection. In Japan and Korea, they are based on an old-boy network formed during college days. The West refers to this as cronyism and complains of lack of transparency. To be sure, there is nothing transparent about it. A businessperson would be reluctant to ask a partner for too much.

Accounting information even if it were reliable, are not asked for because to do so would be to insult the partner's honour. This relationship-based system can work quite well. Such systems have sustained great civilizations for thousands of years; western capitalism has been around only for the last 500 years. A business commitment based on a proper relationship is as solid as anything in this life (although the parties often ask each other to renegotiate). With this background, it is not hard to trace the cause of the Asian financial crisis: investors poured in funds based on (insufficient) public information, rather than cultivating the sort of trust relationship that for millennia underscored investment in that part of the world. It still does in China and Taiwan, which largely escaped the crisis.

In much of the world, cronyism provides the social glue that makes business possible. Far from being immoral, it reflects a highly developed moral sensibility that is often missing in the West. It occurs in relationship-based cultures, in which people place high priority on solicitude for the welfare and feelings of their associates. Maintaining courtesy, respect, loyalty and honor is a fine art. It must be acknowledged, however, that many countries have evolved an uncomfortable blend of Western and indigenous practices. It may be hard to evaluate such cases, and one must look at each one individually.

Nepotism

Nepotism is also standard practice in much of the world. A businessperson from the United States may be asked to hire relatives of the local boss. The proper response is to oblige if the relative

Maintaining Courtesy, Respect, Loyalty and Honor is a fine art.

will work in the host country, but not if he would work in the United States, which has different norms. Hiring relatives, or relatives of friends, has advantages in many cultures. Some may be incompetent, but in any case the boss knows their strengths and weaknesses better than those of other employees, and he can assign them duties accordingly. This is possible because employees are more likely to be managed directly by the boss than assigned to a fixed job description. Also in non-Western cultures, an older relative tends to carry great authority. This can enable the boss to obtain a level of effort and devotion that would not be forthcoming from more competent but unrelated employees.

The main reason for nepotism, however, is the primacy of the family, which is the foundation in many cultures. From this point of view, many people may consider Western family relationships with their broken and troubled histories, as dysfunctional and inefficient.

Bribes

The definition of a bribe varies around the world. Many people regard a kickback as a "commission," not as bribe. A gift of a new BMW after the conclusion of a deal may be viewed as an expression of gratitude rather than a bribe, even if some degree of *quid pro quo* is implied. Bribes, however defined, may be legal or illegal. In China, the punishment for bribery can be death by firing squad. Illegal bribery may or may not be widely practiced. In Singapore, no one dares; in China, it is ubiquitous. The businessperson from abroad must know the local situation.

Bribes may or may not be corrupting for the culture in which they occur. In South Korea, payments in white envelopes are a regular feature of dealings with government officials. In many cases they help to cement a continuing relationship. These relationships are important, because government officials learn which companies are acting properly by cultivating personal ties with their executives. The bribe signals that the executive is serious and will behave himself to avoid upsetting a relationship in which he has invested. Bribes therefore need not be corrupting, although it should be noted that it is 'loss of face' to be exposed for bribery. Koreans seem to realize that bribery could easily get out of hand and become corruption (just as legalism can get out of hand in a rule-based culture, as it has in the United States).

Bribery is usually corruption when it occurs in rule-based Western countries or does not contribute to relationships that are essential to making the system work. It is corruption in Japan, for example, because it undermines loyalty to the group, the foundation of Japanese society. It is largely corruption in China, because it shortcuts *guanxi* and incapacitates the central government. Petty bribery allows many governments to operate, because government salaries are too meager to live on; larger bribes and misappropriation of funds are dysfunctional. The moral status of bribery in Indonesia and Malaysia is less clear. It is widespread in Russia and parts of Eastern Europe, where it is an unmitigated evil. It is far from unknown in the United States. A few years ago, no less a figure than the Chief Justice of a state Supreme Court was impeached and removed from office for taking bribes

Corruption tends to be most prevalent in cultures that have been disrupted by war or colonialism, as for example in some African countries, where bribes are often excessive and harmful to business. Bribery is similarly a legacy of past injustice and violence in Latin American countries, where people regard it as a serious social problem, even those who engage in it. U.S. Foreign Corrupt Practices Act makes it illegal for them to bribe officials of foreign governments. The law does not prohibit bribery of private business people, or payment of extortion money. It also permits "facilitating payments," such as small side payments to officials. The law is vague and unevenly enforced, and it is wise to consult lawyers when in doubt. In fact, when in a foreign country it is wise to avoid, whenever possible, any transactions that might be interpreted as bribes. Locals may know how to do it without getting into trouble, but visitors do not. Bribery tends to be an art that amateurs should not attempt!!

The definition of a bribe varies around the world.

Gender Discrimination

Different cultures can have very different attitudes toward gender equality. A visitor from the United States or Europe tends to notice this right away, because it is a high profile issue back home. A case study called the "Foreign Assignment" (Dunfee and Robertson, 1997) describes a female bank employee in the United States who asked to be transferred to a branch in Mexico City. She encountered patronizing attitudes from male coworkers and, from clients, a lack of respect for her professional competence. Her dilemma was whether to acquiesce in this aspect of the local culture or fight it. She chose the latter with the result that her superiors gave her lukewarm evaluations and her career advance floundered.

Cultural patterns of this sort usually exist to serve a purpose in the larger system. The tradition of *machismo* in Mexico can be traced to Moorish Spain. It is centered on the concept of manly honor. Like so many cultural practices, it is a stress control mechanism. The underlying cause of stress is lack of control over one's fate. A young man growing up in Latin America once faced (and in some cases still faces) a life of danger and violence. To deal with this stress, he learned to take control of the situation. Rather than give in to fate, he took action, often violent. Rather than surrender his wife and children to danger, he protected them by whatever means was necessary. *Machismo* made a virtue of necessity: by facing up to danger "like a man," the Latino experienced life as an occasion to display manly honor rather than to cover with fear. *Machismo* was a way of making a hard life bearable for men and women alike. The patronizing attitude toward women therefore does not imply that women are inferior; only that they have a different role. They nurture the family while men shield it from danger. In fact, the flip side of *machismo* is *Marianisma* (after Mary, mother of Jesus), which views women as morally superior to men. What U.S. women experience as demeaning, traditional Latina women accept as a sign of respect.

In recent times this system has evolved, at least among the upper classes, to an emphasis on devotion to family. A man of honor puts his family first. One way that Mexicans judge whether a business partner is trustworthy is to find out if he is a good family man. In particular he should never let business take precedence over the family. A Mexican businessman will cancel a meeting or miss an appointment to take care of family matters. He may spend a long lunch hour with the family or take several days off to assist an older relative or attend a funeral. This presents a stark contrast with business in the United States, where companies often expect total commitment, as though families did not exist. U.S. business people might well envy the Mexican way when it comes to family.

The Western habit of viewing different cultures as simply more or less advanced is therefore inadequate. Different peoples have made different tradeoffs and arrived at different solutions to life. Every solution favors certain human virtues and develops some aspects of human potential while suppressing others. A Westerner who simply resists a culture that seems retrograde misses an opportunity to develop a side of his or her humanity that is neglected back home.

Relativism

From the discussion of above emerges the concept of ethical relativism. This refers to the differences in interpretations and evaluations of behavior in different cultures. It is said that when in Rome, one should do as the Romans do. This principle is inadequate to guide one's operations in foreign countries. The host countries policies and the local countries policies create conflict. There are many versions of relativism.

Ethical relativism means that actions are morally right within a particular society because law, custom or other conventions of the society approve them. This is not always true. Descriptive relativism means that, as a matter of fact, the value beliefs and attitudes differ from culture to culture. It says that there are differences between the moral beliefs and attitudes of various cultures. However, just because certain cultures approves of rapes does not mean that they are ethical.

Different cultures can have very different attitudes toward gender equality.

Moral relativism means that moral judgments are contextual. It believes in the situational theory. For example lying is immoral. Special circumstances can arise where people have to lie in order to save a life or protect their privacy from intruders.

Relativism is important in multinational contexts involving different cultures. This helps people to make adjustments.

International Rights

The MNCs have to respect the International rights. They must understand the necessity and importance of these rights while operating their business in the host country. Donaldson+ suggests the following ten international rights:

1. The right to freedom of physical movement
2. The right to ownership of property
3. The right to freedom from torture
4. The right to a fair trial
5. The right to nondiscriminatory treatment (freedom from discrimination on the basis of race and sex)
6. The right to physical security
7. The right to freedom of speech and association
8. The right to minimal education
9. The right to political participation
10. The right to subsistence.

MNCs must promote morally just measures even though the host countries standards might be lower. *For example*, DDT is harmful to health, even though in underdeveloped countries the laws are not stringent, company should not promote the product or educate the users about the product.

The transfer of technology across borders and appropriateness of such technology are applicable to MNCs. They transfer outdated technology to underdeveloped countries. Is this ethical? In the automobile industry, outdated models with safety features considered inadequate are introduced in less developed countries so that machineries and plant which are unacceptable in developed countries are used to in under developed regions. Is this to be accepted?

MNCs should look at the appropriate technology while selecting a technology for different countries. Nirma uses semi manual technology to produce detergents while Hindustan Lever uses automated technology. The costs are low for Nirma so also the price of the product. Water coolers work in dry climates in Hyderabad and Pune, but in Chennai they are not effective. Only air conditioners are effective. Appropriate technology refers to the most suitable technology. For example: a country with many poor farmers can make better use of small, single or two wheel tractors that can serve as motorized ploughs, to pull wagons or to drive pumps, than huge diesel tractors. On the other hand, the same country may benefit from the latest micro technology to spread a telephone network. Appropriateness should be examined from scale, technical and managerial skills, materials, environment, capital costs and above all human values.

Bhopal disaster – A case study

Union Carbide is a US based MNC. It has branches all over the world. In 1970, it transformed its pesticide plant in Bhopal from just mixing chemicals to full-scale manufacturing. The company in the home country was fully aware of the dangers of the new technology while transferring the technology. In its main plant in USA they produced Methyl Iso-Cyanate, which was the main poison used in pesticides, particularly used in India. Methyl Iso-Cyanate is a concentrated gas, which burns any

* Donaldson Thomas, The Ethics of International Business, New York : Oxford University Press, 1989, P. 81

Moral relativism means that moral judgments are contextual

Technology should be examined from Scale, Cost , Skill, and Human Values

moist part in the body by affecting throats and nasal passages, blinding the eyes and even destroying lungs leading to death.

While installing the Bhopal plant, Union Carbide did not transfer all the available safety mechanisms. In the USA it used computerized instruments to control the safety systems to detect leaks. But in Bhopal, safety controls were manual.

The Indian Government had told the company that the Bhopal plant should be operated fully by Indian workers. So, Union Carbide USA took some care to give training to the Indian personnel in the USA. It also sent teams of US engineers to India to make regular safety inspections. But in the year 1982, due to financial pressures, the Company reduced its supervision of the Bhopal plant. On their last inspection, the US engineers had warned of many risks and dangers, which finally led to the disaster.

In the subsequent years, safety practices were reduced gradually due to high turnover of employees, failure in giving training to the new employees and lack of technical awareness among the Indian laborers. Due to this, the workers learned more about the dangers of pesticides from their personal experience than from the study of safety manuals. They also forgot the safety practices of US standards. They used only low-level Indian standards of safety practices within their reach.

Reasons for the Disaster

1. As per the Company's safety manual, the tanks used to store Methyl Iso-Cyanate were not to be filled beyond 60% of their capacity. But in the Bhopal plant, the tanks were over loaded to a tune of 75%.
2. As per the policy of the home company, another empty tank had to be placed near the first tank for use as a stand-by in emergencies. But in the Bhopal plant that emergency tank was also filled with a large amount of chemicals.
3. The storage tanks were to be refrigerated to make the chemical less reactive. But in Bhopal, the entire refrigeration unit had been shutdown as a measure to reduce the cost and this led to increase of temperatures to a higher level.
4. Two months before the disaster, due to over supply production of methyl Iso-Cyanate was stopped and all the workers were diverted to plant maintenance. A new worker had been instructed to clean the pipes and filters connected to the storage tanks. He closed the valves to separate the tanks from the pipes and filters, but unfortunately he failed to insert the safety disks, which were meant to prevent leakages. This led to enormous pressure build-up and heat in the storage tanks.
5. According to Union Carbide, one of the disappointed workers unscrewed a pressure gauge on a tank and inserted a hosepipe into it, knowing that it would cause damage, but not to this extent.
6. As a result the Methyl Iso- cyanate gas started to leak. The workers tried to use the vent – gas-scrubber that was designed to reduce the exhaust gas. But that scrubber had also been shut down.
7. So the workers tried a second way. They wanted to use the flare tower, which was designed to burn off the escaping gas missed by the scrubber. But unfortunately, it was also not in an operating condition.
8. Finally, the workers tried to minimize the damage by spraying water up to 100 feet into the air. But the gas was escaping from a stack of 120 feet high. Unfortunately there were no emergency drills or evacuation plans available.

US engineers had warned of many risks and dangers, which finally led to the Bhopal disaster.

As a result most of the gas escaped and formed a cloud in the air and gas spread over 40 sq.m. This led to a death of more than 6000 people in and around the plant and injured more than 7000 people. Approximately 200,000 people had adverse health effects.

This tragedy happened only because of the total un-preparedness of both the US Company as well its branch in the host country. Bhopal holds out lessons for basic concerns of safety, for standards and above all for good sense.

Twenty years after the Bhopal tragedy, the two survivors, Champa Devi Shukla and Rashida were selected for the group of winners for the Goldman Environmental Prize. They were recognized grassroot environmental activists. The two women shared Rs. 53 lakhs as the award. They decided to use it to establish an award in India to recognize individuals who fight corporate crime. To get the global attention, two of them organized a global hunger strike to help sustain international awareness of the lingering effects of the disaster and for fighting to get the Dow Chemicals to pay for the medical care of the survivors and their children, as well as the environmental clean up.Union Carbide became the wholly subsidiary of Dow Chemicals in 1999., fifteen years after the gas leak. The survivors suffered multiple health problems including headaches, shortness of breath, burning sensation, insomnia and bone pain. They were coughing , there are cases of cancer and anaemia. Women showed high concentration of toxins in their breast milk. The efforts of the survivors helped to persuade the Indian Government to pursue criminal charges against the former Union Carbide Chairman, Warren Anderson, who was leading retirement life in New York State. More monetary damages were claimed from Dow, under the terms of an original settlement, the survivors received about $ 55 (Rs. 21,500) and the relatives of those killed got abut $ 2,000. Dow chemicals claimed that they had no involvement in the Bhopal tragedy, but were considering the original terms of the settlement between Union Carbide and the victims. Legal proceedings in the matter are continuing.

The other winners of the 2004 Goldman Environmental Prize was awarded to Margie Richard who successfully led a campaign to get Royal Dutch/Shell to pay for the relocation of people living near Shell Chemical Plant in Norco, Lousiana. In Africa, the prize was awarded to Rudolf Amenga Etego of Ghana, who worked to suspend a water privatization project that would have limited access to drinking water. In South America social worker Libia Grueso Castelblanco, won for securing 2.4 million hectares in territorial rights for rural communities in Columbia, where armed conflict and aggressive development have displaced many. In Europe, Manana Kochladze won the prize for fighting a multi-corporation plan to build the world's largest oil pipeline through Georgia. His work won concessions to protect villagers and forced, a larger examination of the project's environmental and health impact.

HOW ETHICS IS MANAGED IN TEXAS INSTRUMENT (TI) M- A MNC

For many companies, increased competition, stricter government controls and emerging global markets have raised ethical questions that they were unprepared to deal with.

"Ethical questions face business people every day, especially when a company is involved with worldwide markets," says Carl Skooglund, former vice-president and director of ethics, Texas Instruments (TI). "Finding the right answer isn't often easy — one has to balance local customs and laws with laws of the home country."

As an international company with more than 44,500 employees operating in more than 25 countries, TI is global in scope and culture with a time-honored tradition of conducting business in an ethical and legal manner. But, that is an increasingly difficult challenge thanks to the fast changing times, relationships and situations today.

TI's global vision is 'World Leadership in Digital Solutions for the Networked Society.' The company is competing to win at a global level — entering into strategic partnerships, alliances and

Bhopal holds out lessons for basic concerns of safety, for standards and above all for good sense.

joint ventures in every corner of the globe. The success of these relationships depends greatly upon the company's representatives understanding the ethical standards and expectations of others.

Consider these examples of cultural differences from their files:

In the U.S., telephone help lines or "hotlines," as some companies refer to them, are considered a normal part of business. In some parts of the world, however, hotlines may be greatly mistrusted or even viewed as personally offensive and dangerous.

U.S. companies and U.S. citizens are subject to certain U.S. laws wherever they are. Other countries also have a global reach.

Workers in some parts of the world consider the concept of ethics to be very personal and they may not fully understand that it is also a global or company-wide issue to be discussed or even questioned. In many places, the contract negotiation process can be very long and drawn out — and somewhat informal. That's very frustrating for most U.S. companies unless they have a good understanding of what's going on. There may be very good intentions on all parts, but unless everyone clearly understands the process, it may seem that something unethical is happening.

"These types of situations are trying in the best of times. But today, many organizations and people are under enormous pressure to succeed in a very competitive and challenging global economy. Companies are either reducing or eliminating layers of management that made decisions that they are now expecting those on the firing line to make. We are in a world where the ability to communicate rapidly has exploded. It has created enormous opportunities as well as risks. Legal complexities have increased to the point that people simply don't know. In fact, they can't know," says Skooglund. "Our relationships with other companies are changing through alliances, partnerships and joint ventures to the point that at different times we may be dealing with other companies as customers, suppliers or competitors. Yet, we still expect employees to recognize and respect those differences and the legal risks they present."

The challenge in this dynamic environment, with its close calls and uncertainties, according to Skooglund, "is to provide tools to our employees so that they can make the tough, quick decisions on the fly, on the firing line. And, make them correctly. There are two elements to making decisions and taking action on behalf of any organization: a)a clear understanding of the organization's guiding values, principles and ethical expectations and b) a sound personal judgment and ability to make appropriate choices."

To meet these challenges, TI has adopted a three-level approach to ethical integrity on a global level. The first level simply asks: 'are we complying with all legal requirements on a local level?' The next level asks: 'are there business practices or requirements at the local level which impact how we interact with co-workers in other parts of the world? A growing number of local regulations — rigid environmental regulations in some parts of Europe, for example — have a significant effect on products that we ship to and from those countries.' The third level is: 'do some of our practices need to be adapted based on the local laws and customers of a specific locale? What we think is perfectly proper in one country may not migrate well to another. On what basis do we define our universal standards that apply to TI employees everywhere?'

"For example," Skooglund explained, "TI generally follows conservative rules covering the giving and receiving of gifts. However, what we consider to be an excessive gift in the U.S. may differ from what local customs dictate in other parts of the world. We used to define gift limits in terms of U.S. dollars, but this is impractical when dealing internationally. Instead, we emphasize following the

Workers in some parts of the world consider the concept of ethics to be very personal and they may not fully understand that it is also a global.

TI has adopted a three-level approach to ethical integrity on a global level.

directive that gift giving should not be used in a way that exerts undue pressure to win business or implies a quid-pro-quo.

"In today's environment, there is no way that a rulebook or a library of policies is going to guide those actions. A shared understanding of basic values and principles of integrity must guide them. And they must be supported by resources that will help them recognize when the caution lights should come on and to know where they can seek expert advice quickly. TI's reputation is completely in our hands, to be enhanced or damaged by the nature of our actions.", he concludes.

International ethics tools

Some of the issues faced in international practice are similar to those at home. They are made more serious and/or complex by the different and often less ethically demanding foreign work environment. In the area of labour, if you try to act ethically by paying local employees more than the low local pay rate, you can cause a social chaos.

The Indian engineer practicing abroad in USA or Canada could use some tools to help make the best ethical decisions. The International Federation of Consulting Engineers (FIDIC) provides templates for contract format, terms and definitions, as well as policies on practice specifics (e.g. copyright liability). It also has a code of ethics for engineers and their firms. The issue is the codes do not specify if the standards are more demanding than local codes or standards, engineer should follow which standards. This issue is especially critical in such areas as safety.

In addition to the engineering specific codes, there are international ethics initiatives that can also provide useful guidance. United Nations Global Compact, Organisation for Economic Cooperation and Development Anti-bribery Convention, World Bank and International Monetary Fund criteria. Both now screen proposals made to them using ethics criteria, emphasizing avoidance of countries and companies associated with corruption.

Jim Ridler+ offers some guidelines for international practice:

Aim for doing no harm, realizing mutual benefit, having respect for local views and being consistent with your values.

Find the best local people, prove your integrity, build trust and become part of the solution, by being a good corporate citizen and supporting the local community.

Do not participate in corrupt practices and fire employees who do.

Use common sense, good judgment and creative options

If a client is resisting an ethical solution to an issue, explain that your professional standards are as important to you as the client's standards are important to them.

To meet the challenges of globalisation, many companies may require a Chief Globalisation Officer (CGO). The CGO has to maintain a fine balance between global focus and local relevance. He has to globally expand operations, ownership and commitment. He has to champion his cause with the patience, experience, and thick skin, insight, foresight and intuition and communication skills to become a global leader.

ENGINEERS AND THE ENVIRONMENT

Engineering responsibility for the environment is necessarily closely related to the laws governing environmental matters, but environmental degradation was not the subject of serious government regulations until the late 1960's. Until that time, private litigation and the common law, at least in the USA, were the principal tools for controlling pollution. Usually, however, no single individual was sufficiently harmed by pollution to be motivated to bring suit against a polluter. Governments were ineffective in controlling pollution.

---

* Jim Ridler, P. Eng., Problems in International practice, Engineering Dimensions- November/December, 2002

The CGO has to maintain a fine balance between global focus and local relevance.

As a response to this state of affairs, the US Congress passed the National Environmental Policy Act (NEPA) in 1969. The Act inaugurated "a national policy which will encourage productive and enjoyable harmony between man and his environment...." One of the best-known provisions of the NEPA is the requirement for an environmental impact statement, which enumerates the effect of a project on the environment. Congress then created the Environmental Protection Agency (EPA) to enforce its mandates.

In the ensuing decades the U.S enacted legislation to control pollution in four major areas. In order to protect the air, they enacted the Clean Air Act of 1970 and amended it in 1977. The Act set a goal of a 90% reduction for auto emissions. It permitted the EPA to consider economic and technological feasibility in deciding when the goals were to be met, but not in adjusting the goals themselves.

After 1979, the EPA adopted a "bubble" concept as a method of enforcement. According to this policy, an imaginary "bubble" is placed around a plant or even an entire region. Under the bubble concept, industries may reduce those emissions that they can reduce most cheaply. One plant may be able to reduce pollutant A more cheaply, even reducing the level below the minimum level required by law. Another plant may be able to reduce pollutant B more cheaply, reducing it below the level required by law. Then the two plants can engage in trades, whereby the first plant trades some of the "credits" it has in pollutant A for some of the "credits" the second plant has in pollutant B. Since the first plant can reduce pollutant A most efficiently and the second plant can reduce pollutant B most efficiently, the total level of pollution under the bubble can be reduced to designated levels, but in the most economically efficient way.

In 1972 the U.S Congress enacted the Clean Water Act and amended it in 1972, 1977, and 1986. The Act, designed to "restore and maintain the chemical, physical, and biological integrity of the Nation's waters," makes it unlawful for any person, business, or governmental body to discharge any pollutant into navigable waters without a permit. The Act mandated pollution control measures in two stages. By 1977 all plants were to have installed water pollution control devices that represented the best practicable pollution control technology. By 1989 all plants were to have installed equipment that met more stringent standards. Plants discharging conventional pollutants are to apply the best conventional pollutant control technology. Plants discharging toxic or unconventional pollutants are to apply the best available technology economically achievable.

In 1976 they enacted the Resource Conservation and Recovery Act (RCRA), designed to control the transportation, storage, treatment, and disposal of hazardous wastes. The Act requires the generator of a hazardous waste to complete a "manifest," a form that describes the nature of the hazardous waste and its method of disposal. The transporter must sign the manifest and the operator of the disposal site must do so as well, returning the manifest to the generator of the waste. This procedure is supposed to provide a complete record of the disposal of the waste. The EPA is also required to regulate the disposal sites themselves.

In order to facilitate the cleanup of inactive dump sites, Congress enacted the Comprehensive Environmental Response, Compensation, and Liability Act in 1980. The Act empowers the President to clean up abandoned hazardous sites and to provide necessary remedial actions in the case of spills. Finally, Congress has enacted a number of other laws that require businesses to alter products and processes that can have an adverse effect on the environment. The Noise Pollution Control Act of 1972 gives the federal government broad powers to protect the public from excessive noise. The Federal Insecticide, Fungicide, and Rodenticide Act of 1947 and the Federal Environmental Pesticide Control Act that amended it requires manufacturers to register insecticides with the EPA before they can be sold to consumers. The EPA will register a pesticide only if it is properly labeled, does what it claims to do, and will not produce "any unreasonable risk to man or the environment, taking

NEPA requires an environmental impact statement.

into account the economic, social and environmental costs and benefits of the use of any pesticide." The Toxic Substances Control Act (TOSCA) of 1976 establishes a regulatory mechanism for protecting the public against dangerous chemical materials contained in consumer and industrial products.

These are the principal U.S laws that provide the legal context in which decisions regarding the effect of technology on the environment must be made. Similar legislations have also been made or are being made in India and other countries. The laws, however, do not cover many situations, however, so there is the need for individual judgment. Business managers usually make these judgments, so the attitudes of managers toward environmental laws are very important.

Business Managers and Environmental Laws

A recent survey gives us insight into the attitudes of managers towards environmental laws. From 1982 until 1985 Joseph M. Petulla, Director of the Graduate Program in Environmental Management at the University of San Francisco, surveyed a number of industries with respect to hazardous waste disposal. He found that he could classify the companies he investigated into three categories.

The first type of company, consisting of 29% of the firms surveyed, engaged in what Petulla called "crisis-oriented environmental management." Industries in this group tended to have no full-time personnel assigned to environmental concerns, devoted as few resources as possible to such matters, and fought environmental regulations. As one representative of this group put it, "Why the hell should we cooperate with government or anyone else who takes us away from our primary goal (of making money)?" He went on to say that it is cheaper to pay the fines and lobby than to devote resources to environmental matters.

A second group, consisting of 58% of the firms surveyed, adopted what Patulla called "cost-oriented environmental management." Firms in this group accepted governmental regulation as a cost of doing business, but often without enthusiasm or commitment. They usually had established company policies regulating the environmental matters and separate units devoted to them.

A third group, consisting of 9% of Petulla's sample, adopted what he called "enlightened environmental management." In these companies, responsiveness to environmental concerns had the complete support of the CEO. The companies had well-staffed environmental divisions, used state-of-the-art equipment, and generally had good relationships with governmental regulators. One manager said that people in his company saw themselves as good neighbors in the community. "Anyhow," he concluded, "in the long run it's in our own interest, to keep us from lawsuits and generate some good will."

Petulla's findings must be viewed in the light of the fact that many of the attitudes expressed concerned environmental laws and their enforcement and may not have reflected fundamental attitudes towards environmental matters accurately. Many of the managers in the second group may have had a commitment to environmental preservation, but they may have believed that governmental regulations are an inefficient way to protect the environment. Nevertheless the survey suggests that relatively few managers have a firm commitment to preserving the environment.

Engineering Codes and the Environment

In the light of widespread skepticism on the part of managers, what are the responsibilities of professional engineers with regard to the environment? The first canon of the NSPE code requires engineers to "hold paramount the safety, health and welfare of the public in the performance of their professional duties." Insofar as environmental issues have a clear relation to human safety and health, therefore, the engineering profession has already committed itself to a concern for environmental protection and perhaps even improvement. For example, engineers already have an obligation to concern themselves with pollution, when it affects human health.

The codes give little direction, however, as to how this concern should be implemented. What kinds of policies with respect to the environment should engineers advocate? If engineers have an

U.S laws regard the effect of technology on the environment.
Few managers have a firm commitment to preserving the environment.

obligation to promote a clean environment in order to protect human health, how do they determine what is "clean"?

A still wider issue is raised by the fact that some environmental problems do not raise issues of human health. Suppose an engineer is asked to participate in the design of a dam that will destroy a section of a "wild river" and flood thousands of acres of farmland. He may believe that this is an unwarranted destruction of a natural state and even bad social policy. If an engineer objects to such, what should she do so as an engineer or as a concerned citizen? In other words, should the objection to environmental degradation not involving dangers to human health be a matter of professional ethics or personal ethics?

Consider another example. An engineer may be asked to design a condominium project that will be built in a wetlands area. She may be concerned about the resource depletion that will be accelerated by a chemical process, or the destruction of plant species that will result from an engineering project. Can an engineer object to such projects on the basis of her role as an engineer, or should she make clear that she is objecting as a citizen? Again, should such objections be made on the basis of professional ethics or personal ethics?

One of the most explicit statements on environmental matters to be found in an engineering code is in the code of the Institute of Electrical and Electronics Engineers (IEEE). The first canon of the code commits IEEE members: ....

...to accept responsibility in making engineering decisions consistent with the safety, health, and welfare of the public, and to disclose promptly factors that might endanger the public or the environment.

The fact that there is an explicit reference to endangering the environment in addition to endangering "the public" might be taken to indicate that environmental concerns go beyond a concern for human health. This inference might, however, be unwarranted. The concern for the environment might be intended to refer only to matters affecting human health. Furthermore, IEEE members are obligated only to "disclose" possible dangers to the public and the environment. Should such dangers be disclosed only to one's immediate superior? What if one's superior is part of the problem? And does an engineer have any right as a professional to refuse to participate in projects to which she has strong objections from an environmental standpoint? Again, the codes are silent.

Environmental Matters Involving Human Health: How Clean Is Clean?

If we can assume that the engineering profession has already committed itself to a concern for the environment insofar as it is related to human health, how can we ascertain the proper implementation of that commitment? Since this question usually involves environmental pollution, one way to formulate this question is to ask how we can determine an acceptable level of pollution. The question is often asked, "How clean is clean?"

One way of responding to this question is to adopt an approach that is oblivious to costs and keeps the environment as free as possible of pollution. We have seen that the Clean Air Act places safety ahead of the balancing of costs and benefits when dealing with hazardous pollutants. It permitted the EPA to consider economic and technological feasibility in deciding when the goals were to be met, but not in adjusting the goals themselves. The Clean Water Act requires polluters to do the best they possibly can to stop polluting, without reference to cost. The Resource Conservation and Recovery Act requires that standards regulating hazardous waste be based solely on the protection of public health and the environment. The Endangered Species Act is essentially oblivious to cost considerations. Finally, in the famous decision regarding Tellico dam, the U.S Supreme Court forced the dismantling of a dam costing $100 million in order to prevent the extinction of an economically worthless species of perch.

Engineers have obligation to pollution.

There are several problems with this cost-oblivious approach to environmental pollution, even where human health is concerned.

First, it tends to produce disrespect for the law. Manufacturers know that the law is unrealistic and that the regulators determine its practical significance. There is a strong incentive, therefore, to engage in as much deception and hard negotiation as possible, knowing that it may pay off in rich dividends.

Second, in spite of the rigor of the law, the enforcement of the law may be too lax. The disparity between the law and the way it is enforced may be too great. This is because enforcement involves consent decrees with industry. These decrees often allow pollution that is far greater than what the law allows. Thus the net result may be more pollution than an even less stringent law would have allowed.

Third, this approach takes no account of the cost of eliminating the pollution, or the fact that in some cases the threat to human health is unknown or is in dispute. Some pollutants pose far more danger to human health than others, and there are other values that should perhaps be considered as well, such as jobs and the standard of living.

In the light of these objections, some have proposed an approach to the regulation of environmental pollution based on cost/benefit analysis (CBA). CBA is a type of utilitarianism, in that its aim is to maximize human well-being. One aspect of well-being is health, and pollution is a threat to health. Unfortunately, reducing threats to health involves a cost. We cannot improve the environment with respect to human health without devoting resources to the effort, and this requires diverting those resources from other areas. As economist William F. Baxter comments, even though low levels of pollution contribute to human well-being, "so do food and shelter and education and music."

CBA provides an appealing way of resolving conflict problems between the good of reducing pollution and other competing goods which make demands on social resources: we must divert resources to environmental causes only up to that point at which the resources can produce more overall human well-being if used elsewhere. It would be irrational, by the standards of CBA, to devote resources to environmental causes when the resources could produce more overall human well-being if they were devoted to other uses. Thus the goal of CBA is not a totally "clean" environment, but rather an environment such that making it any cleaner would divert financial resources from other areas, where they could promote more human well-being.

The CBA method for determining optimal pollution involves three steps. First, one must assess the problem in terms that are amenable to a CBA. Second, one must calculate the costs and benefits. Third, one must compare the costs and benefits and determine the proper course of action.

We can illustrate this method by means of an example of pollution from a chemical plant.

Suppose there is a large chemical plant near a residential area. The plant emits a number of noxious odors, some of them posing mild risks to health. How do we determine the optimal level of pollution that the plant should be allowed to contribute to the environment?

First, we must analyze the problem. The plant is emitting pollutants into the air, which is a part of the "commons." The commons are those areas, such as the air, rivers, and oceans, which are not owned by anyone in particular. Economists say that the plant is "externalizing" the cost of the pollution by forcing others, such as the surrounding residents, to pay the cost of the pollution. The costs of the pollution must be "internalized," or charged to the plant that produces the pollution. The other costs and benefits of regulating the pollution must be determined in order to arrive at an optimal pollution level.

Second, we must calculate the costs and benefits. If a manufacturer can dump pollutants into a river or into the air and not be liable for any further costs for their disposal, then we do not know the true costs of eliminating the pollutant. In order to internalize the cost, we must first determine the cost of the pollution. One way to get a measure of the cost for the obnoxious

The Environment Law should be enforced.

smells is to compare the costs of homes near the plant with costs of homes in locations which are equivalent, except that the odors are not present. Then some measure of the cost to health would have to be obtained. We would have to estimate the lost earnings from days missed at work, the cost in suffering, and any other costs attributed to poorer health.

There are also costs associated with forcing the plant to eliminate the pollution, because the plant also confers benefits on the community. If the cost of eliminating the pollution produced by a given process is greater than the profits produced by the process, the plant may be forced to terminate the process. This would increase unemployment, and the cost of this increased unemployment would have to be entered into the CBA equation.

Third, we must compare the costs and benefits of regulating the pollution. The plant should eliminate the pollution up to that point at which the advantages to the community of eliminating the pollution are outweighed by the disadvantages to the community of eliminating it. Then the optimum level of pollution will have been reached.

This analysis omits many of the considerations that should be a part of a complete CBA, but it illustrates the method. This same method can, of course, be applied to any other type of pollution. Implementation of policies based on CBA does not guarantee that all pollution will be eliminated, but rather that resources will be used in the most economically efficient way.

There are several objections to the CBA answer to the question, "How clean is clean?" First, the CBA assumes that economic measures of cost and benefit must override all other considerations. CBA encourages only the elimination of pollution that can be eliminated in an economically efficient manner, and this may not be the pollution that is most harmful from an environmental standpoint. Suppose the chemical plant we have been considering is near a wilderness area that is damaged by one of the plant's emissions. It might not be economically efficient to eliminate the pollutant, from the CBA standpoint. Of course the damage to the wilderness area must be included in the cost of the pollution in a CBA, but this cost might still not justify the elimination of the pollution from the CBA standpoint, or even its reduction. In this event, CBA would allow the plant to continue damaging the wilderness area.

Second, it is often very difficult to ascertain the costs and benefits of the many factors that enter into a CBA. If the threats posed by many substances to human health are not known, it is impossible to execute a competent CBA. This problem becomes especially acute if we consider long-term costs and benefits, most of which are impossible to calculate.

Third, CBA often does not take into account the distribution of costs and benefits. Often those who bear the costs of pollution do not share in the benefits. Suppose a plant pays a pollution tax to dump pollutants into a river. By CBA, the costs of eliminating the pollution might not justify its elimination, yet these costs may fall in a disproportionate way to the poor people who often fish in the river and eat the contaminated fish.

Fourth, CBA often leads to conclusions contrary to the moral beliefs of many people. Many manufacturers oppose child labor laws, arguing that the laws would lead to economic inefficiencies. For example, tunnels and shafts in some mines were too small to accommodate adults, shall be seen in the next section, in fact, that most environmental legislation is based on values that transcend CBA.

This observation does not, of course, mean that CBA is wrong. It may be that our moral beliefs that cannot be justified by CBA are wrong. Nevertheless, the counter-intuitive implications of CBA do at the very least raise doubts about its validity as a complete basis for answering the question, "How clean is clean?" Combined with the other problems, this objection becomes even more relevant. In spite of these problems, CBA is a useful method in determining the proper policies for pollution control. The criticisms show that, taken alone, it is not adequate.

The cost and benefit of regulating the Pollution must be compared.
The cost of eliminating pollution might not justify its elimination

If defining "clean" in terms of either a cost-oblivious approach or CBA are both unsatisfactory, philosopher Mark Sagoff suggests a middle ground between them. Sagoff suggests that what is needed is a policy that: might permit the agencies to take technological and economic factors into account, on a case-by-case basis, as long as they act in good faith to make progress toward reducing and, it is hoped, eventually eliminating damage to the environment and risks to human safety and health.

It is not always clear how Sagoff's suggested policy should be applied, but it may be a useful general guideline in determining engineering responsibilities with respect to environmental pollution. As such, it can be a supplement to the almost total lack of specificity in the codes. It shows a blend of RP and utilitarian considerations that is characteristic of many good moral guidelines. That is, it takes into account both the need to protect human health and the need to balance costs and benefits, within certain limits. It also has the benefit of a background in the law. Now let us turn briefly to a consideration of environmental concerns that go beyond considerations of human health.

Engineering Responsibilities to the Non-Human Environment

Contemporary technologically advanced civilization has made massive changes in the environment. Western society has tended to conceive of nature as passive, as the fit object of human manipulation and control. This view of nature as passive is amply reflected in our language about the natural world. Land is to be developed." "Raw" land is to be "improved." Natural resources are to be "exploited" and "consumed." Trees are to be "harvested." The rivers are to be "harnessed" to produce electrical power. The wilderness must be "managed." Nature, like the rest of the non-human world, is to be subservient to human purposes.

The environmental movement, so influential during the last twenty-five years, is a reaction against this attitude toward nature, but there is still a question as to whether the concern for non-human nature should be a part of *professional* engineering ethics rather than an engineer's *personal* ethics. What are some of the arguments for and against including a concern for non-human nature in the professional codes of engineers? Those who believe that professional engineering obligations to the environment should not be extended beyond a concern for factors that endanger human health could make the following arguments.

First, the judgments that would have to be made in this area fall outside the area of professional engineering expertise and as such might be considered a violation of professional responsibility. Suppose an engineer is asked to participate in the design of a condominium that will be built on a wetland area. The engineer objects because she believes that the wetland area is especially important for the ecology of the area. This judgment is not a professional engineering judgment, but rather one more appropriately made by a biologist.

The same problem exists in many other areas related to the environment. An engineer may object to a dam that will destroy a wild river or flood hundreds of acres of farmland. Or he may object to designing a sawmill that is to be built in the midst of an ancient forest. In all of these cases the judgments involve considerations outside the engineer's professional expertise. An engineer may well object to these projects, but he or she should not object as an engineer. To do so is to invite public disrespect for the engineering profession.

Such objections might even be considered violations of engineering codes. The National Society of Professional Engineers (NSPE) code contains the following statement: 'Engineers may express publicly a professional opinion on technical subjects only when that opinion is founded upon adequate knowledge of the facts and competence in the subject matter.'(Section II 3.b) Many objections to environmental matters are not based on professional engineering competence.

Suppose the NSPE code also contained a provision such as this: Engineers must not participate in projects that are unnecessarily destructive to the environment, even if they do not endanger human life or health. The judgments necessary to comply with such a provision would often not be profes-

Concern for non-human nature is a part of Engineering Ethics.

sional engineering judgments, so that implementing such a provision might well involve violating the above section.

Second, an extension of professional responsibility for the environment into areas not clearly related to public health or safety might cause considerable problems for engineering societies. Along with other members of society, engineers disagree over environmental issues, especially where human health is not directly involved. Forcing members of professional societies to take policy stands on such issues will introduce a new source of divisiveness into professional societies. Another aspect of this same objection is that such issues will be especially troublesome for engineering managers who are members of the societies.

Management cannot be expected to be sympathetic to policies that will inevitably result in greater expense for industry. The effect of introducing these issues into the societies may serve to weaken industry support for the societies themselves. There are, however, reasons for believing that engineers should assume a professional responsibility for the effects of engineering work on the non-human environment.

First, a good argument can be made that the very concept of responsibility shows that engineers have a responsibility for environmental problems, even when they do not directly affect human welfare. Philosopher Kenneth E. Goodpaster finds several senses of the term "responsibility," two of which are relevant here. In the *causal* sense of responsibility, we say of a person that he or she is responsible for something when an action or event is brought about at least in part by that individual. By this definition, engineers should share in the responsibility for environmental concerns, because technology has brought about many environmental problems, and it has the capacity to remedy many of them.

Another conception of responsibility is a *role-following* sense, referring to socially expected behavior associated with certain roles. Thus parents have responsibility for children. In this sense also engineers have responsibility for the environment, for many members of the public expect engineers to assume this responsibility.

Second, the engineering profession could make a substantial contribution to the protection of the environment. Engineers are, after all, major participants in virtually all of the projects that affect the environment for good or ill. If even a substantial number of concerned engineers refused to contribute their professional skills to some of the most environmentally destructive projects, the result might well be the cancellation of the projects or at least a modification of them so they will produce less environmental devastation.

We shall leave it to the reader to decide whether engineers should have an obligation as professionals to protect non-human nature. There is, however, another approach to the question. There is a precedent in other professions for allowing professionals to refuse to lend their professional expertise to activities to which they have personal objections.

The morality of abortion is an issue outside the professional expertise of physicians. It is a matter for moral philosophy or theology rather than medicine. Nevertheless, physicians are not usually required to perform abortions if they have moral objections to it. Similarly, perhaps engineers should not be required to participate in environmental projects to which they object. Many engineers already have serious reservations about some projects that damage the environment. Without support from the codes, they may find it difficult to register their objections to the projects or to refuse to participate in them.

Perhaps a provision in the code could be worded like this: 'Engineers should not be required to participate in projects that, in their personal judgment, are unnecessarily harmful to the environment. They also have the right to make their objections known to the proper authorities.' Such a provision

Engineers should share the responsibility of environment.
A Professional Engineer has the Right to object and to refuse to participate.

allows a professional engineer to refuse to participate in (and even to object to) projects which offend her personal values regarding the environment.

(***A Case for Discussion***: *The Chennai-based Orchid Chemicals received an award for environmental and community service. The Rotary Club of Madras gave the award. The company is driven by a corporate philosophy that places people before products and profits. It is 100 per cent export oriented company producing antibiotics.. The company has invested 14 million on capital expenditure in environmental friendly systems. The company has pioneered the concept of Zero discharge in the pharmaceutical sector. The company adopted a technology to break down the effluents it produces by separating heating and cooling and convert them into useful or harmless waste.*

Water can be extracted form liquid waste but solid waste poses the real challenge for the industry. Orchid recovers almost 100 % of the water used in its production process. To minimize solid waste, the company has undertaken bio composting to produce manure, which has been tested and proved to be safe and effective. Normally we hear about kitchen waste but not industrial waste. Industrial waste from a pharmaceutical company is mainly made up of inorganic salts and solvent residues, it doesn't have heavy metals, which makes it possible to convert it to manure.)

COMPUTER ETHICS

Computer ethics is the branch of engineering ethics dealing with moral issues in computer technology. It is becoming increasingly important as computers become the technological backbone of contemporary society.

Computers have become integral part of our life. We are in a knowledge economy, but our managerial and governance system are stuck in the industrial era. What we need is the culture of citizenship with interplay of structures, values and practices, encourage every person to pursue individual excellence and at the same time create, through shared processes of self-governance, an emotional commitment to efforts for the common good. It seeks to break the conflict between self-interest and corporate interest. The practice of citizenship cannot be imposed from above. It must grow out of the actions and beliefs of the citizens themselves.

The era of computers have advantages and disadvantages. Communication has become fast and the reach has increased. New issues of safety and privacy have emerged. Some of the problems are given below:

Technostress: This is stress induced by computer use. Its symptom includes aggravation, hostility towards other humans, impatience and fatigue.

Computers viruses, abuse and crime: Computer abuse is the commission of acts involving a computer that may not be illegal but are considered unethical.

Ethical dilemma of Employee monitoring: Should you monitor a worker who spends more time on internet?.

Rage due to Computer failures: The failure can occur due to hardware or software. Hardware problem do not occur frequently and can be solved, but software errors are very serious as they destroy the entire network. Who is to be blamed?

Cyber crimes+:

The Internet is fast becoming a way of life and also a way of living because of growing dependence and reliance on it. The advent of computers has been a boon to engineers. There have been various kinds of computer and Internet related crimes that are classified as cyber crimes. Unauthorized access to systems, damage to property, theft, fraud, mischief and publication of obscene and indecent material are the types of crimes the Internet revolution has spawned.

Hacking

Hacking is a crime in which a person(s) cracks a system and gains unauthorised access to the data

* Technical note, Journal of Intellectual Property Rights, Vol 9, January 2004, pp. 51-56

Computer ethics deals with moral issues in computer technology.

stored in them. The hacker hacks into the site and change the material. The real tangible threat of hacking comes in when an unauthorized access to a system is done with an intention of committing further crimes like fraud, misrepresentation, downloading data in order to commit infringement of copyright, accessing sensitive and confidential data from the sites etc. One of the common types of fraud on the net is circulation of bogus online investment newsletters, which give biased and untrue advice on stocks and securities.

Hacking is criminal trespass covered under Section 441 of the Indian Penal Code that defines it as ' unauthorized entry into or upon property against the will of the person in possession or lawfully obtaining entry but wrongfully remaining thereon'. Herein a website is considered as a property. Could website be regarded as property is an issue? The world of Internet includes terms like site, home page, visiting a site and traveling on the super highway etc.. Hacking is made a crime punishable under Section 66(2) of the Information Technology (IT) Act, 2000 providing for an imprisonment upto 3 years or with fine up to Rs. 2 lakhs or with both. If a person gains unauthorised access to the property (web site) of another, breaching confidentiality of electronic documents, it is punishable under Section 72 of the IT Act with an imprisonment upto 2 years or fines up to 1 lakh or with both.

Cyber Scams and Frauds

Section 25 of the IPC defines 'fraudulently as an action or deed done with an intention of deceit. One needs to satisfy the deceit or an intention to deceit or to cause possible injury. Internet is being used to defraud people and organization. This is done through online investment newsletters, bulletin boards, e-mail spams. Spam is junk e- mail that is cheap and easy to create. These offenses are treated as fraud and cheating.

In Hyderabad, a case of fraud of on-line cheating was identified The cyber fraud was exposed when a website manager noticed large number of transactions being conducted to a single Internet Protocol (IP). The duplicate of the charge slips of credit cards submitted by customer on petrol bunks was retained and the PIN numbers were noted down . The accused began ordering goods on e bay and paid through the credit card numbers. Subsequently he registered himself as buyer as well as seller. He used to buy and sell goods in different names and credit cards. Many credit card numbers were obtained from nationalized banks also.

Computer Virus

Viruses are introduced deliberately and with *mala fide* destroying or altering the operating systems and database of computer. It is described as mischief as per Section 425 to 440 of the IPC. Loss or damage to the public or person needs to be proved. Chapter XI of the Information Technology Act, 2000 deals with computer crimes and provides for punishments for these offences.

Internet Defamation

If X publishes something, which is an attack on the good name of Y on the internet. Can it be a case of defamation ? Similarly, if wrong information is provided on the net. The jurisdiction is a problem in the net. The issue is what should constitute as publication on net. Suppose you get some bad remarks on e-mail . Can e-mail be regarded as publication ? It is a personal correspondence. Just because internet has jurisdiction problem, is it ethical to publish wrong information or defame somebody.

Software Piracy

Just as in publishing and music, software piracy is a reality. In India computer software falls under copyright laws and therefore, the software is protected under the Copyright Act. The problem is philosophy behind Internet is freedom of information and freedom to information. Some 'die hards' like the proponents of open source software maintain that software copyright protection violates this philosophy.

Cyber squatting relates to registration of a domain name.

Cyber Squatting

Cyber squatting is an offence that relates to the registration of a domain name by an entity that does not have an inherent right to similar or identical trademark registration. In the Sify case, the Supreme Court on a complaint by Sify, the software and ISP major, has restrained another company from using the domain name Sify.

The Internet crimes are increasing at an alarming rate. There is a need for international cyber law due to the problem of jurisdiction since in the Internet geographical boundaries are difficult to define and enforce.

Code of Conduct for Computer Professionals

Computer professional find themselves in various relationships of employer-employee, client - professional, professional-professional and society-professional. These relationships involve a diversity of interests and sometimes these interests come into conflict with each other. To respond to the various problems of computer ethics, the Computer Society of India has evolved their own code of conduct and a set of Ten Commandments has been drawn up. The code of ethics specifies that IT professionals should act with integrity, respect confidentiality of information and be human in their approach. The responsibilities of IT professional towards clients and community have also been specified.

Ten Commandments of Computer Ethics

Created by the Computer Ethics Institute

1. Thou shall not use a computer to harm other people.
2. Thou shall not interfere with other people's computer work.
3. Thou shall not snoop around in other people's computer files.
4. Thou shall not use a computer to steal.
5. Thou shall not use a computer to bear false witness.
6. Thou shall not copy or use proprietary software for which you have not paid.
7. Thou shall not use other people's computer resources without authorization or proper compensation.
8. Thou shall not appropriate other people's intellectual output.
9. Thou shall think about the social consequences of the program you are writing or the system you are designing.
10. Thou shall always use a computer in ways that insure consideration and respect for your fellow humans.

Weapons Development

There are special moral issues intrinsic to the defense industry, such as cost overruns, uncritical proliferation of new weapons and secrecy in military work. Should countries invest in weapon development which is to be used in war? Should engineers get involved in the weapon development and take it up as a career? Engineer are under obligation to erect bridges that do not collapse, and build nuclear power plants that do not emit radiation, they need to carefully consider the consequences. A pacifist may argue that engineers have the right to refuse to get involved in the unethical act of manufacture of devices to kill human beings. Weapon development by itself is not unethical but their use for killing people is unethical and against the principle of human right to live, he may argue.

To us the atom bombs dropped on Hiroshima and Nagasaki are horrible because of deaths and ***destruction they caused. India had nuclear tests in Pokhran. If the use is for societal good then it is ethical. Those who are working in military missiles enjoy the challenging task and are proud***

Ten Commandments for Computer Engineers.

and patriotic. Design, manufacture and deployment of weapons need to include not only their use but also eventual disposal. Engineers and scientists dealing with materials dangerous enough to be considered useful as weapons must consider not only their direct use but also their accidental diversion and ultimate safe disposal.

(***A Case for Discussion***: *In October 1986, Mr. Vanunu, a former engineer at Israel's Dimona nuclear reactor, disclosed to The Sunday Times (London) that Israel had between 100 to 200 nuclear weapons, backing this with evidence and photographs. Following this, he was abducted by Mossad secret agents from Rome, smuggled by sea to Israel and tried behind closed doors. He was imprisoned for 'treason'. His trial and conviction came in for sharp protests from jurists, human rights and peace activists from the world over, including Noble Peace laureates and groups like the International Peace Bureau and the UK Campaign for Nuclear Disarmament. He defended his fundamental rights. Mr. Vanunu insists that he is not a 'spy' or a ' traitor': he merely ' let the world know what was happening' for reasons of conscience. He also said the Dimona reactor should be destroyed – just as Israel bombed Iraq's nuclear reactor in the early 1980's, then under construction. His past contribution to raising awareness about the nuclear danger, especially in West Asia, is both substantial and ineradicable. He is a leader of conscience.*

Comment on Mr. Vanunu may articulate the nuclear disarmament standpoint or work as an activist in the global peace movement.)

Global compact

The Global Compact of UN Secretary-General was launched officially in July 2000. It exhorts individual corporations to advance basic values within their sphere of influence. These basic values are based on nine internationally agreed principles from the fields of human rights, labour and environment. Consultations are underway about the possibility of adding "corruption" as a tenth principle.

The Global Compact's nine principles enjoy universal consensus, having been derived from the following:

The Universal Declaration of Human Rights

The International Labour Organisation's Declaration on Fundamental Principles and Rights at Work

The Rio Declaration on Environment and Development

Human Rights

1. 1.Businesses should support and respect the protection of internationally proclaimed human rights within their sphere of influence; and
2. 2.Make sure that they are not complicit in human rights abuses

Labour Standards

1. 3.Businesses should uphold the freedom of association and the effective recognition of the right to collective bargaining.
2. 4.Eliminate all forms of forced and compulsory labour.
3. 5.Effective abolition of child labour.
4. 6.Eliminate discrimination in respect of employment and occupation.

Environment

1. 7.Support a precautionary approach to environmental challenges.
2. 8.Undertake initiatives to promote greater environmental responsibility; and
3. 9.Encourage the development and diffusion of environmentally friendly technologies.

9 Principles of Global Compact.

Six case studies wherein the Global Compact is violated are presented below:

1. Aventis

Since Aventis signed on to the Global Compact in July 2000, its genetically engineered StarLinkTM corn has illegally contaminated the food supply and seed stock in the U.S. The contamination of other corn varieties significantly impacts links throughout the food chain, from farmers, grain elevators, and food processors to retail grocers and consumers. Without a system of segregation or the ability to control pollen drift, StarLink contaminated much of the U.S. corn supply. The full costs of this contamination continue to emerge; however, current estimates run in the hundreds of billions of dollars.

A look at the company's behavior regarding StarLink shows that before and after signing the Compact, Aventis violated Global Compact's Principle 7, which is drawn from the Rio Declaration and supports "a precautionary approach to environmental challenges."

Source: Institute for Trade and Agriculture Policy

2. Nike

Since 1997, Nike has continually failed to uphold "freedom of association and the effective recognition of the right to collective bargaining," which is Principle 3 of the Global Compact. Nike made a commitment to respect this right in 1997 when it signed the Fair Labor Association voluntary workplace code of conduct along with other giant shoe and garment manufacturers like Reebok, Adidas, Liz Claiborne and Patagonia. Violations of Principle 3 and related accounts of repression, firings, violence and threats are found in Nike production factories in China, Indonesia, Thailand, Cambodia and Mexico. In addition, Nike has been actively involved in lobbying Washington against using trade policy to pressure China to respect workers' rights.

Source: Global Exchange

3. Rio Tinto

In 2000, the Indonesian government's National Human Rights Commission investigated allegations of abuses at the Rio Tinto's Kelian gold mine and found egregious violations. Since the mine opened in 1992, the Commission revealed, the Indonesian military and company security forcibly evicted traditional miners, burned down villages, and arrested and detained protestors. Local people have systematically lost homes, lands, gardens, fruit trees, forest resources, family graves and the right to mine for gold in the river, according to the Human Rights Commission. Kelian employees have also been named in a number of incidents of sexual harassment, rape and violence against local women between 1987 and 1997. These included abuse and rape committed by senior company staff against local Dayak women.

Rio Tinto, which has headquarters in the UK and Australia, also is accused of environmental abuses affecting the health of the surrounding community. The Kelian mine produces over 14 tons of gold per year using the cyanide heap-leaching process, which produces contaminated tailings. The tailings are held in a dam and treated in a polishing pond near the Kelian River. Water from the polishing pond pours into the river through an outlet. The company claims that the water is clean; meanwhile the community says that people cannot drink or bathe in the water because it causes skin lesions and stomach aches.

Two articles on the CorpWatch website (www.corpwatch.org) document that Rio Tinto has violated Principle 1 of the Global Compact, which requests companies to "support and respect the protection of international human rights within their sphere of influence," and Principle 8, which asks business to "undertake initiatives to promote greater environmental responsibility."

Source: Project Underground and Asia-Pacific Human Rights Network

4. International Chamber of Commerce

The International Chamber of Commerce (ICC), a lobby group with over 7,000 corporate members, is a prominent partner in UN Secretary-General Kofi Annan's Global Compact and has played a key role in shaping it from the start. While the ICC has provided momentum to the Global Compact, it also seriously undermines its credibility.

The ICC has a long history of vigorous lobbying to weaken international environmental treaties and these efforts have continued even after the group has pledged support for the Global Compact principles. Examples include the Kyoto Protocol, the Convention on Biodiversity, and the Basel Convention against trade in toxic waste. In all of these UN negotiations, the International Chamber's obstructive lobbying runs counter to the Global Compact principles to which it subscribes.

For instance, rather than "supporting a precautionary approach to environmental challenges," (Principle 7), and rather than undertaking "initiatives to promote greater environmental responsibility" (Principle 8), the ICC promotes a narrow commercial agenda, dominated some of the world's most environmentally irresponsible corporations.

Source: Corporate Europe Observatory

5. Unilever

In March 2001, residents of Kodaikanal, a pretty hill retreat in Southern India, caught the Anglo-Dutch multinational Unilever red-handed when they uncovered a dump site with toxic mercury-laced waste from a thermometer factory run by Unilever's Indian subsidiary Hindustan Lever. The 7.4-ton stockpile of crushed mercury-containing glass was found in torn sacks, spilling onto the ground in a busy scrap yard located near a school. Company officials denied and downplayed the dump site, eventually refusing even to engage researchers in dialogue about the issue.

Unilever's mercury tainted glass was found at this crowded scrap yard in Kodaikanal, India. Photo: Shailendra Yashwant/Greenpeace, 2001.

At Kodaikanal, Unilever's behavior violates the environmental principles of the Global Compact that require signatories to "support a precautionary approach to environmental challenges" (Principle 7); "undertake initiatives to promote greater environmental responsibility" (Principle 8); and promote the "diffusion of environmentally friendly technologies" (Principle 9). Allegations that the company has employed a double standard in relation to worker safety indicate a violation of Principle 6, "the elimination of discrimination in respect of employment and occupation."

Source: Nityanand Jayaraman/CorpWatch

6. Norsk Hydro

Late in 2000, Norsk Hydro, a Norwegian corporation with investments in light metals, oil, petrochemicals and agriculture, faced a crisis in the Eastern Indian state of Orissa, where it is a partner in a $1 billion bauxite/alumina project. On December 16, three tribal men — two aged 25 and one aged 45 — were shot dead near their village. Nine others were seriously injured. The three who died were among several hundred local residents fleeing armed police, who had been called in to quell protests against the project.

Norsk Hydro and its partners did decide to "temporarily curtail" the project "pending a lower level of tension." But that response does not reveal the company's role in fueling tensions leading to the protestors' deaths. Allowing tensions to reach a point where police violently repress dissent reflects a violation of Principle 2, "make sure their own corporations are not complicit in human rights abuses." The failure to abandon the project in keeping with the wishes of the local people is a violation of Principle 1, "support and respect the protection of international human rights within their sphere of influence."

Source: Nityanand Jayaraman/CorpWatch

ENGINEERS AS MANAGERS, CONSULTANTS AND LEADERS

Engineers are generally considered to be technocrats. Technocrats are perceived as professional experts and knowledgeable in their chosen area of specialization and are expected to be result-oriented. Many a generalist believes that engineers have a narrow perspective and are egoistic and not so adaptable. Some engineers harbour a feeling that they are not getting their due share of power and position. In this Chapter we look at the various roles played by an engineer.

ROLE OF ENGINEERS

Let us first understand the variety of roles played by engineer. An engineer wears different hats in different roles.

Figure 1

Different Roles performed by engineer

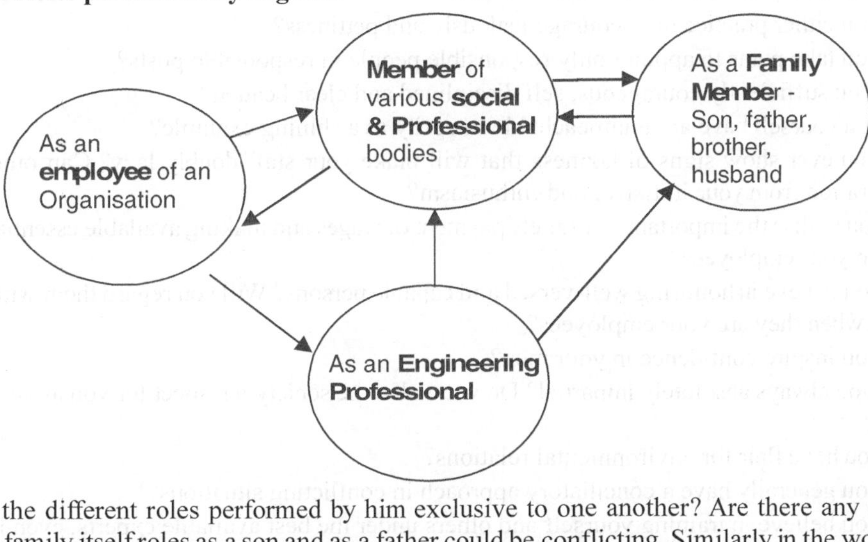

Are the different roles performed by him exclusive to one another? Are there any conflicts? Within a family itself roles as a son and as a father could be conflicting. Similarly in the working life he is a subordinate to somebody and superior to others. How can he discharge disparate responsibilities?

Mr. Sushrut got promoted from being just an engineer to be the CEO of the FTZ Corporation. He had been working in the organization for a number of years and had come up from the ranks. He read an episode in Mahabharata wherein Narada was delivering a code of conduct to Yudhistara before the latter's coronation as the king. The teachings were in the form of questions and answers. Narada tells Yudhistara to ask the questions and find the answers for himself. Mr. Sushrut knew that the teachings were time-tested, and thought that by developing a similar set of appropriate questions and answers for himself, he could become a successful leader.

Engineers are technocrats.

1. Are you a person of high principles?
2. Are you consistent in the practice of economic principles both in business and personal life? Do you avoid excess consumption of wealth and showy living?
3. Have you divided your time rightly between pursuit of virtues, wealth generation and entertainments?
4. After evaluating your strengths and weaknesses, will you keep an updated note of your competitor's strengths and weaknesses too?
5. Do you keep a watchful eye on what your associates, competitors and frustrated employees are doing?
6. Do you ensure that your managers are virtuous? Are they of good family background?
7. Are they thoughtful of your organization's welfare? Are they able to distinguish between what should be done and should not be done? Are your managers well versed in their subjects? Do they know how to keep a secret? Are you sure that they are not susceptible to the influence of your competitors, your subcontractors, your clients or your opponents?
8. In crucial decisions do you consult experienced and wise men? Do you have too many advisors?
9. Do you take blind leaps into the dark? Or calculated jumps with the required precision and precaution?
10. Are you prepared to accept one learned and efficient key man rather than a number of useless fools , so that there is at least one person to help you substantially and usefully? Do you entrust work to undependable and corrupt assistants?
11. Do you either practice or encourage jealously and pettiness?
12. Do you take pains to appoint only responsible people in responsible posts?
13. Are you sufficiently courageous, self disciplined and clear headed?
14. Do you yourself have an unimpeachable integrity as a shining example?
15. Do you ever show signs of laziness that will make your staff doubly lazy? Can others draw inspiration from your initiative and enthusiasm?
16. Do you realise the importance of timely payment of wages and making available essential amenities to your employees?
17. Do you believe in honoring well-versed and capable persons? Will you regard them with respect even when they are your employees?
18. Do you inspire confidence in your men?
19. Are you always absolutely impartial? Do you value the society's respect for you as an impartial man?
20. Do you have flair for environmental relations?
21. Do you generally have a conciliatory approach in conflicting situations?
22. Do you believe in training yourself and others under the best available experts, even if it costs more?
23. Will you be able to watch your men continuously to be sure that they continue to be trustworthy?
24. Do you indulge openly in drinking, gambling and philandering?
25. Do you give gifts to deserving person?
26. Do you have eye for detailing with a touch of perfection?
27. Do you manage your time between external and external affairs?
28. Do you act impulsively?
29. Have you resolved to conduct yourself with dignity everywhere and thereby command respect?
30. Do you punish the guilty and honour the innocent without any consideration for personal likes or relationships?

A set of appropriate questions to be asked to become a successful Leader.

31. Can people deposit their trust in you and feel safe?
32. Are you always a balanced person?
33. Do you believe in teamwork?
34. Do you show serious concern about the welfare of your people?
35. Are you flexible and practical or rigid and stubborn? Do you read and re read important documents?
36. While you expect others to be loyal to you, are you loyal to others?
37. Do you strive to evolve a code of your own high principles which will hold you aloft everywhere?
38. Can you firmly say no with a smile?
39. Do you avoid doing purely personal work in your office during office hours, except as a part of social or professional service?

Models of Professional Roles+

We said that the profession of engineering is aimed at promoting the public good, or as is commonly said in codes of ethics public safety, health, and welfare. Of course, there are different conceptions of the public good, and also different views about how engineers contribute to it. In this section, we list a few of the models that have seemed attractive to some engineers. These are general models that need to be refined, but they serve to organize thinking and crystallize attitudes. We leave for a study question the assessment of the models in connection with thinking about career goals.

1. Savior

Plato believed a philosopher-king was needed in order to create the ideal society. Others have believed that engineers hold the key to creating a utopian society. In part this is to be achieved through technological developments that lead to material prosperity. In part it is to arise through creation of a technocracy in which engineering ways of thinking are applied to large-scale social planning. The representative engineer is a savior who will redeem society from poverty, inefficiency, waste, and the drudgery of manual labor.

2 *Guardian*

Perhaps engineers cannot usher in the Utopia. Yet it is they who know best the directions in which, and pace at which, technology should develop. Accordingly, they should be given positions of high authority based on their expertise in determining what is in the best interests of society.

3 *Bureaucratic servant*

Within the corporate setting in which engineers work, management should make the decisions about the directions of technological development. The proper role of the engineer is to be the servant or handmaiden who receives and translates the directives of management into concrete achievements. The engineer is the loyal organization man or woman whose special skills reside in solving problems assigned by management, within the constraints set by management.

4 *Social servant*

The role of engineers lies exclusively in obedient service to others, but their true master is society. Society expresses its interests either directly, through purchasing patterns, or indirectly, through government representatives and consumer groups. Engineers, in cooperation with management, have the task of receiving society's directives and satisfying society's desires.

5 *Social enabler and catalyst*

This *is* a variation of the social servant model. Service to society includes, but is not exhausted by, carrying out social directives. Ultimate power and authority lie with management; nevertheless, the engineer plays a vital and active role beyond mere compliance with orders. Some-

* Ibid pp. 32-33

Keep a watch on Associates, Competitors and Frustrated Employees.

times engineers are needed to help management and societies understand their own needs and to make informed decisions about desirable ends and means of technological development.

6 *Game player*

Engineers are neither servants nor masters of anyone. Instead they play by the economic game rules that happen to be in effect at a given time. Their aim, like that of managers, is to play successfully within organizations, enjoying both the pleasures of technological work and the satisfaction of winning and moving ahead in a competitive world.

FUNCTIONS OF ENGINEER

An engineer's responsibility encompasses a whole range of functions that are listed below in the Table along with a sample of ethical questions to be asked against each:
advice? Is informed consent required?

Function	Ethical questions to be asked (Illustrative)
Conceptual design	Will the product be useful" Not illegal, as are certain drugs
Market study	Is the study unbiased or is it to attract investors?
Specifications	Do they meet established standards and codes? Are they physically realizable?
Contract	Are cost figures and time schedule realistic? Is it bid made low to get the job, with the hope of renegotiating?
Analysis	Is there an experienced engineer who can judge if a computer program gives reliable results?
Design	Are safe alternatives explored?
Purchasing	Will parts and materials be spot tested for quality upon receipt? Are they as per the specifications?
Manufacturing parts	Is the workplace safe, free of noise and toxic fumes? Is time allowed for quality workmanship?
Assembly construction	Are workers familiar with the purpose and basic functions of the product? Who supervise safety?
Final test of product	Are testers sufficiently independent of manufacture or construction management?
Sale of product	Any bribes? Is advertising honest? Are customers given good advice? Is informed consent required?
Installation, Commissioning	Do users get training? Is the safe exit tested? Are neighbors informed of possible toxic emissions?
Use of product	Are users protected from harm? Are users informed of risks?
Maintenance and repairs	Is maintenance regularly carried out by competent staff? Does the manufacture still carry spare parts?
Product recall	Is there a commitment to monitor the 'experiment' and if necessary to recall the product.
Decommissioning	How are recycling of valuable materials and disposal of toxic wastes handled at end of useful life?

Engineer as a Manager

Many engineers move into management, often after a few years of starting their career. As managers they are responsible for establishing and maintaining a moral climate conducive to professional responsibility and to dealing constructively with conflicts. An approach is suggested herein which could be used by an engineer manager to improve his managerial effectiveness.

An engineer manager is often confronted with a situation in which two or more ethical principles are in conflict causing a moral dilemma. Usually, the five moral dimensions are:

(a) Information rights and obligation,
(b) Property rights,
(c) Accountability and control,
(d) System quality, and
(e) Quality of life.

He/she could use a five-step methodology to analyze a situation. This involves identifying: (1) facts (2) values (3) stockholders (4) options and (5) consequences of action. Once the ethical analysis has been performed to arrive at a judgment, six ethical principles derived from culture, religion and traditions could be applied. They are not hard and fast rules and may not apply to all situations. These principles are:

1. ***Golden rule***: Do unto others as you would have them to do unto you. Putting yourself in the place of the other person(s). Think of yourself as the object of the decision. Think about fairness as it would apply to you.
2. ***Immanuel Kant's Categorical Imperative***: If the action is not right for everyone to take, then it is not right for anyone. Ask if everyone did, could the organization or society survive?
3. ***Descartes' Rule of Change***: If an action cannot be taken repeatedly, then it is not right to take it at all. Once started on a slippery path, you may not be able to stop.
4. ***Utilitarianism***: Is it for the common good?
5. ***Risk Aversion***: Take that action that achieves the highest or greatest value Take that action that produces the least harm or incurs the least potential cost. Some actions have extremely high failure costs with very low probability of failure. (say, building a nuclear generation facility in an urban area)
6. ***Ethical 'No free lunch' Rule***: Assume that virtually all tangible and intangible objects are owned by someone else unless there is a specific declaration otherwise.

After having been only an engineer, a person may be promoted as a manger in an organization. As a manager he would have a number of subordinates working under him and other colleagues working with him. There would also be his superiors. If one has to become a good boss, one needs to be a good subordinate first. This transition from technical to managerial work calls for a number of adjustments. Engineers are preferred as managers because of their strong analytical and problem solving skills and work ethics.

The skills required as an engineer are technical; but when one becomes a manager, managerial skills like motivation, communication, and teamwork are essential. A technocrat may not be a team player. He may be excellent in technology-based solutions, but may lack the skills needed for solving human conflicts. A good technocrat need not necessarily prove to be a good manager. Unless he acquires managerial skills he may not succeed as a manger. But there is always a continuity of moral thread in the transition from being a technical person to being a manager.

Golden rule: "Do unto others as you would have them to do unto you".

As a manger, engineers remain professionals whose primary responsibility is to provide useful products and services while ensuring that they are safe and profitable. He has the responsibility for promoting ethical climate in the organization and resolving conflicts amongst his subordinates. As a manager he has to combine formal organization and policies with informal traditions and practices and personal attitudes and commitments.

Engineer as a Leader

One may work at the middle level or a senior level position. In those positions one would have to take decisions on transfers, promotions and removal. You may be posted in the production department or sales. As one moves up the ladder from the position of engineer to manager to leader, the responsibility and the functions increases and from the technical functions it moves to the function of people management. The following figure depicts the movement and the responsibility.

Figure

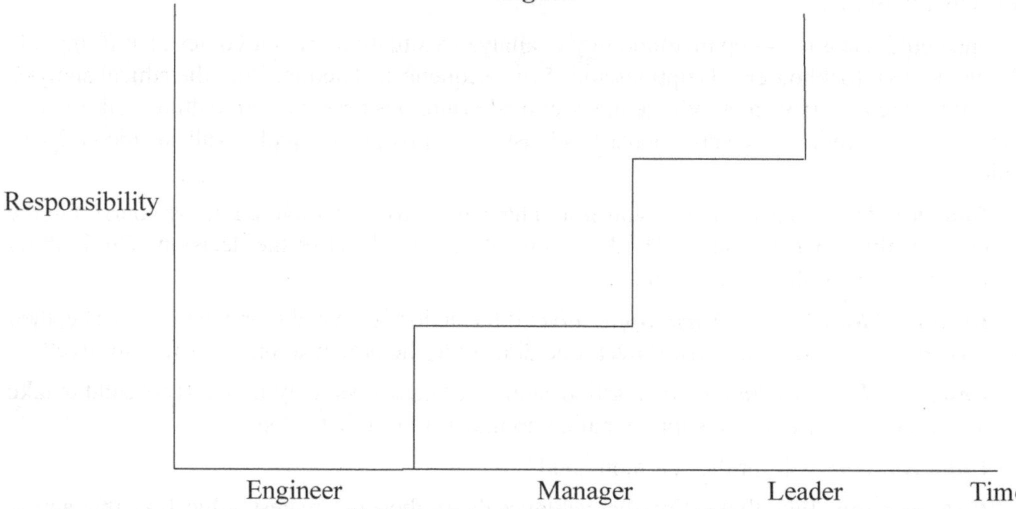

Every manager feels that within him/her there is a leader waiting to burst out. "**Managers do things right and leaders do the right things** "observes Peter Drucker. One of the 'right things' that a leader should do is to offer leadership based on sound principles and values, says Stephen Covey. We have a number of examples of this in India. Two of the most enduring names in corporate India – J.R.D. Tata and Ramakrishna Bajaj are known as much for their humanitarian values as their business acumen. Many of today's business leaders like Narayanamurthy and Azim Premji have taken this concept on board and results are for all to see.

A leader has to develop a Vision and Mission for his organization. Organizational values emerge from this. It is evident from the prominence being accorded to Corporate Social Responsibility (CSR) and 'Societal Mission' that ethics is being given increasing importance in the corporate world. The 'good old days', when 'increasing monetary profits for the share holders' was the only guiding principle of the corporate world, are slowly disappearing. Why is it that Bill Gates, the richest man in the world, is willing to part with a sizeable chunk of his money for charity?

As a leader, an engineer has to build his organization's culture which is its soul. It is the collective values of the individuals who form the organization. Each individual has beliefs which translate into personal values, which expressed collectively shape the organization culture. In living companies, values are clear and operationalised and form the base on which decisions are made. Values provide stability for employees, contribute to insight and direction when facing unpleasant decisions, provide the rudder for steering the organization to higher ethical conduct, respect and dignity for the indi-

Technical functions move to that of people management as he becomes Leader.

vidual and increase employee motivation – all of which jointly provide the 'competitive edge' to the organization.. When employees share organizational values they feel greater loyalty and commitment to the organization and identify more strongly with it.

Jack Welch, the former Chief Executive Officer –CEO of General Electric, stated:

"The success of our company lies in the fact that (our) people understand (our) values. They joined the company knowing these were the values, and they have worked to implement them. This is our life. This is how we behave. If someone cheats in our company, they are thrown out the first time. Some may get second chance, but they don't get third. If they are not open, if they don't share ideas that's bad behaviour. We have translated values into operational behaviour."

Great leaders use and communicate values. Values make the difference between winners and losers. A leader should build an organization that lasts by creating an environment of safety, trust, honesty, loyalty and stability, where workers trust management and each other, where management works in everyone's best interests, where employees are free to focus on their work and the organization cares more about them, where innovations and creativity abound. Fear complex should be eradicated at all costs since fear destroys truth. When people become fearful, they recognize and communicate dangers and not opportunities.

Trust is the foundation of any organization and creating and maintaining that trust is the responsibility of a leader. The founder of Matsushita Electric states:

"I am the soul of this company. It is through me that our organisation's values pass. The statements of the organization vision, mission and policies – however numerous, well crafted and eloquently articulated are futile if the leader's actions and behaviour are inconsistent with these statements. Action speaks louder than words, what the leader does and values set the ethical tone and create the moral environment of the orgnisation."

In India we have had leaders like Swami Vivekananda, Sri Aurobindo, and Mahatma Gandhi who lived for higher values of life. One can learn a lot about leadership from their lives. In one of his articles, Subhash Sharma + proposes the concept of corporate VEDA, ie. Vision, Enlightenment, Devotion, and Action, of leadership.

Figure

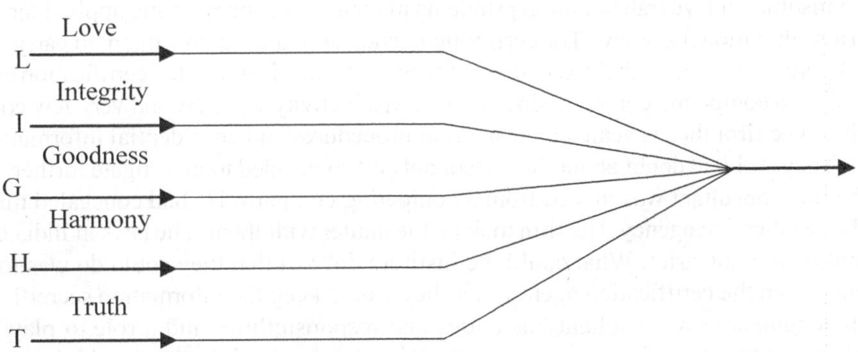

The five human values which were valid in earlier times are equally valid today in the knowledge era. The diagram shows that the noble thoughts and the LIGHT from leaders should spread in all directions. This kind of moral leadership is needed in engineering. Engineers need not necessarily

* Subhash Sharma, Towards Corporate VEDA: Indian Ethos and Corporate Development, Journal of Human Values, 9 (2), pp. 163 - 171

Great leaders use and communicate values.

take up moral leadership only in their own organizations; but they can take up useful leadership roles in social services also.

An example from Tata Steel, given below, shows how ethics are promoted in an organization:

The month of July is celebrated as 'Hamara' ethics month in memory of J R D Tata. The object of this unique initiative is make all employees of the Steel Company, including those based in its far-flung raw material sources aware of the Tata Code of Conduct, the relevance of corporate governance and to adopt an ethical behavior at their work place. The campaign is even more significant today, as many corporate houses in the recent past have failed to maintain ethical behaviour in their business dealings and have lost their esteem and respect as honest, fair and transparent business houses.

The campaign has been called 'Hamara" to create a feeling of belonging and ownership among all individual employee and generate team feeling across the company. Numerous activities were undertaken during this month. Some of them are - hosting of Tata Code of Conduct on the e-Procurement site on the company's Intranet, organising awareness talks on Business Ethics, quiz rounds, and skits on ethics the various departments and locations of the company. Invariably, there is overwhelming response and employees participate in the campaign with great enthusiasm.

Competitions are held during the month for creating slogans and suggestions. Such events are meant to constantly remind everybody to conduct their business in the most ethical way despite various adverse conditions prevailing all around.

Engineer as a Consultant

Consulting engineers usually practice as independents. They are compensated by fees for the services they render, not by salaries from their employees. Because of this, they tend to have greater freedom to make decisions about the projects they undertake. A consulting engineer will face disputes relating to advertising, competitive bidding, contingency fees and giving technical opinions in disputes.

The proposed Engineers Bill and codes of conduct highlight the role and conduct of consultant engineers. (Please see the Annexure Engineers Bill for details). As a consultant one should not release misleading advertisements or endorse false claims of a product. As a bidder, the engineer should not encourage cartel formation in submitting bids. (*When your client makes a false claim for insurance, what should you as a consultant do?)*

An institute in Hyderabad training students in computer programming applied for ISO Certification to a multinational agency. The certifying agency appointed a consultant to carry out the quality audit. Before interacting with the consultant, the institute checked with the certification agency whether he was from a competing company since their area of activity was new and very few consultants were available. The firm then revealed their internal procedures and confidential information to the consultant. They still had doubt about the consultant and so decided to investigate further. It was discovered that the consultant was indeed from a competing company. He had concealed this information from the certification agency. The firm took up the matter with them. The laws in India on competitive information are not strict. What could the institute do? All that they could do was to get a written assurance from the certification agency that they would keep the information secret!!

The engineer as a consultant has duties and responsibilities and a role to play. He should, if possible avoid, working for competing companies. In case he does, he should not use confidential information of one company for the other company. He has to be very careful about what he says and does.

Engineers as Expert Witnesses and Advisers

Engineers at times provide expert testimony in adversarial contexts. The focus may be on past or future. Past may be in the form of causes of an accident, malfunctions etc. or may be about technology

The engineer as a consultant should not work for Competitors and not use Confidential Information.

for future. Should they become hired guns or should they function as impartial seekers and communicators of truth?

Between being a hired gun and being a disinterested observer lie a range of forms of advocacy that are open to abuse. The plaintiff or the defendant in civil or criminal cases may hire an engineer to appear as an expert witness. Some engineers may come as expert witnesses while some others may be appearing as specialists in forensic engineering. Forensic engineering means the application of engineering skills and knowledge in criminal investigations to aid judicial system. They may act as witnesses in the cases concerning defective products, personal injury, damage to properties, traffic accidents and air crashes. Their evidence is considered seriously while awarding compensatory damages, compensation for loss of property or violation of rights.

Engineers are hired by lawyers to serve the interest of their clients. When hired, engineers have a responsibility of confidentiality and act honestly. He may be hired as an eyewitness or an expert witness. As an eyewitness, engineer has to give evidence in the court about what has been actually seen. There is little freedom whereas as an expert witness, he has larger latitude of opinion in the area of his expertise and reporting standards. Although lawyers are supposed to be hiring engineers and paying for their services to unearth the truth and not for giving just supporting evidence favourable to the lawyer's clients, there are many instances the opposite is the case. Let us understand them so that engineers can avoid and protect themselves against them.

Abuses

***1. Hired Guns*:**

When engineers are hired by lawyers to help them to establish the facts in a way favourable to their clients, they are called 'hired guns'. The objective is to get a favourable report. As a hired gun, an engineer may have to stretch the standards of honesty. *For example*: a brand new heating rod gives an electric shock to a user. He is hurt and files a case against the manufacturer. An expert engineer may be called upon to certify that there was no defect in the product. He is expected to examine the rod and give his unbiased opinion; but instead he certifies that there was no manufacturing defect without subjecting the rod to critical examination, and suggests that the consumer would have used it wrongly. Since the manufacturer has hired him, he gives a favourable report. Is this right? He is forced to give a false report since he is a hired gun. This is one kind of abuse of his position as an engineering expert.

2. Financial Biases:

Being paid by one side can create a financial bias. This will influence one's investigation and testimony. The bias will be all the more when the fees are paid only after the case is won. These fees are permitted by law but may lead to bias and hence could be unethical. In some case forensic engineers who act as expert witnesses will always support the lawyer who hired them. Some of these engineers make their living only by serving as expert witnesses.

3. Ego Biases:

Engineers could get influenced by their own perception and ignore other aspects of the case. He would look at the dispute only from his own side. The other side is regarded as guilty without examination. His egoistical stance could greatly influence the opinion given by him. Engineer has to guard himself against this type of bias.

***4. Sympathy Biases*:**

An Engineer feels sympathetic towards a particular party and identifies himself with that party's situation. This is human nature. This bias can upset disinterested investigation of the facts.

To overcome these influences the engineers while serving as expert witnesses, must take efforts to maintain their integrity. (In a particular case, a professional engineer swore an affidavit in support

The objective to hire engineers as hired guns is to get a favourable report.

of a lawsuit. He was not a party to the lawsuit. It was alleged and admitted that the affidavit contained statements the professional engineer knew or ought to have known were false and that would mislead the court. The submission of the affidavit was not within the practice of professional engineering and the conduct was regarded as disgraceful, dishonorable and unprofessional. Hence it was regarded as misconduct.

Engineer as an adviser in planning and policy making:

Expert advice may be called for in a new technology. They may be asked to forecast the usages and users of the technology. In such cases, engineers have to take precautions not to get biased by advocates of a particular view. He may be asked to make a study and evaluate the safety of the technology. The cost benefit aspects would have to be examined. The feasibility has to be looked at from market side as well as from technical aide. They are paid fees for technical studies. They have to be candid in these situations since often public at large are involved and the impact of wrong decisions would be on the public.

As an adviser there are conflicting responsibilities to their clients and also to the general public. To face such conflicting situations, there are some normative models that could be used. .

Value-Neutral Analysis: This model insists that engineers should be impartial. He must avoid any bias and favoritism. Their role is to identify all options and analyse the factual implication of each options. They have to make cost – benefit analyses. They should remain neutral.

Value-Guided Advocates: when they are advocates, they should remain honest and independent in their opinions. They have to consider the responsibility to the public paramount and be honest on all technical facts.

Important requirements for an adviser are virtues like , honesty, competence, diligence and loyalty.

Engineer as an Entrepreneur:

An engineer may decide to start his own enterprise instead of working for somebody; he may decide to work on his own. Since he is basically a technocrat, he should not be carried away by the technology but acquire managerial skills. He has to become a team player. When he is selecting his line of business, he has to look at its impact on society. When choosing the location for his firm, he has to keep in mind environmental issues. *For example*. if he is setting up a chemical factory, he has to invest in pollution control;. treat the water and air, which are let out from the facility. He should avoid selecting products that would have harmful effects. As an entrepreneur, he has responsibilities towards his employees. He must try to create an ethical climate. It is his responsibility to build trust and relationship amongst his people. He needs to pay taxes and duties as mandated by law.

ROLE OF PROFESSIONAL ENGINEERING

The roles might be indirect, such as designing, manufacturing and marketing products for export. It could be direct such as working for an Indian company living in a foreign country. An engineer could be a part of an international engineering services consulting practice. Their success will be based on competence, fairness and high standards of practice and ethics. Indian engineers have made a name for themselves in software development. The direct roles are in design and project management functions like

Technical advisor to a foreign government especially regarding standards
Definer of contract terms of reference and contract negotiation.
Trainer of local personnel for transfer technology to a foreign country, and
Expert witness for contract interpretation.

As an Adviser, Engineers have conflicting responsibilities.
As an adviser, virtues like, Honesty, Competence, and Loyalty are required.

These roles require the Clients to have trust in an engineer's technical competence as well as his integrity and professional ethics.

Role of professional & regulatory bodies

An Engineer plays a significant role as a member of regulatory bodies, professional bodies like the Institution of Engineers, Computer Society of India, and most importantly as a citizen. He has immense responsibilities as a citizen and he is expected to play a positive role in contributing to the development of the country. Engineers may take up jobs in the Government or occupy positions in regulatory bodies. As a member of such bodies he would be responsible for framing appropriate laws and regulations.

The aim of an Engineers body should not be confined to regulating the behaviour of engineer members as per the Engineers' Act, but should also extend to the actions and conduct of engineers outside the practice of professional engineering. They must curb ***incompetence and, professional misconduct*** and enforce a strong ***code of ethics.***

A member must be found ***incompetent*** if he or she displays a lack of knowledge, skills or poor judgment or disregard for the welfare of the public in discharging professional responsibilities. The responsibilities of a professional engineer go beyond acts within the practice of engineering profession. ***Professional misconduct*** is behaviour relevant to the practice of engineering that would be regarded as disgraceful, dishonorable or unprofessional by the engineering profession. At times an engineer may commit fraud or breach of trust not as an engineer, and he could be found guilty of a criminal offence. This is an act of misconduct. Professional engineers are accountable to the public and must be seen to be trustworthy. If a professional engineer has demonstrated untrustworthy behaviour to an extent that it resulted in a criminal conviction, it is reasonable to suggest that he be charged with professional misconduct.

An engineer failed to obey court orders to pay monies owed to another engineer for services rendered by the latter. The former was found to guilty of professional misconduct because the circumstances pertained to an engineering relationship. They were relevant to the practice of professional engineering and failure to obey court orders was both dishonorable and unprofessional. Violation of ***Code of ethics*** is regarded as misconduct and unprofessional. Even if an unethical situation is not covered by the code of ethics, it might still be ruled professional misconduct.

A number of professional engineers are involved in pre-purchase home inspection for residential homebuyers. There are also many non- engineers offering these services. However, engineer offering such services often use the fact of their professional engineering qualification as an indication of superior qualification for such work and to gain competitive marketing advantage over the non-engineers offering the same service. In such circumstances, it is fair to suggest that the pre-purchase home inspection is relevant to the practice of professional engineering. Therefore a professional engineer providing such services could face disciplinary action if the conduct relating to those services were determined to be disgraceful, dishonorable or unprofessional.

As it is company has to deal with so many disclosure norms under the various provisions of the company law. The cost of compliance worries the Indian companies. Indian Credit Rating Agency (ICRA) has started the concept of corporate governance ratings (CGR). The key variables in ICRA's rating methodology for corporate governance include shareholding structure, governance structure and management process, board structure and process, stakeholders relationship, transparency and disclosure and financial discipline.

ICRA conducted a survey of 35 leading institutional investors and large brokerage houses in 2003 to understand the market mood. As per the survey, an overwhelming majority felt that corporate

Violation of Code of Ethics is regarded as Unprofessional and Misconduct.

governance would play a major role in making the capital market safer place for investors. From the investor's point of view integrity of accounting statements and stress on ethical behaviour were identified as the key objectives of good governance. However, the presence of a strong board of directors ,a major focus of corporate governance in most countries featured somewhat lower in the respondents' list of priorities. Over 85% of respondents felt that corporate governance is as important as quantifiable factors such as likely growth in earnings, from the point of view of investment decision.

It is a fact that well governed corporate entities are less likely to indulge in malpractice and are more likely to protect the interests of minority shareholders.

The Corporate Governance Rating (CGR) should be made voluntary or recommendatory and not mandatory in nature. The corporate sector has the fear that CGR will be made mandatory. Companies such as ITC, Wipro, Godrej Consumer Products, PNB Gilts, ESSAP Ltd and Infosys Technologies Ltd have gone ahead with ICRA rating though all have not gone for CGR. The cost of compliance to CGR will improve the cost of capital. Investors are willing to pay a premium for companies that have good corporate governance.

ROLE OF MEDIA

Media can supplement the efforts of mandatory regulations of norms of ethics and play a major role. Media have dual responsibilities. Instances of unethical behaviour should be given wide publicity. The culprits are afraid of media. On TV we see many people covering their face with cloth since they do not want to be identified. But before exposing the culprit investigative research should be done and cross-checked.

Media can also help in mobilizing opinions in society. It can influence decision makers. Press and TV are powerful media which can be used as a tool to bring about awareness about issues. If necessary engineers can also develop appropriate technology for different situations.

Thanks to Mr. Sam Pitroda who was responsible to bring low cost technology for Subscriber Trunk Dialing STD. The communication scenarios changed radically with STD. Every small village has STD. Prof. Jhunjunwalla of IIT Chennai has formed a center which have developed a low cost appropriate technology for rural communication. This has a wider reach.

ROLE OF CIVIL SOCIETY

The issue is how you can involve society in the crusade for ethics. Man is a social animal. He/she wants to operate within the societal norms. Earlier in Chapter I on ethics and environment we discussed the role of engineer as a citizen of India. We have seen how community coming together in the form of co-operatives has been used as successful business models.

Non Government Organisations (NGOs) can play an important role in promoting ethics. An award given by the Rotary Club to Orchid Pharmaceuticals for responsible corporate behaviour vis-à-vis environment. Every year the Confederation of Industries (CII) presents Safety, Health and Environment-'SHE' awards for companies implementing measures to promote safety, health and environmental protection. The aim of the award is to recognize, motivate and facilitate corporates to adopt innovative practices.

Federation of Indian Chamber of Commerce and Industry (FICCI) has a Brand Protection Committee to address the issue of counterfeiting as an industry iossue rather than as a company issue. It is estimated that every year counterfeit brands result in Rs. 2,500 crores loss to companies and Rs. 900 crores loss to the Government revenues. The menace is more in Fast Moving Consumer Goods (FMCG). Textiles, Automobile ancillaries and pharmaceuticals. FICCI addresses the issue of counterfeit through a four-fold strategy. 1. Measuring and publicizing negative economic impact. 2. Open communication channels between the stakeholder to generate awareness and stimulate action. 3. Take action against the offenders and 4. Advocate more effective enforcement of existing laws and regulations.

Media can help in mobilizing opinion in Society and influence decision maker.

FICCI organized a high visibility destruction in Delhi of the counterfeit products worth 10 crores. The committee has lobbied with the State and Union Government for better enforcement of IPR laws, which led to the creation of IPR cells in Maharashtra and Madhya Pradesh.

As a citizen it is the responsibility of engineer to participate in these social organization and contribute to the benefit of the society at large. They can take up issues of industrial pollution, automobile safety and disposal of wastes. Engineers can offer voluntary services to solve the problems of society.

Engineer should be ***rajarshi.*** A rajarshi is a combination of the qualities of a ***raja***, a king and ***rishi***, a sage. The king pleases his subjects. He has the qualities of power and efficiency while rishi has wisdom. A rajarshi therefore has the power and efficiency of a king and wisdom of rishi. His efficiency and energy enables him to perform and his wisdom to achieve welfare of people.

Case 1

Mr.Anil Manibhai Naik joined L & T as a junior engineer and rose to be the first full-time executive chairman in 15 years. He is the first professional to rise from the ranks. Anil was born in a family of teachers. His father was a Gandhian. After completing his education, he joined Nestler Boiler at Byculla in Mumbai. Within a year he was put in charge of the boiler shop, with nearly 350 people working under him. He took up a job in L & T as an Assistant Engineer in the planning department. During the interview, the General Manager asked him "what would you want to become in the company?" The reply was prompt: "Who knows, time will tell."

After 6 months he was given a supervisory role and more and more responsibilities came his way. He succeeded in disciplining the workers at Powai. Anil acted tough with those who refused to fall in line. At the same time, he understood their problems. His toughness ensured higher efficiency and productivity. Anil is a simple man, at heart and in life. The strict vegetarian loves the food prepared by his wife Geeta. Strange for a top-notch executive, he is not keen on dining in five-star hotels. He donated large sum of money to a school in Gujarat. He unwinds by watching Hindi movies and is a great fan of Amitabh Bachchan. He loves volleyball and cricket but mostly plays badminton. He does yoga regularly.

Naik's formula for success as he says is ***Observe, Learn, Think, Introspect and Correct***. He believes that his greatest strength is in making relationships which last. He learnt consistently. The end of the day is spent in introspection about what was done during the day. He said " My passion for relationships and dedication for work did the trick". He benchmarked the company against global standards. It made an aggressive entry into international markets. It started exporting to developed nations like the US and the UK. Anil achieved success in defence and nuclear sectors. Anil decided to concentrate only on core engineering and technology businesses. Accordingly, the cement business was demerged and it became the largest demerger in the history of corporate India. He wants to make L & T an Indian Multinational and fight other multinationals in India and abroad with skill and technology. The Week described him as a ***Gandhian Engineer***.

Questions for discussions

1. What are the different roles Mr. Naik has played?
2. Identify the virtues that are required to be ethical.

Society can act in crusade of Ethics.

Engineer should be Rajarshi. His efficiency and energy enables him to perform and his wisdom to achieve welfare of people.

Case 2

Product Design

Normally the time taken in automobile industry from the drawing board to the showroom is two and a half years. An automobile company had developed a new design for which they wanted to crash the lead-time to two years. The new model of automobile had to withstand an impact at 20 mph from the rear side. The safety standard was increased to 30 mph. This was done to reduce possibility of fire in the event of a collision. There should be no fuel leak with an impact at 30 mph.

The prototypes failed at impact speed of 20 mph. The crash test showed ruptured gas tank and dangerous leaks. After the test there was modification done of the rubber bladder in the gas tank and a piece of steel was inserted between the tank and the rear bumper. Even then the vehicle represented a serious fire hazard when struck from the rear, even in low speed collisions.

The Company had to decide whether to take the risk and introduce the product and meet the time schedule at the risk of consumer safety or they should delay the project and redesign the fuel tank to make it safer.

The losses which included the cost of medical charges, property damages, insurance costs, legal costs, pain and suffering, cost of funeral in the event of death, etc were estimated Rs.2, 00,000 per accident. Benefits in terms of savings if the accidents were avoided were estimated at Rs. 5,00,00,000. The costs of the suggested safety improvements worked out to Rs. 10,00,00,000.

Question for discussions

Assume you are the Managing Director of the Company; what decision will you take and why? (Hint: Use the concepts discussed earlier)

Case 3

Who says honesty doesn't pay?

No dealings in black money. No payment of bribes. Strict adherence to rules and regulations. These are some of the principles that the Chennai based corporate group called Alacrity, a leading name in the business of housing, has unflinchingly adhered to. This account by the founder of the group which Central Vigilance Commissioner N Vittal has termed 'incredible', illustrates that value-based management does absolutely no damage to the profits of a business, that economic growth and social consciousness are not mutually exclusive.

Amol Karnad is the Founder and Chairman of The Alacrity Group of Companies, Chennai, which consists of Alacrity Foundations (P) Ltd., Alacrity Housing Limited and Alacrity Electronics Limited. These are excerpts from the Eighth Shri B V Narayana Reddy Memorial Lecture delivered at the Indian Institute of World Culture, Bangalore.

The Alacrity experience

Alacrity Foundations was launched in 1978 largely as an expression of my own search for an integrated identity in a complex society through the medium of business. Some friends and family members joined the new venture. I recognised that my quality of life was inextricably tied up with the quality of life of the society I lived in and unless the two were harmonised, I would have to live in an eternal state of conflict. Given this objective and given the fact that I was not inclined to go the way of society, I had no option but to think in terms of trying to change society to come my way. My way was simply the sensitive process of unfolding the human being, manager and leader within myself, sharing this experience with my colleagues so that they too could similarly unfold themselves and translating the power thus generated into a successful institutional strategy. To discourage any distraction from this central purpose, I made Alacrity Foundations a private limited company to be fully owned by its employees in proportion to their seniority in the organisational hierarchy. Writing in the inaugural issue of our house journal, Genesis, I had described those early days in the following words: "We had little money, no `connections', not even `contacts'. But we had what mattered: a strong commitment to values and an abiding confidence in our ability to succeed. Steadfast in our mission, we made Alacrity our family, our religion and our community."

The active practice of ethical leadership meant that we had to remove the dividing line between personal life and professional life and be open, predictable and accountable with one another first and then behave similarly with our constituents outside Alacrity. I decided that this need would be best served if we not only worked together but also lived together, which prompted Alacrity's first apartment construction.

This perspective and the related optimism supported, of course, by the dedicated efforts of my colleagues, saw our first project being delivered in record time.As the quality of our flats and especially our prices got wider notice, more opportunities came our way not only from property owners who were happy to be provided with the option of not dealing in black and not losing sleep and hair in the bargain, but also from customers who responded warmly to our advertisements that said: "When you are investing for a lifetime, you need a builder you can trust." Encouraged by these opportunities, we decided to formally enter the field of urban housing and formulated our long-term strategy for this purpose. Explaining the strategy at the First Annual General Meeting of the shareholders of Alacrity Housing Limited, I had said: "Housing is a universal need: in other words, it is a need that no popularly elected government can afford to ignore or fail to support. That makes legislation on housing quite predictable, even if it is not immediately enabling, no matter which party be in power. By following a policy of strict adherence to laws and regulations with total avoidance of both dealing in black money and paying bribes to get sanctions or approvals, we have established a workable formula that cannot lose under any condition. The only risk involved is that an unwittingly misguided administrator or bureaucrat may unfairly delay or deny a sanction occasionally. When that happens we have a cast iron case which has every reason to be supported by the judiciary. Besides, should a representative of the government choose to get involved for whatever reason, not only would it make good copy for the press, but it would also encourage the political opposition to raise in the Assembly the issue of an honest builder being unnecessarily harassed. Thus our risks in a notorious area of conflict would be minimised, which only proves that the institutional cross-checks and balances provided for in our Constitution have indeed been designed to ensure that honesty does pay!"

With a reputation built around honesty, we readily attract customers who are naturally conscious of securing their investment of a life-time with a builder they can trust. Recognising that it is the responsibility of entrepreneurs to absorb risk, as far as possible, and not expose security-conscious customers to risk, we offer a fixed price and underwrite all escalations thereafter, and also compensate by way of liquidated damages for any delay in the delivery of a project, even if the delay is on account of factors beyond our control. The validity of these considerate policies has found concrete endorsement in the findings of a recent market survey carried out by an independent agency, which reported that when respondents were asked to prioritise the builders preferred by them, over 60 per cent had named only Alacrity. Thus even amidst the rough and tumble of the marketplace, there has been striking confirmation of the old adage, 'Honesty begets honesty.' And what is more, the Alacrity record over a decade proves that economic growth and social consciousness are not mutually exclusive.

Today, the Alacrity brand carries as much value in government departments as elsewhere in the marketplace. We have thus hopefully demonstrated that our public departments are only as corrupt, as ineffective and as inefficient as the rest of us. If dealing with the government departments in an ethical manner is considered one end of the ethical business spectrum, the care and consideration shown to the less privileged and the underdogs may be seen as the other end: A migrant contract labour force which today is nearly 2000-strong has been offered the opportunity to settle down by ensuring regular employment and fair wages, membership of the company's provident fund trust as also medical insurance and other welfare support to the workers and their families.

In the past, whenever I had shared the human dimension of the Alacrity experience, I have been invariably asked if there is not a price to pay in terms of reduced profits or even losses. We have needed to balance it, of course, with superior performance in the conventional business functions. And I must say here that we do have a team of deeply committed people in planning, designing, development and implementation. But to understand the economic risk better, I have to take you back to my own early insights into business uncertainty. I had realised that the very fact of business being risky and uncertain establishes that there is no formula to guarantee profit all the time. Therefore, to enter business without adequate psychological preparation to deal with a loss situation was surely asking for trouble either in terms of being under pressure to misreport results or simply going under. So long as we were not able to raise our volumes to an optimal level, we had to provide for losses. But with a clear understanding of the principle of venture capital, we could justify these losses as the development cost of establishing an ethical business. Later, when we decided to go public with Alacrity Housing Limited, to increase our equity base, promising fair returns to the shareholder, sections of the popular press, drawing attention to the accumulated loss, called us scamsters and frauds. However, when we addressed a meeting of the Tamil Nadu Investors' Association, we were pleasantly surprised at the overwhelmingly favourable reception we got. Not only was the hall packed unprecedentedly but the president of the association also chose the occasion to harmonise his own position with ours. "I spoke to the association's auditor," he said, "and asked him about the loss. The auditor, who is not a regular investor himself, told me that when you consider investing in Alacrity, it has to be not on the basis of profit or loss but for the cause, and he had himself decided to invest. I have therefore decided to depart from my usual discipline of not speaking for or against any issue and ask you today to invest your mite in this honest company."

Has Alacrity's honesty finally paid off?

1. The Alacrity group's current annual turnover is in the region of Rs 100 crores.
2. Alacrity Housing Ltd is an overwhelming market leader among flat builders in the city of Chennai. It has paid steady dividends to its shareholders from the first full year of its operations. (Over 140 projects and 2500 flats have been completed and delivered in strict compliance with development regulations).
3. Alacrity Electronics Ltd which has a significant presence in the field of energy management with the well-established Krykard brand, has also opened its dividend record last year.
4. Alacrity Foundations Pvt Ltd has emerging businesses in the fields of primary health care and education.
5. Even more striking has been its social performance.
   - Alacrity is in a position to say today that more than 30 per cent of flat building activity in Chennai is in strict accordance with Development Control Regulations and free from black money.
   - Nearly 30 per cent of Alacrity's labour force has shown itself capable of sustained employment and earnings, thereby opening the prospect of an extended market for housing and growing opportunities for employment to cover the less privileged in our society.
   - Alacrity's top managers mostly stay in Alacrity flats, travel by two-wheelers or public transport and draw salaries much less than what they would command elsewhere in the market. In the process, they demonstrate that a moderate lifestyle does not stand in the way of excellence in business performance.

In conclusion, you might as well ask me: "Are you not making it all sound a little too smooth and rosy?" We have had our problems and crises. To meet such demanding standards over long years, Alacrity's managers have to sustain a level of self-discipline, commitment and self-renewal that can, at times, become quite stressful, especially at the higher levels. This would perhaps explain a recent development which tested the institutional strength: a group of senior employees departed from the Alacrity fold and we came through this test as well as ever. There is enough evidence to show that the institution has only grown wiser and stronger after every fresh crisis. And we continue to have the conviction that no wealth or power can be more valuable than our dignity, no loss of profit can be more critical than the loss of our credibility, no skills or qualifications can substitute the integrity of our character. As a result, the dangers and risks are turned into opportunities, and the failures become the proverbial stepping stones to success."

In 1990, Mr. Gopi a Non Resident Indian (NRI) settled in the US had invested in a flat of Alacrity looking at the ethics of the company. The company was the only promoter who received all the payments through cheque. The company was known for good quality construction and delivery of the flat promptly as per the due date. There were no price escalation clauses.

After over a decade he was looking at the financial results of Alacrity. The company was making financial losses. Many of their projects came to a halt. The company was failing to meet delivery schedule of flats. Mr. Gopi remembered reading the excerpts a few years back in a magazine. However, in recent years, the company has been incurring heavy losses. He was wondering what went wrong in Alacrity. He had heard that they had acquired land at high prices and the land prices had since then crashed. Was that the reason or was company paying the price for being ethical? Should he believe that the person who is ethical will have to suffer during a testing time, but in the long run ethical companies will survive and do well.

Questions for discussions:

What alternatives does Alacrity have?

What should Alacrity do and why?

'***Code of ethics***' and '***code of conducts***' are often used interchangeably. However, there are some differences between them. Code of ethics are broader while later is more specific to person or company. Code of conduct is a part of code of ethics. These codes are based on five principles or canons of ethics. These are: ***Integrity, competence, individual responsibilities, professional responsibilities and human concerns.*** The members are expected to act according to the code of conduct laid down. Violation of the code may result in penalties / de recognition as a professional. Doctors have their medical council, lawyers have bar council, chartered accountants and engineers have their institute.. Once a qualifying degree is obtained they become a professional and member of their respective bodies.

1. AMERICAN SOCIETY OF MECHANICAL ENGINEERS (ASME)

Code Of Ethics Of Engineers

Fundamental Principles

Engineers uphold and advance the integrity, honor, and dignity of the Engineering profession by:

1. Using their knowledge and skill for the enhancement of human welfare;
2. Being honest and impartial, and serving with fidelity the public, their employers and clients; and
3. Striving to increase the competence and prestige of the engineering profession.
4. Supporting the professional and technical societies of their disciplines.

Fundamental Canons

1. Engineers shall hold paramount the safety, health and welfare of the public in the performance of their professional duties.
2. Engineers shall perform services only in areas of their competence.
3. Engineers shall continue their professional development throughout their careers and shall provide opportunities for the professional development of those engineers under their supervision.
4. Engineers shall act in professional matters for each employer or client as faithful agents or trustees, and shall avoid conflicts of interest.
5. Engineers shall build their professional reputation on the merit of their services and shall not compete unfairly with others.
6. Engineers shall associate only with reputable persons or organizations.
7. Engineers shall issue public statements only in an objective and truthful manner.

2. THE AMERICAN SOCIETY OF CIVIL ENGINEERS (ASCE)

Code of Ethics

Fundamental Principles

1. Engineers uphold and advance the integrity, honor and dignity of the engineering profession by:

2. Using their knowledge and skill for the enhancement of human welfare and the environment;
3. Being honest and impartial and serving with fidelity the public, their employers and clients;
4. Striving to increase the competence and prestige of the engineering profession; and
5. Supporting the professional and technical societies of their disciplines.

Fundamental Canons

Engineers shall hold paramount the safety, health and welfare of the public and shall strive to comply with the principles of sustainable development in the performance of their professional duties.

1. Engineers shall perform services only in areas of their competence.
2. Engineers shall issue public statements only in an objective and truthful manner.
3. Engineers shall act in professional matters for each employer or client as faithful agents or trustees, and shall avoid conflicts of interest.
4. Engineers shall build their professional reputation on the merit of their services and shall not compete unfairly with others.
5. Engineers shall act in such a manner as to uphold and enhance the honor, integrity, and dignity of the engineering profession.
6. Engineers shall continue their professional development throughout their careers, and shall provide opportunities for the professional development of those engineers under their supervision.

Guidelines to Practice Under the Fundamental Canons of Ethics

CANON 1.

1. Engineers shall hold paramount the safety, health and welfare of the public and shall strive to comply with the principles of sustainable development in the performance of their professional duties.
2. Engineers shall recognize that the lives, safety, health and welfare of the general public are dependent upon engineering judgments, decisions and practices incorporated into structures, machines, products, processes and devices.
3. Engineers shall approve or seal only those design documents, reviewed or prepared by them, which are determined to be safe for public health and welfare in conformity with accepted engineering standards.
4. Engineers whose professional judgment is overruled under circumstances where the safety, health and welfare of the public are endangered, or the principles of sustainable development ignored, shall inform their clients or employers of the possible consequences.
5. Engineers who have knowledge or reason to believe that another person or firm may be in violation of any of the provisions of Canon 1 shall present such information to the proper authority in writing and shall cooperate with the proper authority in furnishing such further information or assistance as may be required.
6. Engineers should seek opportunities to be of constructive service in civic affairs and work for the advancement of the safety, health and well-being of their communities, and the protection of the environment through the practice of sustainable development.
7. Engineers should be committed to improving the environment by adherence to the principles of sustainable development so as to enhance the quality of life of the general public.

CANON 2.

1. Engineers shall perform services only in areas of their competence.
2. Engineers shall undertake to perform engineering assignments only when qualified by education or experience in the technical field of engineering involved.
3. Engineers may accept an assignment requiring education or experience outside of their own

fields of competence, provided their services are restricted to those phases of the project in which they are qualified. All other phases of such project shall be performed by qualified associates, consultants, or employees.

4. Engineers shall not affix their signatures or seals to any engineering plan or document dealing with subject matter in which they lack competence by virtue of education or experience or to any such plan or document not reviewed or prepared under their supervisory control.

CANON 3.

1. Engineers shall issue public statements only in an objective and truthful manner.
2. Engineers should endeavor to extend the public knowledge of engineering and sustainable development, and shall not participate in the dissemination of untrue, unfair or exaggerated statements regarding engineering.
3. Engineers shall be objective and truthful in professional reports, statements, or testimony. They shall include all relevant and pertinent information in such reports, statements, or testimony.
4. Engineers, when serving as expert witnesses, shall express an engineering opinion only when it is founded upon adequate knowledge of the facts, upon a background of technical competence, and upon honest conviction.
5. Engineers shall issue no statements, criticisms, or arguments on engineering matters which are inspired or paid for by interested parties, unless they indicate on whose behalf the statements are made.
6. Engineers shall be dignified and modest in explaining their work and merit, and will avoid any act tending to promote their own interests at the expense of the integrity, honor and dignity of the profession.

CANON 4.

1. Engineers shall act in professional matters for each employer or client as faithful agents or trustees, and shall avoid conflicts of interest.
2. Engineers shall avoid all known or potential conflicts of interest with their employers or clients and shall promptly inform their employers or clients of any business association, interests, or circumstances which could influence their judgment or the quality of their services.
3. Engineers shall not accept compensation from more than one party for services on the same project, or for services pertaining to the same project, unless the circumstances are fully disclosed to and agreed to, by all interested parties.
4. Engineers shall not solicit or accept gratuities, directly or indirectly, from contractors, their agents, or other parties dealing with their clients or employers in connection with work for which they are responsible.
5. Engineers in public service as members, advisors, or employees of a governmental body or department shall not participate in considerations or actions with respect to services solicited or provided by them or their organization in private or public engineering practice.
6. Engineers shall advise their employers or clients when, as a result of their studies, they believe a project will not be successful.
7. Engineers shall not use confidential information coming to them in the course of their assignments as a means of making personal profit if such action is adverse to the interests of their clients, employers or the public.
8. Engineers shall not accept professional employment outside of their regular work or interest without the knowledge of their employers.

CANON 5.

1. Engineers shall build their professional reputation on the merit of their services and shall not compete unfairly with others.
2. Engineers shall not give, solicit or receive either directly or indirectly, any political contribution, gratuity, or unlawful consideration in order to secure work, exclusive of securing salaried positions through employment agencies.
3. Engineers should negotiate contracts for professional services fairly and on the basis of demonstrated competence and qualifications for the type of professional service required.
4. Engineers may request, propose or accept professional commissions on a contingent basis only under circumstances in which their professional judgments would not be compromised.
5. Engineers shall not falsify or permit misrepresentation of their academic or professional qualifications or experience.
6. Engineers shall give proper credit for engineering work to those to whom credit is due, and shall recognize the proprietary interests of others. Whenever possible, they shall name the person or persons who may be responsible for designs, inventions, writings or other accomplishments.
7. Engineers may advertise professional services in a way that does not contain misleading language or is in any other manner derogatory to the dignity of the profession.

Examples of permissible advertising are as follows:

(a) Professional cards in recognized, dignified publications, and listings in rosters or directories published by responsible organizations, provided that the cards or listings are consistent in size and content and are in a section of the publication regularly devoted to such professional cards.

(b) Brochures which factually describe experience, facilities, personnel and capacity to render service, providing they are not misleading with respect to the engineer's participation in projects described.

(c) Display advertising in recognized dignified business and professional publications, providing it is factual and is not misleading with respect to the engineer's extent of participation in projects described.

(d) A statement of the engineers' names or the name of the firm and statement of the type of service posted on projects for which they render services.

(e) Preparation or authorization of descriptive articles for the lay or technical press, which are factual and dignified. Such articles shall not imply anything more than direct participation in the project described.

(f) Permission by engineers for their names to be used in commercial advertisements, such as may be published by contractors, material suppliers, etc., only by means of a modest, dignified notation acknowledging the engineers' participation in the project described. Such permission shall not include public endorsement of proprietary products.

(g) Engineers shall not maliciously or falsely, directly or indirectly, injure the professional reputation, prospects, practice or employment of another engineer or indiscriminately criticize another's work.

(h) Engineers shall not use equipment, supplies, laboratory or office facilities of their employers to carry on outside private practice without the consent of their employers.

CANON 6.

1. 1.Engineers shall act in such a manner as to uphold and enhance the honor, integrity, and dignity of the engineering profession.
2. 2.Engineers shall not knowingly act in a manner which will be derogatory to the honor, integrity, or dignity of the engineering profession or knowingly engage in business or professional practices of a fraudulent, dishonest or unethical nature.

CANON 7

1. Engineers shall continue their professional development throughout their careers, and shall provide opportunities for the professional development of those engineers under their supervision.
2. Engineers should keep current in their specialty fields by engaging in professional practice, participating in continuing education courses, reading in the technical literature, and attending professional meetings and seminars.
3. Engineers should encourage their engineering employees to become registered at the earliest possible date.
4. Engineers should encourage engineering employees to attend and present papers at professional and technical society meetings.
5. Engineers shall uphold the principle of mutually satisfying relationships between employers and employees with respect to terms of employment including professional grade descriptions, salary ranges, and fringe benefits.

As adopted September 2, 1914, and most recently amended November 10, 1996.

The American Society of Civil Engineers adopted THE FUNDAMENTAL PRINCIPLES of the ABET Code of Ethics of Engineers as accepted by the Accreditation Board for Engineering and Technology, Inc. (ABET). (By ASCE Board of Direction action April 12-14, 1975)

In November 1996, the ASCE Board of Direction adopted the following definition of Sustainable Development: "Sustainable Development is the challenge of meeting human needs for natural resources, industrial products, energy, food, transportation, shelter, and effective waste management while conserving and protecting environmental quality and the natural resource base essential for future development."

3. INSTITUTE OF ELECTRICAL AND ELECTRONIC ENGINEERS (IEEE)

Code Of Ethics (*Revised October 1990*)

IEEE is a non-profit technical professional association of more than 360,000 individual members in approximately 175 countries.

We, the members of the IEEE, in recognition of the importance of our technologies in affecting the quality of life throughout the world, and in accepting a personal obligation to our profession, its members and the communities we serve, do hereby commit ourselves to the highest ethical and professional conduct and agree:

1. to accept responsibility in making engineering decisions consistent with the safety, health, and welfare of the public, and to disclose promptly factors that might endanger the public or the environment;
2. to avoid real or perceived conflicts of interest whenever possible, and to disclose them to affected parties when they do exist;
3. to be honest and realistic in stating claims or estimates based on available data;
4. to reject bribery in all its forms;
5. to improve the understanding of technology, its appropriate application, and potential consequences;
6. to maintain and improve our technical competence and to undertake technological tasks for others only if qualified by training or experience, or after full disclosure of pertinent limitations;
8. to seek, accept, and offer honest criticism of technical work, to acknowledge and correct errors, and to credit properly the contributions of others;
9. to treat fairly all persons regardless of such factors as race, religion, gender, disability, age, or national origin;

10. to avoid injuring others, their property, reputation, or employment by false or malicious action;
11. to assist colleagues and coworkers in their professional development and to support them in following this code of ethics.
12. In the end, engineers must be ever cognizant of both their actions and inactions as professionals.

4. INSTITUTE OF ENGINEERS (INDIA)

The Institution of Engineers has set up a "Safety and Quality in Engineer Forum" that aims to ensure greater safety and improve quality in the profession. The Forum will be based in the Capital and will network with national, regional and local Government bodies to inculcate the concepts of safety and quality among engineers. The Forum will create awareness about the significance of safety and quality, assist governments and municipal bodies in developing codes and norms for construction, develop courses on safety engineering and quality management systems. It will also conduct training courses on safety quality standards, create awareness on legal compliance requirements and conduct research.

Code of Ethics for Corporate Members

1.0 Preamble

1.1 The Corporate Members of the Institute of Engineers (India) are committed to promote and practice the profession of engineering for the common good of the community bearing in mind the following concerns:

1.1.1 Concern for ethical standard;

1.1.2 Concern for social justice, social order and human rights;

1.1.3 Concern for protection of the environment;

1.1.4 Concern for sustainable development;

1.1.5 Public safety and tranquility.

2.0 The Tenets of the Code of Ethics

2.1 A Corporate Member shall utilize his knowledge and expertise for the welfare, health and safety of the community without any discrimination for sectional or private interests.

2.2 A Corporate Member shall maintain the honour, integrity and dignity in all his professional actions to be worthy of the trust of the community and the profession.

2.3 A Corporate Member shall act only in the domains of his competence and with diligence, care, sincerity and honesty.

2.4 A Corporate Member shall apply the knowledge and expertise in the interest of his employer or the clients for whom he shall work without compromising with other obligations to these Tenets.

2.5 A Corporate Member shall not falsify or misrepresent his own or his associates qualifications, experience etc.

2.6 A Corporate Member, whenever necessary and relevant, shall take all reasonable steps to inform himself, his employer or clients, of the environment, economic, social and other possible consequences, which may arise out of his actions.

2.7 A Corporate Member shall maintain utmost honesty and fairness in making statements or giving witness and shall do so on the basis of adequate knowledge.

2.8 A Corporate Member shall not directly or indirectly injure the professional reputation of another member.

2.9. A Corporate Member shall reject any kind of offer that may involve unfair practice or may cause avoidable damage to the ecosystem.

2.10 A Corporate Member shall be concerned about and shall act in the best of his abilities for the maintenance of sustainability of the process of development.

2.11 A Corporate Member shall not act in any manner which may injure the reputation of the Institution or which may cause any damage to the Institution financially or otherwise.

3.0. General Guidance

The Tenets of the Code of Ethics are based on the recognition that–

3.1 A common tie exists among the humanity and that The Institute of Engineers (India) derives its value from the people so that the actions of its Corporate Members should indicate the member's highest regard for equality of opportunity, social justice and fairness;

3.2 The Corporate Members of the Institution hold a privileged position in the community so as to make it a necessity for their not using the position for personal and sectional interests.

4.0 And, as such, a Corporate Member–

4.1 should keep his employer or client fully informed on all matters in respect of his assignment which are likely to lead to a conflict of interest or when, in his judgement a project will not be viable on the basis of commercial, technical, environmental or any other risks;

4.2 should maintain confidentiality of any information with utmost sincerity unless expressly permitted to disclose such information or unless such permission, if withheld, may adversely affect the welfare, health and safety of the community;

4.3 should neither solicit nor accept financial or other considerations from anyone related to a project or assignment of which he is in the charge;

4.4 should neither pay nor offer direct or indirect inducements to secure work;

4.5 should compete on the basis of merit alone;

4.6 should refrain from inducing a client to breach a contract entered into with another duly appointed engineer;

4.7 should, if asked by the employer or a client, to review the work of another person or organization, discuss the review with the other person or organization to arrive at a balanced opinion;

4.8 should make statements or give evidence before a tribunal or a court of law in an objective and accurate manner and express any opinion on the basis of adequate knowledge and competence;

4.9 should reveal the existence of any interest–pecuniary or otherwise–which may affect the judgement while giving evidence or making a statement.

5.0 Any decision of the Council as per provisions of the relevant Bye–Laws of the Institution shall be final and binding on all Corporate Members.

5. INDIAN INSTITUTE OF MATERIALS MANAGEMENT (IIMM)

To promote the high standard of commercial morality and just and honourable practice in the conduct of business in all matters amongst its members.

To observe the following code of conduct and ethics

1. To consider first the TOTAL interest of one's organisation in all transactions without impairing the dignity and responsibility of one's office;
2. To buy without prejudice, seeking to obtain the maximum ultimate value for each Rupee of expenditure.
3. To subscribe and work for honesty and truth in buying and selling to denounce all forms and manifestations of commercial bribery, and to eschew antisocial practices.
4. To accord a prompt and courteous reception, so far as conditions will permit, to all who call upon a legitimate business mission.
5. To respect one's obligations and those of one's organisation, consistent with good business practice.

6. INSTITUTE OF ELECTRONICS AND TELECOMMUNICATION ENGINEERS (IETE)

The Institution of Electronics and Telecommunication Engineers (IETE) is India's leading recognised professional society devoted to the advancement of Science and Technology of Electronics, Telecommunication & IT. Founded in 1953, it serves more than 50,000 members through various centres, whose number is 51, spread all over India and abroad. The Institution provides leadership in Scientific and Technical areas of direct importance to the national development and economy. Government of India has recognised IETE as a Scientific and Industrial Research Organization (SIRO) and also notified as an educational Institution of national eminence. The objectives of IETE focus on advancing electro-technology. The IETE conducts and sponsors technical meetings, conferences, symposia, and exhibitions all over India, publishes technical journals and provides continuing education as well as career advancement opportunities to its members.

THE PROFESSIONAL ENGINEERS BILL

The Professional Engineers Bill seeks to regulate the engineering profession and matters connected therewith. The Bill has become inevitable in the present context due to concerted moves in the US, Australia, and European countries to restrict entry of professionals from India, China and other Asian countries. Restrictions are likely to come up as discriminatory barriers regarding the competence of personnel, international recognition of qualifications, continuing education and requisite age. This assumes importance since we have to consolidate our potential by seeking national as well as international recognition through partnerships and certifying competence at par with professionals from any other country.

The main objective of the Bill is to ensure that only competent persons take up engineering and technology activities. Recognition of competence of engineers and technologists on the basis of a degree obtained at one point of time is not considered enough in the West. Hence, a mechanism needs to be developed and installed for imparting relevant continuing development and integrating the same with the process of certification. For this purpose, it is necessary to properly regulate the practice of engineering to protect health, safety and welfare.

The aims and objectives of the Bill pertain to technology being visualized to play a key role in socio-economic development. Efficient use of resources – physical, financial and human- will be a determining factor in raising the rate of growth and it has to be ensured that activities of engineering and technology are performed by competent person. It is also important that engineers and technologist take professional decisions with due honesty and integrity.

For the operation of the Bill, an implementing agency shall render life-long support for the professional growth of engineers. The Bill, (Annexure) will become an Act after approval by the Parliament, is to provide for the constitution of the Engineering Council of India and the maintenance of National Registers of Professional Engineers , Associate Professional Engineers and Consulting Engineering Organizations, and regulate engineering profession and matters connected therewith.

EXERCISE

Debate on globalisation.

Identify code of conduct of some Indian engineering companies.

Debate on Pros and Cons of Engineers Bill.

Debate an whether the concern for non human environment should be a part of professional engineering ethics or personal ethics.

SHORT QUESTIONS

1. Define Multinational Corporations with examples.
2. How are computer used as an instrument of unethical behaviour.
3. What do global issues mean?
4. What do you learn from the 6 examples?
5. Give an account of the Bhopal disaster

6. What is environmental protection?
7. What is computer ethics?
8. What is CGO?
9. What is a hired gun?
10. What are the various abuses that engineers faces as an expert witness?
11. What are the various normative models that engineers can use when faced with conflicts as an adviser?
12. What does forensic engineering mean?
13. Who is a consultant engineer?
14. What are contingency fees?
15. What are the changes involved in transition from engineer – manager – leader?
16. Who is an expert adviser? Give examples.
17. Define professional misconduct.
18. Define code of ethics.
19. Define incompetence.
20. What is a code of conduct?
21. Identify some of the basic principles of ethics on which codes of conduct are generally framed.
22. Code of conduct are required only by professional bodies. Discuss.

LONG QUESTION

1. Write a note on Global Compact.
2. Discuss cyber crimes.
3. Discuss the environmental ethics with examples.
4. Discuss the Ten Commandments of Computer ethics.
5. Discuss the role of engineering in global trade.
6. What is moral leadership?
7. Discuss the various roles played by engineers.
8. What are the functions as an engineer?
9. Give examples of ethical issues faced by a consultant engineer.
10. How can a engineer manager/ leader create an ethical climate?
11. Discuss the models of professional roles of an engineer?
12. Explain leadership qualities diagrammatically.
13. Present the salient features of Engineers Bill.
14. Develop a code of conduct for a large size company employing software engineers.
15. Identify the differences between the various codes of conduct.
16. Write a note on CBA technique.

REFERENCES

Mike W. Martin and Rolan Schinzinger, Ethics in Engineering, Tata McGraw Publishers, 2003

John Hooker, Some Business-Related Ethical Issues in Engineering, Carnegie Mellon University, May 2000

ANNEXURE

The Engineers Bill, 2003 Aims and Objectives of the Bill

Technology is visualized to play a key role in socio-economic development. Efficient use of resources-physical, financial and human-will be a determining factor in raising the rate of growth. It has to be ensured that activities of engineering and technology are performed by competent persons.

Recognition of competence of engineers and technologists on the basis of a degree obtained at one point of time is not enough. Mechanism has to be developed and installed for imparting relevant continuing development and integrating the same with the process of certification. For this purpose, it is necessary to properly regulate the practice of engineering by an Act of Parliament in order to protect the public health, safety and welfare.

It is also important that engineers and technologists take professional decisions with due honesty and integrity.

For the operation of the Bill, an implementing agency shall render life long support for the professional growth of engineers.

The Bill, which will become an Act after approval by the Parliament, is to provide for the constitution of the Engineering Council of India and the maintenance of National Registers of Professional Engineers, Associate Professional Engineers and Consulting Engineering Organizations and regulate engineering profession and matters connected therewith.

CHAPTER I

PRELIMINARY

1. SHORT TITLE, EXTENT AND COMMENCEMENT

1.1 This Act may be called the Engineers Act, 2003.

1.2 It extends to the whole of India.

1.3 It shall come into force on such date as the Central Government may, by notification in the official Gazette, appoint.

2. GENERAL PROVISIONS, AIMS AND PURPOSE

2.1 In recognition of the vital impact which the rapid advance of knowledge of the mathematical, physical and engineering science as applied in the practice of engineering is having upon the lives, property, economy and security of our people and national defence, it is the intent of legislature, in order to protect the public health, safety and welfare, that the privilege of practicing as professional engineers be entrusted only to those persons duly licensed, registered and practicing under the provisions of this Act.

2.2 In order that the country and members of the public may be able to identify those duly authorized to practice as professional engineers and fix responsibility for work done or services rendered or acts performed in the practice as professional engineers, only licensed and registered persons shall practice, offer or attempt to practice engineering or call themselves or be otherwise designated as any kind of a "Professional Engineer" as a professional, business or commercial identification, title, name, representation, claim or asset.

2.3 In furtherance of intent and purpose of the Legislature, the practice of engineering is hereby declared a learned profession to be practiced and regulated as such, and its practitioners in the Indian Union shall be held accountable to the State and members of the public by high professional standards in keeping with the ethics and practices of the other learned professions in this country.

Legislature also intends to ensure that engineers take professional decisions with due honesty and integrity. A mechanism will be set up under this Act for laying down the norms of professional conduct, updating the same from time to time and taking appropriate action for failure to follow them.

Various engineering associations have repeatedly emphasized the need for statutory regulation so that only professionally qualified engineers are able to undertake the complex engineering designs and thus safeguard the health and safety of general public. With the passing of this legislation, it will be unlawful for any person to practice engineering profession unless he is registered under the Act. This will also help in recognition of Indian professional engineers in other parts of the world in view of increased global opportunities. The legislation is generally on the same lines as similar Acts in other countries.

2.4 It is the intent of the legislature to make participation in continuing development programmes mandatory for all registered engineers so that their expertise is updated.

2.5 A mechanism will be set up under this Act for laying down the norms of professional conduct, updating the same from time to time, and taking appropriate action for violating them.

2.6 The Engineering Council of India will be the organizational mechanism for attaining the aims and objects of this Act.

3. DEFINITIONS

In this Act, unless the context otherwise requires:

3.1 "Associate Professional Engineer" means a person who has been duly registered by ECI as an Associate Professional Engineer.

3.2 "Certificate of Registration" means the certificate issued by ECI granting the privilege of practicing as a registered Professional Engineer, Associate Professional Engineer or Consulting Engineering Organization;

3.3 "Chairman" means the person appointed to be the Chairman of the Council of ECI and its Executive Committee;

3.4 "Consulting Engineering Organization" means an organization or division of an organization (Commercial company/Partnership/Proprietorship/Co-operative or non-profit Society/NGO/Govt. Department) employing one or more professional engineers and technologists, which is primarily dealing with engineering related consultancy, and which is duly registered by ECI;

3.5 "Council" shall be the body consisting of all Members whose names are standing in the Register of Members of ECI;

3.6 "Engineer" means a person who has graduated with a Degree or equivalent in engineering or technology from an institution recognized by the All India Council for Technical Education, Government of India or any other appropriate body and such other qualifications as may be approved by ECI;

3.7 "Engineering Council of India" means the Engineering Council of India (herein called "ECI") constituted under this Act;

3.8 "Executive Committee" means the Committee constituted for managing the day-to-day functioning of ECI;

3.9. "Practice" means any service or creative work adequate performance of which requires engineering and technology education, training and experience in the application of special knowledge of mathematical, physical and engineering sciences to such services. The project could be on effective use of natural, financial and human resources. It includes, but is not limited to consultation, studies, investigations, evaluation, conceptualization planning, design and supervision of engineering projects and systems, which are to be backed by information technology where required. Teaching along with research/consultancy in any engineering discipline in a recognized Institute or Engineering Research Organization shall be considered as part of practice;

3.10 "Professional Engineer" means an Engineer who has been duly registered by ECI as a Professional Engineer;

3.11 "Regulation" means a regulation made under this Act by ECI.

3.12 "Rule" means a rule made under this Act by the Central Government;

3.13 "Secretary and Director General" means the person appointed as Secretary and Director General (herein called "SDG") of ECI;

3.14 "Vice-Chairman" means the person appointed to be Vice-Chairman of the Council of ECI and its Executive Committee.

CHAPTER II

ENGINEERING COUNCIL OF INDIA

4. CONSTITUTION OF ECI

4.1 The Central Government shall, by notification in the official Gazette, constitute, with effect from such date as may be specified in the notification, a statutory Council to be known as the Engineering Council of India (hereinafter called "ECI"), which shall be a body corporate, having perpetual succession and a common seal with power to acquire, hold and dispose of properties, both movable and immovable, and to contract and may by that name sue or be sued. The existing Engineering Council of India will stand dissolved on the creation of the statutory body, its assets and liabilities will be transferred, registration with it will continue to be valid and the National Registers and Databases will become National Registers and Databases of the statutory body.

4.2 The Head Office of ECI shall be in the National Capital Territory of Delhi and ECI may, with the previous approval of its Council, establish offices at other places in India.

5. OBJECTS, POWERS AND FUNCTIONS

5.1 ECI will work for the advancement of science and practice of engineering and technology in the country; enhancing the image of engineers and technologists in the society; certifying the competence of engineers and technologists and consulting engineering organizations for undertaking professional activities both inside the country and outside and meet all relevant obligations under the international charters; and laying down strict norms of professional conduct and taking appropriate action against violations

5.2 Specific objectives and functions in the attainment of the objects stated in Sub-section 5.1, for which the Engineering Council of India will exercise powers are:

(i) To standardize criteria and procedures to be adopted for according the status of "Professional Engineer", "Associate Professional Engineer" and "Consulting Engineering Organization" and to accord registration/license/accreditation to practice engineering and technology in India.

(ii) To maintain a National Register of "Professional Engineers", a National Register of "Associate Professional Engineers", and a National Register of "Consulting Engineering Organizations", and databases of any other types of engineering and technology manpower considered necessary for the attainment of objectives.

(iii) To promote the practice of continuing education and training to upgrade the quality of engineering professionals.

(iv) To establish a code of ethics for engineers and technologists and consulting engineering organizations registered with ECI, for adoption and to evolve the strategy for its enforcement.

(v) To identify and undertake various activities for the promotion of engineering profession.

(vi) To interact with the Government at State and Central levels and help adoption of policies for the betterment of engineering profession.

(vii) To represent Indian engineering profession at national and international levels and to act as a nodal body representing India for recognition of "Professional Engineers" and "Consulting Engineering Organizations".

(viii) To develop standards and criteria for facilitating cross-border mobility of experienced Professional Engineers and Consulting Engineering Organizations among signatories of International agreements and to establish such committees, as may be necessary, for reciprocal/ joint activities with similar professional bodies in other countries who are signatories of international agreements.

(ix) To network and cooperate with other such national and international bodies/fora who are engaged in similar activities, and, if necessary, to enter into agreements with them.

(x) To perform any or all other acts, deeds and things, which may become necessary to be performed at any stage to achieve the main objectives of improving the image of the engineering profession, and to serve the needs of the society.

6. MEMBERSHIP OF THE COUNCIL

6.1 Membership

The Council will comprise of nominated members, co-opted members and ex-officio members.

6.2 Nominated Members

Members will be nominated as described below.

(i) Nodal Ministries/Departments/Organizations of Central Government (4)

One nominee each from the following:

- Planning Commission
- Human Resource Development
- Commerce
- Science and Technology

(ii) Major Employing Ministries/Departments/Organizations of Engineers in Central Government (6)

One engineer each to be nominated by 6 Ministries /Departments/Organisations by rotation from the following:

- Urban Development and Poverty Alleviation
- Road Transport and Highways
- Railways
- Telecommunication
- Water Resources
- Power
- Defence
- Heavy Industry
- Civil Aviation
- Information Technology
- Council of Scientific and Industrial Research
- Defence Research and Development Organization
- Atomic Energy Commission
- Indian Space Research Organization

(iii) Organizations of Technical Education (4)

One engineer each to be nominated by the following Organizations :

- All India Council for Technical Education
- Three educational institutions imparting education in engineering and technology, to be selected by the Ministry of HRD

(iv) State Governments (5)

One engineer from each State as follows:

- One State from northern region, by rotation
- One State from western region, by rotation
- One State from southern region, by rotation
- One State from eastern region, by rotation
- One State from north-eastern region, by rotation

(v) Industry Associations (2)

One engineer each from two associations by rotation from the following:

- Federation of Indian Chambers of Commerce and Industry
- Associated Chamber of Commerce and Industry
- Confederation of Indian Industry
- National Association of Software Service Companies
- Standing Conference of Public Enterprises

(vi) Engineering Professional Associations / Societies (26)

One nominee each from the following Associations/Societies:

1. Aeronautical Society of India
2. Association of Consulting Civil Engineers (India)
3. Broadcast Engineering Society (India)
4. Computer Society of India
5. Construction Industry Development Council
6. Consultancy Development Centre
7. Consulting Engineers Association of India
8. Indian Building Congress
9. Indian Concrete Institute
10. Indian Geotechnical Society
11. Indian Institute of Chemical Engineers
12. Indian Institution of Bridge Engineers
13. Indian Institution of Industrial Engineering
14. Indian National Academy of Engineering
15. Indian Society for Trenchless Technology
16. Institution of Surveyors
17. Institute of Urban Transport (I)
18. International Council of Consultants
19. The Indian Institute of Metals
20. The Institute of Marine Engineers (India)
21. The Institution of Electronics & Telecommunication Engineers
22. The Institution of Engineers (India)

In addition to the nominees of 22 organizations listed above, 4 engineers may be nominated by multi-discipline associations/societies e.g. The Institution of Engineers (India), to represent disciplines un-represented or not adequately represented otherwise.

The Government may, through a notification, add or delete certain organizations in the list above of nominating organizations.

6.3 Co-opted Members

The Council may co-opt up to two eminent engineers as members.

6.4 Ex-officio Members

Chairman, Vice Chairman and SDG will be ex-officio members. SDG will discharge the functions of Secretary of the Council and Executive Committee.

If there is no SDG, Chairman may nominate a member of the Executive Committee to perform the functions of Secretary of the Council and the Executive Committee. In that situation, the member so nominated will be referred to as Member Secretary.

6.5 Incorporation of the Engineering Council of India

A body corporate as by the name of Engineering Council of India is hereby constituted by all Council Members specified in Section 6.2 of this Act.

7. COUNCIL

7.1 All the Members described in Section 6 shall constitute the Council. Nominated and co-opted members will have a term of three years. If a vacancy of a nominated or co-opted member arises for any reason whatsoever, the concerned organization shall nominate or the Council shall co-opt, as the case may be, another person to fill up the vacancy for the remaining period.

7.2 The Council will consider all the policy issues covered under the objects and functions in Section 5 as may be brought before it by the Executive Committee or any Member. The Council shall give suitable directions to the Executive Committee for implementation/action on such issues.

7.3 Meetings of the Council will be held in accordance with the procedures laid down in the Regulations.

8. EXECUTIVE COMMITTEE

8.1 Membership of Executive Committee

The Executive Committee shall comprise of Chairman, Vice Chairman, Secretary and Director General, and twelve members.

8.2 Constitution of Executive Committee

The Executive Committee shall be constituted after the Council has been formed.

Members of the Executive Committee, other than Chairman, Vice Chairman, Secretary and Director General, and co-opted member, will be appointed by election by the Council from amongst its members as laid down in the Regulations.

Provided that elected members will represent the various constituencies as follows:

i) Three members from:
- Nodal Ministries / Departments / Organizations of Central Government,
- Major Employing Ministries / Departments / Organizations of Engineers in Central Government, and
- State Governments

(ii) Two members comprising one each from:
- Organizations of Technical Education, and
- Industry Associations

(iii) Six members from:
- Engineering Professional Associations / Societies

In addition,

One eminent engineer may be co-opted by the Executive Committee

8.3 Tenure of the Executive Committee

The normal tenure of the Executive Committee will be 3 years ending on 30th June. The new Executive Committee should normally be constituted by that date. In exceptional cases even after the expiry of this tenure, the Executive Committee in office shall continue to function till a new Executive Committee is constituted.

8.4 Functioning of the Executive Committee

The Executive Committee will function in accordance with the provisions of relevant Regulations.

9. POWERS OF THE EXECUTIVE COMMITTEE

9.1 The Executive Committee will have such powers as are delegated to it by the Council to do such things as it may consider necessary or expedient for the purpose of carrying out the objects of ECI.

10. INCOME, EXPENDITURE AND ACCOUNTS

10.1 ECI will have the power to receive income from different sources as registration and renewal charges, grants, donations, gifts, corpus fund, sponsorship charges, consultancy charges for services provided or for any other purpose consistent with its objects and functions.

10.2 The income and property of ECI, howsoever derived, shall be applied towards the promotion of the objectives set forth in this Act, subject nevertheless in respect of the expenditure of grants or donations made for any specific purposes as may be desired from time to time by the donors. No portion of the income and property of ECI shall be paid or transferred, directly or indirectly, by way of dividends, bonus or otherwise or by way of profits to any person/persons, who at any time are or have been members of ECI or to any of them or to any person claiming through them, or any of them provided that nothing herein contained shall prevent the payment in good faith of remuneration to any member or other persons in return for any service rendered to ECI.

10.3 The Executive Committee shall cause to be maintained proper Books of Accounts of ECI as required by the Act.

11. AUTHORITIES OF ECI

11.1 The Authorities of the ECI will be

(i) Chairman

(ii) Vice Chairman

(iii) Secretary and Director General

11.2 Chairman and Vice Chairman

11.2.1 The Chairman and Vice Chairman will be eminent engineers. The Chairman and Vice Chairman will be nominated by the Council from amongst panels of names suggested by a five-member Search-cum-Selection Committee appointed by the Council. The members of the Search-cum-Selection Committee as also the persons empanelled by it may be from within the Council or outside. They will be appointed as per procedure laid down in the Regulations.

11.2.2 Provided that on the first constitution of the Council under this Act and until the Chairman is appointed as per the procedure laid down in the Regulations, a member of the Council nominated by the Council shall discharge the functions of the Chairman.

11.2.3 The Chairman and Vice Chairman of ECI will have a term of 3 years and exercise powers as detailed in the Regulations.

The Chairman, on the recommendation of a selection committee set up by the Executive Committee and with the approval of the Executive Committee, will appoint a Secretary and Director General. The salary and service conditions of the SDG will be governed by Regulations.

11.3 Duties of the Chairman and Vice Chairman

The Chairman, when present, shall preside at the Council meetings, and the Executive Committee meetings, and conduct the meetings as per Regulations of ECI. The Chairman will also be responsible jointly with the SDG for proper records of the minutes of all meetings in which he/she is present. In the absence of Chairman, Vice Chairman will perform the functions of Chairman.

11.4 Duties of the Secretary and Director General

The Secretary and Director General will convene meetings and maintain records of proceedings of the Council and the Executive Committee, and shall perform such other duties as the Chairman may decide. SDG will also function as Administrative Head.

12. BODIES OF ECI

ECI will have the following bodies as provided in this Act.

(i) Council

(ii) Executive Committee

(iii) Board for Registration of Professional Engineers and Associate Professional Engineers

(iv) Board for Registration of Consulting Engineering Organizations

(v) Board for Development of Professional Engineers and Consulting Engineering Organizations

(vi) Board for Ethics of Professional Engineers and Consulting Engineering Organizations

(vii) Appellate Board

12.1 Functional Boards

The main functions of ECI will be to grant appropriate certificates of competency to Professional Engineers and Consulting Engineering Organizations, ensure their up-gradation of knowledge and skills, and regulate the profession of engineering through a code of ethics. To ensure the fulfillment of these objectives, ECI shall constitute Functional Boards included at S.Nos. (iii) to (vii) in Section 12.

12.2 Constitution and Functions of Functional Boards/Committees

All the Functional Boards shall be constituted by the Council with experts drawn from within the Council and outside. In consultation with the Council, all the five Functional Boards shall frame procedures for performance of their respective functions which will include maintenance of "National Register of Professional Engineers", "National Register of Associate Professional Engineers" and "National Register of Consulting Engineering Organizations", removal of names from these registers, disciplinary action such as suspension and revocation of status of Professional Engineers, Associate Professional Engineers and Consulting Engineering Organizations. If the Functional Boards so recommend, necessary changes in their own constitution, functioning, nomenclature, activities, etc, would be made by the Council after due consideration.

12.3 Other Boards/Committees

The Council may constitute other Boards/Committees as may be found necessary with such terms of reference as may be required for serving the objectives of ECI.

13. ORGANISATION STRUCTURE

13.1 ECI may establish an organization consisting of full-time or part-time officials, which may be headed by a Secretary and Director General on full time basis who will be the Administrative Head.

13.2 Duties and responsibilities as well as the pay and other conditions of the employees below the level of Secretary and Director General shall be approved by the Executive Committee. SDG shall enjoy his powers as per this Act and such specified powers as the Executive Committee may delegate to him and cause to be recorded in its minutes.

14. CUSTODY OF DOCUMENTS

The Executive Committee shall cause all important documents such as title deeds, securities and investments etc. to be kept in safe deposit and/or with a scheduled Bank for realization of interest or dividends to the credit of the ECI Account. The Executive Committee shall be entitled to transfer such securities and investments to the name of the Bank, if they so desire.

15. LEGAL PROCEEDINGS

ECI may sue or be sued in the name of Secretary and Director General as per the provisions of this Act.

16. FINANCIAL YEAR

The financial year of ECI shall be from 1st April to 31st March of the following year.

17. AUDIT OF ACCOUNTS

The accounts of ECI shall be audited by a duly qualified Chartered Accountant appointed by the Council every year.

CHAPTER-III

REGISTRATION OF ENGINEERS

18. CATEGORIES OF REGISTRATION

Under the provisions of this Act, registration shall be made for the following categories:

18.1 Professional Engineer (PE)

A person who is entitled to undertake independent practice (excluding practice being restricted by any other law) on matters such as planning, research, design, analysis, execution, manufacturing, maintenance, testing, evaluation, quality assurance, management and/or guidance thereof, certification work and such other matters which require professional abilities in engineering and technology, which ECI may decide from time to time and include in its Regulations.

18.2 On having been registered as a Professional Engineer and included in the National Register of Professional Engineers, the person concerned shall be entitled to work in his specified area of operation throughout India and no further registration at State/local level will be required for the purpose of practice, subject however to any special statutory requirements applicable to practice in a particular field. Any certificate to be issued by the Professional Engineer in the discharge of his specified functions shall carry the stamp of authorization by ECI and shall be valid before any accepting authority in Government, Public or Private Organization.

18.3 No person other than a Professional Engineers would be authorized to:

(a) certify an engineering drawing/design/process/system/cost estimates/time schedule/resources forecast/budget allocation for any engineering work/product/process;

(b) certify the design quality of a product/process/project;

(c) certify the adequacy of safety measures and environmental protection; and

(d) certify that the quality of construction/product process is in accordance with the design.

Provided that this condition may not apply to Engineers of disciplines who, under some other Act, are permitted certification work to the extent the relevant Act permits.

18.4 Associate Professional Engineer(APE)

A person who has acquired educational qualifications required for APE and takes up engineering work under the supervision of a Professional Engineer may apply, in the prescribed form accompanied by requisite fee as specified in the Regulations, submitting therewith the consent of the said supervisor. On the approval of his application his name will be entered in the National Register of Associate Professional Engineers.

18.5 Consulting Engineering Organization (CE)

Any organization that undertakes, in accordance with its objectives, work on matters such as planning, research, design, analysis, execution, testing, evaluation, quality assurance and such other matters which ECI may approve from time to time and include in its Regulations and/or guidance thereon, which require professional abilities in engineering and technology, under the supervision of Professional Engineers.

18.6 On having been registered as a Consulting Engineering Organization and included in the National Register of Consulting Engineering Organizations, the firm concerned will be entitled to work in its specified area of operation throughout India and no further registration at the state/local level will be required for the purpose of practice, subject however to any special statutory requirements applicable to practice in a particular field.

19. CRITERIA, STANDARDS AND PROCEDURES FOR REGISTRATION

The Council will lay down criteria, standards and procedures for the registration, and its renewal, of Professional Engineers, Associate Professional Engineers and Consulting Engineering Organizations. The procedures for registration of Professional Engineers may include appearing in examinations, interviews, etc. as may be considered necessary.

20. PUBLIC AND PRIVATE WORKS

20.1. Any Government or Private organizations/agencies or authorities or officials or employees thereof shall not engage in the practice of engineering involving either public or private property without the project being under the direct charge and supervision of a Professional Engineer as provided for the practice of a profession of this Act. The Government may, however, exempt any government agency or private organization or type of public or private works from this provision.

20.2 The Government may, by issuing a notification, exempt for the certification work of engineering Engineers working in Central/State governments, public sector undertakings, and other organizations working under government control, from registering as Professional Engineers for a period specified in the notification.

21. REMOVAL FROM REGISTER

21.1 ECI may, by order, remove from the National Register the name of any Professional Engineer/Associate Professional Engineer/Consulting Engineering Organization for reasons, and following procedures, laid down in the Regulations.

22. DISCIPLINARY ACTION - REVOCATION, SUSPENSION, FINE OR REPRIMAND

ECI shall have the power to take disciplinary action as may be decided by the Executive Committee and accordingly reprimand any Professional Engineer/Associate Professional Engineer/Consulting Engineering Organizations or suspend, refuse to renew or revoke the Certificate of Registration, or levy a fine, on being found guilty of acts stated in the Regulations.

23. VIOLATIONS AND PENALTIES

ECI will have the power to take appropriate legal steps against any person, firm, partnership, organization, association or other entity of violation of any provision of the Act or as spelt out in the Regulations so that the guilty may, upon conviction, be sentenced by a court in accordance with the laws.

24. SURRENDER OF CERTIFICATES

A person or organization whose name has been removed from the National Register under Sub-section 21.1 or where such person is dead or the organization has ceased to exist, his/its legal representative, as defined in the appropriate Section of the Code of Civil Procedure, shall forthwith surrender his/its Certificate of Registration to the Director General.

25. RESTORATION TO REGISTER

ECI may at any time, for reasons appearing to it to be sufficient order that upon payment of such fee as may be prescribed by Regulations, the name of the person or organization removed from the National Register shall be restored thereto.

26. ISSUE OF DUPLICATE CERTIFICATES

Where it is shown to the satisfaction of the Director General that a Certificate of Registration has been lost or destroyed, the Director General may, on payment of such fee as may be prescribed by the Regulations, issue a duplicate in the form prescribed under the Regulations.

27. PRINTING OF NATIONAL REGISTERS

As soon as may be after the last day of January in each year the Director General shall cause to be prepared copies of the National Registers as they stood on the said day in printed or electronic form and such copies shall be made available to persons applying therefore on payment of such fee as may be prescribed by Regulations and shall be evidence that on the said date and persons/firms whose names are entered thereon were Professional Engineers/ Associate Professional Engineers/Consulting Engineering Organizations.

CHAPTER-IV

MISCELLANEOUS

28. AUTHORIZATION TO PRACTICE AS CONSULTING ENGINEERS

28.1 The practice of or offer to practice engineering by Consulting Engineering Organizations registered under this Act, by more than one person acting individually, through a firm, corporation , co-operative, institution or private practitioner employing others, referred to hereinafter as a firm, is permitted provided that the person in direct control or having personal supervision of such practice and all personnel who certify on behalf of the organization in professional matters are registered under this Act as Professional Engineers.

29. PROFESSIONAL CONDUCT

29.1 ECI may by Regulations prescribe standards of professional conduct and etiquette and a Code of Ethics for Professional Engineers/Associate Professional Engineers/Consulting Engineering Organizations.

29.2 Regulations made by ECI under Sub-section 29.1 may specify which violations thereof shall constitute infamous conduct in any professional respect, that is, professional misconduct, and such provision shall have effect notwithstanding anything contained in any law for the time being in force.

30. PENALTY FOR FALSELY CLAIMING TO BE REGISTERED

If any person or organization whose name is not for the time being entered in the Register falsely represents that it is so entered, or uses in connection with his or its name any words or letters reasonably calculated to suggest that his or its name is so entered, he or it shall be punishable with fine as may be decided by the court.

31. PROHIBITION AGAINST USE OF TITLE

31.1 After the expiry of one year from the date appointed by ECI and specified in Regulations, no person other than a registered professional engineer, shall use the title and style of Professional Engineer or P.E., no person other than a registered Associate Professional Engineer shall use the title and style of Associate Professional Engineer or A.P.E., and no organization other than a registered consulting engineering organization shall use the title and style of Consulting Engineering Organization or Consulting Engineers.

31.2 If any person or organization contravenes the provisions of Sub-section 31.1, he/she or it shall be punishable.

32. FAILURE TO SURRENDER CERTIFICATE OF REGISTRATION

If any person or organization whose name has been removed from the Register fails without sufficient cause forthwith to surrender his or its Certificate of Registration, he or it shall be punishable with fine and, in case of continuing failure, with an additional fine for each month after the first during which he or it has persisted in the failure.

33. COGNIZANCE OF OFFENCE

33.1 No court shall take cognizance of any offence punishable under this Act, except upon complaint made by order of ECI or a person authorized in this behalf by ECI.

33.2 No judicial authority less than a judge of a High Court shall try any offence punishable under this Act.

34. INFORMATION TO BE FURNISHED BY ECI AND PUBLICATION THEREOF

34.1 ECI shall furnish such reports, copies of its minutes, and other information to the Central Government as the Government may require.

34.2 The Central Government may publish, in such manner as it may think fit, any report, copy or other information furnished to it under this Section.

35. PROTECTION OF ACTION TAKEN IN GOOD FAITH

No suit, prosecution or other legal proceeding shall lie against the Central Government, ECI or any Member of Council, the Executive Committee or any other Committee or Officers and other employees of ECI for any thing which is in good faith done or intended to be done under this Act or any Rules or Regulations made thereunder.

36. MEMBERS OF ECI AND OFFICERS AND EMPLOYEES TO BE PUBLIC SERVANTS

The Members of the Executive Committee of ECI and officers and other employees of ECI shall be deemed to be public servants within the meaning of Section 21 of the Indian Penal Code.

37. POWER TO REMOVE DIFFICULTIES

37.1 If any difficulty arises in giving effect to the provisions of this Act, the Central Government may by order published in the Official Gazette, make such provisions, not inconsistent with the provisions of this Act, as appear to it to be necessary or expedient for removing the difficulty.

Provided that no such order shall be made under this Section after the expiry of two years from the date of commencement of this Act.

37.2 Every order made under this Section shall as soon as may be after it is made, be laid before each House of the Parliament and the provisions of Sub-section shall apply in respect of such order as it applies in response of a Rule made under this Act.

38. POWER OF CENTRAL GOVERNMENT TO MAKE RULES

38.1 The Central Government may, by notification in the Official Gazette, make Rules to carry out the purposes of this Act.

38.2 Every Rule made under this Section shall be laid, as soon as may be after it is made, before each House of Parliament, while it is in session for a total period of thirty days which may be comprised in one session or in two or more successive sessions and if, before the expiry of the session immediately following the session or the successive sessions aforesaid, both Houses agreed in making any modification to the Rule or both Houses agreed that the Rule should not be made, the Rule shall thereafter have effect only in such modified form or be of no effect, as the case may be; so, however, that any such modification or annulment shall be without prejudice to the validity of anything previously done under that Rule.

39. POWER OF ECI TO MAKE REGULATIONS

ECI may make Regulations, not inconsistent with the provisions of this Act or the Rules made there under, to carry out the purpose of this Act.

Chapter

7

Professional Ethics

Issues and implications

The objective of this chapter is to integrate and summarise all the earlier chapters and present an integrated view of the subject. It highlights briefly the issues and implications.

The era of globalisation has thrust ethical issues to the forefront. This is not accidental. The success and even survival of any enterprise are crucially dependent on its withstanding the rigours of competition. It has to cope with challenges in every direction and benchmark itself constantly against the best practices and business models. Expectations of stake-holders – investors, creditors, collaborators, suppliers, distributors and customers – are getting to be more and more exacting. Advances in technologies are breath-taking in scope and scale. The market place throngs with diverse kinds of players not all of whom are interested in promoting public good. Without a degree of control over the base elements of human nature, there is a danger of free market economy ending up as a free-for-all, no-holds-barred and no-punches-pulled economy. In the last two years, innumerable instances of unbridled greed causing havoc have been exposed in industrialised countries. In turbulent times, when all the time tested assumptions, conventions and notions are going overboard, and governments and institutions have to navigate uncharted and stormy seas, the eternal verities of ethics provide the only sure and steady beacon light.

Dharma and ethics

The average Indian, more than anyone else, should be able to grasp this point easily. From ancient times, in all the corpus of literature, reflecting the country's unrivalled religious and cultural heritage, the emphasis is on ethics. The overarching ancient concept of *dharma* itself embodies a comprehensive set of ethical and moral prescriptions governing the conduct of human beings pertinent to every conceivable situation. Gautama Buddha's eight-fold path — right views, right intentions, right communication, right speech, right action, right living, right effort and right conduct — is nothing but ancient wisdom in a capsule form. All elaborations of kingship in all languages give pride of place to ethics. In short, there has never been any doubt at any time about the cardinal importance of adherence to canons of ethics in any field of human endeavour.

In its simplest form, a code of ethics is nothing but a kind of mission statement for human beings to live by. It flows out of the overriding necessity to ensure that any given task is undertaken and completed in conformity with the principles of accountability, equity, propriety, prudence, probity, rectitude, honesty, integrity and transparency, and paying due regard to the imperatives of national security, public safety, health and sanitation, environmental protection and ecological balance. These fundamental requirements admit of no compromise. They are sacrosanct not only in themselves, but also for the reason of being at the very heart of rights and entitlements on the one hand and duties and obligations on the other. Except when anchored in these verities, there is no assurance of either the former being safeguarded or the latter being carried out for the common good.

With the increasing complexity and sophistication of human enterprises, brought about by technological advances and knowledge explosion, it has become necessary to further refine and fine-tune this omnibus definition of ethics to suit the mind-boggling variety of activities falling within the broad canvass of development. The ongoing processes of globalisation, liberalisation and privatisation have thrown the doors wide open for the inter-play of innumerable actors on the world stage. When so many contend and compete for the cake of a limited size in terms of technical, financial, material and natural resources, infrastructure, markets and trade mechanisms, it becomes all the more necessary to formulate and enforce criteria that will guarantee a level playing field and an equitable share of opportunities whether in the form of access, employment, investment or return. They should be applicable not merely to the availability of resources and opportunities, but also the manner in which they are put to use. In other words, the optimal utilisation of the factors of production, and unclogged operation of the channels of supply, sales and distribution at fair prices and by fair means to the end users also come within the ambit of ethical architecture.

Governance and ethics

That is what makes governance in all its aspects the prime issue to be addressed in any discussion on ethics. Good, sound and effective governance is what enables a host of institutions, in both the public and private sectors, all the way from *panchayats* at the village level to governments in the States and at the Centre, to deliver to the people services in tune with their responsibilities and commitments. The parameters of such governance are rooted in ethical considerations. Indeed, the first and the basic element of ethical conduct is the timely fulfilment in letter and spirit and in their entirety of promises made or expectations roused relating to the quality of the service or product and the overall performance. In a context in which corporates have begun to dominate a preponderant proportion of trade, commerce and industry, and thereby determine the course of the economy, corporate governance and business ethics have become the obverse and reverse of the same coin.

Importance of ethics for a soft state

An inviolable ethical framework is all the more compelling in India because of certain adverse features that have come to characterise the polity, preventing it from emerging as a full-fledged modern state. First, preferences and prejudices based on caste, community, region and language still continue to influence perspectives, leading to favouritism, nepotism and cronyism. This makes decision-making erratic and opaque. Second, while there is no dearth of laws, rules and regulations, their enforcement is poor. Third, the mindset is still feudal and authoritarian, with the result responsiveness, empathy, mutual reinforcement, team spirit and loyalty become casualties. Fourth, criminalisation of politics is defiling representative institutions into which a good number of law-breakers is gaining entry to become law-makers. Fifth, the traditional exemplars — parents, teachers, elders, and preceptors — are losing their hold. Finally, there has been a crumbling of values and norms all round due to increasingly competitive, consumerist, combative and even predatory pulls and pressures. Corruption is threatening to become a way of life.

The only antidote to these corrosive disabilities of a soft state is a well-devised ethical compass to help steer institutions and organisations in the right and proper direction for the betterment of society as a whole. An ethical compass in itself will be of no avail, unless it is derived from the intrinsic values that are integral part of daily lives and unless it reflects social conscience, social commitment and social responsibility.

Holistic connotation of ethics

Ethics in whatever profession or avocation does not stand by itself. A human being too cannot be ethical in certain respects and unethical in certain others. He is either ethical or he is not. That is why it becomes necessary to adopt a holistic approach to it. Its full importance cannot be understood by viewing it apart from the entire sweep and range of factors and characteristics that contribute to societal well-being. It stems from, and is enlivened by, certain basic values which need to be im-

Gautama Buddha's eight-fold path is ancient wisdom in a capsule form.

planted in individuals who are collectively engaged in performing their assigned functions in their respective walks of life. Indeed, its durability over the long-term is conditional on the awareness of those values. As such, a brief discussion of this aspect may not be out of place.

Attributes of an ethical personality

1. *Giving of one's best*

The first and foremost distinguishing feature of an ethical personality is the spirit of service itself. It basically comprises seven ingredients:

Spirit of Service comprises of 7 ingredients

(a) *Sensitivity,* that is, sensing intensely, instinctively and instantly the feelings, emotions and reactions of other human beings, and avoiding anything that will alienate people, and going out of the way to anticipate and help.

(b) *Empathy,* that is, the ability to view and understand things by putting oneself in the other person's shoes.

(c) *Responsiveness,* that is, being receptive to ideas, suggestions and requests in a positive, "will do" spirit.

(d) *Vigour,* that is, being dynamic, energetic, tireless in performance;

(e) Integrity, that is, being honest and straightforward in dealings.

(f) *Commitment,* that is, being passionately dedicated to cause or task and total identification with it.

(g) *Excellence,* that is, being a little ahead of, and doing a trifle better than, requirements. Achieving a little more than what is strictly expected.

All of these fall within the definition of being true to oneself, by maintaining the highest standards of conduct and behaviour and constantly upgrading oneself in what the *Bhagavad Gita* calls skill in action (*karma sukausalam*). This precept simply means that one should keep one's faculties sharp and shining and mental antennae up and active, so as to be able to realise one's potential to the maximum. The striving for excellence, whatever be the nature of responsibilities and functions, regardless of status or rank, should become the second nature for every achiever. This comes from devotion to one's duty and the inner urge to give of one's best, stretching oneself to, and even beyond, the outermost limits of one's capabilities. That is how one will be able to stamp one's personality on whatever one does.

2. *Loyalty to team associates*

Second in importance is building up the self-esteem, competence and capabilities of one's associates. The paramount aim of everyone in any field of endeavour is to be an inspiration and an exemplar. No one who aspires to lead or manage can afford to lose sight of the fact that human beings are the most precious assets of any organisation. One of the findings of science is that fusion unleashes vastly more energy than fission; it is the same in organisations. Synergy is the outcome of the fusion of the energies of human beings in full measure and the most powerful motive force in helping organisations realise their goals and objectives. Harmonious team work, strict discipline and total involvement are the mainsprings of achievement.

3. Loyalty to customers

Third is putting in the maximum efforts to live up to the essence of what has come to be known as 'customer delight'. No one has defined this ethical imperative so pithily as Mahatma Gandhi. His famous tribute to the greatness of the customer is of eternal relevance and bears quotation: *"A customer is the most important visitor on our premises. He is not dependent on us. We are dependent on him. He is not an interruption on our work. He is the purpose of it. He is not an outsider on our*

> **A code of ethics a kind of mission statement for human beings to live by.**
> **Achievement springs from harmonious team work, strict discipline and total involvement.**

business. He is a part of it. We are not doing him a favour by serving him. He is doing us a favour by giving us an opportunity to do so."

Sensitivity to the feelings of customers is the hall mark of decent and civilised business culture. It is not without its material rewards. It makes for loyal customers who help enlarge the market share by attracting new ones by their endorsement of the quality of the product or service. As such, it is worthwhile taking due note of the framework for strengthening relations with customers (*given in **Appendix I** of this chapter).*

4. Social responsibility

Fourth is the sense of social responsibility. That is what distinguishes a human being or organisation from a pack of animals. The justification for this rests on a number of important considerations. At the very minimum, a socially conscious individual or organisation discharges a moral obligation by giving back to society what he or it has knowingly or otherwise had taken from it in terms of resources. The immeasurable goodwill earned thereby raises his or its moral influence and authority as well as social standing, and concomitantly, his or its effectiveness. Tangibly, social responsibility also makes business sense, from the standpoint of corporate entities in any sector, as it is an essential pathway to good public relations and general acceptance.

There are, of course, costs of ethical or socially committed behaviour that may eat into profits. Adherence to ethics, entails avoidance of short cuts or cutting corners, and sticking to principles. Refusal to pay bribes, circumvent laws or bend rules may mean forgoing a lucrative business opportunity. Some costs are inherent in any form of philanthropy, social service, or community uplift. If the attempts to do good are sporadic, irrelevant or unsuited to needs, or ineffectually carried out, they may even become counter-productive. Corporates must, therefore, build up the in-house expertise to make the right choices or evolve the right yardsticks to measure the benefits that accrue from their initiatives.

It is hoped that the illustrative checklist and the diagrammatic sketch that are given as ***Appendices II and III*** to this chapter will be of help in gaining a greater understanding of the indicators for appraising corporate social behaviour and the concrete directions along which the various actors should channel their efforts.

Ethics in professions

These overall considerations, no doubt apply to professions as well, but at the same time it has to be remembered that they are a class apart in some important attributes. According to the dictionary, they are characterised by, or conform to, the technical or ethical standards of a calling requiring specialised knowledge and often long and intensive academic preparation; they are also expected to exhibit a courteous, conscientious, and generally businesslike manner in the workplaces. The hall marks of professionalism are precision, clarity, objectivity, mastery of facts and data, forming conclusions on a logical and rational evaluation of all available information painstakingly collected, being on top of advances in knowledge and technology and result-orientation. Generally, any deviation in these respects has more serious consequences in professional enterprises than in non-professional ones.

Pre-eminence of engineering profession

Each profession has its own specialised and distinctive nature marked by a high degree of differentiation and sophistication, and governed by its own performance criteria. The pre-eminence of the engineering profession derives from its being the propellant of the economic regeneration for which the country is gearing itself. Every activity in this direction calls for close involvement of the profession in planning, executing and commissioning of projects of all descriptions in all sectors and ensuring that they are completed within the prescribed time frames and allocated funds. The profession encompasses a variety of disciplines and draws on complex and fast-changing technologies. For

Sensitivity to the feelings of customers is the hallmark of business culture.

instance, within the ambit of the engineering profession itself, with which we are concerned here, there are a number of branches: civil, mechanical, electrical, electronics, communications, signaling and the like. It is also slated to absorb a significant proportion of the heavy investment both in educational facilities for meeting the requirement of quality professionals and in research and development for putting the country on par with, if not ahead of, achievements in other countries.

An engineer's multi-faceted responsibilities

In the course of carrying out the tasks entrusted to him, an engineer may be undertaking a variety of responsibilities: Selection of sites and putting in place physical infrastructure; project appraisal; choice of technology; getting designs prepared and tested; purchase and procurement of materials; negotiations for financial and technical collaboration; determining modalities for optimum deployment of resources; enlisting the cooperation of different stakeholders such as owners, vendors, contractors, consultants, bankers and regulators; ensuring safety, security and protection; conflict and crisis management; resolving industrial disputes; motivating associates, co-workers and other professionals to put in their best; public relations; and participation in policy formulation.

The effectiveness of an engineer in coping with these multi-faceted responsibilities and carrying people with him is in direct proportion to the respect commanded by him by virtue of his honesty of purpose, transparency of dealings, easy accessibility and ability to instill the needed sense of accountability. This book has comprehensively dealt with the ethical framework the engineering profession is required to function in.

Crucial role of project managers

An Engineer has multi-faceted responsibilities

However, it is considered worthwhile in this chapter to highlight the special ethical considerations applicable to project managers who are a class by themselves and who play a crucial role in providing the underpinning to the economy of the country and contributing to its acquiring the status of a developed nation. Project management embraces activities of both concept and commissioning on the one hand and operations and maintenance on the other. The quality and caliber of project managers and the vision and sense of mission they are imbued with can make a vital difference to the progress of the country itself in all directions. It has been estimated that the savings by avoidance of cost and time over-run, and efficient operation and maintenance, can add a clear three percentage points to the gross domestic product. Ensuring that benefits reach the people on this monumental scale is in itself the core component of accountability which stems from overarching ethical sense of all those who run projects. Hence, a few quintessential ingredients forming the code of ethics have been extracted from published sources and given in ***Appendix IV***

Monitoring, supervision and enforcement

There is no point in formulating and circulating a Code of Ethics in any organisation unless it is made binding. It should be backed by a mechanism to enforce it and impose sanctions and penalties for transgression. As regards government departments and the public sector undertakings, there is usually a Vigilance Department manned by their own senior employees, reporting directly to the head of the organisation. The Code of Corporate Governance for companies in the private sector requires them to set up Ethics Committees at the Board level, working in close conjunction with the Audit Committee.

For these mechanisms to function effectively, it should have the means of getting to know of violations as soon as they occur, and conducting the necessary enquiries, so as to arrive at a just and fair finding and recommending appropriate penal action. They should have the authority and the power to summon witnesses and call for the relevant documents. They should enjoy absolute functional independence, and any attempt to interfere in their working should in itself be considered a breach of the code, attracting retributive action.

The starting point of the whole process of enforcement of the code is, of course, the availability of information. Sources of such information are many and varied, and it may be useful to make a brief mention of each of them with reference to its nature and follow-up action:

(1) **Anonymous/pseudonymous complaints**: These are from aggrieved or disgruntled employees, contractors or self-righteous busybodies, and should be handled with discretion. Generally, they should be disregarded, unless there contain concrete facts which are verifiable and actionable.

(2) **Regular complaints in which the complainants disclose the identities**: These certainly cannot be ignored; on the contrary, they should be taken seriously and pursued vigorously. Placing complaints boxes to bring to notice deviations from norms, rules and procedures can by itself act as a deterrent to most persons prone to yield to temptation.

(3) **Media reports**: These too can open the eyes of the bodies enforcing the code of ethics to the actual, imminent or potential occurrence of misdeeds. However, in view of the possibility of their having been planted or being the offshoot of misdirected journalistic exuberance, it is better to exercise caution and assess their veracity before initiating formal enquiries.

(4) **Matters formally referred by the heads of departments, or the chief of the setup:** There is no question that these should be attended to, as the top functionaries have already applied their minds and formed their judgment about the need for action.

(5) **Internal audit reports:** Besides providing valuable clues, they can also help stop a mischief before it assumes larger dimensions and ramifications.

(6) **Annual audit reports:** Although not so very proximate to the objectionable event as the internal audit report, they can offer leads to trained eyes for further examination.

(7) **Inspection reports:** Each organisation should revive the old practice of periodical inspection of the working of the various departments, wherever it has fallen into disuse, as this again plugs loopholes and brings suspicious activities to light.

(8) **Mounting surveillance and engaging watchers:** This is a proactive technique employed by vigilance, intelligence and investigative bodies by way of supplementing the other efforts.

(9) **Whistle-blowing:** Departures from ethical behaviour are often brought to light by ethically motivated persons within the organisation. The subject has been covered in detail elsewhere in the book, and does not need any elaboration at this point.

In short, if only there is a will to strictly enforce ethical conduct, there are ways in which the task can be accomplished to the benefit of the organisation, the society and the nation. In the ultimate analysis, however, nothing else will avail, without the organisational culture being conducive to the creation, preservation and maintenance of an ethical ethos. The core aspect of the culture is the setting of the right and impressive examples by the top. Without that happening, not all the books and lectures on ethics can change things for the better.

Short Questions

1. Identify the sources of information for enforcement of code of ethics.
2. What are the various responsibilities of engineer?
3. Discuss the role of Governanace in Ethics.
4. What are the 8 fold path of Gautama Buddha?
5. What is Dharma?

Long Questions

1. Identify and discuss the various attributes of an ethical personality.
2. How do you inculcate "customer delight" into work culture?
3. Identify the indicators of Corporate Social Behaviour.
4. With the help of diagram, explain the Corporate Social Responsibility

Code of ethics needs to be monitored, supervised and enforced.
The core aspect of the culture is the setting of the right examples by the top.

Appendix–I

Framework to build 'customer delight' into work culture

1. Core components

1. Inclusion of obligations to customers in the credo of the organisation and its induction manual for new entrants
2. Written exhortation under the personal signature of Board of Directors, emphasizing its vital importance
3. Making it the theme of address at gatherings on special occasions
4. Devoting special issues of House Journals to the different dimensions of the subject earmarking a section for customer complaints and appreciation
5. Incentives for prompt attention to complaints and removal of defect
6. Attending to serious complaints at the level of the CEO
7. Periodical (e.g., monthly) Customer Delight Sessions held by CEO:
   - with his executives, (both from headquarters and the field) to review complaints, suggestions and follow up action
   - with batches of customers to develop better understanding
   - with representatives of customers'/consumers' organisations and federations
8. Special newsletter for circulation to customers
9. Inviting customer relations experts from outside to address employees
10. Periodical visits to customers' place of work/residence to enquire about the quality of product/service
11. Immediate replies to comments and complaints appearing in the media indicating the remedial action taken
12. Making customer delight the centerpiece of the training course, with highest level executives, including the CEO, participating in discussion groups and taking classes
13. Replacement/recall of defective items without demur
14. Generous compensation for injury or damage without harassment
15. Rewards to customers for best suggestions to improve product/service
16. Deterrent punishment for indifference to customers on the part of employees
17. Frequent sensitivity sessions with dealers/retailers during tours and through workshops/meetings held in the corporate office.
18. Sharing of information with customers on the basic features, strengths and weaknesses of technologies used.
19. Separate divisions/personnel for product-related and service-related customer contacts.
20. 24-hour customer service centre

Appendix–II

Corporate Social Behaviour -Checklist of Indicators for Appraisal

(Source: Publications and reports available on websites)

I. Community involvement

1. Inclusion

1. General philanthropy : Corporate support of educational institutions, cultural activities, recreational programs, health and community welfare agencies, and similar eleemosynary organisations.
2. Public and private transportation : Alleviating or preventing urban transportation problems including the provision of mass transportation of employees.
3. Health services : Providing health care facilities and services and the support of programmes to reduce disease and illness
4. Housing : Improving the standards of dwelling, the construction of needed dwellings, and the financing of housing renovations and construction
5. Aid in personal and business problems : Alleviations of problems related to the physically handicapped, child care, minority businesses, disadvantaged persons, and the like .
6. Community planning and improvement : Programmes of urban planning and renewal, crime prevention and the like.
7. Volunteer activities : Encouraging and providing time for employees to be active as volunteers in community activities.
8. Specialised food programs : Provision of meals to meet the dietary needs of the aged, the infirm, the disadvantaged child, and other groups.
9. Education : Development and implementation of educational programmes to supplement those of the public or private schools, such as work study programs, and employee services on school boards, schools authorities, and college university trustee and advisory boards.

II. Human Resources

1. Employment practices : Providing equal job opportunities for all persons, creation of summer job opportunities for students, and recruiting in depressed areas.
2. Training Programmes : Programmes for all employees to increase their skills, earning potential, and job satisfaction.
3. Promotion policies : Recognising the abilities of all employees and providing equal opportunities for promotion.
4. Employment continuity : Scheduling production so as to minimize retrenchment and recalls, maintaining facilities in efficient operating conditions so that they will not have to be abandoned.

5. Remuneration : Maintaining a level of total salaries and wages plus benefits that is in line with others in either the industry or community.
6. Working conditions : Providing safe, healthful, and pleasant working environment.
7. Drugs and alcohol : Providing education and counseling for employees to prevent or alleviate problems in these and similar areas.
8. Job enrichment : Providing the most meaningful work experiences practical for all employees.
9. Communications : Establishing and maintaining two-way communication between all levels of employees to secure suggestions, to provide information s to what the company is actually doing and how each department's activities relate to the total corporate activity, and to inform employees families and friends of corporate activities.

III. Physical resources and environment contributions

1. Air, Water and Noise: Refraining from causing pollution.
2. Solid waste: Disposal of solid waste in such a manner as to minimise contamination, reduce its bulk and the like, and the design of processes and products that will minimize the creation of solid waste.
3. Use of Scarce resources: The conservation of existing energy sources, the development of new energy sources, and the conservation of scarce materials.
4. Aesthetics: The design and location of facilities in conformance with surroundings and with pleasing architecture and landscaping.

IV. Product or service quality assurance

1. Completeness and clarity of labeling, packing, and marketing information to make sure that methods of use, limitations on use, hazards of use, shelf life, quantity of contents, and quality cannot be misunderstood.
2. Warranty provisions : Adherence to all stated or implied warranties of a product with implementation through timely recalls, repairs, or replacements.
3. Responsiveness to consumer complaints : Prompt and complete responses to all complaints received.
4. Consumer Education : Literature and media programmes to keep consumers informed of product or service characteristics, methods and areas of use of products, and of planned products changes or discontinuances.
5. Product Quality : Quality Assurance through adequate and effective checks and controls.
6. Product Safety : Design or formulation and packaging of products to minimize possibilities of harm or injury in product use.
7. Content and frequency of advertising : Giving full consideration to the omission of any media material that may be adverse or offensive and the avoidance of repetition to the extent that it becomes repugnant.
8. Constructive research : Orienting technical and market research to meet defined social needs and to avoid creating social and environmental problems.

Appendix–III

Corporate Social Responsibility

Flow Chart of Roles of Different Participants

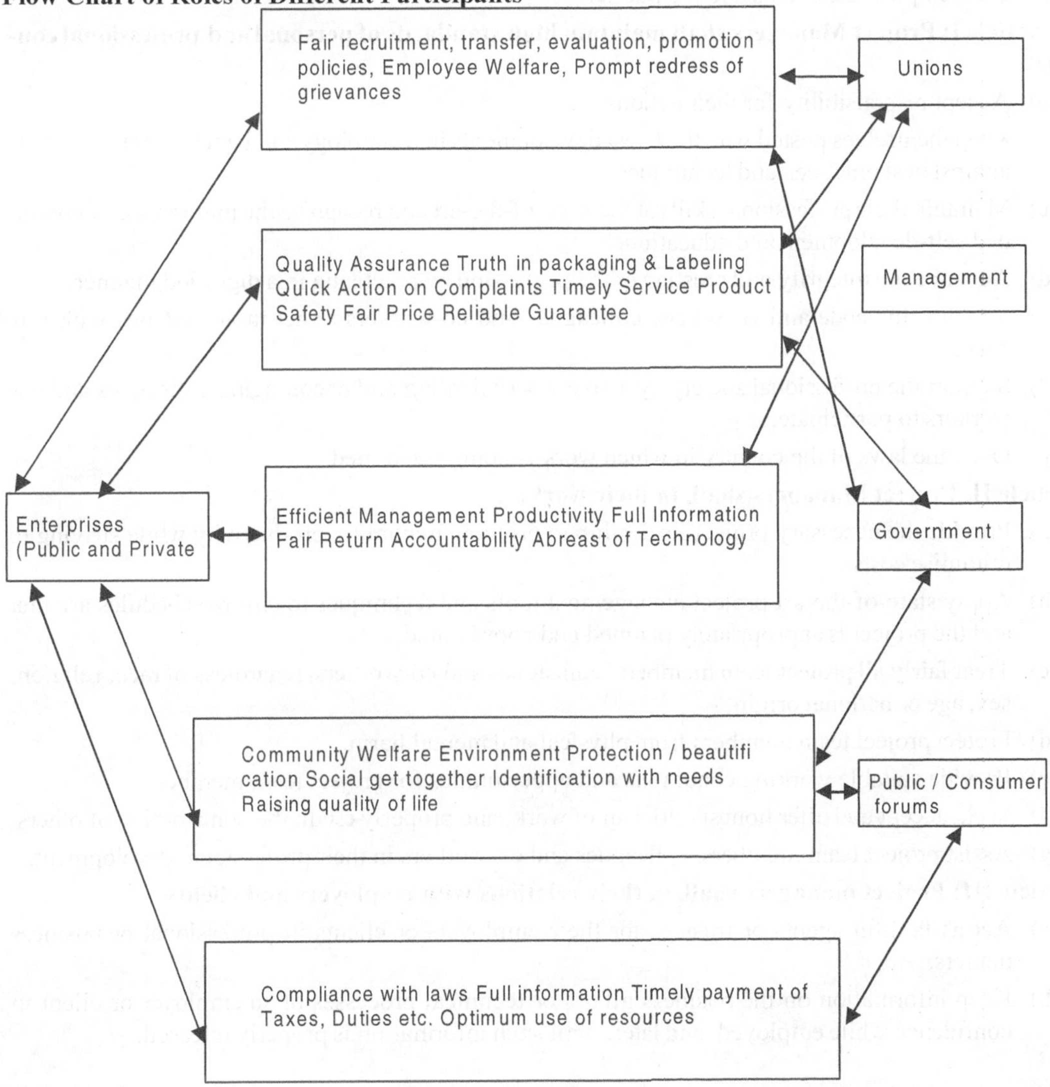

Appendix–IV

Code of Ethics for Project Managers

Preamble: Project managers, in the pursuit of their profession, affect the quality of life of the people. Hence, it is vital for project managers to earn and maintain the confidence of team members, colleagues, employees, clients and the public.

Article I: Project Managers shall maintain high standards of personal and professional conduct.

(a) Accept responsibility for their actions.

(b) Keep themselves posted with the latest developments in technology and benchmark themselves against best practices and techniques.

(c) Maintain their professional skills at the state-of-the-art and recognise the importance of continued self-development and education.

(d) Advance the integrity and prestige of the profession by practising in a dignified manner.

(e) Support this code and encourage colleagues and co-workers to act in accordance with this code.

(f) Support the professional society by actively participating and encouraging colleagues and co-workers to participate.

(g) Obey the laws of the country in which work is being performed.

Article II. Project Managers shall, in their work:

(a) Provide the necessary project leadership to promote maximum productivity while striving to minimise costs.

(b) Apply state-of-the-art project management tools and techniques to ensure schedules are met and the project is appropriately planned and coordinated.

(c) Treat fairly all project team members, colleagues and co-workers, regardless of race, religion, sex, age or national origin.

(d) Protect project team members from physical and mental harm.

(e) Provide suitable working conditions and opportunities for project team members.

(f) Seek, accept and offer honest criticism of work, and properly credit the contribution of others.

(g) Assist project team members, colleagues and co-workers in their professional development.

Article III: Project managers shall, in their relations with employers and clients:

(a) Act as faithful agents or trustees for their employers or clients in professional or business matters.

(b) Keep information on the business affairs or technical processes of an employer or client in confidence while employed, and later, until such information is properly released.

(c) Inform their employers, clients, professional societies or public agencies of which they are members or to which they may make any presentations, of any circumstances that could lead to a conflict of interest.

(d) Neither give nor accept, directly or indirectly, any gift, payment or service of more than nominal value to or from those having business relationships with employers or clients.

(e) Be honest and realistic in reporting project cost, schedule and performance.

Article IV: Project Managers shall, in fulfilling their responsibilities to the community:

(a) Protect the safety, health and welfare of the public and speak out against abuses in those areas affecting the public interest.

(b) Seek to extend public knowledge and appreciation of the project management profession and its achievements